# IDEAL BEAUTY

# IDEAL BEAUTY

## THE LIFE AND TIMES OF GRETA GARBO

LOIS W. BANNER

RUTGERS UNIVERSITY PRESS

*New Brunswick, Camden, and Newark, New Jersey*
*London and Oxford*

Rutgers University Press is a department of Rutgers, The State University of New Jersey, one of the leading public research universities in the nation. By publishing worldwide, it furthers the University's mission of dedication to excellence in teaching, scholarship, research, and clinical care.

Library of Congress Cataloging-in-Publication Data

Names: Banner, Lois W., author.

Title: Ideal beauty : the life and times of Greta Garbo / Lois W. Banner.

Description: New Brunswick : Rutgers University Press, [2023] |
    Includes bibliographical references and index.

Identifiers: LCCN 2023008702 | ISBN 9781978806504 (hardcover) |
    ISBN 9781978806511 (epub) | ISBN 9781978806535 (pdf)

Subjects: LCSH: Garbo, Greta, 1905–1990. | Motion picture actors and actresses—
    Sweden—Biography. | Feminine beauty (Aesthetics)

Classification: LCC PN2778.G3 B36 2023 | DDC 791.4302/8092 [B]—dc23/eng/20230505

LC record available at https://lccn.loc.gov/2023008702

*A British Cataloging-in-Publication record for this book is available from the British Library.*

References to internet websites (URLs) were accurate at the time of writing. Neither the author nor Rutgers University Press is responsible for URLs that may have expired or changed since the manuscript was prepared.

♾ The paper used in this publication meets the requirements of the American National Standard for Information Sciences—Permanence of Paper for Printed Library Materials, ANSI Z39.48–1992.

rutgersuniversitypress.org

For my grandchildren
Owen Banner and Eleanor Banner

# CONTENTS

# IDEAL BEAUTY

# *Prologue*

## Who Was Greta Garbo?

> When she was in the mood to be happy,
> there was no one more fun or lighthearted.
> —Gray Horan, Garbo's niece

> There's not been a day in my life that
> I've felt completely well.
> —Greta Garbo

*L*EGENDARY HOLLYWOOD FILM star and ideal beauty Greta Garbo was born Greta Gustafsson in Stockholm, on September 15, 1905. Her parents were impoverished workers, still close to their peasant roots. In 1923, when she was a scholarship student at the Swedish Royal Dramatic Academy in Stockholm, the famed Swedish director Mauritz Stiller discovered her for films. He starred her in *The Saga of Gösta Berling*, changed her surname to Garbo, and negotiated contracts for them with Louis B. Mayer, head of the Hollywood branch of Metro-Goldwyn-Mayer (MGM), a major American film studio. Arriving in Hollywood with Stiller in August 1925, Garbo was Hollywood's first Swedish female star.[1]

Ten months later, in a stunning reversal of fortune, Mayer fired Stiller. Demoralized and ill, Stiller returned to Sweden in 1927 and died a year later, while Garbo became a top Hollywood star. In 1942, at the age of thirty-six, after making twenty-four MGM films, she left the studio, moved to New York, and became a celebrity, "the queen of the international set" led by Greek shipping tycoon Aristotle Onassis.[2] In

1965 she joined the circle around Cécile de Rothschild, an openly lesbian member of the famed Rothschild family. Garbo died in 1990, at the age of eighty-four.

Despite the publication in 2021 of two biographies of Garbo, one by Robert Gottlieb and the other by Robert Dance, Garbo's role in the histories of beauty, gender, ethnicity, and sexuality remains unexamined.[3] Yet she was central to the cultural history of Europe and the United States between World War I and World War II. In that interwar era of social, political, and demographic shifts, beauty was redefined, with Garbo at its center. It's time for a new interpretation of her, focusing on her beauty, gender, ethnicity, and sexuality, and on analyzing her internal self, her career, and her sexual orientation.

These aspects of Garbo's persona and her cultural context are key to understanding her. Why did many U.S. journalists find her unattractive when she arrived in the United States in 1925? And why, only five years later, was she the West's preeminent female beauty? Issues remain about her "whiteness" and its connection to her day's racism as well as her chronic illnesses and their relation to her health.

I have written two books on the history of beauty: *American Beauty* (1983), on physical appearance in the United States from 1800 to 1920, and *Marilyn: The Passion and the Paradox* (2012), on Marilyn Monroe and the 1950s. Having skimmed over the 1920s and 1930s in those books, I decided to investigate these decades in depth, with Garbo as my guide and her biography part of my narrative. As in all my work, I brought a feminist sensitivity to the task, charting Garbo's contribution to women's emancipation, an ongoing project during her lifetime. And I regard the subject of human beauty as broad in scope, including such components as dress, personality, age, health, consumer products, and individual taste.

In this prologue I will outline Garbo's persona and the theories of beauty in the media of her day, especially in the movie fan magazines. These date from the 1910s, and by the 1930s there were over a dozen such magazines in the United States alone, circulating in the millions of copies.[4] These magazines have been called untruthful, but many of their writers strove for legitimacy at a time when "legitimate" theater productions were regarded as high art, and films were often dismissed as formulaic mass entertainment. And the movie magazines covered more than just films. Including photos and articles on the clothing and appearance of film actresses as advice for readers, they were also beauty magazines, searching for ideal female beauty. The media both hugely praised and sharply criticized Garbo's appearance; she became central to the quest for ideal beauty.[5]

As a child, Greta Gustafsson dreamt of being a great actress—a goal she pursued with typical Swedish determination, even though she developed chronic ailments: anemia, insomnia, menstrual issues, and a manic-depressive syndrome, mostly with depressive lows. She chain-smoked from the age of seventeen on, and she dieted throughout her film career. To alleviate stress, she swam and hiked. Together, her dieting and vigorous exercising led to anorexia nervosa, the disorder that triggers the body's starvation response and can lead to uncontrolled dieting and even death. It was a problem for Hollywood actresses in this era, when thinness was considered central to female beauty.[6]

Garbo's character was rooted in paradox. Raymond Daum, a New York walking companion, called her "a puzzling physical specimen, who could seem both frail and robust."[7] Often stubborn, she could display an iron will. But she was shy and lacked self-confidence, and she liked being led. Ruth Harriet Louise, her first MGM photographer, described her as a "creature of many moods." The magazine editor Jane Gunther, a close friend, called her "Scandinavian, quite matter of fact," but "responsive and funny, mocking and full of jokes." The writer Mercedes de Acosta, a sometime lover of Garbo's, described her as shaped by Sweden's cold winters, by "wind, rain, and dark brooding skies." "She's hard to classify," mused film star Eleanor Boardman, "because, like Chaplin, she was man, woman, and child."[8]

Garbo had sensitive hearing and hated noise. She went to forests and deserts for their silence as well as their beauty. Like most Swedes, she loved nature, referring to "the grandeur and everlasting patience of mountains" and "the feeling [oceans give] of the infinite, of eternal life, of liberty."[9] It's a myth, however, that she always wanted to be alone. She had friends; she went to parties and plays. She wanted to be left alone—by fans, journalists, and street photographers. And she had a phobia about strangers. When someone she didn't know entered a room she was in, she became a frightened animal, running for cover. Actress Tallulah Bankhead called her fear of strangers "a disease." Garbo said that she was "forever running away from somebody or something."[10]

Throughout her career, Garbo called herself "he," "the boy," "the bachelor," or "Garbo." She disliked the feminine name Greta; she often thought of herself as male. Moreover, as an adult, she sometimes became a child, speaking in a childlike manner, telling childish jokes—as though she was a Peter Pan who never grew up. And she was a rebel. She was a pacifist, an advocate of healthy living, and an explorer of Eastern religions, especially Hinduism. A dress reformer, she made trousers and turtleneck shirts acceptable attire for women. (Turtlenecks had previously been worn only by jockeys and prize fighters.) She wore no bra long before 1970s feminists discarded it. She criticized Hollywood materialism and misogyny—by wearing male clothing and, as her friend actress Pola Negri put it, by being "the dowdiest woman in Hollywood . . . where smartness and an air of being well-groomed is a religion with even the poorest extra girl."[11] Yet, in Sweden, she had been a saleswoman in the women's clothing department of Stockholm's elite department store and a mannequin in fashion shows there. Once a film star, she tried to play cross-dressed and even male roles.

She was among the few MGM actors to successfully challenge L. B. Mayer, a tough, Jewish man who had immigrated to America as a child with his family from Eastern Europe, fleeing poverty and anti-Semitism. Shrewd and bold, Mayer and other men like him went from poverty to owning working-class nickelodeons, which charged a nickel to see a silent film, to building huge studios to make films for millions of patrons. Film historians call them "the moguls." In 1927, Garbo defeated Mayer over being typecast as a vamp, a female figure who seduced men to destroy them. She had played a vamp in her first three MGM films: *The Torrent* (1926), *The Temptress* (1926), and *Flesh and the Devil* (1927). But she detested playing vamps so much that she went on strike from the fall of 1926 to the spring of 1927 to force Mayer to cast her in dramatic roles. It was an extraordinary action on her part.

After she won her first conflict with Mayer, Garbo made a series of feminist movies, beginning with *A Woman of Affairs* (1928) and *The Single*

*Standard* (1929), which challenged Victorian sex restrictions and called for free love, free divorce, companionate marriage, and the "Single Standard." That was a slogan for ending the double standard, in place for centuries, under which men could have sex with impunity, while women had to remain virtuous. "Free love" meant the right for women as well as man to have multiple sex partners. Or it referred to the belief that as long as there is no jealousy, having multiple sex partners could purify individuals and, ultimately, society.[12]

Once woman suffrage was achieved by 1921 in Scandinavia, Germany, and the United States, many feminists focused on achieving gender equality in sex, as Garbo did in early films. I call them her "new woman" films, employing the term used from 1890 to 1940 for women who disregarded Victorian norms to enter higher education, the workforce, and the public sphere in general.[13]

In his history of early Hollywood, Lewis Jacobs called Garbo "the prototype of the ultracivilized sleek and slender, knowing and disillusioned, restless and oversexed and neurotic woman who leads her own life."[14] Jacobs' attack on Garbo was an anomaly in his discussion of women's influence in early Hollywood. They were heavily represented in studio story departments, judging novels and plays as potential films. They were the writers and readers of the fan magazines. They were 85 percent of movie audiences and many of the studios' screenwriters. According to Frances Marion, a top MGM screenwriter, the female screenwriters provided "the fodder for a revolution in [female] mores, attitudes, and dreams."[15]

Once Garbo's new woman films were released, women became a majority in her audiences, especially young women, who identified with her—while heterosexual men left her audiences in droves. Fan magazine writers reported that men were afraid of Garbo, who had won her struggle with one of the nation's most powerful men and had created a powerful persona for her films.[16]

In 1934 Garbo reached the peak of her career in playing the title role in *Queen Christina*, a biopic about the seventeenth-century Swedish queen who cross-dressed and was bisexual. It was the major Hollywood film featuring female cross-dressing until 1982, when Julie Andrews starred in *Victor / Victoria* and Barbra Streisand in *Yentl*. But the censors removed *Queen Christina* from the screen six months after it was released. L. B. Mayer, conservative and homophobic, changed the film's financial records to make it appear a box office failure.[17] After this seeming disaster, Garbo abandoned innovation and focused on achieving financial independence. She never played her favored cross-dressed figures— Joan of Arc and George Sand—or her favored male, Dorian Gray, from Oscar Wilde's novel *The Picture of Dorian Gray*.

Garbo's Hollywood career wasn't easy. In her early Hollywood years, she underwent the hazing sometimes visited on overseas actors who threatened the livelihood of American performers. The film censorship board often constrained her sexual assertiveness. And she refused to comply with the expectation that stars owed fans a lot of attention, instead holding her right to privacy paramount. Her fans ignored her desire to be left alone. They mobbed her, thrust autograph books at her, and even tore off pieces of her clothing. To avoid them, she wore disguises, often dressing as a boy.

And there was a continuous male backlash, led by powerful men like L. B. Mayer. They expected sex from starlets, while they supported Hollywood's culture of prostitution, with brothels, courtesans, and streetwalkers. In Marilyn Monroe's autobiography, the great Hollywood star of the 1950s called Hollywood "an overcrowded brothel, a merry-go-round with beds for horses." She was correct for much of the history of Hollywood.[18]

### Theories of Beauty

Movie magazine writers used many theories of beauty in analyzing Garbo's appearance.[19] Foremost among them was proportional theory, also called symmetry. Dating to ancient Egypt and based on architecture and mathematics, it defined beauty in terms of a ratio between body parts, generating the term "well-proportioned" for a beautiful body. In the sixth century B.C.E., the Greek sculptor Polykleitos in his "canon of beauty" defined the perfect height of a body as equal to the length of its face, from hairline to chin, multiplied eight or nine times. He also defined ideal ratios between facial features and between body parts—hands to arms, feet to legs, distance between the eyes, and so forth.[20]

Both Michelangelo and Leonardo da Vinci used proportional theory, but they defined their own ratios, as did many artists. The theory was taught in art academies, using books of engravings of classical sculptures, with their proportions included. In fact, proportional theory is flexible, since its results depend on the person being measured and the proportions being used. If the measure is eight faces to the body, it can result in a figure six feet tall, like the famed Venus de Milo statue from ancient Greece, now in the Louvre Museum in Paris.

The renowned Hollywood makeup artist Max Factor used proportional theory in the late 1920s in defining the ideal face as dividing vertically into three equal parts and horizontally into five eye widths. In 1933, writing in the movie magazine *Screenland*, illustrator Rolph Armstrong defined beauty in symmetrical terms as "a rigid, definite combination of architecture and mathematics—so many inches from brow to chin, from cheekbone to jaw; just so much space between the eyes—proportions immortalized centuries ago by Greek sculptors."[21]

Over its long history symmetrical theory was often challenged, and many of those challenges appeared in the debate over Garbo's beauty. Seventeenth-century English philosopher Francis Bacon wrote: "There is no excellent beauty without some strangeness in its proportions." Even more relative was the belief that "beauty lies in the eye of the beholder." Some writers contended that beauty is spiritual, not physical, produced internally and beamed through the eyes, not the body.

The eighteenth-century philosopher Edmund Burke distinguished between "the beautiful," meaning feminine delicacy, and the sublime, meaning an awe-inspiring entity, often male. The artist William Hogarth, Burke's contemporary, revised the "line of beauty." Classical authors had defined it as straight, as in Greek temples, but Hogarth proposed that it is curvy, as in the baroque style of his era—and in the undulations of snakes.[22]

Burke's delicate female led to the nineteenth century's small and demure Victorian female ideal, while Hogarth's curving line was cited to justify tight-lacing female corsets to produce a curvy body. And his serpents weren't forgotten. In the late nineteenth century the French actress Sarah Bernhardt's sensual movements were called serpentine, as were the writhings of Italian divas / vamps, meant to ensnare and then punish the men who had abused them. Garbo used that writhing in playing the title role in *Mata Hari* (1931), about the World War I courtesan and spy.

Women also contributed to defining female beauty, as editors of fashion magazines, dressmakers and couturiers, and models and mannequins. Rebellious female models helped the English Pre-Raphaelite painters of the mid-nineteenth century to find beauty in tall, uncorseted women, launching a dress reform movement. Paris couturiers led the Euro-American fashion world, with actresses, wealthy women, and courtesans their major patrons. Such fashionistas popularized French styles from the reign of Louis XIV in the late seventeenth century until the mid-twentieth century. They used the phrase "jolie laide" (the beautiful ugly) and the word "chic" to describe plain women with flair.[23]

In the 1920s, the film star Gloria Swanson claimed that everyone used the word "chic" without understanding it.[24] Indeed, the language of fashion can be ambiguous. Take the word "glamour." It was coined by ancient Celts to mean witches' dark spells, and later used in the late nineteenth century to describe Paris courtesans—well-known figures who starred on the stage, rode in open carriages on the boulevards, and were featured in newspapers and magazines. Given these associations, fashion magazine writers didn't use the word "glamour," because they feared it might offend their readers. But Hollywood publicists and movie magazine writers, without such constraints, applied it to Swanson in the early 1920s, and when her career declined by the late 1920s, Howard Strickling, MGM's head of publicity, associated it with Garbo.[25]

In addition to symmetrical theory, movie fan magazine writers used the theory of types, dating to the nineteenth century, when botanists, physiologists, anthropologists, and psychologists used the words "species," "race," "genre," and "type" to organize plants, animals, ethnicities, illnesses, and sexualities into categories. To simplify casting plays, theatrical producers separated actors into types. Film producers followed suit, implying that a range of ideal beauties existed, not just one.

For actresses in Garbo's era, the types included ingenue, or innocent adolescent; soubrette, or saucy adolescent; siren; leading lady; character actor; vamp; and flapper, although the last two categories went in and out of fashion.

With ties to the movie studios and to beauty companies and designers, movie fan magazines advertised their products while featuring the clothing and cosmetics of movie actresses. Their writers claimed that any woman could be beautiful by finding the actress who was her type and adopting the beauty practices of that actress. The magazines described those regimens, including the products actresses used, which were advertised in the magazines and used by cosmetic companies in marketing their wares.[26]

Movie fan magazine writers assumed that styles in fashion, like styles in art, cycled over time. The small, flirtatious beauty of the Rococo era, wearing an elaborate white wig, gave way to the tall and slender beauty of the French Revolution and Napoleon's era (1789–1815). She wore a shift gathered under the bosom and falling to the ankles, in the "empire style." By 1820 a conservative reaction to an era of political upheaval brought the small woman, with an hourglass figure, into vogue. By 1840 she resembled England's tiny Queen Victoria, wearing a tight-laced corset and a bell-shaped skirt held out by petticoats made of stiffened crinoline, and by 1850, by a steel hoop. By 1870, a straight dress front with a bustle on the backside was the ideal fashion in female dress.

By then, dress reform had appeared, as women wore suits with skirts for shopping; shirts and long skirts for working; and bloomers for exercising. The tall Pre-Raphaelite woman led to the statuesque woman of the painters of the 1890s. That tall figure also appeared as the ideal beauty in illustrations drawn by the Pre-Raphaelite illustrator George du Maurier for the British humor magazine *Punch*, and in those of his follower Charles Dana Gibson, for the American humor magazine *Life*. The famous Gibson girl was born.

In the 1900s, Cole Phillips, Howard Chandler Christy, and scores of other illustrators in Britain, France, and the United States followed Gibson but drew smaller, less patrician beauties like the Phillips girl and the Christy girl, who were named after their creators. By 1920, the flapper had taken over. That adolescent figure had appeared in the nineteenth century in working-class dance halls and in fashions marketed for adolescent girls.

Most dominant models of beauty arise from a multiplicity of models before becoming hegemonic. "Hegemony" implies that the dominant beauty of any era is temporary, not fixed, and that alternative types exist. Any of them may rise to the top because of historical developments, social change, the dictates of designers, or the popularity of iconic individuals. According to the *Vogue* editor Edna Woolman Chase, "fashions evolve; they do not leap."[27] Yet, the final change may seem revolutionary. The French designer Jacques Patou is often credited with creating the "new look" of 1930, involving an elegant tall model in long skirts. But height and elegance as fashion standards for women were already emerging by 1925, and Garbo may have been their source.

Garbo's position as both beautiful and unattractive suggests many interpretive strands. In chapter 1 I will follow some of those strands by analyzing the most famous photograph taken of her—by Edward Steichen in 1928 for *Vanity Fair* magazine.[28] MGM photographers usually photographed Garbo: Ruth Harriet Louise from 1925 to 1930, and Clarence Bull from 1930 to 1942, when Garbo left MGM. Occasionally, a well-known lensman like Steichen photographed her.

Steichen was the day's most prominent transatlantic photographer. He had brought modern art from Paris to New York in the 1910s and modernity to photography, adding a hard edge to the prevailing soft-focus style. In 1924 he became head photographer for *Vanity Fair* and the three *Vogues*—in New York, London, and Paris, all overseen by the New York office. Steichen shot celebrities for *Vanity Fair* and mannequins for *Vogue*, creating a prototype of the modern woman.[29] His 1928 photograph of Garbo influenced later photographers of her, and it led to the 1930s glamour school of Hollywood photography. As Christian Peterson maintained, the image of a movie star in Garbo's era was usually "a particular portrait."[30] Given the widespread popularity of Steichen's portrait, it served that purpose for Garbo.

I will present Garbo's biography chronologically, pausing periodically to comment on its connection to the history of beauty. I find Garbo's acting and her beauty powerful, but my discovery of the negative attitudes toward her is perhaps my most important finding. It led me to investigate the Garbo-maniacs, an important fan group in the history of films. They dressed and behaved like Garbo, saw her films numerous times, and defended against attacks on her in the fan magazines. Unlike other prominent Hollywood stars, Garbo had no fan clubs.[31]

Reading the sources on Garbo in depth, I discovered that she suffered from chronic illnesses, including painful inflammations of her ovaries and cervix. Those inflammations were probably caused by gonorrhea, a condition that MGM publicists hid and that writers on Garbo have overlooked. The inflammations often caused her insomnia and motivated her continual travels for rest to mountains and desert spas in the United States, and to Sweden, her beloved homeland. Because regular doctors had no cure for these ailments until sulfa drugs were discovered in the late 1930s, she often consulted practitioners of alternative medical therapeutics, like osteopaths and chiropractors, as well as natural healers and fitness gurus. Moreover, she frequently dated closeted homosexuals, men who wouldn't demand sex but who would firm up her reputation as a heterosexual woman—a reputation important to female success in Hollywood. And she often thought of herself as male, and sometimes as a homosexual male.

Garbo was tall and slender, with large deep-set, almond eyes, high cheekbones and sunken cheeks, a large nose, luxurious light brown hair, and a masculine silhouette. Her look, adopted by fashion mannequins and women of wealth, has remained hegemonic until the present. It can be seen in the insouciant and insolent stance of models on fashion runways today and of stylish women featured in fashion magazines. Requiring dieting and strenuous exercise, it is as dangerous and difficult to achieve today as it was in Garbo's day.

It was as true for Garbo as for famous beauties today. Fame did not necessarily bring her happiness, although she engaged in sports and nature, achieved her childhood dreams, and was friends with major figures of her era. Gray Horan, her niece and frequent companion in her later years, commented, "When she was in the mood to be happy, there was no one more fun or light-hearted. "And Garbo herself said, "You know, I've lived a fabulous life." But she also said, "There's not been a day in my life that I've felt completely well."

# PART I

# THE STEICHEN PHOTO

Edward Steichen, Garbo, 1928. © 2022 The Estate of Edward Steichen / Artists Rights Society (ARS), New York

# 1

# Garbo Glorified and Demonized

*I*N AUGUST 1928 Edward Steichen photographed Greta Garbo for *Vanity Fair* during a brief break in the filming of *A Woman of Affairs*—Garbo's eighth film for MGM and her first new woman film, after playing vamps, lovers, a spy, and an opera diva. Photographing Garbo wasn't easy. Because of her shyness, she might freeze in front of a camera, and Steichen had little time to establish a rapport with her. That rapport was crucial to bringing out her photogeneity—the magical glow of skin and eyes to which a camera responds, like a lover responding to a beloved.

When Steichen met Garbo for the photo shoot, she seemed to him like a frightened child or a wild animal ready to run, so he calmed her down and let her pose herself. Then he mentioned that her hair was messy—a frequent annoyance of hers. Riled up, she responded with a stunning pose. Covering her body and arms with a dark cloth, she swept her hair back with her hands, holding it on the sides of her head, while registering a complex expression on her face. I see that expression as elegant and earthy, spiritual and sad, masculine and feminine, but with no joy, not the hint of a smile.[1]

Garbo's pose in the Steichen photo resembled the pose for desperation in the Delsarte acting system. Invented by François Delsarte, a speech teacher in Paris in the mid-nineteenth century, it specified facial expressions and body positions for every human emotion. Garbo had studied the system in drama school and used it in her acting.[2] Despite her popularity by 1928, Garbo was desperate that summer. She feared her chronic illnesses—depression, anemia, bronchitis, menstrual issues. She still mourned the death of her adored older sister, Alva, two years previously, and her rejection by Mimi Pollak, her romantic lover in acting school, who married a man. Mauritz Stiller, her mentor, had returned to Sweden, and her romance with John Gilbert, Hollywood's top male star, was falling apart.

Before she sat for Steichen, Garbo had been filming a difficult scene in *A Woman of Affairs*, when her character, Diana Merrick, watches her new husband commit suicide on their wedding night by jumping out a second-story window, while she lies in bed in the room, waiting for him.[3] As an actress, Garbo became the character she played, both on- and off-screen. When Steichen photographed her, he was shooting both the traumatized Diana Merrick and the desperate Garbo. Facing a famous photographer, Garbo was perfecting her signature sorrowful look, which she had already used in films and photos and would continue to use throughout her acting career. She was defining herself as MGM's greatest tragic actress, although she was only twenty-two years old.

Does the Steichen photo of Garbo reflect themes of the 1920s, the decade in which it was shot? And how did contemporary writers, especially film magazine journalists, describe Garbo's appearance? Answering these questions led me to the Garbo-maniacs, as well as to how Garbo, a young woman still connected to her peasant and working-class roots, reacted to the discourse about her in the movie magazines, some of which she read.

In the first place, the Steichen photo bears scant relationship to popular descriptions of the 1920s as "the roaring twenties," an era of dancing, drinking, and sex, or as "the era of the flapper," referring to the androgynous adolescent girl who symbolized the decade's youth rebellion. Instead, the photo relates to a third definition of the 1920s, as dominated by a disillusioned "lost generation" shaped by the huge loss of life in World War I and in the flu pandemic that followed it.[4]

Recovering from World War I was difficult, especially in Europe, where it was fought on native ground, with new weapons of mass destruction: airplanes, bombs, machine guns, tanks. The Allied and Axis armies remained deadlocked for years, with both sides bivouacked in trenches stretching for miles on either side of France's northeastern border. The trenches were muddy, with poor sanitation. They were open to bombs, grenades, and diseases carried by insects and rats. Post-traumatic stress disorder was common. It was called shell shock and believed to be the result of an unmanly character.[5]

"Beneath the superficial frivolity of the 1920s," wrote the English author Leslie Baily, "the postwar generation was haunted and worried by the problem of death." The specter of death pervaded war memorials and cemeteries, the prosthetic masks worn by men with faces disfig-ured by bombs, and the black mourning clothes widows wore.[6] The war was fought by men. With huge casualties on both sides, it created a pop-ulation imbalance in many European countries—more women than men. It would take more than a decade to reduce that imbalance, which meant that many widowed women were unable to remarry.

Garbo's sad, sculpted face in the Steichen photo might be a death mask, with her sadness reflecting postwar suffering—"the ache which is the mainspring of human consciousness," as a contemporary writer described it. The journalist James Fidler opined: "With her great mourn-ful eyes and hollow cheeks, she has the face of a medieval martyr." Lou-ise Brooks, the Hollywood actress and chronicler, called Garbo a mater dolorosa, the mother of Christ mourning for her son who had died on the cross.[7]

How did other writers perceive her? They mostly celebrated her beauty, finding her screen presence mesmeric, while the sadness in her eyes made her seem vulnerable, needing solace and support. A writer in *Time* magazine stated that she infused the screen with a "white light," caused by her intensity and her photogenic glow. The playwright and journalist Robert Sherwood called her "the dream princess of eternity" and "the knockout of the ages." Writers rhapsodized over her smolder-ing, half-lidded eyes, her long eyelashes, and her "fascinating, wide mouth." Publicists devised titles for her: "the most beautiful woman in the world"; "a legend in her own time"; "a woman of fire and ice." The last title referred both to the Swedish climate (arctic in the winter and warm in the summer) and to her supposed passion beneath a cold exterior, a frigidity that could be awakened to ecstasy—the ultimate sexual fantasy.[8]

Garbo was often called "the mystery woman of Hollywood," a phrase that could be read as an invitation to try to define her. Her manager, Harry Edington, contributed the title "divine," which was associated with the French actress Sarah Bernhardt and a long list of opera divas and theater tragediennes. John Gilbert, Hollywood's top male star in the late 1920s and Garbo's lover, described her in an interview: "She can be the most alluring creature you have ever seen. Capricious as the devil, whimsical, temperamental, and fascinating.... What magnetism she gets in front of the camera! What appeal! What a woman! One day she is child-like, naïve, ingenuous, a girl of ten. The next day, she is a mysterious woman a thousand years old, knowing everything, baffling, deep. Garbo has more sides to her personality than anyone I have ever met."[9]

Writers discerned that Garbo's appearance crossed age categories: she could look like an ingénue or a sophisticate. Such age crossing appealed especially to Europeans. The French believed that, like fine wine, women needed to mature beyond the age of thirty to be beautiful. Because Garbo, with the right makeup, could appear to be almost any age, she could play an older women involved with a younger man, a relationship central to the European "novel of initiation," in which an older woman initiates a young man to romance and sex. It is a theme in novels by Balzac and Flaubert; it was often a theme in Garbo's films. The European market for Hollywood films produced 35 percent of U.S. sales; United Artists' 1936 *Black Book* listed Garbo as the major star in twenty-six of thirty European countries.[10] Irving Thalberg, in charge of production at MGM, kept the European market in mind in choosing films for the Swedish actress. That market was essential to maintaining her stardom—and MGM's profits.

When Garbo first came to Hollywood, writers described her in terms of Norse mythology, in line with her Swedish background. She was called a Valkyrie, a powerful Norse goddess who finds slain heroes on battlefields and brings them to Valhalla, the home of the gods. She was soon identified with ancient Greek and Roman goddesses, who were central to the heritage of many Western nations. Her smooth white skin and angular face, often tanned to an apricot color, looked as though it had been carved out of marble. She could pass as a modern version of an ancient classical divinity, especially Venus, the Roman goddess of beauty, and specifically the Venus de Milo, a major symbol of ideal female beauty for over a century since the statue was discovered on the island of Melos in 1832. Garbo's admirers called her height "statuesque," a word coined in the early nineteenth century, when classical statues of large women were especially admired.

A classical revival also flourished in the 1920s and 1930s, as artists turned to ancient Athens as a place of order and stability, the home of Western philosophy and democracy, an antidote to the chaos of the world war they had experienced.[11] Influenced by the classical revival, Picasso and other artists in the early 1920s painted and sculpted monumental women, using classical sculptures as their models. Many Paris couturiers, fashion setters for the Euro-American world, based their designs on the draped tunics and chitons worn by women in ancient Athens.[12] The classical goddesses appeared in illustrations in fashion, movie, and general-circulation magazines. Readers recognized them because classical mythology was featured in children's books and taught in schools. "Olympus Comes to Hollywood" was the title of a 1928 article in *Photoplay*, the major movie fan magazine.[13]

In addition to being called a goddess, Garbo was also described as exotic, Slavic, a blonde Oriental, glamorous, patrician, or as eccentric or odd-looking. All these descriptions focused on her height, sloe eyes, high cheekbones, sunken cheeks, and long nose and neck. In negative descriptions of her, racist and nativist tropes appeared, even though Garbo was Swedish, usually a praised immigrant group in the United States.

By 1930 Garbo was receiving 5,000 fan letters a month, and in 1932 the writer Helen Parde gained access to them. In the letters she read, Parde found that "exotic" was the word most often used to describe Garbo. Parde also reported that the Garbo fan mail "bristles with additional connotations of the word 'exotic': foreign, mysterious, glamorous, Orchid-like." John Gilbert called Garbo's facial expression "half Occidental astuteness and half Oriental passion."[14] Journalist Margery Wilson asserted that "Garbo brings to mind the half-authentic, half-legendary stories of the Mongolian 'hordes of Attila the Hun,' who

Statue of the Venus de Milo. agefotostock / Alamy Stock Photo

swept over Europe. The last vestige of their physical impress on the Western world is found in the peculiar slanting eyes of certain ... North Germans, Swedes, and Norwegians."[15]

The word "exotic" fits Garbo's physiognomy: slanting, deep-set eyes; high cheekbones; and sunken cheeks. In her films she played Spanish, French, and Russian aristocrats, divas, and courtesans, but rarely working women, except for prostitutes. Mercedes de Acosta thought that Garbo looked Slavic, although in using the term "Slavic," Mercedes specified that she meant the Russian aristocrats, some 250,000 in number, who had fled Russia during the Revolution of 1917. That usage avoided the presumption in contemporary texts about race that Slavic peasants were inherently inferior. In his book on the female Russian aristocrats who fled to the West, Alexandre Vassiliev noted in passing that the beauty ideal in Nordic lands, especially in Sweden, resembled Slavic looks.[16]

The word "exotic" dates to the sixteenth century, when it meant "foreigner." Over time, it acquired a sexual connotation. In Garbo's era it was believed that Asian, African, and even European women were deeply sensual, while U.S. women were puritans.[17] Ghislaine Wood contended that the word "exotic" often meant "primitive," and like that word, it wasn't derogatory. Rather, it suggested "an exciting vision, carrying colonialism into a global future. It promoted fantasies of erotic toleration." Webster's 1934 dictionary defined primitivism as a belief in the superiority of primitive life. That was a common assumption in artistic circles and among the avant-garde in the 1920s and 1930s.[18]

In other words, this argument held that the attraction between individuals of differing appearances and ethnic backgrounds could result in cross-ethnic relationships promoting racial equality. The famed U.S. anthropologists and public intellectuals Franz Boas and Ruth Benedict promoted this argument, while the Afro-American revue performer and French screen star Josephine Baker put it into practice by adopting children of differing ethnicities. She called them her "rainbow tribe."[19]

Yet, racism was hegemonic in the 1920s and 1930s. It was based on an interpretation of Darwin's evolutionary theory positing that evolution had produced a hierarchy of races, with whites at the top, and that mixing whites and people of color would produce "mongrel" (inferior) individuals. The U.S. Congress passed laws ending the prewar influx of immigrants from Eastern Europe and the Mediterranean region into the United States. Hitler used eugenic theories devised by U.S. scholars to justify exterminating Jews, Gypsies, and homosexuals.[20]

What about Garbo's pale skin? Was she the "white goddess" of the racists? She was Hitler's favorite actress, but she was neither racist nor anti-Semitic.[21] Mauritz Stiller, whom she adored, was Jewish, as were her later mentors and companions, the actress Salka Viertel and the New York businessman George Schlee, a White Russian émigré from the Russian Revolution. Garbo often called herself a "wandering Jew," a literary character who wandered the world and had no home. She loved jazz—in New York she went to Harlem nightclubs; in Los Angeles she went to jazz clubs on Central Avenue near downtown, the heart of the Black community. In *The Torrent* (1926), her first Hollywood film, she identified herself with a Black entertainer in a nightclub. When Hitler came to power, she fantasized about killing him.

Garbo wore white makeup in her early films because the film stock then in use registered pale skin as dirty.[22] Moreover, for centuries Japanese geishas had painted their faces white, and the fashion spread to the West in the late nineteenth century, when Japanese styles came into vogue after U.S. Commodore Matthew Perry and four gunboats sailed into Tokyo Harbor in 1856 and "opened" Japan to the West. Garbo used a white makeup with silver in it, which made her face shine and covered her freckles, which were considered blemishes.[23] White makeup was also used to signify purity, spirituality, or illness.

The *Vanity Fair* associate editor Clare Boothe Brokaw drew on an old tradition of listing the ideal beauties in history when, in an article on Garbo in *Vanity Fair*, she called her the era's Helen of Troy. She continued: "Garbo is the only one our decade has to offer, with the possibility of joining the elite ranks of Cleopatra, Salome, the Queen of Sheba, Mary, Queen of Scots, and others."[24]

We don't know what Helen of Troy, Cleopatra, Salome, and the Queen of Sheba looked like, but most of them came from the Near East and some of them probably had dark skin. The Queen of Sheba did, and so did the ancient Queen Nefertiti of Egypt, the chief consort of the pharaoh Ikhnaton in the fourteenth century B.C.E. Garbo was often compared with her because of a similar physiognomy: high cheek-bones, sunken cheeks, sloe eyes, and a long neck. Nefertiti's appearance was revealed when in 1924 a life bust of her found by German archeologists in the remains of the ancient Egyptian royal city of Amarna was put on display in Berlin's Neues Museum. It was a major cultural event that furthered a fascination with ancient Egypt in the Western world.[25]

Garbo was also identified with the *Mona Lisa*, painted by Leonardo da Vinci in the seventeenth century; with Jane Morris, the major model for the mid-nineteenth-century Pre-Raphaelite painters; and with the tall, abstract woman in art deco illustrations in the 1920s, particularly those by Edouard Benito.

The name "Mona Lisa" translates into English as "My Lady Lisa," the name of the woman who sat for this painting. In the nineteenth century the *Mona Lisa* became a symbol of female beauty when poets and painters, especially those of a decadent bent, identified her as a femme fatale, a figure that fascinated them. Most of them focused on her haunting smile. In 1873 the English essayist Walter Pater, who used decadent themes, described the *Mona Lisa*'s beauty as frightening and her smile as dangerous. He wrote: "Like the vampire, she has been dead many times, and learned the secrets of the grave and has been a diver in deep seas."[26] The *Mona Lisa* was also called the Gioconda, which refers either to her married surname, del Giocondo, or is a wordplay on *la gioviale*, meaning "the jovial one." That was an ironic title, since the woman in the painting looks sad, not happy.

The Pre-Raphaelite painters, a group of English painters led by Dante Gabriel Rossetti, rebelled not only against the conventions in painting in their day but also against the Victorian preference for small women with round cheeks and eyes. Jane Morris, their favorite model, was tall and thin with a long neck and high cheekbones. She wasn't African, but George Bernard Shaw thought that she looked as though she came from an Egyptian tomb. Her contemporaries found her looks "odd" and "ugly" and thought that her high cheekbones and sunken cheeks were signs of illness. On the other hand, Rossetti called her beauty "genius."[27]

Garbo was also identified with the tall female figure in art moderne illustrations, especially those drawn by the fashion magazine illustrator

Leonardo da Vinci's *Mona Lisa*. IanDangall Computing / Alamy Stock Photo

Edouard Benito. Benito and other art moderne illustrators were especially influenced by the elongated and abstract women painted by the artist Amadeo Modigliani. Art moderne (called art deco since the late 1960s) was the major design style of the 1920s and 1930s. An eclectic style, it included cubism, functionalism, and design styles from pre-state societies, including motifs of masks from Africa and Mexico.

The style became associated with Hollywood, especially with MGM, whose art director, Cedric Gibbons, used it in many films, including Garbo films. Advertising illustrators in the 1920s adopted the art moderne woman as a template. The historian Roland Marchand has proposed that with their wide reach through mass market magazines, the advertising illustrators made American women into art moderne figurines. Yet, other influences were involved in creating the ideal female beauty in the United States, including drawings by the fashion magazine illustrators.[28]

The well-known British photographer Cecil Beaton, who often wrote about female beauty, was obsessed with Garbo during much of his adult life. He usually praised her looks, but he sometimes criticized them with such venom that for a long time she refused to meet him. In his *Book on Beauty* (1930), Beaton applied Walter Pater's description of the *Mona Lisa* to Garbo: "With her slightly insane look, eyes that are thinking strange thoughts and weary smile, she is Leonardo's Gioconda, a clairvoyant who, possessed of a secret wisdom, knows all and sees all." In 1934 he revealed that Garbo bought much of her clothing at army-navy stores where sailors and homosexuals shopped, hinting at her gender crossing, which resembled his own in reverse—she liked to wear male clothing; he liked to wear female clothing. He didn't know Garbo in 1934; her friend Mercedes de Acosta, who was close to Beaton, provided him with information about her.

Beaton also called Garbo a clown, which wasn't pejorative. The faces of clowns had long been symbols for both comedy and tragedy, and clowns often appeared in the art of the 1920s and 1930s, representing "rebellion, protean passion, and problematic perceptions."[29] Clowns were androgynous tricksters, sometimes beyond gender. Beaton described Garbo as a double for Jean-Gaspard Deburau, who in the 1830s finalized the figure of

Pierrot in the commedia dell'arte as sad and androgynous, connected to the moon. The commedia, which emerged in sixteenth-century Italian theater and spread throughout Europe, was developed by actors improvising from stock masks and characters and books containing scenarios and jokes. The Zanni were wily servants often played by acrobats; the character Harlequin, masculine and strong, was developed from them as a gentleman's valet. Columbia was a rustic maiden, often a prostitute, who was chased by Harlequin and Pantaloon, a pedantic merchant. She was a forerunner to the soubrette. The commedia was the precursor of much modern comedy, including the English pantomime, slapstick comedy, and Charlie Chaplin's Little Tramp.[30]

In 1934 Beaton wrote that, like Deburau as Pierrot, Garbo was "pale, forlorn, ethereal, and fecklessly gay."[31] By 1934, the word "gay" could mean homosexual. Beaton himself was a gay trickster who sometimes hid homosexual motifs in his photographs. In 1946 Garbo sat for Beaton as Deburau's Pierrot. Garbo often called herself a clown, referring to her childish playfulness and implying that she was a trickster and a fool, both wise and easily duped.

Masks, like clowns, were popular in the 1920s, especially tribal masks. The well-to-do collected them, mostly African varieties, while avant-garde artists used them as subjects in their work. Masks were also a way to assume differing identities. "We all wear masks as a form of protection; modern life forces us to," wrote Noël Coward, the English playwright whose plays defined the sardonic sophistication of many writers in the 1920s, and who, like Garbo, masked his gay sexual identity. In 1935, when he and Garbo were both in Stockholm, they pretended to be lovers, playing a joke on journalists.[32] In the Steichen photo, Garbo seems to hold a mask of her face over her face, suggesting that she is a trickster, hiding a real self beneath a mask.

Was Garbo's beauty an illusion created with makeup? A case can be made for this possibility. When she removed her eye makeup, she looked strange. Her eyelashes were naturally white, making her appear to be, as she put it, an "albino," considered at the time to be freaks. Each morning she put mascara on her eyelashes. They were so long that when darkened, they cast shadows on her cheeks.[33] They also veiled her eyes, giving her a look of "smoldering passion," according to some observers.

Fred Basten, Max Factor's biographer, wrote that before Garbo became prominent, women didn't pay much attention to their eyes. But once she was well known, "even our nicest people began wearing mascara and eye shadow. Just a slight time before, it would have been called a devil's trick."[34]

Garbo also drew a black line above her eyelashes on each eyelid, as well as a line on her upper eyelids, a practice she derived from actors in Chinese theater. In addition to her long eyelashes, the lines on her eyelids were her trademark. And she could raise one eyebrow, an ironic gesture she used to great effect in her acting.[35] Garbo had studied the art of makeup in drama school, and she had worked with makeup artists in Stockholm and Berlin film studios when she made a movie in each city: *The Saga of Gösta Berling* in Stockholm and *Joyless Street* in Berlin. In making up her face, she knew what she was doing. In the Steichen photo her long mouth is highlighted, and her lips have a "cupid bow" or "bee stung" curve, a sendup of the Victorian beauty ideal.[36]

Garbo's eyes, large and luminous, stand out. Projecting her changing emotions in a remarkably clear way, they dominated her acting, especially in close-ups, a central feature in silent films, when the camera slowly moves toward an actor's face, capturing its full meaning in a riveting way. The *New York Evening Herald* in 1928 found flaws in Garbo's acting, but it praised her close-ups: "Miss Garbo takes a close-up like no other big star in Hollywood."[37]

In holding her hair back with her hands in the Steichen photo, Garbo replicated the Eton haircut, whether by accident or design. In the Eton cut, introduced in 1925, the hair was shingled with a razor and parted on one side, copying a male haircut. "Eton" referred to the elite English boys' public school identified with homoeroticism at the time. The Eton cut signaled the height of female masculinity in female fashions in the 1920s. After 1925, femininity slowly took over.[38]

Except for several scenes in *The Torrent*, Garbo didn't wear her hair short in her films, rejecting the bobbed haircut that was all the rage in the early 1920s. Her hair was naturally straight, but for her films it was curled with a curling iron. In 1928 she created "the long bob," with her hair shoulder length. It took women by storm.[39] It was part of the feminine masquerade she assumed in her films to downplay her masculinity, especially by 1930, after she displayed her masculine voice in *Anna Christie*. Yet, in regular life, she often dressed in male clothing and left her hair straight. Street photographers shot her groomed that way, creating an anomaly that puzzled fans and appealed to studio publicists, who liked to present stars as bifurcated in nature to encourage the public to purchase tickets for films and figure out the stars themselves.[40] The street photographers sold their photographs to the movie magazines.

Why did a major star, a trendsetter in her films, disregard fashion in her daily attire? Louis B. Mayer insisted that MGM stars dress fashionably on the streets, but Garbo paid no attention to his decree. Before 1930, journalists hypothesized that Garbo wore men's pants and shirts for walking and horseback riding or as a disguise to hide from fans. Both theories were correct. Not until 1930, after *Anna Christie* revealed Garbo's masculine voice, did they suggest that it might be a form of lesbian cross-dressing. Although journalists speculated that Garbo was lesbian, whether she was or not is debatable. One can be a cross-dresser without being gay or lesbian.[41]

Most writers on Garbo in her day praised her appearance, but some criticized it. In 1930 Herbert Cruikshank called her "an anemic, overslender girl, with straight and rather stringy tresses, a skin kissed to washed-out pallor by the cold Northern Lights, shoulders too broad and angular for her frame, over-sized extremities and a mouth knifelike to the point of cruelty." Her appearance was often called "odd," since a small woman with round eyes and fleshy cheeks, a small nose, and a small mouth was considered the female ideal. In the 1920s Mary Pickford and Clara Bow were at the top of the polls in the surveys conducted by movie theaters of their audiences to rank the top actors and actresses. In *Vanity Fair* in 1934, Maddy Vogtel wrote that Garbo wasn't beautiful. "She is an intense, gauche, romantic child, with a one-track devotion to whatever man her director wants her to be attracted to. Garbo's laugh is the laugh of a child. Thwarted, she is a child, sullen, petulant, ugly."[42]

Some writers disliked the features of her face; others disliked her awkward body. She had broad shoulders, a bulky frame, and a slouch that she had assumed at the age of twelve, when she reached her adult height, to hide it from her classmates who teased her about it. Her movements were awkward and her stride was long and masculine, until her mentors taught her to assume a sexy glide. She was a natural athlete, but a poor dancer.

Once a negative evaluation of Garbo was published, the negativity sometimes escalated, with writers seeming to try to outdo one another. In the 1920s and 1930s, large shoulders and muscular arms were anathema for women, who were encouraged to exercise but not to enlarge their muscles. In 1930 journalist Mollie Merrick wrote that Garbo's arms were like those of a male dock worker, although Merrick noted that the fashion that year was "to be high-shouldered and broad, so Garbo plays to better luck."[43] Merrick didn't seem to know that Adrian, MGM's head costume designer in the 1930s, had created that fashion, based on Garbo's body. In her films, Garbo and her cinematographers often tried to downplay her bulky body and broad shoulders, but they are often evident.

Even Garbo's feet were attacked as ungainly. What shoe size she wore was debated. The outline of her foot in the Mercedes de Acosta papers indicates a size eight narrow. (Garbo traced the outline so that Mercedes could buy slippers for her.) The shoes in the sale of her possessions at Bonham's auction house in Beverly Hills in 2012 were mostly size nine. Even if changes in shoe sizing over time are considered, these were large sizes in an era when Mary Pickford wore a size three and Joan Crawford a two and a half.[44]

Journalists discovered Garbo's insomnia and her anemia and they criticized her languorous acting, charging that she sleepwalked through her films. Given her contempt for many of those films, plus her chronic insomnia, that criticism wasn't out of line.[45]

Nativist rhetoric was used in criticizing Garbo. Swedish immigrants to the United States were usually praised, but they were also criticized as lazy, dumb, and too tall. That criticism, according to Swedish historian Erika Jackson, stemmed from jokes created by older Swedish immigrants to send up more recent immigrants who didn't speak English well. The jokes were picked up by performers in vaudeville, a popular form of theater replete with ethnic stereotypes.[46] From there, they spread to newspapers and then throughout the nation.

The journalist Ruth Biery, who usually praised Garbo, criticized her in 1932: "Fate played a weird trick on Garbo when it gave her the talent of a [Sarah] Bernhardt with the physique of a peasant. We can all recall pages upon pages of quotations from the tongue of Garbo—wisecracks upon her use of our language."[47] "I think I go home," which Garbo borrowed from Mauritz Stiller and often said when about to leave a film set, was reported in dialect by the press as "I t'ink I go home," becoming a national joke. Louella Parsons, doyenne of the Hollywood columnists, wrote in 1933: "Garbo was the most criticized and frequently ridiculed star in Hollywood." The columnist Jimmy Starr agreed: "Gossips, columnists, and wise-crackers never seem to let up on Garbo."[48]

Older ideas about good looks also influenced the debate on Garbo's appearance. In rural areas, high cheekbones and sunken cheeks were associated with old age, poverty, and illnesses like anemia and tuberculosis, which can curb appetite to the point that severe weight loss occurs, causing cheeks to cave in and outlines of bones to show. Loss of teeth, common in previous centuries among the poor and the elderly, can also cause sunken cheeks. In his popular 1925 book on female beauty, Henry Finck was critical of high cheekbones: "They interrupt the regular curve of beauty, are coarse and inelegant, reflect the loss of adipose tissue under the skin that gives the impression of starvation, suggest age and decrepitude, and replicate these as well as the clumsy jaws of apes and savages." Many physiologists maintained that round cheeks and plump bodies indicated both good health and a beautiful face and body.[49]

Some writers contended that Garbo had an unattractive, asymmetrical face; others cited the popular aphorism articulated by the seventeenth-century English philosopher Francis Bacon: "There is no excellent beauty without some strangeness in its proportions." When the film director Jean Negulesco drew a portrait of Garbo, he found the features in her face to be asymmetrical. She has, he said, "one eyebrow higher than the other, a generous mouth, with a much too liberal a lower lip, a perfect nose slightly on the side in full face." But, as Michael Bruni contended, "producers looked for actresses from abroad with off-beat faces."[50] Los Angeles was full of women with symmetrical faces from throughout the United States, local beauties who had come to Hollywood hoping to break into the movies. Asymmetrical faces were unique. Moreover, even Garbo fans disagreed over whether her beauty was physical or spiritual—a product of her facial features, her soul, or her personality.

Garbo's audience in provincial America was limited; her films were popular in Europe and U.S. cities, where high cheekbones and sunken cheeks were often regarded as signs of aristocratic "good breeding." Such an anomaly, in which body features are considered beautiful in one region or group and unattractive in another, is not unusual in the history of human beauty. In 1929 the Jungian psychologist James Oppenheim wrote that none of the Miss Americas selected in the yearly contest in Atlantic City, New Jersey, resembled Garbo. They were "good fellows, open and frank of face," while Garbo was "Mona Lisa, with a mysterious smile, offering the lure of the unknown."[51] On the other hand, according to Oppenheim, the American people were beginning to like subtlety in acting, as Garbo became their "soul image," a Jungian term for an archetypal image that is widely influential. Beauty commentator Larry Carr agreed about the changing image. Not until 1929, according to Carr, did Americans respond to the beauty of sculpted faces.[52] Neither Oppenheim nor Carr explained why the change occurred, but it was in line with the change in the female beauty ideal in 1930.

In the Steichen photo, Garbo may represent a clown, an aristocrat, an ancient goddess, or an exotic woman, but she radiates power. She looks directly at the viewer, controlling the gaze. Her femininity is downplayed, and her masculinity and androgyny appear in her large nose, slicked-back hair, and lack of traditional feminine sensuality, except for pouty lips, suggesting that she is both immortal and beyond gender.

Why did Garbo elicit negative criticism? It was a minority opinion, but it was strident. Fan magazine writers had their own egos. They prided themselves on creating stars. So did fans, who went to the movies and wrote fan letters. Indeed, the star designation was based on box office receipts and amount of fan mail, which was sent to the studios, which served as the stars' official addresses. The writers of negative appraisals of Garbo eventually realized that she didn't respond to them, although they might draw the ire of the Garbo-maniacs. Garbo's silence was, over time, disliked by both journalists and fans, who called her "conceited" and "high hat." Moreover, to discipline their actors, the film moguls planted negative articles about them in the movie magazines. And Garbo was not just an actress. She had reached the top of the polls by 1928.

Garbo refused requests to appear on the radio, the stage, or television, preserving her reputation for mystery but inviting more criticism and jokes. She didn't seem to mind caricatures—her angular face and body invited them. In the 1920s they were regarded as high art; performers considered it an honor to be caricatured by a renowned artist.[53] In 1930 Clarence Bull, Garbo's MGM photographer from 1929 until she left the studio in 1942, burlesqued her by transposing a photograph of her face onto the body of the Egyptian sphinx, a symbol of mystery. Bull feared that this image might offend Garbo, but when he showed it to her, she laughed uproariously.

The controversy over Garbo's beauty increased her fame. Her detractors were vocal, but so were the Garbo-maniacs. They dressed like her and copied her makeup and hairstyle as well as her sadness and languor, her so-called world-weary look. They saw her movies multiple times, increasing her box office receipts. Their presence explains why, as director Clarence Brown noted, her films had large grosses when they were first released, but those profits soon declined.[54] Even the Garbo-maniacs became tired of seeing the same movie over and over.

Writing in 1929 in *Life* magazine, then mostly a humor magazine, Robert Sherwood described the appearance of a group of Garbo-maniacs he encountered in a New York department store: "They are drooping their eyelids, thrusting their heads back and their shoulders forward, training their lengthening hair to fall all over on one side and to curl slightly at the ends; they are whitening their faces in simulation of interesting anemia; they are looking out at the world through the eye of disillusionment; they are doing a great deal of silent smoldering."[55]

Garbo communicated with the Garbo-maniacs through her clothing, behavior, and especially her hairstyle, which she changed for every film. In 1930 journalist Helen Ludlum described an opening night for *Anna Christie* at which Garbo was present, wearing a disguise. Dozens of Garbo imitators were in the audience, but they had styled their hair

Garbo as the Sphinx. ARCHIVIO GBB / Alamy Stock Photo

after Garbo's hairstyle in *The Kiss*, her previous film, not her style in *Anna Christie*. Ludlum concluded that Garbo always kept one step ahead of her fans.[56]

In the early 1930s, scholarly studies were done on the impact of screen stars on teenagers, because of fears that the movies were sexualizing them. These studies found that teenage girls learned sex techniques through watching Garbo's sex scenes, especially those in *Flesh and the Devil*; they then practiced her techniques at home with their girlfriends. Raymond Daum described Garbo's many young female fans as having "schoolgirl crushes on her" that "defined a national idolatry." And knowledge of Garbo's non-heteronormative sexuality was spread through lesbian networks "from coast to coast." Moreover, the 1920s was an era of commercial expansion in which the ranks of saleswomen and typists, careers dominated by young women, increased. These women made enough money to see a movie more than once. They identified with female stars and liked to see them in powerful roles.[57]

After the 1928 shoot Steichen didn't photograph Garbo again, although in 1932 he combined a photo of her he had taken with one of his photos of Marlene Dietrich for *Vanity Fair*. The picture accompanied an article by Maddy Vogtel that criticized Garbo's appearance—and also criticized the way Dietrich looked. Titled "Both Members of the Same Club," Vogtel's article implied that Dietrich and Garbo went beyond cross-dressing into lesbianism.

In the 1928 photo session, Steichen didn't find Garbo an easy subject. When they met before the shoot, she snarled and whimpered, seeming to Steichen like a wild animal or a petulant child. She was exhibiting what Tallulah Bankhead called "a disease."[58] What caused it? The problems I noted above made her desperate—her sister's death; Mimi Pollak's marrying a man; Stiller's return to Sweden; problems with John Gilbert. She hated the possessive attitude of fans in fan letters, which she rarely read, and the criticisms of her in the movie fan magazines, which she read. They made her angry and depressed; she paced her home muttering profanities. Or she went to bed, saying, "They make damn fool out of me." Sometimes the letters she read were "smutty," and they frightened her. But she rarely read the letters, which studio secretaries answered and then burned, at Garbo's request. Nor did she reply to the criticisms in print, although she told screenwriter Anita Loos that "her appearance sometimes made her feel like a freak." Beneath Garbo's assertiveness lay fears. She told Mercedes de Acosta, "I'm frightened of everything—even in trains, at night, in taxis."[59]

As is usual in neurotic adult behavior, the cause of Garbo's fears lies partly in her childhood. She was raised in poverty, and she hated school. Contemporary writers speculated that something dreadful had happened to her as a child.[60] Indeed, at the age of twelve she was probably raped by a stranger on a Stockholm street, a terrible experience. Like many such victims, she tried to repress her memory of the attack. But as is not unusual, it haunted her in the form of a recurring dream. Her dream was about two men slaughtering a sheep on a country road near Stockholm.

In chapter 2, on Garbo's childhood, I will discuss that dream.

# PART II

# MATURING

Greta Gustafsson, circa 1918. PictureLux / The Hollywood Archive /
Alamy Stock Photo

# 2

## *Childhood*

"$\mathcal{G}$ RETA WAS A show all by herself," marveled Elizabeth Malcolm, a childhood friend of Greta's, reflecting on her outgoing nature. Greta's maternal grandmother, who lived on a farm near Stockholm, called Greta "eccentric"—often a loner, often with curious ideas. Once, when visiting that farm, Greta tested her grandmother's patience to the limit by tying a thick rope between two trees and announcing that she was going to become a tightrope walker, frightening every adult on the farm.

"Tightrope walker" became another circus metaphor, in addition to "clown," that Garbo used to describe her adult self in the movies; acting in films was like a balancing on a tightrope, and one could easily fall off.[1] Kaj Gynt, another childhood friend, was in Greta's class in elementary school and in her class at the Swedish Royal Dramatic Academy. Her birth name was Lena Cederström. She remembered Greta as shy and sensitive. "Her spirit was like a harp," Gynt recalled, "on which the slightest thing had an effect." At the age of twelve, Garbo called herself arrogant and self-centered, and she later spoke of her efforts to control her volatile personality.[2]

Many of her childhood traits were part of her persona as an adult, such as her shyness and assertiveness. Given the lack of family papers, however, it's difficult to trace those traits to her ancestors, aside from her parents. But the Swedish Genealogical Society constructed an ancestry table for Garbo based on her family's broad descent patterns. It shows that her forebears weren't only peasants, as Garbo biographers have claimed. The table lists nobles on her broad family tree. Some were military officers in the Thirty Years' War (1618–1648) involving France, Spain, Sweden, Denmark, and numerous German states. Queen Christina, who ruled Sweden then, sold crown lands and titles of nobility to raise money to bring acting troupes and opera companies to Stockholm and to support Swedish artists. For the seventeenth century, the ancestry table includes a chef, a witch, and a professor at Uppsala University. That background may help explain Garbo's complexities.[3]

Greta's parents, Anna and Karl Gustafsson, were peasants born and raised on farms southwest of Stockholm. In 1898, in their late twenties, before they met, they separately joined the migration from Sweden's overcrowded farming south. They both settled in Stockholm, not far from their birth families. They hoped to find jobs in the city, where the industrial revolution was in full force, and Anna also hoped to find a husband.[4]

They were also attracted by Stockholm's beauty. Called the Venus of the North, it was built on fourteen islands between Lake Mälaren and the Baltic Sea, near an archipelago of 24,000 islands and skerries. There were bridges over its canals and inlets, and ferries crossed its large waterways. The city had palaces, parks, cathedrals, and large public buildings, some dating from the seventeenth century, when Stockholm was the capital of a Swedish empire controlling much of Northern Europe. This walking city, not that large, was an ideal place for the precocious Greta Gustafsson to fantasize about her future.

Soon after arriving in Stockholm, Karl and Anna met and married. Within seven years they had three children: Sven, born in 1898; Alva, in 1903; and Greta, in 1905. But Karl was mostly a failure. Because he dropped out of school at a young age to work on his family's farm, he cut off the possibility of professional employment. In his mid-twenties he contracted kidney disease, perhaps a form of tuberculosis, which can assume differing symptoms in different parts of the body. TB, a lingering disease, was then epidemic in Sweden, as elsewhere in Europe and in the United States.[5] With weak health and a lack of education, Karl found employment in Stockholm only as a casual laborer. Anna did odd jobs and cleaned apartments while she cared for her family.

Karl and Anna had few advantages to pass on to their children, with one major exception: both had striking looks. Anna was small, but she had long white eyelashes.[6] She had an ancestor from the Sami people in Sweden's far North, known for their sloe eyes and high cheekbones. Greta's father was six feet tall. He had high cheekbones, a large nose, and broad lips—all Garbo features. Greta's girlfriends, who sometimes came to the Gustafsson apartment after school to gossip and play games, thought that he was the most handsome man they had ever seen. They wove stories about him—that he was a prince in disguise; that he came from a distant land. Often working nights and staying home days, he sang songs in a resonant baritone voice and told them stories when they visited. When he and Greta took walks together, people stared at them because of their beauty.[7]

The Gustafssons lived on Södermalm, Stockholm's southernmost island, called the South Side or Söder for short. Today Söder is chic, and its residents are mostly young professionals. But in Greta's day they were mostly laborers, living in housing so dilapidated that Söder was sometimes called a slum. Surrounded by water, it connects to the main Stockholm islands by bridges. It was so separate in Garbo's day that its children had their own slang and a reputation for being independent and tough.[8]

The Gustafssons lived in a three-room flat on the fourth floor of a tenement, with running water but without gas or electricity. They cooked on a woodburning stove, which also heated the three rooms. To bathe, they used a tub in a shed in the courtyard behind the building or they went to public bathhouses. Greta and Alva slept in the kitchen; their parents in the living room; Sven in the third room. When the weather was freezing, as it often is in Sweden's long winters, they sometimes all slept near the stove. For toilets, they used chamber pots or outhouses in the back courtyard.[9] Greta accepted her family's living arrangements, which were like those on the farms from which her parents and the parents of her friends had come. "There were no children of the rich on Stockholm's South Island," she stated, claiming her peasant and working-class roots, which she usually tried to conceal.[10]

Because of the influx of farm people into Stockholm, the city was over-crowded. The city council had new roads constructed and encouraged contractors to build houses and tenements; Sweden's welfare state, providing housing and financial support for the needy, was in the future.[11] In *Remember the City*, the third volume of Per Anders Fogelström's series of novels on the history of Stockholm, which are often set on Södermalm, Fogelström described the city in 1905, the year of Greta's birth, as "still just an overgrown small town." But it had an entrepreneurial spirit. With Sweden's resources of copper, timber, and coal, construction was everywhere. Fogelström concluded: "The birth pangs of modernization were underway."[12]

The Gustafsson children attended the local public school, played on the grounds of the local church, and skated on Stockholm's waterways when they froze in the winter. Honoring the Swedish love of nature, Stockholm's city council, like those of many Swedish cities, assigned garden plots to the poor on the city outskirts. The Gustafssons had a plot in Enskede, on Söder's southern border, where they raised vegetable and fruits. Yet, their finances were precarious. When Greta was born, Karl's employer offered to adopt her to ease their poverty. Anna refused. If God sent us a child, she said, he will provide bread.[13]

In warm weather, Greta sat on the bottom rungs of an old staircase near their apartment building, creating a fantasy world. She imagined that the staircase was Jacob's ladder, from the Bible story in the book of Genesis in which angels ascend and descend a ladder from heaven to earth, celebrating the patriarch Jacob, whom God has selected to lead the Israelites, his chosen people. Those angels might honor Greta for participating in the local church. Like most Swedish churches, it was Lutheran, Sweden's official religion since the Protestant Reformation of the sixteenth century.

Greta went to Sunday school, where she studied the Bible and Lutheran doctrines, which she also studied in public school. From the age of nine, she sang in the church choir with her father. Shortly after his death in 1920, she was confirmed as a member of the church. She could now take Communion, a central rite of the church, in which the minister gives celebrants wafers to eat and sips of wine from a large chalice, symbols of Christ's body and blood, shed in his crucifixion to save humanity from their sins. After Karl died, Greta continued to sing in the choir, which performed during High Mass Sunday mornings and evensong Sunday evenings.[14] Greta's faith waned as she matured, although she retained her Lutheran sense of sin and guilt, a heavy burden. In her later life, those self-denying emotions led her to search for a God and a religion in which she could believe.

In addition to Bible stories, Greta based her fantasies on folktales told by her mother, a storyteller in the Scandinavian tradition of storytelling. Anna Gustafsson was even-tempered and practical; she bargained with shopkeepers to keep her family financially afloat.[15] Greta internalized Anna's frugality so fully that her stinginess was legendary in Hollywood. But Anna also had a mystical side. She came from the province of Värmland, "rich in lore and legend." Her conversation was filled with aphorisms like "If you let the devil on board, you must row him to the shore," and "If you start by having too much faith in it, it will end by going to hell."[16] Greta adopted those maxims. Counseling submission to fate, they imply a predetermined future. So did the folk songs that Anna sang. They were sometimes joyful, but, usually in a minor key, they were often melancholy.

The folktales could be frightening. They featured witches, the devil, and trolls, associated with disorder. Usually ugly, with three heads, trolls can shape shift, taking on differing forms. If you venture out after dark, warns one tale, trolls may capture you in their nets made of dew-drenched spiderwebs and take you to their mountain kingdom. The Skogsraet, a female vixen, bewitches men. Mara the Nightmare passes through locked doors and attacks sleeping people with nightmares.[17]

Kaj Gynt, who was raised on the folktales, stated that "the strange legends" became "part of the soul of children who have heard them when young." As an adult, Garbo told folktales to her friends. Cecil Beaton heard them a lot. So did Laila Nylund, the daughter of Max Gumpel, the wealthy owner of a construction company, who was Garbo's first lover—when she was fifteen and he was thirty-one—and a lifelong friend. In 1946 she visited Max and his family at his estate near Stockholm. Laila remembered her saying, "My best subject is trolls. They are kind of spooky, but they're friendly." Garbo, then forty-one, seemed to Laila to be a child who wanted life to be a fairy tale. Many of Garbo's friends experienced her that way.[18] Laila also said that Garbo looked like a man. That was another frequent description of her, especially when she wore male clothing.

Greta based some of her childhood fantasies on the kings and queens in her history lessons at school. "Following my fantasies," Garbo remembered, "I might shorten the life of a cruel king and replace him with a romantic knight or reawaken an unhappy queen centuries after her death." But Greta disliked school. She felt oppressed there, having to study subjects she didn't like. She became upset when her teacher reprimanded her for being lost in her fantasies and threatened her with a spanking after she ran away several times. Her sister, Alva, intervened to stop the spanking. Lutheranism, which permeated Swedish culture, recommended harsh punishment for misbehavior.

Greta also fantasized about becoming a Hollywood star and a celebrity. She acted out these fantasies with Elizabeth Malcolm on the tin roof covering the outhouses in the courtyard behind her family's apartment building. "We are on a glistening white beach on the Riviera," Greta would say, "lying near aristocrats and millionaires who are vacationing here." In her fantasy, the backyard was a windswept ocean, and the children playing in the yard were swimmers in the ocean. The gramophone music coming through the open window of an apartment was "sweet melodies from a fashionable casino orchestra."[19]

Tall and muscular, Greta was a natural athlete. No one could swim as far or as fast as she, "with that lightening speed of hers, with those true, powerful strokes." She loved skating—"skimming madly through the keen, cold air, while the wind whistles in your ears, and you feel light—light and swift." Along with her world of dreams, she loved the winter sports of her country. But she told Sven Broman that she was a sickly child, and her mother gave her cod-liver oil, a remedy for anemia, from which Greta suffered. She also had a weak stomach, with a deficiency in hydrochloric acid, which made it hard for her to digest certain foods, like shellfish and papayas.[20]

She was also a trickster. She told Cecil Beaton that as a child, she was the leader of a gang that played tricks on adults, such as ringing the doorbells of the apartments in her apartment building and then

Greta at Katarina Sodra School, in white dress at center. ARCHIVIO GBB / Alamy Stock Photo

disappearing before someone answered the bell. Mrs. Emmanuel Lonn lived next door to the Gustafssons. Lonn remembered Greta as full of life and bossy, ordering everyone around.[21] "Young as I was," Garbo said, "I always had my own opinions." She was so self-willed and opinionated as an adolescent that everyone in her family came to her for advice.

Greta wore her brother's cast-off clothes and sometimes passed as a boy. She said that she was a tomboy, who played leapfrog and had her own bag of marbles. One evening when she was eight, walking on a street near her home, she encountered two men scuffling with each other. Both were drunk, reeking of alcohol. One man was large, the other small. She pulled on the large man's sleeve, and he stopped fighting. Relating this experience to journalist Ruth Biery many years later, she stated, "If I hear two people quarreling, I get sick all over."[22] Did she know the men who were fighting? Was her father one of them? That's been alleged, although she told Biery that her father wasn't involved.

As a child, Greta often thought she was a boy. Was she transgender, identifying herself as male? That's possible, although the word "transgender" wasn't used in her day; individuals with imprecise genitalia were called hermaphrodites, and gender crossers were androgynes. From childhood on, she called herself "he" and "the boy"; she later called herself a bachelor. Her favorite pseudonym as an adult was Harriet Brown. "Brown" had no special meaning; it was a common, anonymous surname. But "Harriet" came from the Swedish poet Harriet Löwenhjelm, who thought she was male, not female. In Garbo's favorite Löwenhjelm poem, the poet identified her lover as female:

The children of the world go dancing now,
treading the boards of vanity,
but I wind the yarn of dreams
along with the roses and the lily
I never did see my own true love
save only in my dreams
Green was the dress she wore
green with rosy seams.[23]

Greta wrote intense letters to Eva Blomqvist, a student in her confirmation class. She told Eva that "her heart was lost to masculinity." She chided Eva for trying to take over her friends, describing herself as "haughty and complicated by nature." Yet, she also wrote Eva that she yearned for her. "Eva child," she asked, "what do you feel for me? Write and tell me your life story."[24]

Do these letters express simple adolescent emotionalism? Or do they indicate a deeper attachment? It's possible. Romantic friendships between adolescent girls were frequent in Sweden in this era, as they were in much of Europe and the United States. They were extensions of the "best friend" relationship of adolescence, which still exists today. The Swedish feminist Ellen Key, known worldwide for her feminist writings, noted in 1911 that same-sex romantic love was increasing. She defined it as "the passionate worship between persons of the same age—or of an elder by a younger member of the same sex."[25] It involved kissing and hugging and perhaps genital contact, although the proof for that is limited.

What did Greta mean when she wrote to Eva that "her heart was lost to masculinity?" Was she referring to Max Gumpel and her affair with him? Or did she mean that she felt herself to be mostly male and she wanted to take on a masculine role with Eva? Her desire for that position would emerge in her affair with Mimi Pollak.

As a child, Greta was an adventurer, despite her anxieties and her anemia. From the age of eight, she roamed Söder's streets. She soon discovered the Mosebacke and Söder theaters in North Söder, an hour by foot from her home, not far from the palisades that mark Söder's northern boundary. The Söder theater featured serious plays; the Mosebacke was a cabaret. Both were on Mosebacke Square, Stockholm's Montmartre, a place of dining, drinking, dancing, and entertainment. Once she reached the square, Greta stood outside the stage door of the Mosebacke theater, which was often open. She listened as the actors played their roles, and she smelled the backstage smell of "greasepaint, powder, and musty scenery," as she described it.[26] Like many theater devotees, she loved that smell. Greta's senses—smell, touch, hearing—were especially sensitive, which affected her acting and her life.[27]

Greta's love of acting was also inspired by the photos of actors that covered a wall of Agnes Lind's newspaper and tobacco shop, on the first floor of an apartment building near the Gustafssons' building. Fascinated by Lind's photos, Greta developed a crush on Carl Brisson, a Danish actor who had been Europe's middle-weight boxing champion. In 1918 he headlined a Mosebacke theater production as "the King of Söder," with a troupe of chorus girls called "Brisson's Blue Blondes."

Stockholm had been a theater city from the days of Queen Christina in the mid-seventeenth century, when the queen brought an opera company and acting troupes to Stockholm. She commissioned Swedes to write plays and sometimes performed in them herself. She gave stipends to composers and singers.[28] In the late eighteenth century, Gustav III, called the Acting King, wrote, directed, and acted in plays. In 1787 he founded the Swedish Royal Dramatic Theater and its acting school. The efforts of Queen Christina and King Gustav III were in line with the trend among European rulers to found theaters, and opera and ballet companies, for entertainment and to promote their countries.[29]

One winter night, Greta brought a bunch of out-of-season violets to the Möseback theater for Carl Brisson. Charmed by the gift, he gave her a pass to his performances. When she attended one and clapped loudly, he appointed her his "claque"—to start the audience singing when he wanted to hold a sing-along.[30] Greta also wrote plays. She, her siblings, and her friends played the parts in them, and she produced them in living rooms in the neighborhood. In her plays, she stated, she was sometimes an evil spirit. Her sister would kill herself out of jealousy; her brother, out of despair. Sometimes she would kill herself to make her lover happy.[31] Her plots resembled those of the melodramas of her era, with sensationalism, overblown emotions, and stereotyped characters. She organized an acting group, which she called the Attic Theatre, and played roles in its productions—especially male roles. She did a sketch in which she was both a sheik and a dancing girl. Elizabeth Malcolm called Greta "a show all by herself."

Greta's involvement with the theater may not have been that unusual. By 1910, Stockholm had more theaters per capita than any other city in Europe. Small theaters were common, sometimes located in hotels and large houses.[32] What Pers Anders Fogelström had identified in 1905 as the birth of modernization in Sweden was expanding, as the middle class continued to increase in size and museums and monuments were built. Swedes were inventors—of searchlights, explosives, and the Electrolux vacuum cleaner, for starters. The Swedish author August Strindberg began publishing his many novels, essays, and plays in the late 1870s;. Selma Lagerlöf's first work, *The Saga of Gösta Berling*, was published in 1891. In 1909 she won the Nobel Prize in Literature, the first woman and the first Swede to win the prize. Henrik Ibsen, from Norway, was the third dramatist in a triumvirate, along with Strindberg and Lagerlöf, which brought Scandinavia world acclaim.

Hollywood movies as well as films made by the few Swedish studios then in existence appeared in Stockholm by 1910. As an adolescent, Greta loved films. She especially liked Mary Pickford in Hollywood films and Mary Johnson in Swedish films. Both were small and determined tomboys. When Greta learned that Mary Pickford had risen from poverty to fame, she decided to do the same.[33] It was bravado on her part, but she put into action a plan that worked. By the age of fifteen, she was selling women's hats and clothing in Stockholm's premier department store, modeling clothes in fashion shows, and acting in minor movies. She was then admitted to the Royal Dramatic Academy in Stockholm, a stunning achievement. Finally, Mauritz Stiller, the famed Swedish film director, noticed her.

In the story of Garbo's childhood that I have related, she seems carefree and assertive. But the story has a dark side. Greta may have been strong-willed, but she easily became shy and insecure. Prone to up-down moods, she probably suffered from a condition that is today called bipolar disorder, with manic and especially depressive periods. She told the journalist Ruth Biery that even as a child, "at one moment I would be happy and the next plunged into sorrow and despair."[34] Many successful artists and writers throughout history have had bipolar disorder. The hypomanic state between depression and elation, in particular, can produce a controlled creativity, providing incentive and self-discipline.[35]

By the age of twelve, Greta had reached her adult height of five feet, seven inches. She towered over her classmates, who teased her about her height, as did people on the streets. "Everywhere I went as a child I was pointed at because I was so big, so very big," she wrote.[36] She tried to look smaller by slouching. She never lost that affectation; she later incorporated it into her acting. Fortunately for her, slouching was in fashion in the 1920s, as a characteristic of the rebellious flapper, and many actresses adopted it. Yet, the young Garbo wasn't concerned about her chubby body, which is apparent in her communion photo of June 1920.

When Mauritz Stiller auditioned her in 1923 for *The Saga of Gösta Berling*, he told her that she had to lose a lot of weight to succeed in films. During the next several months, she lost over twenty pounds. Her weight—and her dieting—would remain issues for her throughout her career, as she struggled with obesity and anorexia nervosa.

In 1930, Greta wrote a brief memoir of her childhood for her friend the Swedish journalist Lars Saxon, which he published in his magazine *Lektyr*. It reveals some of the difficulties of her childhood. "Extreme poverty always ruled our lives," she began, referring to her family. She portrayed a typical evening in the Gustafsson's living room. The long winter nights, she wrote, were always gray. Karl would be sitting in a corner, scribbling figures on a newspaper. Her mother would be repairing old clothing, always sighing. The children would be talking in low voices because anxiety was in the air. She described their neighborhood. The houses and apartment buildings looked alike; the grass was dying, as were the children in her neighborhood. (Her statement about children dying probably referred to the 1918 flu pandemic, which caused more deaths than World War I did.)

Calling her childhood "brutal" in a conversation with Cecil Beaton, Garbo told him about a terrible experience she had when she was twelve. Walking on a country lane near Stockholm, she came across two men slaughtering a sheep. She watched them, horrified and mesmerized. She had never seen an animal slaughtered. One man hit the sheep on the head, killing it. Then the two men cut the animal open and drained its blood into a pan. Finally, they took the carcass away to cut it into pieces, ready for market. Once she finished telling the story to Beaton, she said again and again: "Oh, how awful life is." The killing of the sheep so traumatized her that she often couldn't stop herself from thinking about it in her later life.[37]

Did Greta actually see the killing of a sheep? Greta visited her grandparents' farms, where animals were slaughtered for food. After her parents moved to Stockholm, her father worked as a butcher at a slaughterhouse; the family photo album contained a picture of him with three other slaughterhouse workers, standing in front of a row of animal carcasses.

Or was Greta's recollection of the killing of the sheep a "screen memory"? Sigmund Freud coined the term "screen memory" for a memory the brain creates to conceal a worse reality. Memory can be tricky, holding incorrect images, although memories of traumatic experiences rarely disappear completely, for they trigger high levels of adrenaline and other stress hormones, imprinting the experience on the brain. Trauma may produce insomnia and anxiety attacks.[38]

Garbo's memory of the killing of the sheep also raises the possibility that she was the sheep, that she was sexually abused as a child. Sheep are symbolic of sacrifice, as in the Bible passages about sacrificing sheep to honor God and about Christ as the Lamb of God who was sacrificed to exonerate the sins of humans. Abused girls may blame themselves for attacks. They may develop an aversion to sex or a drive for it, which is today called sex addiction. They may develop a sadomasochism in which they identify with powerful individuals and try to destroy them. Low self-esteem may exist beside megalomania. These symptoms can appear immediately after an attack or later in life. Such possibilities offer ways of understanding Garbo.

Many individuals close to the adult Garbo thought that something dreadful had happened to her as a child. Ramon Novarro, her friend and co-star in *Mata Hari*, said, "Someone must have frightened her at the very beginning." Ruth Biery had the same reaction to Garbo when interviewing her, while Garbo told Nicholas Turner, a close New York friend, that at the age of twelve she had been raped by a Swedish man, a stranger she didn't know, on a deserted Stockholm street. She told Turner that it had left a bad taste in her mouth for a long time. The Hollywood star Dolores del Rio, who was a cousin of Ramon Novarro's and Garbo's close friend, referred in an interview to Garbo's terrible childhood: "Someone had injured her. And you can't put a torn petal back on a rose." Del Rio continued: "It was as though she had diamonds in her bones, and her interior light struggled to come out through the pores of her skin."[39]

Aside from Nicholas Turner, Del Rio was the only person among Garbo's close friends to speak so freely about Garbo's childhood, but Cecil Beaton referred to it when reporting that Garbo told him: "I had a very troublesome time in my youth, and I learned a lot of other things then. It doesn't do to ask an eye for an eye." In other words, it's foolish to demand vengeance against someone who has wronged you. In making that statement, she said that she was thinking of the Bible passage "Vengeance is mine, saith the Lord, I will repay." She added, "Not that I've read the Bible since I was a child and was shocked by all that incest."[40] (The Old Testament includes brother-sister marriages and father-daughter intercourse.) Her panic attacks as an adult—when she snarled and fled from a room if a stranger entered it—seem to have been related to a trauma involving a stranger.

Some Garbo biographers maintain that her father was an abuser, that he was alcoholic and couldn't control himself when drunk. It's probable that Karl sometimes drank too much. The Stockholm journalist Sven Broman, who interviewed neighbors of the Gustafssons for his 1968 biography of Garbo, concluded that Karl sometimes came home tipsy. When Anna confronted him, Karl contended that drinking liquor was the only way he could stand his work. In fact, Swedish employers often rewarded their workers with beer or aquavit, a Swedish liquor with a high alcohol content. This practice resulted in high rates of alcoholism among Swedish working-class men. But a strong temperance movement in Sweden in the early twentieth century reduced the amount of drinking in the country.[41]

Karl was often described as sensitive and intelligent. Garbo remembered his sense of humor and his ability to cheer people up. His only regret, aside from his illness, was that he had to end his schooling before graduating from elementary school to help support his natal family. But he read newspapers and books, and he had a store of knowledge. To deal with his illness he took long walks, sometimes taking Greta with him, inaugurating her love of walking. He sang in the church choir with her on Sundays, and they cared for the fruits and vegetables in their family's garden allotment together.[42]

During Greta's last year in grammar school, Karl lay dying, while World War I raged in Europe. Sweden was officially neutral, but the

Allied blockade of the North Sea prevented food and other necessities from reaching the country. The Salvation Army, which was active in Sweden, set up a soup kitchen in Greta's neighborhood. Following Army procedures, its leaders recruited local people to participate in revues to lift their spirits and as an incentive to join their organization. Greta portrayed a Chinese girl in a Salvation Army revue.

During that year, her older brother Sven impregnated a local shop-girl. The mother and child moved into the Gustafsson apartment, badly straining family finances and living space.[43] To help out, Greta found a job as a lather girl in a nearby barbershop, massaging the faces of men waiting to be shaved and putting lather on their cheeks and chins. Sweden had a tradition of women barbers, and it was respectable for a Swedish girl to work as a lather girl; it was a way to become a barber and eventually to own a barbershop.

Greta said that when she began the job she experienced "a certain feeling of degradation," but she overcame it. Everyone at the shop liked her, and customers asked for her. "Students and soldiers often came to be soaped by her when they didn't need it at all." She learned how to stop unwelcome advances. Sally Ekengren, the sister of the shop's owner, said, "I can picture her now, the future Garbo, changing her coat for a white smock in a small cubicle, neatly arranging her hair, with a pink silk ribbon." She turned the cubicle into a portrait gallery, plastering the walls with photos of Carl Brisson. "She found his wavy hair and boyish dimples irresistible," said Ekengren," and she never concealed her childhood infatuation. She always blew a kiss to his portrait before she skipped into the shop to lather the raspy chin of one of her own devout admirers."[44]

Meanwhile, Karl's health became worse, and Greta became his major caretaker. Even though his illness frightened her, she loved him deeply. He was only forty-eight. The postwar flu pandemic was also frightening. In her *Lektyr* memoir, she wrote of children dying in her neighborhood; the pandemic probably caused the deaths. She took Karl to a public clinic for treatment, but she hated the task, especially having to deal with the admitting clerk, who scorned them as indigents. Sensitive to slights, Greta felt humiliated. She vowed never to be poor when she was an adult, never to be demeaned in such a way. The fear of poverty and its corollary, the drive for wealth, remained with her throughout her life. And she later identified Louis B. Mayer with the conceited admitting clerk at the public clinic. In later life, she nursed friends who were ill, bringing them food and water, sitting by their bedsides and putting cold compresses on their foreheads—replicating her care for her father again and again, in what was her most humanitarian activity.[45]

Did Greta join any of the reform movements in Stockholm in the 1910s and 1920s? There were temperance movements, women's rights and women's suffrage groups, and strong labor unions. Scott Reisfield, Garbo's grandnephew, asserted that Greta's childhood nickname, Kata, usually attributed to her mispronunciation of "Greta" when learning to talk, came from Kata Dahlström, a Swedish socialist and labor union leader. According to Reisfield, Garbo was so forceful that she reminded her family of Dahlström, who was known as the "mother of the Swedish working-class movement."[46]

Along with her mother, Greta became involved with the Salvation Army. She acted in its productions, and she sold its newspaper door to door. When she played a Goddess of Peace at her Attic Theater, wearing a white sheet, she sang a Salvation Army song: "Why must people fight? / Why must blood flow?"[47] Absorbing the antiwar sentiments of the Salvation Army, Greta was a pacifist throughout her life. Pacifism as a movement to end war hardly exists today, but pacifist organizations were strong after World War I. They were often led by women, as was the Women's International League for Peace and Freedom.

Sweden also had a strong feminist movement. The writer Ellen Key was known worldwide, as was Selma Lagerlöf. Key called for state support of unmarried women with children and for men to become gentler and more emotionally open. Lagerlöf delivered the main speech at the plenary session of the Sixth Congress of the International Woman Suffrage Alliance in 1911, held in Stockholm, with delegates from twenty-six countries. Speaking before an audience of over a thousand women and men, Lagerlöf argued—as she would in *The Saga of Gösta Berling*—that women's compassionate nature would benefit the leadership of the state and society at every level. Lagerlöf supported woman suffrage and wrote novels and stories with strong women characters both within the home and outside of it.

Both she and Ellen Key wanted men and women to become more alike, to form what Key called a "third sex." The idea of appealing not only to women but also to men to promote change, not only in society as a whole but also within themselves, was a goal of this early feminist movement.[48] In 1911 Greta was six years old, but the ideas presented at this major conference in Stockholm reverberated throughout Sweden for years. In 1923, Greta's first major film role would be in Mauritz Stiller's version of Lagerlöf's *Saga of Gösta Berling.*

Why did Garbo describe her childhood as brutal to Cecil Beaton? Did she refer only to her family's poverty and her father's illness? Did her hatred of quarrelling stem from family disputes? In their small apartment, arguments would have been dreadful. Greta was close to Alva and Sven. Sven let her wear his clothes, and he acted in her productions. Alva intervened at her school to prevent her from being spanked, and she helped Greta find employment. She worked as a secretary downtown, but she also was cast in walk-on roles in Swedish films. Greta must have hoped that both she and her sister would succeed in films, like Norma and Constance Talmadge and the several other sister pairs who were Hollywood stars. Greta was also close to Karl's brother David, a taxicab driver. He sometimes drove her home from the Mosebacke theaters at night, worrying about her being alone in the evenings on public streets.

What is suspicious in Greta's childhood are her walks in the evenings between central Söder and Mosebacke. Blekinggaten Street, on which the Gustafsson apartment building was located, is close to Gögaten Street, Söder's main road running north to south. In Greta's childhood there were barbershops, movie houses, saloons, and dance halls on Gögaten Street; it wasn't entirely safe. Greta's walks on that street and in the Mosebacke area worried her parents, but they couldn't stop her; she was too independent. When she stayed out too late, Karl or Sven—or her uncle David—went out to find her and bring her home.

An article on Stockholm's female newspaper reporters in the 1900s clarifies the nature of Stockholm's streets in Greta's era. As the first women reporters in the city, these women walked the streets, pursuing stories. They dressed like respectable women, wearing suits, blouses, hats, and gloves. But they feared the streets, which had long been forbidden to women like them. Stockholm had a fair number of prostitutes, and by Greta's day, the system of regulated brothel prostitution had been abolished. Streetwalking was the norm.[49]

Some men regarded women on the streets as fair game. They followed the women reporters, soliciting them for sex. They whistled and made lewd remarks, and they pounded their walking sticks on the street. The women reporters avoided nightclubs and the backstages of theaters, where prostitutes solicited customers.[50] Did Greta encounter any such women at the Mosebacke theater? Did she meet men bent on mischief as she walked the streets on her way to Mosebacke? The evidence about the women reporters, plus the concern of the other Gustafssons about Greta, suggests that Mosebacke and the streets around it weren't safe for women alone. Greta was bold—or foolhardy—in walking there and staying at the Mosebacke theater until the evening performances ended.

What can be concluded about Garbo's childhood? Was it a joyful time, as she played sports, produced plays, and led the neighborhood gang in mischief? Was it gloomy, filled with violence? Cecil Beaton asked her those questions and recorded her answers: "She talked about her youth and how unhappy she was. I interjected: But you've always told me you were such a tomboy and had so much fun leading the other children into mischief. She replied: Cecil Beaton, how can you say such things! There are 365 days in the year!"[51]

Garbo's reply to Beaton's question sounds like Garbo at her humorous best, using irony to avoid a direct answer. She probably found her childhood both happy and harrowing; both these reactions colored her later life. But its traumas never left her. She couldn't stand quarreling, and she trained herself to remain calm when disagreements arose. There was also her terrible fear of strangers, not only in crowds but also in intimate settings. As she aged, books with violence in them frightened her. She always felt as though she was running away from someone or something.[52] These aspects of her character sound like holdovers from a violent experience as a child.

Yet, she could be playful and jokey, childlike and joyful. And she could take problems in stride. When a group of fans mobbed her after the opening of *Camille* in 1936, she wrote to her mentor and close friend Salka Viertel, "I guess I can't complain. After all, I'm just a circus lady." She included in the letter a picture she had drawn of herself as a tight-rope walker, with a parasol in one hand.[53] It was reminiscent of her stunt at her grandmother's house when she had tied a rope between two trees. It was an appropriate metaphor for her career as a Hollywood actor, balancing between directors and producers, finding a path between concealing and revealing who she was.

Greta in Paul U. Bergström's department store film *How Not to Dress* (1921).

# 3

## *PUB, Dramaten, and Mimi Pollak*

$\mathcal{G}$RETA WAS DEEPLY upset by her father's death, but she maintained her composure, controlling her volatile nature. She disliked her family's mourning, as they cried and moaned, railing against fate, indulging in behavior that she found undignified. She mourned in private, quietly crying herself to sleep many nights. She often visited Karl's grave in Woodland Cemetery, at the end of the South Island trolley line. Yet, influenced by old tales of people being buried while still alive, she had to stop herself from visiting Karl's grave in the middle of the night, when ghosts and ghouls supposedly roamed the land, to make certain he was still in his grave.[1]

But Greta wasn't immobilized by Karl's death. She didn't return to school; she had never liked it. Instead, a month after her father died, she applied for a position as a saleswoman at Paul U. Bergström's department store in downtown Stockholm, called PUB after the initials of its founder. It took nerve for a girl from Söder to apply for a position there, since PUB was an elite store. Greta's sister, Alva, who worked downtown as a secretary, gave her the courage to apply.

Built in 1889, PUB was one of the "cathedrals of consumption" and "universes for women" that were constructed in European and American cities in the nineteenth century. Those stores carried items like clothing and household products in separate departments under one roof. With tearooms and fashion shows, and carrying the latest styles, department stores appealed to the wives and daughters of the growing business and professional classes, as well as to the expanding numbers of young unmarried women employed as typists and salesclerks. In cities in Europe and the United States, going shopping and then to a movie matinee became a favorite leisure activity for women.[2]

A position at PUB especially appealed to Greta because film directors and actresses shopped there. As a saleswoman, she might persuade one of them to promote her acting career. She was still passionate about acting. Greta was only fourteen, but her shy smile, interesting appearance, mature demeanor, and startlingly low voice won her a job at PUB, just as they had won her several positions as a lather girl and would contribute to her later successes. She celebrated July 26, 1920, the day she was hired at PUB, as the beginning of her acting career.[3]

A dressmaker who lived in the Gustafsson's apartment building made Greta simple dresses for work—mostly black, the uniform of the saleswoman. Black stockings and low-heeled black shoes completed the outfit. Greta's mother, ecstatic over her daughter's new job, called PUB "paradise" because Greta as a saleswoman was joining the female working-class elite. In fact, Greta had become a "new woman," working in a semiprofessional job while unmarried. To save money, she continued living in the Gustafsson apartment, but it was mostly a place to sleep and store possessions.[4]

She was good at her job. Magdalena Hellberg, her supervisor, praised her. "She was very ambitious, quiet, and always took great care with her appearance," Hellberg enthused. "But she was always dreaming of movies and the theater." When Greta was acting, Hellberg stated, "her shyness disappeared." Hellberg was sympathetic to Greta's dreams, although she was perplexed that Greta didn't join the PUB acting group. But Greta was tired of amateur acting; she wanted to be a professional.

When the store's owner asked Hellberg to choose a saleswoman to model hats for the store's 1921 catalogue, she chose Greta. "She always looks clean and well-groomed and has such a good face," Hellberg enthused.[5] Greta modeled five hats in the catalogue, which was sent to 50,000 Swedish addresses, publicizing her face throughout the country. She was next chosen for a role in a brief PUB advertising film, *How Not to Dress*, in which she played a comic young woman who has difficulty fitting into regular-sized clothes. She impressed Ragnar Ring, the film's producer, who thought she showed a talent for comedy, especially slapstick. Despite her shyness, she had a hearty laugh and a manic energy. Ring thought she had a future as a fat lady in vaudeville.

While making *How Not to Dress*, Greta had an affair with Max Gumpel, the wealthy construction company owner. He came to PUB to watch his nephew play a role in the film. Like many others, Max was smitten by Greta. She was fifteen; he was thirty-one, another older man. Not only was he wealthy, but he was also a champion swimmer and a member of the Swedish Olympic water polo team. They began dating, and she had dinner with him at his apartment in Stockholm's wealthy district. She was fascinated by his bathroom, which had a flush toilet, faucets that she thought were made of gold, and a large bathtub. Suggesting that they were intimate, she described taking a bath in the bathtub. Max turned on the tap and filled up the tub, adding bubble bath to it. Greta said that she had never experienced anything so nice.[6]

She later said that her relationship with Max was a typical younger woman–older man affair, based on her attraction to his sophistication and his attraction to her youth and good looks. Max initiated Greta into sex. A leader in Stockholm's "swinging singles," he was sexually experienced. They may have discussed marriage, but Garbo wanted to continue her career, and in 1923 Mauritz Stiller entered her life. She and Max remained lifelong friends.[7]

While Greta worked at PUB, she modeled clothing in fashion shows and was cast in walk-on roles in several films, including *The Gay Cavalier*, made by the independent producer Eugene Nifford. "She was plump in those days," Nifford remembered, "but I was attracted by her soft, rounded curves. I was fascinated with the thick long curling lashes fringing the most unusual eyes I have ever seen. They were smoldering grey blue eyes that glowed like moonlight on a blue lake when she looked up at me and said, 'It must be wonderful to be a star.'"[8]

After Greta made *How Not to Dress*, the independent producer Erik Petschler cast her in a film. Known as the "Mack Sennett of Swedish films," Petschler made low-budget slapstick comedies modeled after those made by the Hollywood director Sennett, featuring policemen or firemen and attractive young women in bathing suits, combining symbols of male authority with female youth and beauty. When walking on a street near PUB, Petschler noticed Greta gazing at a display in a shop window. Struck by her appearance, he stopped and looked her up and down. She thought he was a "masher," a man with sex in mind, and she brushed him off. After he left, she realized that he was a film director whose movies she had seen.

The next day at work, Greta waited on several Petschler actresses. Engaging them in conversation, she asked them if they thought he might be interested in her for his next film. Liking her shy smile and interesting face, they gave her his phone number. She called him the next day, inquiring about a role. She said that it was the hardest phone call she had ever made. But he remembered their encounter outside the shop window, and he was encouraging. Several days later, after auditioning her, he cast her as one of three bathing beauties in his next movie, *Peter the Tramp*, filmed in the spring of 1922. Petschler played the two male roles in the film—a fireman who is a dandy, in fashionable attire, and the tramp named Peter, in ragged clothes. The film features the fireman wooing Greta and antics by the bathing beauties. It is brief and amusing, but everyone in it badly overacts. Petschler continued to be drawn to Greta. He remembered that during the filming "a sudden rain squall burst over us and Greta improvised a wild Indian dance in the pouring rain. It was a sight for the gods."[9]

Was Greta flirting with Petschler, hoping to charm him into promoting her acting career? From the time she approached Carl Brisson, she had used her beauty and shy vulnerability to attract older men influential in theater and films. Petschler suggested that she contact Mauritz Stiller, who was known for liking attractive women and for casting unknown actors in his films. Conquering her shyness, she went to Stiller's home. When he came to the door, she asked him for a screen test. He wasn't interested, but he told her to come back when she was older. In fact, after he met her, he watched her in productions at the Dramatic Academy.

Magdalena Hellberg became concerned about Greta's seductive behavior toward older men, cautioning her that they were probably interested in her for sex, not acting. But Greta didn't agree. She replied to Hellberg that she might learn something from them. It's also possible that since her father had died, she was looking, perhaps unknowingly, for a father figure to replace him. That need for a father figure continued throughout much of her life, as did a desire for a replacement for her mother, once she met educated, powerful women.[10]

When Greta left Söder in the mornings for downtown Stockholm and PUB and when she returned home in the late afternoon, she went down Birger Jarlsgaten, a broad avenue that was then an elegant street, lined with apartment buildings that had small theaters and chic shops on the first floors and luxury apartments on the floors above. It was called "snob alley."[11] And twice a day, she passed near a large Beaux-Arts building that housed the Swedish Royal Dramatic Theatre (called Dramaten) and its Dramatic Academy. It was built in 1907 to replace Gustav III's 1787 theater, which had fallen into disrepair.

Building a new Dramaten was important for a city "whose sheer volume of play-going was one of its most notable distinctions among European cities."[12] The structure contains an 800-seat theater and several smaller stages, which are still used today. It was built of marble, grandiose and sturdy. When George Bernard Shaw first saw it in 1909, he thought that it was a bank.[13] With an international reputation, it was one of the preeminent theater centers in Europe. By 1920, Stockholm had large churches, banks, museums, department stores, and theaters. It was vying for prominence with Europe's major cities.

As she passed near Dramaten twice a day, it took center stage in Greta's dreams. Its drama school, the Swedish Royal Dramatic Academy, was in two large rooms at the top of the building's central tower, up a long staircase. One room was a classroom, filled with desks, with a small stage along one wall. The second room was mirrored, with ballet barres across the mirrors. It was designed as a dance studio for ballet and movement classes. The teachers at the academy were mainly actors and directors from Dramaten's repertory company. No fees were charged for the school, which the government subsidized. The program lasted for two years, and "premier" students were awarded a third year. No matter the difficulties involved, Greta aimed for the top. With Petschler's encouragement, she entered the competition for admission to the academy in August 1922.

In the audition, seventy individuals competed for twelve places; six men and six women would be chosen. The judges were Dramaten actors and directors plus several theater critics. Most applicants came from well-to-do families, had attended high school, and had theater experience. Greta didn't have these credentials; her film roles had been minor roles in minor movies. But they were something, and Petschler was known in Stockholm theater circles.

To help her prepare the three scenes from plays she was supposed to have ready for the audition, Petschler found her an acting coach— Signe Enwall, the daughter of a former head of the academy. Enwall chose Greta's scenes and rehearsed them with her. Her first scene was from Ibsen's *Lady from the Sea*, about the failing marriage of a woman fascinated by the ocean. The second was from Selma Lagerlöf's *The Fledging*, about an insecure girl who has "no blood in her veins, only tears."[14] The third was from Victorien Sardou and Emile Moreau's comedy *Madame Sans-Gêne* (*Madame Devil-May-Care*), about a washerwoman who has married a count in Napoleon's court; in the scene chosen for Greta, the countess tells off the other wives in the court who claim to have noble ancestors but who, like her, come from the working class.

The reaction of the judges to Greta was mixed, but her luck held. Karl Martin, another candidate in the auditions, overheard one judge praise her low voice. Martin also heard Nils Personne, "the grand old man of the Swedish theater," remark that Garbo's audition wasn't that impressive but there was something special about her, and she should be admitted. Personne had directed plays at Dramaten for many years. His opinion carried the day.[15] Greta joined the class of twelve.

The teaching day at the school began with calisthenics, followed by classes in dance and movement, fencing, elocution, theater history, makeup, and play interpretation. Students were given passes to plays at

Dramaten and theaters nearby. They performed minor roles in Dramaten productions and produced plays on their own. A copybook in Garbo's handwriting at the Swedish Film Institute in Stockholm indicates that she studied the Delsarte system of acting.[16] Like Konstantin Stanislavski, the famed Russian innovator in acting technique, Delsarte disliked the acting system in which students copied the actors who taught them—which was used at many acting schools. At the famed Conservatoire de Paris, teachers taught the classic system of declamation and precise rhetoric designed for the plays of seventeenth-century playwrights Pierre Corneille and Jean Racine, who wrote their plays in rhymed couplets.

Other teachers used another traditional acting system that was constructed around bold gestures and building emotions to culminate in speeches called "points." Expressing a "point of view," the speeches resembled operatic arias. A few acting teachers taught a new psychological style of acting in which actors determined the traits of the person being portrayed and internalized those traits. That style was appropriate for the realist plays of Henrik Ibsen and the early work of August Strindberg.

In the nineteenth century, experts catalogued plants and animals, illnesses, and emotional states into types, species, races, and genres. Linking himself to that effort, Delsarte called his system "scientific." He specified body movements and facial expressions for every emotion. Such an acting system wasn't new, but Delsarte spent many years perfecting his. He watched people on the streets and in interior spaces. He studied human anatomy, corpses in morgues, and statues in museums. His system isn't simple, especially since he decided that individuals could modify it to fit their needs. But it had to be so internalized that its use on the stage was unconscious. On this point, Delsarte sounds like Stanislavski, although the Russian innovator regarded predetermined gestures as clichés. In other words, he found Delsarte's system too rigid.[17]

Isadora Duncan, a founder of modern dance, incorporated Delsarte movements into her routines, as did other dancers who were designing new systems of dancing for the modern age. But at this point in Greta's life, she liked neither the movements nor the calisthenics and ballet taught in morning classes. Given her awkward body, she wasn't good at doing them, while she was embarrassed displaying her body in gym clothes in a mirrored room, which magnified her awkwardness. Yet, she later incorporated Delsarte movements and ballet steps she had learned at the Dramatic Academy into her film acting.[18] They gave her a foundation on which to build her technique.

At first, Greta was quiet and restrained in acting school, hiding her working-class background, her residence in Söder, and her lack of education. But when no one at the school seemed to care, she became lively and funny. Wanting to seem impressive, she dressed in black and wore a black velvet men's cloak. She became as rebellious as she had been in elementary school. She often skipped the morning movement classes, claiming that she stayed out late at night attending plays at theaters on Birger Jarlsgatan and then had to sleep late the next morning. But Mimi Pollak remembered that Greta often went to cabarets and coffeehouses in the evenings.[19] This was the 1920s, and Stockholm had dance halls, nightclubs, movie theaters—and dating among young people.

Greta's teachers grumbled about her absences, but they didn't scold her. She had a photographic memory and quickly learned scripts. That skill, plus her resonant alto voice, her ability to play both young and old characters, and her striking looks made up for her deficiencies. Aware of her sensitivity to criticism, her teachers were gentle with her. Maria Schildknecht, who taught dramatics, remembered that: "She always gave a beautifully clean performance, but she suffered from a kind of indolence."[20] Critics of her acting in Hollywood films made the same comment. Yet, she must have impressed her teachers. When she completed two years, they judged her a premier student and awarded her another year.

On her first day at drama school, Greta met Mimi Pollak. They soon became romantic friends. Both were outsiders. Greta came from Söder; Mimi from Karlstadt, in Värmland. Mimi's father was Jewish and her mother was Austrian. Those differences from Karlstadt's Swedes elicited so much comment that the entire Pollak family, all

Dramaten acting students, 1922. Garbo is at the far right, with Mimi Pollak below her. ARCHIVIO GBB / Alamy Stock Photo

of whom had been Catholic, converted to Lutheranism. Mimi's father, an engineer, was then appointed head of the city's transportation department.

Mimi thought that Greta liked her because she had traveled extensively and wore expensive clothes—suggesting that Garbo was already attracted to wealth. Mimi fell for Greta because she was beautiful and dynamic, "thoughtful, afraid, unafraid, curious about life and quick to laugh." Although Greta was the youngest student in the class, she often seemed the oldest, which also had been the case with her siblings when she was growing up.[21]

In the accompanying photo of Garbo's acting class, Greta and Mimi are at its right edge, holding hands, boldly signaling their relationship. It's not evident from the photo, but Greta was tall and Mimi small. Greta gazes obsessively down at Mimi, who looks straight ahead, with a mischievous glint in her eyes. Mimi seems in control, as she will also appear to be in their correspondence.

Mimi introduced Greta to smoking cigarettes. It was a symbol of adult sophistication, but it was also an addiction that Greta was unable to end, even after she developed chronic bronchitis. And she soon became a chain-smoker, smoking one cigarette after another, often as many as a pack a day. In Greta and Mimi's relationship, they called Mimi "Mimosa," the name of a flowering tree with multiple species, derived from the Greek words for actor and for resemblance. They called Greta "Gustaf," a male name derived from Gustafsson, or "Gurra," a nickname for Gustaf. When Greta was Gurra, she became masculine, joking, and rowdy. Their classmate and friend George Funkqvist thought that Greta was lesbian. She once told him, referring to Mimi, that she was meeting her fiancée.[22]

Both Mimi and Greta told jokes and played pranks. They double-dated, each with a boyfriend along. They loved zany adventures, as when they went with male escorts to an elegant Stockholm restaurant and pretended that they were ladies in a Viennese operetta. Their male escorts wore black tie, and they all ate duck served on a silver platter. Greta's date, Gösta Kyhlberg, fell madly in love with her. Noticing that her clothes were sometimes threadbare, he bought her a dress to wear to a masquerade ball. Greta was something of a party girl in drama school.

Yet, both Mimi and Greta were, as Mimi put it, "in the middle of our most difficult years. Greta and I were often listless, soggy, felt ugly, were burdened by feelings of inferiority."[23] That statement sounds typically adolescent, but it might indicate deeper psychological issues. In March 1925, when Stiller was angry with Garbo because of her negotiations for a contract with Universum Film AG (UFA), Germany's major film studio, Greta wrote to Mimi that her "unfortunate, inherent nature" had taken her over, and her nasty temperament was destroying everything. She wanted Mimi to come to Berlin to calm her down. She could hear Mimi saying, "I understand you, Gurra." But Mimi had a temperament like hers, which was "dangerous" because "anything could disturb it."[24]

Greta and Mimi both became infatuated with Tora Teje, a star of Swedish films who acted in Dramaten productions. Teje had dark hair and a low voice, and she exuded sensuality. They followed her to her home, just as Garbo's fans later followed her when she was a Hollywood star—behavior she hated. While Mimi and Greta were students at the Dramatic Academy, Teje played Anna Christie in a Dramaten production of Eugene O'Neill's play *Anna Christie*, about a Swedish-American prostitute in New York. Whenever they could miss classes, Greta and Mimi watched Teje rehearse the play. In 1929, in her first sound film, Garbo would play Anna in *Anna Christie*.

According to Harriet Bosse, an actress who taught at the dramatic academy and who was the third wife of August Strindberg, the acclaimed Swedish writer, Teje "combined the grandeur of classical acting [its precision and "points"] with the psychological depth of contemporary plays, like those by Ibsen and Strindberg."[25] Teje starred in films directed by Mauritz Stiller. Given the control he exerted over his actors, he must have influenced Teje, who, in turn, influenced Garbo, especially in her interpretation of Anna Christie in 1929.

Greta and Mimi also became close to Alf Sjöberg, a Dramaten student and a socialist who wanted to make the theater into a revolutionary force. "He came into our world like a storm wind—with his visions, his new ideas, and his rebellion against the old." By 1920, new forms of theater were appearing. At the Moscow Art Theatre, Stanislavski stressed using memories of one's experiences when acting, creating the beginnings of method acting. In England, Gordon Craig, son of the famed British actress Ellen Terry and a partner to Isadora Duncan, devised a new stagecraft that focused on sets and costumes and downplayed actors. In Berlin, Max Reinhardt organized huge spectacles as well as small theater and cabaret performances, as expressionism became popular. In expressionist art and theater, reality is distorted to conform to the inner ideas of artists and playwrights. The little theatre movement in New York, Paris, and other cities appeared, with new kinds of plays and new audiences. It's not surprising that Stockholm theater students dreamt of effecting social change through the theater.[26]

Alf Sjöberg also ratified what Greta had learned about the oppression of labor and of women from growing up in reform-minded Stockholm.

Mimi, Greta, and Alf were reformers, but they weren't activists; they didn't participate in demonstrations and strikes. The theater absorbed them. At graduation, Alf, like Greta, was named a premier student and awarded a third year. He later became a director at Dramaten and at the Svensk Filmindustri (Swedish Film Industry, SFI), Sweden's major film studio. Unlike Alf and Greta, Mimi Pollak didn't attain premier status, but she eventually became a permanent member of the Dramaten acting company and a well-known actress and theater director in Sweden.

Greta and Mimi remained romantic friends, but they were often separated. Mimi acted in plays in Stockholm theaters, but she often performed in theaters out of town or visited relatives who lived at a distance from Stockholm. By the time Mimi became a member of the Dramaten company, Greta had left Stockholm for Hollywood. When Mimi wasn't close by, Greta missed her terribly. That is evident in her letters to Mimi. Most of Greta's early letters discuss their adventures with boys and other girls and especially their drinking and smoking, which symbolized their relationship to them as a madcap adventure. The letters are often silly, filled with adolescent humor. In 1923 Mimi became engaged to Nils Lundell, a Stockholm actor and director, and she married him in early 1927.

In her letters to Mimi before the marriage—and after it—Greta expressed undying love for Mimi, depression with her own life, dislike of Hollywood once she moved there in 1925, and the hope that Mimi might become her permanent partner, despite the obstacles involved in achieving that goal. Above all, Greta didn't want to lose Mimi, who was her major Swedish confidante until she met Countess Hörke Wachtmeister in 1929 on the steamship returning to Sweden from New York.

Sometimes Mimi wavered in her commitment to Nils, as when she wrote a love letter to Greta from Venice in 1924 that awakened "a storm of longing" in Greta, who was then employed at Dramaten. She told Mimi that if she took twenty baths a day, she wouldn't forget her. To her, their relationship was mystical, existing on a spiritual plane as well as a physical one. She wanted to put a world of longing in her letters for Mimi to experience.[27]

The letters sometimes refer to other women. Greta worried about Mimi's involvement with Doris Nelson, a Stockholm actress who resembled Greta, while she admitted that she had been spending time with a stylish actress named Frau Mayer. But Frau Meyer was leaving Stockholm, and Greta feared that she would never see her again. "Now I believe," she wrote, "that men live in a little hell when they see a soft, stylish woman and can't have her." She advised Mimi that they should stop criticizing men for their aggressively sexual natures because she had experienced an overwhelming sexual attraction to Frau Mayer.[28]

The letters express heterosexual desire as well as same-sex love. That duality was part of the culture of female romantic love, although most analysts of that culture have overlooked it, seeing only its single-sex side.[29] Young women had boyfriends as well as girlfriends. Greta stated that she had a "jolly time" on a date with Hans Spiro. She also had a boyfriend, Gösta Kyhlberg, who worked in a bank. According to Eugene Nifford, she was also involved with Einar Hanson, an actor who was a matinee idol in Stockholm and one of Stiller's young male actors. Garbo had been among the young women who waited for Hanson outside the theater after he performed, hoping for an intimate glance. Hanson had singled out Greta for attention, although other sources indicate that he was involved with Mauritz Stiller, not with Greta.[30]

She wrote to Mimi in 1923, while filming *The Saga of Gösta Berling,* that she now loved a wonderful man. "Ack! What eyes, what lips, kiss, kiss." Yet, despite her involvement with men, she was devastated when Mimi became engaged to Nils Lundell, who was nicknamed "Nisse." She tried to deal with the engagement by extending her love to Nils: "I love you and you love Nisse," she wrote Mimi, "so I love him too."[31] She later suggested that the three of them form a trio and live together, although that never happened.

Mimi didn't visit Garbo in Hollywood, and L. B. Mayer didn't give Garbo a leave of absence until the end of 1928. When she visited

Stockholm—in 1929 and later—she spent time with Mimi. Yet, despite Garbo's invitations to her friend to visit her in Hollywood, Mimi never traveled there. Since Mimi's letters to Garbo have disappeared, we don't possess her side of the correspondence. From Garbo's letters to Mimi, however, Mimi seems in control, as she is in the photograph of students at the acting school.

Greta's enthusiasm for the theater continued before she left Stockholm for Hollywood. In the months before and after filming *The Saga of Gösta Berling* in 1923, she acted in plays—at the dramatic academy, on Dramaten's central stage, and in theaters nearby. She played young women, older women, prostitutes, and wives, exhibiting her flexibility in portraying age. She was especially praised for her portrayal of Hermione in Shakespeare's *A Winter's Tale*. Hermione is the wife of the king of Sicily. When he falsely accuses her of infidelity, she pretends to be dead and goes into hiding at the home of her friend Paulina. Years later, she reappears as a middle-aged woman with wrinkles, but she is still attractive, and the king welcomes her back.[32]

If Greta had stayed in Sweden, she probably would have succeeded on the stage, given her success at the theater academy. But Mauritz Stiller predicted that if she went to Hollywood with him as his protégée, he would turn her into the world's greatest actress, and that's what she wanted. Still, it's puzzling that once in Hollywood she never again appeared on the stage, even though throughout her career critics disparaged her for acting only in films, which many considered an inferior dramatic form. The only reason she gave for quitting the stage was that she didn't have the strength to perform in a play night after night. In fact, as she became older, her chronic illnesses, especially insomnia, bipolarity, and bronchitis, became more persistent, while she developed menstrual issues accompanied by intense pain. She was speaking truth when she said that her weak body kept her from performing on the stage.

Yet, her life was soon to change drastically when Mauritz Stiller came back into it in a powerful way, taking her over and making her into the successful actress she wanted to be. When Stiller asked Dramaten's director to recommend two of its best female students to him to audition for roles in his new film, *The Saga of Gösta Berling*, Greta was one of those chosen. Or perhaps Stiller asked for Greta directly, since he had, in fact, been watching her for some time. From the beginning, he was attracted by her appearance, even though many of his colleagues at the Swedish Film Institute found her to be only an ordinary young woman, not appealing at all.

Greta in *The Saga of Gösta Berling* (1924). Classic Picture Library / Alamy Stock Photo

# 4

## Beauty and the Beast

### Garbo and Stiller

$I$N THE SPRING of 1923 Mauritz Stiller cast Greta Gustafsson as Countess Elizabeth Dohna, a central character in his film *The Saga of Gösta Berling*, adapted from the novel by Selma Lagerlöf. Greta was again lucky. She was a neophyte actor, but Stiller liked to cast beginners in his films because he could mold their acting styles. He also liked to cast actors whose looks matched those of the characters in the novels and stories he filmed. In *The Saga of Gösta Berling*, Elizabeth Dohna is Italian. With Greta's deep-set eyes and light brown hair, she could pass as Italian.[1] The countess is also innocent and spiritual, and Stiller saw those qualities in Greta. Liking her looks, he disagreed with associates at the Swedish Film Industry who thought she was ordinary, "just an awkward, mediocre novice." He proclaimed that "the screen reflects a face like hers only once in a generation."[2] Dramatic in his life as well as on the stage, Stiller could become very emphatic in trying to prove a point.

Realizing the exotic nature of Greta's beauty, Stiller told her: "With your broad shoulders, narrow hips, and sleek head, you can take on the glamour of the Egyptian beauties of old. But you must get slim. Slim like a match."[3] Thus began the most powerful relationship of Garbo's life, destined to make her into the world's greatest actress and its most beautiful woman, and to plunge her into despair when Stiller died just before she was going to see him in Stockholm at the end of 1928, probably to marry him. Unfortunately, Stiller's statement that she was overweight for films motivated her extreme dieting, which led to anorexia nervosa.

In 1923, after ten years of directing Swedish films, Stiller was at the height of his fame, as was the Svenska Biografteatern, the studio where he worked. Located on an island not far from downtown Stockholm, it began its climb to fame in 1910, when the newsreel photographer Charles Magnusson became its executive producer.[4] Magnusson assembled a small but first-rate company. Julius Jaenzon, his cinematographer, was among the world's best. Without Jaenzon's skill, Greta might have failed soon after she began acting in films. He used lights to heighten the features of her face and to magnify the shadows created by her eyelashes and her high cheekbones—techniques later cinematographers used in filming her.

In 1912 Magnusson hired Mauritz Stiller and Victor Sjöström (anglicized to Seastrom) as his directors. At Svenska Bio, as at most European film studios, directors, not producers, controlled filming, in contrast to Hollywood, where producers were in control by 1925. Seastrom was calm and good-natured. He didn't direct comedies, but he played comic characters, like Thomas Graal in Stiller's comedies *Thomas Graal's Best Film* (1917) and *Thomas Graal's First Child* (1918), which satirize filmmaking through the comic misadventures of Thomas Graal, a film director. Like many Swedish artists, Seastrom was influenced by the mysticism and struggle between man and nature inspired by Sweden's landscape of mountains, forests, and lakes, and its long dark winters and brief warm summers.[5] In Seastrom's *The Outlaw and His Wife* (1917), an Icelandic outlaw and his wife climb ever higher in stark mountains to escape from an avenging sheriff; Seastrom's *Girl from the Marsh Croft* (1917) is about the travails of a servant girl on a farm who is made pregnant by her employer.

In 1923 Seastrom went to Hollywood to direct films for MGM, attracted by the studio's large salaries and its advanced equipment. Having spent part of his childhood in the United States, he spoke English and was familiar with American mores. Through his deferential calmness, he charmed Hollywood producers while directing several acclaimed films, including the circus melodrama *He Who Gets Slapped* (1924) and *The*

*Scarlet Letter* (1926), adapted from Nathaniel Hawthorne's novel about Puritan morality in colonial Massachusetts.

The screenwriter Charles Brackett called Seastrom "slow, plodding, gracious, and very likely to be right most of the time."[6] If Mauritz Stiller had adopted Seastrom's diplomatic ways, he might have avoided his disastrous year at MGM, when L. B. Mayer fired him. The two Swedes were friends, but they weren't intimates. Seastrom was married, with children, while Stiller was homosexual and a major figure in Stockholm's homosexual circle. In the early 1930s, Seastrom returned to Sweden, where he directed and acted in many films, including Ingmar Bergman's *Wild Strawberries*.

Stiller possessed a range of abilities. He was a comedian, a dramatic actor, a director, and, with a strong baritone voice, a singer in operettas. Influenced by the innovative American director D. W. Griffith, he introduced technical innovations into Swedish filmmaking—close-ups, fade-outs, new camera angles. He was six feet tall, with large hands and feet and a gnarled face. He was forty years old when he met Greta, who was eighteen. The workers at Svenska Bio called Greta and Stiller "Beauty and the Beast." But they had much in common. Tragedy had stalked both their childhoods. Greta had grown up in poverty, and her father died when she was fourteen. Stiller was born and raised in Helsinki. His mother committed suicide when he was four, and his father died soon after that. Jewish by birth, he was raised by Jewish foster parents. They weren't especially observant, although he attended a Hebrew school and changed his birth name Movsha Stiller to Mauritz Stiller, which was better suited to the international career he intended to have.[7]

Like Garbo, Stiller began acting as a teenager in local productions. Finland was then a duchy in the Russian Empire. As a young man, Stiller was conscripted into the Russian army, but he acquired a forged passport and escaped to Sweden, where, knowing Swedish, he acted in plays and sang in operettas. He moved back and forth between Finland and Sweden with impunity; the Russian authorities left him alone.

Stiller could be domineering and eccentric. Once he was a success at SFI, he bought a house and a yellow sports car, dubbed the Yellow Peril because he drove it at full speed around Stockholm, which was still a small city. Called the Grand Duke, he dressed like a dandy, wearing a long yellow fur coat, ties made from antique waistcoats, and gold rings set with precious stones. The conservative suits he wore were tailored in London, a world center for men's tailoring, as Paris was for women's clothing. Restless and adventurous, he traveled to Berlin, Paris, and London to see plays and films in those cities.

Stiller had an up-down temperament. He was often depressed, but when he was elated, he had "a pixie sense of humor, mixed with a deadpan appreciation of the ridiculous."[8] He had a fatalism about life, although he was drawn to beautiful women and young men. He had mesmeric gray eyes and a low, soothing voice, which became loud and demanding if he was angry. Victor Seastrom said that "so many men were gathered within him."[9]

By the time he auditioned Greta for *The Saga of Gösta Berling*, Stiller had directed forty films. Like most silent films, most of his films were brief. They included peasant dramas, spy stories, and vamp movies—a genre of film introduced by Danish film directors, who were leaders in early European cinema.[10] In these films, powerful women seduce weaker men and ruin them financially and/or emotionally. The vogue of the vamp (or female vampire) began in the mid-nineteenth century among male artists drawn to the male vampire, a figure in East European folklore who feeds on human blood and turns his victim into slaves. Some artists made the figure female.[11] Because they frequented prostitutes, these men feared venereal disease, which was then epidemic in Europe. They blamed prostitutes for its spread, not themselves. They also feared the woman's movement, which they saw as a threat to men.[12]

In the 1910s, Hollywood actress Theda Bara was known for playing vamps, but she was only one among many actresses—in Italy, Germany, Sweden, and the United States—who played the destructive type. In Italy, vamps in films had a heroic side; they moved in an irresistible serpentine manner to seduce the corrupt males who had victimized them, in order to punish those men.[13] Even Stiller made vamp films. In *Vampyren* (1913), an army officer is obsessively in love with an egocentric opera diva. After Garbo made her first MGM film, *The Torrent* (1926), she was typecast as a vamp / siren. She objected to the typecasting and then modified the type, adding spirituality to the vamp's destructive nature.

Some Stiller films are masterworks. In *Love and Journalism* (1916), a young female journalist disguises herself as a teenager in order to be hired as a chambermaid in the home of a famous Arctic explorer. She intends to find the manuscript he has written about his latest Arctic adventure and leak it to the press. The film is as zany and sophisticated as any of the Hollywood screwball comedies of the 1930s, in which male and female protagonists engage in pranks and witty quips before falling in love.[14]

In *Erotikon* (1920), Stiller brought to the screen the Austrian *Kammerspiel*, a sexual comedy of manners. In the film, which stars Tora Teje, Stiller examined the merits of marriage versus free love through the story of a professor of etymology who is studying a colony of promiscuous insects. Obsessed with his research, he fails to notice that his wife is having an affair with his best friend. The film ends with the wife leaving the professor for her lover, while the professor settles down with his vivacious niece.

Stiller took care in expressing sex in his films. Only one—*Vingarne*—has a homosexual theme, but the film focuses on the relationship between an older woman and a younger man—the novel of initiation motif. Sodomy was then illegal in Sweden, as it was in most European countries and in the United States—by state laws. Many of Stiller's films end with a chaste kiss between the female and male protagonists after an exposition promising more. Reflecting Sweden's Lutheranism, the nation's film industry had the strictest censorship code of any European country.

In 1917, in a triumph for Svenska Bio, Victor Seastrom persuaded Selma Lagerlöf to allow the studio to film one work of hers every year. Swedes revered Lagerlöf, whose novels and stories were considered national treasures. In 1919 Magnusson assigned Lagerlöf's short story "Sir Arne's Treasure" to Stiller. He made it into a breathtaking film about lust, love, and murder in the seventeenth century, set in winter snow in Swedish forests and in a village beside the ocean. In 1923 Stiller was assigned Lagerlöf's *Saga of Gösta Berling*. Set in the 1820s, it tells the story of Berling, an alcoholic defrocked minister who is irresistible to women. He joins a group of aging male adventurers, former soldiers in the Napoleonic Wars. Spending their time drinking and carousing, they live in a wing of the manor house of a wealthy older woman who owns several coal mines. Lagerlöf called her "as gruff as a man and as powerful as a queen."[15]

Cynical, humorous, and dramatic, *The Saga of Gösta Berling* is set in Värmland, where Lagerlöf was born and raised, as was Garbo's mother. Värmland is famous for its folklore tradition; the tales of the region, like Lagerlöf's novel, are replete with witches, sprites, and the devil. Against this background, the characters in the novel confront fate, human idiosyncrasies, and a decaying class structure. Elizabeth Dohna's marriage to the foppish Count Dohna is annulled, and she marries Berling, who promises to abandon his errant ways and work for reform. Elizabeth joins with his former female lovers to make him keep his promise. *The Saga of Gösta Berling* is an epic tale that is critical of the male epic tradition, rooted in adventure and combat. Instead, in *Gösta Berling*, women band together to guarantee a humane and peaceful social order.

In addition to directing films, Stiller directed plays, including plays written by Swedish playwright August Strindberg, whose huge output of essays, plays, and novels from the 1880s until his death in 1912 deeply impressed his contemporaries. He was one of Garbo's favorite authors. Yet, because he took controversial stances, he was both revered and reviled. As a young adult, he attacked bourgeois conventions before becoming a symbolist, using metaphors and dreams to explore moral and social issues. In his early work he favored women's rights, but after a conservative women's group sued him for blaspheming Christianity, he turned against the entire women's movement. He won the court case, but it soured him on women, causing him to regard them as an unfortunate necessity in men's lives. He suffered from mental illness, which he overcame through a process of self-analysis.[16]

Determined to become Europe's premier playwright, in 1888 he wrote *Miss Julie*, partly in response to Henrik Ibsen's 1879 *A Doll's House*, a major text for European feminists. *A Doll's House* is about a woman stifled in a marriage who leaves her husband and children to be free. In *Miss Julie*, Strindberg focused on what he saw as a woman's insatiable sex drive. Miss Julie, an unmarried upper-class woman, can't stop herself from having sex with a virile male servant, although sex was forbidden in Sweden outside of engagement and marriage. Fearful of being stigmatized for having illicit sex with a servant and desperate because he won't elope with her, Miss Julie kills herself.

In 1912, the year Strindberg died, Stiller took over Strindberg's Theatre Intima in Stockholm. How he interpreted Strindberg's plays is largely unknown, although a Swedish journalist reported that he directed Strindberg's *Dream Play*, a symbolist work, in an "ambitious modernist style."[17] In his films, Stiller often interpreted Strindberg's "war of the sexes" as amusing, not threatening. Men in Stiller's films are sometimes fools; the stolid Victor Seastrom played that persona in Stiller's Thomas Graal comedies.

Stiller was sympathetic to feminism. Some of his films make a brief for gender equality and male sensitivity, and he celebrates powerful women, like the female coal mine owner in *The Saga of Gösta Berling*. In *The Tyrannical Fiancée* (1913), the heroine proclaims, "We are free; we are modern women." The male protagonist in that film is persuaded to address an audience of women. When he proclaims that a woman's place is in the home, the audience responds with jeers and a barrage of household utensils. In *The Modern Suffragette* (1913), Stiller satirizes the suffragists' husbands as much as the female activists.[18]

Women found Stiller attractive, and he had close women friends. The Finnish writer Alma Söderjhelm, who often lived in Stockholm, helped him write his screenplays. Söderjhelm and Stiller were physically affectionate; in her diary she wrote that she sat on his lap, and they kissed and hugged. According to her, he proposed marriage, but she refused him. Although he was homosexual and she was lesbian, they might have contracted a "lavender" marriage—one without sex—but he was too dictatorial for her. Söderjhelm contended that he turned his young male lovers into slaves.[19]

How did Stiller treat Greta Gustafsson? He appreciated her beauty, but like Nils Personne, "the grand old man of the Swedish theatre," who was ambivalent about Greta's acting at her Dramaten audition, Stiller wasn't certain about her when she auditioned for him. Since she had impressed her teachers in drama school, she was probably so frightened by Stiller that she froze. After filming began on *Gösta Berling*, Greta was often so exhausted that she had to lie down during breaks. Her anemia had flared up. Stiller worried that she wasn't strong enough to play Countess

Elizabeth. Not until he realized her acting ability—or she achieved it through his training—did he trust her skill.[20]

Stiller was harsh in directing Greta. "I'm ruthless with her," he told a friend. "Wait until I've broken her in." This harsh technique resulted partly from his ambivalence about her acting, but for some time he had been looking for an actress to shape into a Trilby to his Svengali, in line with George du Maurier's popular novel *Trilby*. In that novel, the mysterious Svengali mesmerizes Trilby, a Parisian cocotte, into becoming the world's greatest singer. The novel inspired plays about women transformed by powerful men, such as George Bernard Shaw's *Pygmalion*, in which a professor transforms a Cockney girl into a lady.[21]

According to Sven Borg, who studied drama in Stockholm and was Garbo's interpreter during her first years in Hollywood, it was common knowledge in Stockholm theater circles that Stiller was looking for a beautiful female puppet through which to express himself. After Stiller made *Erotikon*, according to Victor Seastrom, he was obsessed with this idea. He had suggested his scheme to several Swedish actresses, but they turned him down.[22] When he cast Greta in *Gösta Berling* she was more than twenty years younger than he, and while he was famous, she was unknown; surely, he could mold her. To become the clone of a teacher violated the Delsarte system, but Greta was overwhelmed by her swift promotion from a neophyte to the world's greatest actress, which was what Stiller promised her she would become as his protégée.

He also wanted to mold her into a version of his female self. Stiller was masculine and tough, but he had a feminine side. Since he wasn't willing to represent it himself, which might reveal his homosexuality, he decided to create a woman in his image. According to Victor Seastrom, Stiller wanted his ideal woman to be sophisticated, scornful, and superior, but humanely warm, like Tora Teje, with the deep emotion and mysticism that Mary Johnson displayed in *Sir Arne's Treasure*. In using these words, Seastrom described not only the mature Greta Garbo but also the ideal beauty of Garbo's era: sophisticated, scornful, and superior, but humanely warm, and deeply emotional and mysterious—in other words, "glamorous," which was Hollywood's watchword in the 1930s.

In coaching Greta, Stiller acted out her scenes for her, and then, when she did them, he praised her extravagantly one minute and criticized her severely the next, to break her down and reshape her.[23] During the filming of *The Saga of Gösta Berling* he put her through many retakes. Garbo said that she went through Gethsemane in making that film—a reference to Christ's dark hour in the garden of Gethsemane before the crucifixion.

Sometimes Greta broke down, calling Stiller names and crying, until he put his arms around her and soothed her. "Moje knows what is best for you," he would say. ("Moje" was his nickname.) When he was displeased with anyone, Stiller would say, "I think I go home now," meaning where he lived. Nils Asther, who studied with Stiller and serviced him sexually, stated that "Stiller had demonic control over all of us." Silent film star Emil Jannings called him "the Stanislavski of the cinema."[24] In the Stanislavski method, actors go deep into their memory to use their past experiences to create the characters they play. Konstantin Stanislavski was a director at the Moscow Art Theatre, not that far from Stockholm; Stiller must have known about his technique.

Garbo identified with Stiller. While they were in Stockholm, he taught her how to dress, to wear makeup, to walk and talk. He took her to fine restaurants and introduced her to his friends, who were surprised by how much she copied him. She went with Stiller in his roadster to towns and villages around Stockholm, buying antiques for the manor houses in *The Saga of Gösta Berling*. It was Stiller who first said, "I think I go home." That phrase, rendered in dialect as "I t'ink I go home," became a famous "Garboism," the silly sayings American journalists attributed to her.

Stiller refused to give interviews about his past or his private life, and Garbo eventually adopted that stance, too. She picked up "his pixie sense of humor, mixed with a dead-pan appreciation of the ridiculous," as well as his perfectionism and his ironic attitude toward life. Yet, her identification with Stiller was never complete. When filming *The Torrent*, her first MGM film, she wrote to Mimi Pollak that she couldn't stand having anyone control her, although she added that she felt as though she was married to Stiller—or she was his unmarried widow, a confused explanation of their complex relationship.[25]

After she auditioned for Stiller, he told her that she had to lose weight, and she obeyed him. She is plump in her confirmation photo and in *The Saga of Gösta Berling*. In stills from *Joyless Street*, a film she made in Berlin in 1925, she has lost weight, and in photos taken of her in New York and

Hollywood later that year, she is even thinner. She loved heavy Swedish food, but she cut back on calories and exercised diligently to lose twenty pounds in the year after Stiller told her to lose weight. By 1920, thinness was an obsession with stylish women. Garbo eventually lost so much weight that anorexia nervosa, "the starvation illness," became an issue for her.[26]

Were Garbo and Stiller lovers? It's doubtful, although Garbo said that Stiller taught her everything she knew about acting, and she was among Hollywood's most sensual actresses. She told Cecil Beaton that Stiller believed that the most important form of sex was the platonic relationship between a powerful teacher and an adoring student.[27] Like Alma Söderjhelm, she sometimes sat on Stiller's lap. She would smoke his cigarette, "taking it away from him for a puff with coquettish little giggles." Greta knew about his male lovers. The circle of homosexual actors, directors, and craftsmen at SFI was no secret in the industry. During their stay in New York in 1925, Stiller had a male secretary with him.[28] Moreover, Garbo was still involved with Einar Hanson, and Hanson, one of Stiller's young male actors, was also one of his lovers.

Stiller also took the place of her father. After Karl Gustafsson's death, Garbo often became involved with older men, who introduced her to adult life, taught her needed skills, and made decisions for her. The Greta Gustafsson who had been the decision maker in her family and who seemed the oldest student in her drama school class never disappeared, but the more Garbo achieved, the less secure she seemed to be. Stiller brought out her latent power to express her emotions through her eyes, to perform for the camera, to be sensual and spiritual at the same time. But he also instilled in her the need to have someone to guide and nurture her.

While filming *Gösta Berling*, Stiller told Greta to change her name. "Greta Gustafsson" was too long for theater marquees, and Gustafsson was a common Swedish surname. As a star, she needed her name to stand out. Exactly who found "Garbo" is unclear, although Mimi Pollak claimed that a friend of hers at the Stockholm name registry office recommended it to them because Swedes rarely used it. It sounds like *garbon*, a Swedish sprite who comes out at night to dance in the moonbeams. The *garbon* is a descendent of the dread *gabilun*, who breathes fire and can assume any shape it chooses.[29] In Italian and Spanish, *garbo* means "grace." In Spain it was applied to matadors, who engage in the deadly sport of bullfighting, moving with a singular grace as they swing a cape to anger and confuse the bull.

The new surname also implied that Greta had to create a new self to match her new name. Under Stiller's tutelage, that's what she was doing. As Greta mused over the surname "Garbo," she drew from her practical and joking sides to remark that because her initials would remain GG, the impecunious Garbo would have no need for new monogrammed towels.

Surprisingly, *The Saga of Gösta Berling* wasn't a success in Sweden. Both Selma Lagerlöf and Swedish critics complained that Stiller had taken too many liberties with the novel—such as cutting out characters and writing his own subtitles rather than using phrases from the book. But the film was a hit in Germany, and Stiller took Garbo with him to Berlin in August 1924 for a screening there. It was her first trip outside Sweden. She liked German audiences because, she said, they adored her from a distance and didn't bother her. In fact, most German film stars came from the theater, where they were regarded as artists. Unlike Hollywood actors, they weren't typecast, and their personal lives weren't revealed to the public. Their fans respected them and left them alone.[30]

Returning to Stockholm after the Berlin trip, Garbo went back to Dramaten and the Gustafsson apartment. Several months later, Stiller contacted her and told her that they needed to go to Berlin again, to meet Louis B. Mayer, who had approached him about becoming a director at MGM. Stiller was interested. He and Mayer agreed to meet in Berlin in December 1924.

As a studio, MGM had been formed in early 1924; it was part of a trend toward amalgamation among Hollywood film studios, influenced by the move toward monopoly in U.S. business. The heads of Metro Productions and Samuel Goldwyn Studio, plus Louis B. Mayer, the head of his own small studio, Louis B. Mayer Productions, came together to create it—ergo Metro-Goldwyn-Mayer. Mayer, who was an able administrator, was chosen to head the Hollywood branch. He would deal with actors, staff, and the New York office. It was also a package deal. Irving

Thalberg, Mayer's chief associate, would head film production. Although only twenty-four, Thalberg brought films in on budget, in the allotted time. He could run the Hollywood facility while Mayer was in Europe.

Wanting to look like a successful director when meeting Mayer, Stiller booked a suite at the top Berlin hotel where they were to meet. Mayer, who was shrewd, saw through him. He checked out Stiller with Seastrom, who praised him, but others may not have been so positive. When they arrived in Berlin, Stiller arranged for Mayer to view *The Saga of Gösta Berling*. After he saw it, Mayer offered contracts to several of its actors, including Mona Mörtenson, a friend of Garbo's from Dramaten.

Some writers contend that Mayer realized star potential in Garbo when he first saw her, but the harsh treatment given to her in New York and in her first years in Hollywood suggests that he wasn't certain about her. When Mayer's adolescent daughter Irene, who was with him in Europe, saw Garbo in the hotel elevator, she took her for a poorly dressed middle-aged woman. Garbo stated that Mayer paid no attention to her when he and Stiller discussed contracts in her presence. She told Jack Gilbert that Mayer wanted Stiller, not her. She later said about Mayer that "anyone who has a continuous smile on his face conceals a toughness that is almost frightening,"[31]

Mayer and Stiller disliked each other, though both were middle-aged Jews born in Eastern Europe—Mayer in Ukraine (then part of Russia) and Stiller in Finland—another Russian duchy. Both were egocentric and domineering; they were too much alike to get along. Stiller was accustomed to controlling the films he directed, while at MGM, producers were in charge. Meyer was homophobic, and Stiller was homosexual. Yet, Stiller negotiated MGM contracts with Mayer for himself and Garbo; Garbo's contract was for three years.[32] Soon after the meeting, Stiller tried to void their MGM contracts when he received an offer from Paramount Pictures, MGM's chief competitor. But Mayer threatened to ruin Stiller if he didn't honor their agreement. Frightened by the threat, Stiller backed down. He soothed Garbo by telling her that they would stay in Hollywood only for a year. Neither realized what they were getting themselves into.

After a few days in Berlin, Garbo and Stiller went to Constantinople to scout locations for a projected film, "The Odalisque from Smolna," about a Russian noblewoman fleeing the Bolsheviks during the Russian Revolution of 1917. She is on her way to safety in Constantinople when she is captured by pirates, who sell her to a Turkish sheik for his harem, and she escapes. Such a plot sounds implausible, but given the existing situation, it could have happened. The Russian Revolution ended with the Bolsheviks in power, and many Russian nobles, plus their families and supporters, followed the Menshevik army as it retreated to Constantinople. Two hundred and fifty thousand individuals joined the exodus from Russia. The women among them were prey to sexual predators.

Several weeks after they arrived in the Turkish city, Stiller's funding for the film fell through, and he rushed back to Berlin to raise more money, leaving Garbo behind in Constantinople, along with several other actors, including Einar Hanson, who was slated to play a leading role in the projected film. But Garbo didn't mind being left behind. The mix of ethnicities in the city fascinated her, as did the mosques and minarets, the Muslim call to prayers, and the unfamiliar scents in a Middle Eastern city. She liked walking Constantinople's narrow, winding streets, with shops and bazaars open to the street. Hanson was with her; he protected her. Stiller was unsuccessful in raising money. The Swedish consul in Constantinople paid for Garbo's trip back to Berlin.

Garbo's adventures with Stiller weren't at an end. In Berlin, the German director G. W. Pabst caught up with them. He had seen Garbo in *The Saga of Gösta Berling*, and he wanted to cast her as a young working woman in his film *Joyless Street*. Stiller needed money; Garbo accepted the role. The film explored the terrible postwar inflation in Central Europe and the social destruction it caused, through the story of women who are so desperate for food that they turn to prostitution to earn money. Pabst is viewed today as a major figure in the movement of "new objectivity" in German art and films, a new realism in reaction to the expressionism that dominated German art and films in the early 1920s. *Joyless Street* was only Pabst's second film, but he was being hailed as a genius. A socialist, he was called "Red Pabst."[33]

Unlike Stiller, Pabst was empathetic as a director. He was calm and cajoling, not gruff and outspoken. Nor did he act his actors' parts for them; he suggested movements and expressions. Yet, he filmed *Joyless*

*Street* in a month, keeping the actors filming sixteen hours a day. When Stiller tried to direct the film from the sidelines, Pabst barred him from the set. The irrepressible Stiller then coached Garbo in the evenings. *Joyless Street* would ultimately be ranked as one of the great works of the post–World War I German cinema. Garbo's combination of sadness and spirituality as a young woman struggling for money to buy food for herself and her family, trying to avoid selling her body but deeply attracted by a luxurious fur coat, vaulted her to stardom in Europe. A young American soldier, played by Einar Hanson, rescues her from the brothel where she is trapped.

What impact did Berlin have on Garbo? Its citizens had endured losing World War I, followed by a severe economic depression and then a soaring inflation. With savings wiped out twice, many young Berlin residents went wild. The "roaring twenties" reached an extreme there, as a new democratic government after the war abolished censorship.[34] Prostitutes were everywhere. Some of them looked like "fierce amazons, strutting in high heels made of green glossy leather." Others dressed like schoolgirls in pigtails, carrying schoolbooks. "Any Berlin lady of the evening might turn out to be a man."[35] Cross-dressed women and men danced at cross-gendered balls. Many women wore male haircuts, suits, and ties.

At the same time, the arts in general were flourishing in Berlin. In her autobiography, Salka Viertel, then an actress in the city, described Berlin's "Babylon," but she also described advances in art, music, and theater in the city. There were exhibitions of the paintings of Wassily Kandinsky and Paul Klee. The modernist music of Arnold Schoenberg and of Anton von Webern was gaining recognition. There were exciting performances at Max Reinhardt's theaters and cabarets.[36]

Berlin was also a center of homosexual organizing. It had fifty lesbian clubs, several lesbian magazines, and a homosexual rights movement.[37] Magnus Hirschfeld, famed for his writings on homosexuality and transvestitism, had founded the Institute for Sex Research in a large building in the center of the city. It contained a museum and a research institute on homosexuality. (The Nazis destroyed Hirschfeld's institute after Hitler took power in 1933.) In her spare time in Berlin, Garbo wandered the streets, especially Unter den Linden, Berlin's main street, because it was straight for miles, and she wouldn't get lost on it. Yet she couldn't have missed the sexual spectacle—or the lesbian clubs. Valeska Gert, a German actress who played the brothel madam in *Joyless Street*, performed a "socio-critical dance pantomime," a frenzied expressionist dance, at Bertolt Brecht's cabaret, The Red Grape.[38]

Aside from working on *Joyless Street*, Garbo's and Stiller's activities in Berlin are largely unknown. Did he steer her away from the city's Babylon? Did they go to movies, plays, and upscale cafes? Edgar Sirmont, a friend of Stiller's, wrote him a letter referring to their good times in Berlin and asking him about Garbo. "How is that darling girl, Greta Garbo? Are you married already? [She is] so sweet and not like the usual actresses." In other words, Sirmont didn't find Garbo self-centered and haughty, and she and Stiller seemed to him to be in love. Garbo wrote to Mimi Pollak that she was depressed in Berlin. She held her temper responsible for her quarrels with Stiller over her contract negotiations with UFA, the major German studio, which he forbade when he found out about them. But then, Garbo often wrote depressed letters to Mimi.[39]

In her conversations with the Swedish journalist Sven Broman, Garbo told Broman that she loved the roller coaster at Berlin's Luna Park, the city's amusement park. When the actors in *Joyless Street* took her there as a treat, she rode it fifteen times. Roller coasters appealed to the child in Garbo. Despite her endemic anxiety, she was never frightened on them. And "she never tired of going on the roundabout or of shooting at the bull's eye" in the targets at carnival booths.[40]

After finishing *Joyless Street*, Garbo and Stiller returned to Stockholm. Garbo went back to Dramaten and the Gustafsson apartment. Stiller contacted her after several months to go to New York and Hollywood with him to fulfill their contracts with MGM. Garbo wrote to Mimi Pollak that she didn't want to leave her, but Stiller had predicted that she would soon be an international star. Besides, Mimi was involved with a man, and Garbo didn't know how to handle the situation. Moving to a new continent and a new life might bring her happiness.

# PART III

# THE STAR

Genthe's photo of Garbo. Bill Waterson / Alamy Stock Photo

5

# Hollywood

*I*N JUNE 1925 Garbo and Stiller went by train from Stockholm to Göteborg, on the southwest coast of Sweden, where steamships sailed to New York. They were on the first leg of their journey to Hollywood. It took ten days to cross the Atlantic Ocean to New York by steamship, then four days by rail across the American continent to Los Angeles, with a transfer in Chicago. Commercial air travel across the ocean and between New York and Los Angeles wasn't in place until the mid-1930s.[1]

Given the stature of Stiller and Garbo in Europe, they expected a gala welcome in New York, a city known for its receptions for celebrities, which movie studios arranged for their stars. In 1923, Pola Negri, from Germany, the first European star to sign with a Hollywood studio, was met by a score of reporters and photographers and a "mob of fans" when her ship docked in New York. A police escort with "blaring sirens" accompanied her limousine to her hotel, the elegant St. Regis. But Negri's reception wasn't spontaneous. Publicists for Paramount Pictures, her studio, had arranged it—they had hired the police escort, the limousine and its driver, and film extras to play "fans." All the New York newspapers covered Negri's arrival.[2]

Garbo and Stiller didn't receive such a welcome. Negri's last German film, *Passion*, had been a hit in the United States, but neither of Stiller's recent movies—*Sir Arne's Treasure* and *The Saga of Gösta Berling*—had yet played in America. Besides, L. B. Mayer was angry with Stiller because he had attempted to cancel the contracts that he and Garbo had signed with MGM in order to accept an offer from Paramount, MGM's major Hollywood rival.

Hubert Voight, a junior publicist at MGM–New York, was assigned to take care of them during their time in New York, and he was told to keep costs down. Meeting them at the dock where their ship was anchored, Voight had with him Greta's sometime friend Kaj Gynt. In Sweden, Gynt had been a member of Garbo's elementary school class and her acting class at Dramaten, under the name Lena Cederström. In the United States she had appeared in several Metro films, but she hadn't made much of an impression. Fluent in English, she could ease Garbo's transition to the new country. She was jealous of Garbo's success, and they didn't get along. Jimmy Sileo, a freelance photographer whom Voight had hired that morning, was also with him at the dock. Realizing that the Swedish pair weren't an MGM priority, Sileo took only a few photos of them—which appeared in only two of New York's sixteen daily newspapers.[3]

Voight registered the two Swedes at a hotel near Grand Central Station, and according to Voight, the New York executives treated Garbo as a joke. "They couldn't even remember her name." Howard Dietz, the head of publicity in New York, called her "excess baggage." Edward Bowes, vice president at MGM, called her "an awkward peasant type" and declared that she would be back in Sweden within six months.[4]

Based on the photo that Sileo took of Stiller and Garbo leaning on the railing of their docked ship, journalists concocted the story that Garbo was badly dressed. In the years to come, movie magazines would feature the photo and the story of Garbo's sloppy dressing when she arrived in New York as proof that MGM designers had turned Garbo from a poorly dressed foreigner into an elegant Hollywood actress, with the suggestion that any woman could do it for herself if she followed the magazine's advice. The story of the raggedy Garbo was often embellished. One journalist claimed: "Everyone knows the story of how the MGM officials who met the boat gave one look at the awkward, gangling girl dressed in an ill-fitting check suit and fainted dead away."[5]

Yet, Garbo seems up to date by 1925 fashions. She wears a suit belted around her hips; a knee-length skirt; silk stockings showing her legs; and a cloche hat—a typical flapper outfit. When Irene Selznick saw the

Stiller and Garbo on the steamship from Sweden, docked in New York.
Allstar Picture Library Ltd / Alamy Stock Photo

photo, she thought that Garbo looked well-dressed, not like the heavy-set, poorly dressed woman she had seen in the elevator of their Berlin hotel.[6] But Garbo, still frugal, had probably purchased cheap copies of stylish clothes—that's what Voight concluded.[7] Still, he thought she was beautiful. He enjoyed taking her to see the sights, along with Stiller, who kept a close watch on her.

The two Swedes sweltered during a hot and humid New York summer, waiting to be summoned to Hollywood. Garbo soaked in cold baths, trying to cool off. Voight took them to Broadway plays; to New York's air-conditioned movie theaters; and to Coney Island, where Garbo rode the roller coaster again and again. "She ate hot dogs and popcorn and taffy and shouted like a little boy over everything." But she had moods that Voight found "frightful"—"She simply crawled into her shell." Showing manic-depressive behavior, she made up for her depressions with highs. "She would be rollicking and so much fun."[8]

Despite Voight's efforts, Garbo was ambivalent about New York. She had expected to find it filled with "carpets of flowers," a metaphor for a magical city, but she found it overcrowded, with too many automobiles and too much noise, which bothered her acute hearing, although she later stated that she had found the city fascinating. She went shopping with Kaj Gynt, who found Garbo "as imperious and sure of herself as an empress." But Kaj may have exaggerated Garbo's behavior because she was jealous of her success, although she provided Adela Rogers St. Johns with insightful stories about Garbo's childhood.[9]

Garbo liked Coney Island, and Voight introduced her to Harlem, in uptown Manhattan, which had recently transitioned from an upper-class white area to one dominated by African Americans. It was the capital of African American culture and the United States' center of jazz singing and dancing. It was very popular in the 1920s, and Garbo loved it. The screenwriter Anita Loos, a friend of Garbo's, described Harlem's attractions: "Every block was a pleasure zone and Lenox Avenue a permanent carnival. No one wanted to stay indoors; tenants spilled over into the streets, where jazz was in the air; new rhythms were being extemporized that were giving America its first serious standing in the world of music." There were also bawdy dives and "sex circuses" where intercourse was performed, but Voight didn't take Garbo to those places.[10]

Stiller often went to the MGM offices, trying to finalize transportation to Hollywood. But the officials there put him off; they couldn't do anything until they had instructions from Mayer. Except for Adele Whitely Fletcher, few journalists requested an interview with Garbo. In her interview with Fletcher, Garbo said that Gloria Swanson was her favorite Hollywood actress and that she hoped to play characters like the ones Swanson played, "silken ladies wearing luxurious clothes." Or she could do "funny acting," like what she had done for Erik Petschler in Stockholm. But she didn't want to play flappers or vamps; she was adamant about that.[11]

To keep Stiller quiet, the New York executives arranged a screen test for Garbo, but they didn't like the results. They told her that her appearance was too unusual for Hollywood. For once, she blamed Stiller, writing to Lars Saxon that she was upset with Stiller for "making trouble and causing delays." Then a friend of Stiller's referred him to the photographer Arnold Genthe, known for his photographs of stage legends like Isadora Duncan and his many photos of Asian immigrants. Genthe was fascinated by Garbo's face, with its exotic look, and he talked her into an immediate photo session. Genthe spoke German, which Garbo liked, and he had a subtle sexual appeal, which brought out her photogeneity. In their session, he shot some of the best photos ever taken of her. Seeing Genthe's photos of Garbo in the window of his studio, an MGM executive exclaimed, "Is this the blonde we saw hanging around?"[12]

Genthe's photos brought out the drama in Garbo's face and made her body appealing. In the accompanying photo she is sensual and in control. Her body looks thin, challenging reports that she was chubby. Genthe speculated, "Maybe it was part of her inner soul I captured, the part she shields so carefully."[13] Disillusioned after waiting for two months in New York, Stiller and Garbo booked passage back to Germany, although Stiller, in a last-ditch effort, sent the Genthe photos of Garbo to Victor Seastrom at MGM, asking him to show them to Mayer. When Seastrom did that, Mayer took a good look at the photos and summoned the two Swedes to Hollywood. Genthe sold one of his Garbo photos to *Vanity Fair*, and it appeared in the magazine's November 1925 issue.[14] When Garbo and Stiller left for Hollywood in late August, Garbo's film career seemed assured.

Problems emerged when they reached Los Angeles. A crowd of journalists and photographers met their train at the station, attracted by an item in a local newspaper calling Garbo "a star in Europe." In describing her appearance in their newspapers, those journalists were as critical as the New York MGM executives had been. They reported that she had a run in a stocking and run-down heels on her shoes. They howled with laughter when she was asked where she expected to live in Hollywood, and she replied that she hoped to find an inexpensive room with a nice family. No real movie star lived that way; stars lived in luxury. Garbo's reply about housing became, according to *Photoplay*, "a classic among screen legends."[15]

For her first several weeks in Los Angeles, MGM publicists booked a room for Garbo in the elegant Biltmore Hotel downtown, although she told both Cecil Beaton and Mimi Pollak that after a day there, she went to Santa Barbara, a beach city two hours north of Los Angeles, where she met a man and almost married him.[16] She then moved to Santa Monica, to the Miramar Hotel, a residence hotel close to the beach, which is now a luxury hotel. Most Scandinavians working in Hollywood films lived in Santa Monica. They liked its cool climate and its location on the Pacific Ocean, reminiscent of their homelands, and only a half hour from the MGM studio, in Culver City, where most of them worked.

Living in Santa Monica, Garbo swam in the Pacific Ocean and hiked in the coastal hills of the Santa Monica Mountains. A spur of high hills, they run from the northern edge of the Santa Monica beach east through the northern edge of downtown Los Angeles, passing through Bel-Air, Brentwood, and Hollywood, where they become the Hollywood Hills. By 1925 film luminaries were building mansions in those hills.

Garbo liked the Santa Monica pier, which had a merry-go-round, a roller coaster, and carnival games, and was walking distance from the Miramar Hotel. She went to downtown Los Angeles, to the Central Avenue African American district, which had authentic jazz clubs. She bought a used car for her travels. Several years later, when she became a star, she purchased a used limousine, acquiring a cheap version of the elegant limousines of other stars. Her African American servant James Rogers became its driver. She remained frugal, sending money to her mother and saving money to achieve her goal of financial independence.

Stiller rented a bungalow near the Miramar Hotel, and he and Garbo spent evenings sitting on its porch, eliciting comments that they were a dowdy "grandmother and grandfather." They occasionally went to parties and to the opera. "She was a lovely, soft, ethereal girl then," wrote *Los Angeles Times* reporter Elza Schallert in 1931. "At the opera, she wore a silvery wrap with a fox collar, not the heavy ulster, roughneck sweater, and mannish skirt of today."[17] (As a star, in her everyday clothing Garbo cross-dressed and wore mannish clothes, which she bought at the inexpensive army-navy store.) Victor Seastrom and his wife Edith Erastoff, leaders of Hollywood's Scandinavian community, also lived in Santa Monica, and Garbo became close to Erastoff, who had been an actress at the Swedish Film Industry.

Garbo and Stiller met with L. B. Mayer and Irving Thalberg, but the two producers were cool to them. They put Stiller to work writing screenplays, and they had Garbo take another screen test, but they didn't like the results. The Genthe photos seemed forgotten. According to MGM publicist Katherine Albert, no one on the lot knew why Garbo was there. "She was gawky, too tall, with none of the requirements of a great actress."[18]

The criticisms of Garbo expressed by the New York executives reached Hollywood and were expanded by MGM employees on the lot. Garbo was called Stiller's "folly" and his "glad-hand girl," brought along for sex.[19] Sven-Hugo Borg, Garbo's interpreter, was appalled by the anti-Swedish slurs aimed at her: "square head," "flat foot," "peasant," "skyscraper." The individuals making them thought that Garbo didn't know English, but she knew enough to understand them. Studio flunkies pulled her from movie sets, calling her "the Swede." If Garbo resisted them, they taunted her, saying that she had been a latherer in a Stockholm barbershop, implying that the job included sex. "Everywhere she turned, people were unkind to her," Borg wrote.[20] *The Saga of Gösta Berling*, with English subtitles, was screened at the studio, but the audience laughed at it. The sensitive Garbo was deeply hurt. She was especially insulted by Max Factor, who told her that Swedish women needed to be taught beauty care.[21]

Mayer and Thalberg were busy assembling the studio, which was barely a year old. They were hiring and firing personnel, closing some departments, and creating others. They wanted to make MGM into the world's preeminent studio, with "all the stars in the heavens." They worried about the reports they received on Garbo's interviews. Stilted and uncertain, she giggled like a child, laughed loudly, and criticized MGM, which Mayer had forbidden. Calling herself a little Swedish girl, wanting people to like her, she eagerly signed autographs. She wrote to Mimi Pollak that she was frightened because she was "not old enough for all of this."[22]

The publicity department had "cheesecake" photos taken of Garbo, standard for newcomers, ignoring her protests that she was a star in Europe. She was photographed in a sunsuit on the Venice boardwalk and beside a real lion, who was the model for MGM's onscreen logo of a roaring lion. Garbo was terrified. On an athletic field of the University of Southern California, she huddled under hurdles and then a high jump while hurdlers and jumpers went over her. Joan Crawford, hired by MGM in early 1925 from a Broadway chorus and photographed in the same poses as Garbo, said that newspaper editors loved these photos of half-dressed young women.[23]

Becoming friendly with Pola Negri, Garbo often visited her at her home. "She would sprawl on the rug," Negri remembered, "and rail against MGM. She was very tall, almost like a man with her large shoulders, and she would mourn: 'I came here to conquer, and I guess I have to suffer. Someday I will be like Lillian Gish [MGM's top actress], and then I will tell them all to go to hell.'"[24] She never forgot how badly she was treated when she first came to Hollywood.

In analyzing Garbo's appearance, Michaela Krutzen contended that Mayer ordered extensive cosmetic surgery on Garbo's face. To the contrary, the changes were minor. Garbo's front teeth were straightened, a small bump on her forehead was removed, and Max Factor redid her hairdo and her makeup, decreasing her makeup rather than increasing it.[25] Both Pola Negri and Val Lewton, then an MGM publicist, contended that Garbo had modified her appearance when she realized that she didn't look like other Hollywood actresses.[26] She had, after all, studied the art of makeup in drama school, at the Swedish Film Industry in Stockholm, and at UFA in Berlin.

In the spring of 1925, MGM–New York producers hired Lillian Gish, who had been one of D. W. Griffith's famed actresses, to add luster to the studio's roster. Gish was appalled by Mayer's treatment of Garbo, whom she regarded as a younger version of herself. Like Garbo, Gish was tall and, again like Garbo, she was both assertive and shy. She talked Mayer into giving Garbo another screen test, using cinematographer Hendrik Sartov and his soft-focus lens, which she regarded as crucial to her success in films.[27]

This time, the test was successful; it showed Garbo's photogeneity, her magical aura. Mayer and Thalberg were impressed; they now had to find a film for her. But they couldn't decide if she was an ingénue—the type she had played in her European films—or a siren / vamp, which the Genthe photos suggested. Then they saw a solution. Alma Rubens, slated to star in a film called The Torrent, was hospitalized for heroin addiction, and Aileen Pringle, Mayer's next choice, had rebuffed a sexual advance on Mayer's part. He was so angry at Pringle for this rejection that he took the role in The Torrent away from her and gave it to Garbo.[28]

Garbo portrayed both an ingénue and a temptress in The Torrent, and Mayer and Thalberg could take their pick in typing her. Film audiences had become increasingly sophisticated, and they were laughing at stereotyped vamps, while stars like Aileen Pringle were complaining publicly about having to play them.[29] Given the spirituality Garbo projected, she could create a more sympathetic vamp. After five MGM executives watched a screening of *The Torrent*, they agreed, "She can either be an actress or found a religion."[30]

In the first half of *The Torrent*, Garbo played a naïve Spanish peasant girl named Leonora who is involved with the local landowner's son, played by Ricardo Cortez. In the film's second half, she becomes a famous Paris opera star called La Brunna (The Dark One), sophisticated and worldly. *The Torrent* was also a "Latin lover" movie, following Rudolph Valentino's stunning success in the early 1920s playing that type. Ricardo Cortez, who resembled Valentino, was Garbo's co-star in *The Torrent*. His real name was Joseph Krantz; he was Jewish and from the Bronx, but in silent films, Hollywood studios changed the ethnicity of their players with impunity, since accents were irrelevant and only looks mattered.

*The Torrent* featured a flood that threatened the lovers, giving the movie its title, while the natural disaster served as a crude metaphor for passion as a torrent. Filming began in late November 1925, without Stiller as its director. Mayer and Thalberg feared that, given his ego and his temper, Stiller wouldn't obey them. They had encountered these problems with Erich von Stroheim, the brilliant director of such movies as *Greed*, and they didn't want to face them with Stiller, who reminded them of von Stroheim. To direct *The Torrent*, they chose Monta Bell, known for directing romantic comedies. Garbo was terrified when she lost Stiller as her director, but he secretly coached her at night, as he had during the filming of *Joyless Street* in Berlin.

William Daniels, the cinematographer on the film, was as skilled as SFI's Julius Jaenzon. He used innovative camera angles and lights to slim Garbo's body and to turn her fatigue—expressed in half-lidded eyes and a general languor—into sensuality. Garbo recognized his ability; he would be the cinematographer on sixteen of her twenty-four MGM films. Realizing that Garbo was sensitive and shy, Thalberg took care in assigning filmmakers to her, rejecting the studio's aggressively masculine directors.

Critics praised Garbo in *The Torrent*, although some called her appearance "odd." The box office on the movie was positive, and Mayer and Thalberg cast her in two more vamp films, *The Temptress* and *Flesh and the*

*Devil*. In essence, they typecast her as a vamp. Actors hated typecasting because it could limit them to playing only one type of character. But L. B. Mayer liked it because he could use it to control actors.[31]

Garbo possessed classic vamp characteristics. She was tall, and she could look mature and sensual. According to Adela Rogers St. Johns, the blonde Swedish actress Anna Q. Nilsson, who freelanced in Hollywood, and who played a vamp in 1923 in the movie *Panjola*, had been the first Hollywood blonde to play that type. She had thus ended what St. Johns called the "stupid convention" that vamps had to be brunettes and ingénues blonde. Garbo could thus be a vamp. In fact, Garbo's hair was light brown, but she was called a blonde—an error she pointed out, although no one listened. The blonde color in her hair was a sheen produced by beaming light directly on it.[32]

*The Torrent* wasn't a typical vamp film. Playing the ingénue Leonora in the first half of the film, Garbo is spiritual. She prays to a statue of the Virgin Mary that she will meet Don Brull, played by Cortez, who is her lover and the son of the local landowner, and that her singing voice will bring wealth to her parents. Love and achievement are thus established as the main themes of the film. Before Don Brull kisses her, she crosses herself, the Catholic sign for piety. After he rejects her, as she leaves for Paris to seek fame through her singing, her mother gives her a cross for protection.

Unlike the typical vamp, Leonora doesn't try to destroy Don Brull. The real villain is his mother, who comes between Leonora and her son. In the final scenes of the film, some years after Leonora has become a famous opera star, Don Brell wants her back. But by then, he has changed from a beautiful youth into a pudgy middle-aged man, married, with three children, while Leonora is still beautiful. The last scenes of *The Torrent* are striking. Leonora's hair is black, in an Eton haircut, slicked down with pomade. Wearing a white fur coat with a large black-and-white collar, tall and commanding, she resembles an art deco icon. In her last close-up in the film, she looks spiritual and sad, elegant and earthy, masculine and feminine, as she will in the Steichen photograph two years later.

Garbo began her next film, *The Temptress*, in the spring of 1926. An authentic vamp film, it has feminist overtones, which was not unusual in vamp films, since by destroying men, vamps by implication attacked patriarchal values. Garbo plays Elena, who is married to a French marquis. She causes havoc among the men in the film: she is responsible for the death of her husband and of Fontenoy, a banker; several duels; and the destruction of the dam in Argentina that Robledo, her lover, is building. The film moves from what a subtitle calls "the female luxury of Paris" to Argentina, where tough men are taming a continent. Antonio Moreno, authentically Spanish, plays Elena's lover.

Elena justifies her behavior by telling Robledo that her husband sold her to Fontenoy, the banker, for a large sum of money. "Men have wanted my body not for my happiness, but for theirs," she laments. Repenting her deeds, she prays to Christ, who "taketh away the sins of the world," to have mercy on her. Unable to resist the temptress, Robledo wants her to elope with him, but she leaves him instead. She is unwilling to destroy his noble effort to build a dam to bring water to a barren land. With this action, Elena reveals her true noble character.

In the film's final scenes, Elena is in Paris; she has become a prostitute and a drunk. Robledo, now a famous engineer, is also in Paris, and he comes across her as she sits at a bistro table outdoors. He wants to help her, but she refuses him. He buys her a drink, probably absinthe, which can cause hallucinations. She drinks the liquor and sees a vision of Christ at the next table, but her Christ is an ordinary man. Signifying her self-destruction, she gives the anonymous man the emerald ring that Robledo gave her when they first met and fell in love.

*The Temptress* exalts male adventure—while disparaging men's treatment of women. It also contains several perverse scenes. The major one involves a duel with whips between Robledo and a robber who had tried to destroy the dam. Their upper bodies are naked, and the slashing of the whips they wield produces gashes in their flesh. While Elena watches, horrified, Garbo actually looks perplexed. The movie produced a furor, but it wasn't a smash hit at the box office. Films usually took about five weeks to make, but after Stiller was fired and a new director hired, *The Temptress* took three months. Garbo's acting in it is wooden. She needed more training, a better co-star, and more sleep.

Thalberg and Mayer next cast Garbo opposite John Gilbert, MGM's top male star, to see how she would fare. Gilbert could carry the

Garbo in *The Torrent* (1926). Photo 12 / Alamy Stock Photo

film; they wanted to see if Garbo could measure up to him, if she really was a star.

Garbo was no happier in Hollywood than she had been in New York. She hated the negative comments made about her on the lot; she disliked Hollywood's methods of filming; and she found the MGM lot ugly. In the fall of 1925, she wrote to Lars Saxon, "The studios are hideous, and everything is so crowded."[33] She had a point. She kept getting lost in the mammoth studio. Its forty-five buildings stretched over forty-three acres, with three miles of paved streets and fire and police departments. Its back lot contained replicas of city streets, historic buildings, and a large lake.[34] In the documentary of the MGM lot made in the summer of 1925, it appears gloomy and overcrowded, with narrow walkways, few trees, and not much grass. Dominated by cinder-block production studios with glass roofs to catch the sun's rays, it resembles a prison.[35]

The gloom of the lot reflected Garbo's reaction to Hollywood, which she found crass, with everyone trying to make a fortune and living beyond their means. Consumer capitalism, which dominated the U.S. economy in the 1920s, had taken over Hollywood. The studios operated like factories: producers and directors were managers; actors were workers; and profits were the main goal. In *Prater Violet*, a satire of the Hollywood studio system, Christopher Isherwood, novelist, screenwriter, and later a friend of Garbo's, described the typical Hollywood studio as a "palace of the sixteenth century": "There one sees what Shakespeare saw: the absolute power of the tyrant, the courtiers, the flatterers, the jesters, the cunningly ambitious intriguers. There are fantastically beautiful women, there are incompetent favorites. There are great men who are suddenly disgraced. There is the most insane extravagance [and] horrible squalor hidden behind the scenery. There are vast schemes, abandoned because of some caprice."[36]

Misfortune now seemed to follow Garbo. Not only was she mocked on the lot, but Stiller wasn't directing her. He wasn't chosen to direct *The Torrent*, and he was laid off after two weeks of directing *The Temptress* because he disobeyed Thalberg and went over budget. Several months later, he was hired by Paramount Pictures, where he successfully directed

Pola Negri in *Hotel Imperial*, about a female servant at a hotel in Austria who saves the life of an Austrian soldier.

Garbo tried to stop Mayer from firing Stiller, and when that didn't work, she tried to break her MGM contract and follow Stiller to Paramount, but Mayer now saw a star in her, and he enforced her contract and wouldn't let her go.[37] He also refused to grant her a leave of absence to visit Stockholm when her beloved sister, Alma, died during the second week of filming *The Temptress*. Not for two and a half more years—until the end of 1928—did Mayer give Garbo a leave of absence to visit her family in Sweden.

In February 1926 Garbo wrote to Lars Saxon that talking to Mayer was like "hitting your head against a brick wall." By March, when her sister died and Stiller left MGM, Greta was desperate. She wrote to Saxon: "I don't understand why God suddenly meant me such harm. It's as though a part of me has been cut away." She wrote to Mimi Pollak that a spell came over her in which she thought she was a failure as an actress. She begged Mimi to visit; she felt like a machine in making her films. She thought of trying the theater again, taking Mimi with her and forcing her to get a divorce. Or maybe Mimi could bring her fiancé along, and the three of them could live together.[38]

Then insomnia hit. Night after night she paced the floor, unable to go to sleep. Reviewing Garbo in *Flesh and the Devil*, journalist Herbert Moulton saw extreme fatigue in her face. "Our methods of filmmaking are seriously interfering with her sleep," Moulton wrote. "She is not used to making films in five or six weeks."[39]

But Garbo was determined to become a great actress, so she did what Mayer wanted, even though she detested meeting with him. He was too domineering, although she didn't realize that he resembled Stiller in that behavior.[40] Mayer alternately praised her, threatened her, and treated her like a child. Unable to control him, Garbo used Stiller's techniques. She refused to engage in conversation and stated that she was going home. Sometimes she acted like a child. But she rarely prevailed—until she met John Gilbert.

Meanwhile, as she filmed *The Temptress*, she constructed a diva persona in public, like La Brunna in *The Torrent*. Hubert Voight, the MGM publicist who had befriended her in New York, was dumbfounded when he visited Hollywood in the spring of 1928 and found Garbo acting like a diva, "unapproachable, stern, haughty."[41] That persona was important; it became central to her life and her acting, as a way of coping with situations beyond her control. But there was also the childish Garbo, who acted like a clown and dressed in adolescent male clothing, partly as a disguise, but also because she liked to cross-dress and to act like a clown. Or she could be dramatic, crying and raging on request. There was also a depressed Garbo, who exercised to relieve her melancholy, or when life seemed too difficult, simply went to bed.

L. B. Mayer was five feet four inches tall and stocky, with the body of a wrestler. A Russian Jew born in poverty in Ukraine, he had immigrated with his natal family as a young child to Nova Scotia, where his father opened a junkyard. Mayer spent his early years searching for scrap metal and fighting off anti-Semitic ruffians. After migrating to Boston as a young man, he opened his own scrap metal yard. Realizing the potential of the movies, he bought a dilapidated movie theater, refurbished it, and showed films.

Mayer made his major money by acquiring the New England distribution rights to D. W. Griffith's *Birth of a Nation* (1915). A racist epic about the South during Reconstruction, it was a huge box office success. It glorified the Ku Klux Klan and portrayed freed African American slaves as villains, unable to control their supposed savage natures. One might argue that Mayer, who presented himself as an American patriot, was racist. In 1918 he moved to Hollywood and set up a small production company.[42]

Aggressive and domineering, Mayer is alleged to have punched out Erich von Stroheim, Charlie Chaplin, and Jack Gilbert in disagreements. I don't doubt those claims, although Mayer more often used salaries and contracts as control mechanisms. If actors didn't have rights over directors, actors, and scripts in their films written into their contracts, Mayer took control. He pleaded and even cried to get his way, but he was manipulative and cruel, and he never forgot an insult—whether actual or imagined.[43]

Irving Thalberg was more likable. He was twenty-six to L. B. Mayer's forty-six when Garbo came to MGM. He was a German Jew from a New

York family with pretensions to gentility. As a child, he often stayed home from school because of a defective heart and a bout of rheumatic fever. He taught himself, spending his time at home studying, eventually taking courses at New York University's business school. He was not expected to live past thirty, but he refused to accept the diagnosis; he lived to be thirty-seven.

Through family connections, he became secretary to Carl Laemmle, head of Universal Studios. He showed his brilliance by turning the failing studio into a success. Drawing from his business school courses, he increased the role of the producer in filming and introduced the continuity script, which included dialogue, stage directions, lighting, sets, and intertitles—a complete production outline.[44] Thalberg was soon called "Hollywood's boy genius."

At MGM, where fifty films were made each year, he supervised every film through assistant producers who reported to him, while he reedited the movies himself. He required directors to stick to the budget for a film and to report to his producers. In other words, he applied the continuity script and what he had learned at NYU business school to MGM, pleasing the Wall Street bankers who were financing films—and demanding tighter production methods. He had films previewed in cities near Los Angeles, and he then reedited them himself, using written comments from the preview audience as the basis for his reediting. At first, L. B. Mayer thought of him as the son he never had. Deferring to Thalberg's intellect, he let him select the films for production; Mayer dealt with actors and the New York office.

Calm and gracious, Thalberg maneuvered actors and writers into submission. Many individuals working under him regarded him as a father. Yet, he could be tough; it was said that "he pissed ice water." Because his illness had stunted his growth, he weighed 120 pounds as an adult and was five feet six inches tall. He liked strong women, and he often hired women as screenwriters. He married featured MGM actress Norma Shearer. Aware that women were a majority of filmgoers, he backed "new woman" films.[45]

But Thalberg often assigned too many writers to one screenplay, in a chaotic process that could produce a weak film. He held endless story conferences with producers and writers, although he always prevailed.[46]

Twenty writers worked on *Susan Lenox: Her Fall and Rise*, starring Garbo. But the writing was so bad that she walked off the set six times. Seven writers worked on *Queen Christina*, seventeen on *Marie Walewska*, about the romance between Napoleon Bonaparte and the Polish countess Marie Walewska, which was one of Garbo's last films. Despite his education, Thalberg wasn't an intellectual; most MGM films of this era had a glossy texture that reflected, more than anything else, the amount of money spent on them.

Mayer and Thalberg weren't the only problems for the insecure Garbo. She detested being called into conferences with MGM executives. Facing a group of powerful men, she felt overwhelmed. "I used to quake at the knees when the studio called me up—they'd sit around the table, cigars in their mouths, and they'd growl and bark." She didn't rage or throw tantrums if she disagreed with them; she simply walked out. "She did not argue at the top of her voice, as other stars did." She was conquering her temper and developing irony and humor as means of self-assertion. Cecil Beaton was impressed by her methods; he wrote that he was "amused at her way of knowingly mystifying the officials at the studio."[47] And her relationship with John Gilbert, which lasted for three years, turned out to be partly an exercise in self-control.

The criticisms of Garbo didn't go away. At the premier of *The Torrent*, she came on the stage after the film ended to be introduced to the audience. The theater's manager presented her and said, "Miss Garbo doesn't speak a word of English." "No," Garbo said, "Not von vord." The audience broke out in guffaws. Having just seen her on the screen as a sophisticated woman of the world, the audience was nonplussed by the awkward woman with a thick Swedish accent now on the stage.[48] That was enough for Garbo. Soon after *The Torrent*'s premier, she wrote angrily to Mimi Pollak that the Americans were stubborn; they never understood anyone and they never showed compassion. She was especially enraged that she had a reputation as a fuddy-duddy because she didn't party with the young Hollywood crowd. "Me, who always sat up half the night drinking with you at home. As long as I am allowed, I will always be Mimosa's Gurra."[49] Several weeks later, she met John Gilbert, substantially complicating her life.

Garbo and Gilbert. ARCHIVIO GBB / Alamy Stock Photo

# 6

## *The Agony and the Ecstasy*

### Garbo and John Gilbert

IN DECEMBER 1925, while Garbo was filming *The Torrent*, she and Mauritz Stiller went to a dinner party at the home of Paramount producer Erich Pommer, who had hired Stiller for Paramount when L. B. Mayer fired him at MGM. Among the guests that evening was director Rowland Lee, who had mentored Hollywood star John Gilbert. Lee began talking about Gilbert, and Garbo asked question after question about the handsome star known as the Great Lover. Like many women, she had a crush on him. According to Rowland Lee, Garbo's knowledge of English was limited, but she knew all the complimentary phrases, which she applied to Gilbert.[1]

Soon after the dinner, Garbo wrote to Mimi Pollak, longing for her as usual. When she dreamt of having a cognac with Mimi at the elegant Strand Hotel in Stockholm, she felt as though she had been thrown out of paradise. She complained about MGM—the long hours; the production methods; the egotism of its actors. She cautioned Mimi that her fiancé Nissi (Nils Lundell) must stay healthy, "now that he has my girl." She also told Mimi that she was no longer involved with Einar Hansen, whom Stiller had hired for Paramount.[2]

In August 1926 John Gilbert entered Garbo's life when she played opposite him in *Flesh and the Devil*, and they fell in love. Their relationship would last for three tumultuous years, until Jack ended it because Garbo wouldn't marry him.

John Gilbert—often called Jack—was born in 1897 to an actress in an acting company that toured the American West. His father managed the company, but soon after Jack's birth his parents divorced, and his father left. Friends of his mother often cared for him; one was a prostitute in whose room Jack slept while she serviced clients. "I was only seven, but I knew more about the world than many people ever discover," he said.[3] He taught himself to read and write; throughout his life he loved reading. When he was eight, his mother married an actor named Walter Gilbert, who adopted him, giving Jack his surname, but that marriage also ended in divorce. When Jack was sixteen, his mother died.

Having acted in his mother's company, he went to Hollywood, hoping for a career in films. Both talented and lucky, he either acted in or directed sixty films. In this era when Rudolph Valentino fascinated women, Gilbert was a Valentino type, dark-haired, with "flashing black eyes" and a slender muscular body. In 1924 he landed a contract with MGM; two years later, he was a superstar.

Jack was kind and friendly. Screenwriter Ben Hecht described him as being "as unsnobbish as a happy child. He swaggered and posed but it was never to impress anyone. He was being John Gilbert, prince, butterfly, Japanese lantern, and the spirit of romance." Hecht called him democratic in sleeping with both prostitutes and film stars.[4]

Loving to talk, Jack could deliver a monologue on many subjects. Deeply emotional, he cried easily. But he had an underlying rage, resulting from his troubled childhood. A binge drinker, and sometimes abusive when drunk, he was bipolar, drinking to self-medicate. He often fell for his co-stars, and he married several, although the marriages ended in divorce.[5] After achieving a large salary, he had a Spanish-style mansion built for him in the Hollywood Hills, with a tennis court, a swimming pool, and views of Los Angeles and the ocean. On Sundays he held a brunch for "Hollywood intellectuals"—like the writer Adela Rogers St. Johns, director King Vidor, producer Arthur Hornblow Jr., and actors

Lilyan Tashman and Edmund Lowe, who were married. As many as thirty people came to Jack's brunches.

Given Jack's tendency to fall in love with his co-stars, it's not surprising that he fell for Garbo. In fact, co-stars involved in loving on the screen carried their romance into their regular lives so often that the advice to them was not to marry until after they had played in two more films with other co-stars, although an off-screen affair between co-stars was considered beneficial to the one they were playing on the screen. The Gilbert biographer Eve Golden claimed that Gilbert and Garbo were mostly friends, but actor Jack Larson disagreed. "Jack was a major womanizer," Larson said to me. "He would never have let Garbo deny him sex."[6] Seven years older than Garbo, Gilbert fit the profile of her Stockholm mentors, who were older professionals in films and the theater. "I could not have managed without him," she said. "He has temperament, but he is so fine an artist that he lifts me up and carries me along."[7]

Gilbert coached Garbo in acting and helped her deal with MGM. But he continued to frequent Hollywood's sexual scene. His exploits in that scene were topped by reports that every so often he took a group of male friends—directors and producers mostly—to MGM's brothel in the Hollywood Hills, which was maintained for MGM's male executives and actors and visiting male dignitaries.

Gilbert told his friend Irving Thalberg that Garbo was a wonderful lover.[8] In Stockholm she had dated women and men, including Max Gumpel, a member of Stockholm's "swinging singles," with whom she had an affair. She had lived in Berlin, a mecca of free love, when she filmed *Joyless Street*. She commented on the sex scene in Hollywood: "The thing I like about Hollywood is that it is the one place in the world where you can live as you like and nobody will say anything about it, no matter what you do."[9]

Was she thinking of "living in sin" with Gilbert? Was Stiller on her mind? She went to him for comfort when Jack drank too much. In the process, she formed a triangle with Gilbert and Stiller, which she controlled. Such triangles often appeared in her films and her life. Did she do it on purpose? She had difficulty making decisions, but she could be calculating. Like many of her friends, Jack found her childlike—a girl of ten, bewildered by Hollywood—although she could be mature and demand-

Garbo and Gilbert in *Flesh and the Devil* (1926). World History Archive / Alamy Stock Photo

ing. She called Stiller "the big man," but she never told Jack that he was homosexual, stoking Jack's jealousy.[10]

When filming *Flesh and the Devil*, Garbo and Gilbert radiated sex, continuing their love scenes after filming on them had ended. Clarence Brown, the film's director, was astonished: "It was the damnedest thing you ever saw. They were alone together in a world of their own. It seemed like an intrusion to yell 'Cut!' I used to just motion the crew over to another part of the set and let them finish what they were doing. It was embarrassing."[11]

Garbo was assertive in those scenes, in which she and Gilbert often lay in a horizontal position, sometimes with Garbo on top. She initiated sex, including open-mouth kissing, which was rarely seen in Hollywood films. The censors didn't cut those scenes, citing her spirituality and her suffering as justifying them. Yet Garbo would soon be restrained, since the censors had banned open-mouth kissing and limited the duration of a kiss.

Set in Prussia before World War I, *Flesh and the Devil* featured Garbo as Felicitas, who is married to an older man, and two young soldiers: Leo, played by Gilbert, and Ulrich, played by the Swedish star Lars Hanson. Felicitas seduces Leo, who kills her older husband in a duel and is exiled to Africa. He returns several years later to find her married to Ulrich, who is wealthy and provides the luxury she craves as a vamp. Ulrich and Leo are close; Felicitas comes between them, which may be her first sin.

The film expands on its title, *Flesh and the Devil*. A subtitle explains: When the devil wants to corrupt a man, he often uses a femme fatale as his agent. In a church service, Garbo as Felicitas kneels next to Leo at the communion rail. When the pastor gives them the communion cup, in turn, to drink the wine that represents Christ's blood, Garbo places her lips on the spot where Leo had placed his. Leo can't resist such a temptation. He and Felicitas resume their affair, and Ulrich, finding out about it, challenges Leo to a duel. But Felicitas repents. Running across a frozen lake to stop the duel, she falls through the ice and drowns.

The film featured an adolescent girl named Hertha, who is Ulrich's sister. She is small, with the innocent face of the "sweet young thing." This character, a type often appearing in women's dramas, was a rival and a confidante to Garbo in *Flesh and the Devil*. She reminded viewers that there were other types of female beauty besides Garbo's exoticism. A different ending for conservative markets was shot for *Flesh and the Devil*. In that ending, after Felicitas falls through the ice and drowns, Hertha wins Leo, suggesting that she was always the right woman for him.

Reviewers of *Flesh and the Devil* focused on the Garbo-Gilbert sex scenes. *Variety*'s reviewer wrote that they made audiences "fidget in their seats and their hair rise on end." Delight Evans, the editor of *Screenland*, wrote: "Ecstatic audiences stayed through the movie twice to see these scenes, and we wrote our own dialogue for the Gilbert-Garbo kisses."[12] Women especially liked the scenes: Garbo not only initiated sex, but she also controlled it, rejecting women's passivity in lovemaking. *Variety*'s reviewer wrote: "The girls get a kick out of the heavy love stuff. They come out of the picture with their male escorts and an 'I wonder if he's learned anything' expression."[13] Garbo soared in popularity. John Gilbert and *Flesh and the Devil* made her a star. Scores of young women saw

the film to learn sex techniques; many became Garbo-maniacs. The journalist Malcolm Oettinger wrote that Garbo brought sex "to every hamlet,
village, and farm in the land."[14]

After completing *Flesh and the Devil*, Garbo moved in with Gilbert in his
home in the Hollywood Hills, keeping her hotel rooms in Santa Monica
to forestall criticism of her for living with a man to whom she wasn't
married—and to remain independent. The dynamic Gilbert brought
Garbo out of her shell. They went to nightclubs, hiked in the hills, and
attended a party at Pickfair, the mansion of Mary Pickford and Douglas
Fairbanks, a hub for the film industry's high society. They were part of the
Hollywood crowd one weekend at the mansion of newspaper magnate
and film producer William Randolph Hearst, up the California coast.
Hearst's estate, known as San Simeon, included a mansion filled with
European antiques, a zoo, and hundreds of acres for hiking and horseback
riding. Hearst lived openly with the much younger Marion Davies, a former Ziegfeld Follies chorus girl; his wife wouldn't give him a divorce. He
established Cosmopolitan Pictures on the M.G.M. lot, mostly to produce
Davies' films. She was kind and generous and beloved by so many in Hollywood. Garbo and Gilbert could be open about their affair at San
Simeon, but in Gilbert's house they hid it, with a secret staircase between
their bedrooms.[15] Fans and journalists could be anywhere.

Garbo was Gilbert's pal as well as his lover. Both loved sports; both
liked to play jokes; both hated L. B. Mayer. Garbo sometimes hosted
Jack's Sunday brunches, although she didn't always show up due to the
large number of guests, using her shyness as an excuse. Yet, screenwriter
Carey Wilson, who was living at Gilbert's house while waiting for a
divorce, never knew the shy Garbo. "I only knew a fascinating young
creature." He and Garbo discussed everything from radio programs to
Ibsen's plays: No one knew the depth of her reading," Wilson said. And
"she wanted to know everything about Jack. She was in love with Jack
and he with her." She often dressed like Gilbert and Wilson, in a loose-
fitting polo coat. "Now I'm one of the boys," she would say.[16]

Jack often proposed marriage to Garbo. She would accept him and
then back off. She told her close New York friend Nicholas Turner that
she did this three times. Suddenly indecisive, she feared that if Jack was

her husband, he would try to control her.[17] Control was always an issue for Garbo. Part of her wanted to be independent, but she also liked to be dominated by an older person who made decisions for her and took care of her. Mauritz Stiller had filled that need, as Salka Viertel, Mercedes de Acosta, and George Schlee would in her later life.

Garbo biographers debate whether she agreed to marry Jack in a double wedding with director King Vidor and actress Eleanor Boardman several weeks after she met Gilbert, and then didn't show up. When L. B. Mayer, a guest at the event, called Garbo a tramp, Gilbert punched him. Most conclude that Garbo was too shy to agree to a wedding so soon after she met Jack, and the brawl with Mayer never happened. But new evidence I found indicates that both Eleanor Boardman and King Vidor stated that it was supposed to be a double wedding, that Garbo never appeared, and that Jack did punch Mayer.[18] Garbo could be capricious in matters of love, as in previously agreeing to marry a man in Santa Barbara and then disappearing.

The journalist and screenwriter Adela Rogers St. Johns, who was close to Jack, thought that Garbo and he were deeply in love, although "they went through cycles of bliss and disaster, surrender and withdrawal."[19] It wasn't easy for Garbo. She had to deal with the mercurial Jack, a new country, a new language, and a new film studio. And Gilbert was jealous of Stiller, who was six feet tall (hence why Garbo called him "the big man") whereas Gilbert was five feet eight inches tall. Garbo never told Jack that Stiller was homosexual, an omission that gave her leverage over Jack. She also kept Mimi a secret.

The language issue affected their relations. Given her photographic memory, Garbo learned languages easily; she was fluent in German when she came to Hollywood, but she had to learn English, which she found difficult. She used her growing knowledge of the language as a control mechanism, making up words and phrases and adopting slang expressions that she found amusing, even though others were sometimes baffled by her idiosyncratic speech. Salka Viertel called it her "baby language." Amused by it at first, Salka came to detest it. Cecil Beaton said that she often spoke on the level of "a children's fable."[20]

Jack showered Garbo with gifts, as though he felt guilty about his drinking and womanizing. Garbo liked the cabin and the waterfall he had constructed behind his house—to remind her of Sweden. She appreciated the account he established for her at a Stockholm bookstore. But she disliked the yacht he bought after he named it *The Temptress*, copying the title of her second MGM film. That name reminded her of her sister's death and Stiller's firing during its filming. Given her disdain, Jack sold the yacht. In an interview, Garbo explained why she stayed with Jack. "Suppose the man you love does something to hurt you. You think you will break it off, but you don't. It's easier just to forget the trouble and continue on."[21]

Given Jack's experience in films, he was an excellent acting coach. When L. B. Mayer cast her in another vamp role after *Flesh and the Devil*, she refused the part, and Mayer suspended her. Jack had Harry Edington, his manager, advise her on what to do next. A genius at negotiations, Edington agreed with Garbo that she should go on strike for a new contract with a higher salary, fewer films a year, and the promise of dramatic roles. Garbo retained Edington as her manager / agent.

Garbo, Gilbert, and Edington together plotted Garbo's mysterious image. To intrigue moviegoers, publicists often described stars as mysterious.[22] But no other star went as far as Garbo, who stopped giving interviews, signing autographs, and attending public events. Fan behavior could be dangerous. In January 1927, for example, a crowd of fans at the Los Angeles premier of *Flesh and the Devil* almost knocked her down. The police had to intervene.[23]

The press covered Garbo's struggle with Mayer extensively, amazed that this young foreigner would initiate "a showdown on rights between studios and stars." Mayer called her an ungrateful immigrant and declared that under the terms of her contract, she had to obey him. He threatened to have her deported. Ruth Biery wrote that many slanders against Garbo were published "as the gospel truth."[24] Yet, the criticism increased her popularity among young working women, a major audience of hers. They had learned from the press that in Stockholm she had been a lather girl and a saleswoman. Those were working-class occupations, which furthered their identification with her.

*Flesh and the Devil* was a hit, and Mayer capitulated; profits were his bottom line. Garbo's new contract, for five years, gave her what she wanted: a larger salary, fewer films a year, and the promise of dramatic roles. Once Garbo signed her new contract at the end of April 1927, she broke down. She had feared for months that her body would give way under the strains of her sister's death, Stiller's firing, her rebellion against MGM, and juggling Gilbert, Stiller, and Mimi Pollak. Then, in April, Stiller almost killed Gilbert. Looking for Garbo, Jack went to her Santa Monica apartment, heavily drunk. When he rang her doorbell and she didn't appear, he climbed up a drainpipe to get in through the balcony. Stiller was there, and he threw Gilbert over the side. Jack wasn't hurt, but the police were called. They put him in a jail cell to sober up. They were used to Jack's antics.

The incident dominated newspaper headlines. Mayer got Gilbert out of jail and into filming *Seven Miles Out*, a movie about rum-running off the California coast. Garbo was filming Tolstoy's *Anna Karenina*, but she often disagreed with the film's director, Dmitri Buchowetzki, and she collapsed on the set. Her doctor diagnosed acute anemia; she was very underweight.[25] She stayed in bed for five weeks and ate a high-calorie diet. She gained fifteen pounds.

Mark Vieira is the only Garbo scholar to have analyzed her 1927 break-down. He attributed it to a botched abortion, citing as proof "vague Hollywood rumor."[26] That may be true, but her doctor's report about weight loss and subsequent bed rest and a diet rich in calories indicates that she may have developed anorexia nervosa. By the 1920s it was recognized as a specific illness, although doctors didn't know much about it. They—and the public—were more familiar with anemia, which involves a lack of healthy red blood cells—which anorexia can cause. There was also her insomnia, anxiety, depression, and the lack of hydrochloric acid in her stomach, which meant that she couldn't digest certain foods, like shellfish. She often suffered from colds and bronchial infections.

She was still exercising; it kept her focused, helped her to sleep, and alleviated her depressions. But excessive exercise can contribute to the onset of anorexia because it reduces the amount of fat in the body. A healthy amount of body fat triggers menstruation, and a lack of body fat may lead to anorexia. There was also her chain-smoking, which contributed to causing her frequent colds and bronchitis and probably to her other health issues. Smoking was endemic in Hollywood; it was considered a relaxant, good for health. It was still linked to sophistication, while the cigarette had become a phallic symbol. When Garbo seduced Gilbert in *Flesh and the Devil*, she smoked a cigarette to attract him.

At some point in 1927, she came down with menstrual difficulties, including irregularity, a heavy flow, and great pain. According to the producer David Lewis, "she might look like hell for about a week. You'd have to shoot around her and not do close-ups."[27] Moreover, she had developed an ovarian inflammation, which Vieira mentioned but didn't investigate, even though it is a key to understanding her physical difficulties. In most cases, it is caused by gonorrhea, a venereal disease. In 1927 there was no cure for gonorrhea; the major treatment involved injections into the blood stream of mercurochrome, a sanitizing agent, even though it contained mercury, a poisonous substance. Sulfa drugs, especially Prontosil, were curatives, but they weren't in use until the late 1930s. A complex disease, gonorrhea can be mild, asymptomatic, or intermittent.[28] In other words, one can have gonorrhea and not know it.

It was at epidemic proportions in the 1920s, but it was referred to humorously as well as seriously. It was called "the clap," a name in use as early as the fifteenth century, when it was presumed to be connected to prostitution. It can be prevented if a man wears a condom during intercourse, but some men do not like to do that since the sheath reduces male sexual pleasure. Marlene Dietrich made that clear in her discussion of sexual behavior in Hollywood with her daughter, Maria Riva, who published what her mother told her in her memoir of Dietrich.[29]

Melvyn Douglas co-starred with Garbo in three films: *As You Desire Me* (1932), *Ninotchka* (1937), and *Two-Faced Woman* (1941). In his autobiography, Douglas praised Garbo for possessing the "plastic, luminous face that sculptors adore." But in his unpublished interview with a film scholar for the Columbia University Oral History Project, he had a different opinion of Garbo. "No one could be more difficult than Garbo," he said. "She took three to four days off on each film, with little advance notice, because of an internal problem."[30]

I interpret "internal" as meaning that her ovarian inflammation had flared up. Garbo tried to conceal it; she called it "the problem" and cited only anemia and bronchitis as recurring illnesses of hers. As censorship forces gained increasing control over films, it was best to stay clear of admitting to gynecological issues, especially one connected to sex. From the etiology of the disease and statements made by Garbo and her friends, her attacks of inflammation were episodic, but they were painful. Mercedes de Acosta described them: "She could be gay and look well and within five minutes she would be desperately depressed and apparently terribly ill."[31] Moreover, her bouts of ovarian pain challenge the common assumption that Garbo was a hypochondriac. The ailments she suffered from were real; many seemed incurable. They frightened her, and it's not surprising that she talked with friends about them. She was heroic in coping with them.

Garbo never revealed who had infected her. Marlene Dietrich later contended that Rouben Mamoulian, the director of *Queen Christina*, had given her gonorrhea, but much evidence suggests that she initially contracted it in 1927, long before she met Mamoulian in 1933. It explains her frequent breaks from films, which have puzzled scholars.[32] It also explains why she so often consulted physicians and healers outside the medical establishment, why she so often had massages and steam baths, and why she went to desert and mountain resorts. Regular doctors couldn't do much for her.

Was Jack Gilbert involved? The descriptions of Jack as a "great lover" and a "womanizer" put a positive spin on his behavior, as though his sexual exploits were triumphs. Given his overactive sex drive, I suspect that he suffered from sex addiction, an obsession recognized by psychologists today as the inability to control one's sex drive, to the extreme of trying to seduce any available attractive woman.[33] My criticism is not aimed at John Gilbert, but at a patriarchal culture fixated on the male phallus, holding the very masculine man as the male ideal. It's called toxic masculinity today.

Garbo had recovered from her breakdown in the spring of 1927 by the following summer, and she began filming a new version of *Anna Karenina*, with John Gilbert as Vronsky, Anna's lover. The original version was scrapped, and the title was changed to *Love*, so that theater marquees read: "Garbo and Gilbert in Love." Irving Thalberg now pampered Garbo. She was excused from story conferences and rehearsals. An extra who resembled her did her long and tedious costume fittings and lighting tests. She was given a mobile dressing room, which was parked on the edge of her sets, so that she could rest between filming. She was allowed to leave filming each day at 5:00 P.M.[34] Her fragility, acute hearing, and need for quiet were recognized.

William Daniels, her cinematographer on *Love*, as on most of her films, now barred visitors from her sets and surrounded Garbo with black screens during filming so that she didn't see anyone. She was having difficulties concentrating, which was key to her acting, as the softer lights now used for filming made spectators on the set easy to see, while her physical issues bothered her. She needed such quiet that her directors began communicating with her through a hole in one of the black screens.

That sounds like an extraordinary concession, but by now Garbo mostly directed herself in her films, with her official directors providing a comfortable environment. She once said, only partly in jest, that she would prefer it if her director left the set and let her determine her movements and expressions herself.[35]

Throughout her affair with Jack Gilbert, Garbo corresponded with Mimi Pollak. In November 1926, three months after she met Jack, she wrote to Mimi about him, since newspapers were publishing articles about them and she wanted to have some influence over Mimi's reaction. Journalists expected her to marry him, she said, but she told Mimi that she couldn't do that. Marriage didn't suit her; she was too temperamental. She called herself "naughty" because she had made many false promises to Gilbert. He had everything—a swimming pool, servants, a lovely house—and still she went to her hotel rooms. She told Mimi that she didn't know why she did that, but other sources reveal that his drinking troubled her. Garbo had disliked the alcoholism in Sweden, and she disliked it in Hollywood. Other behaviors of Jack's troubled her. There were reports that he threatened her with a gun and that he pushed her off his porch, causing her to fall down a hill.[36]

Even after Mimi married Nisse in early 1927, Garbo still wrote to her. In June, she asked Mimi to buy a decanter and a set of glasses for her that she had seen in a Stockholm store and wanted to give Jack for Christmas; she hadn't given up on him. In September, after *Love* wrapped, she wrote to Mimi that she longed to see her—and to touch her, "of course." She thanked Mimi for sending photographs of herself: "You are just as small and fine and delicate." In November, she wrote that she dreamed of living in a Stockholm apartment with Mimi and a bottle of champagne beside them.[37]

Garbo assured Mimi that she wasn't involved with another woman, but women at that time and writers ever since have thought otherwise. The Hollywood actor and chronicler Louise Brooks claimed that she had a one-night stand with Garbo in the summer of 1928 and that she was a "masculine dyke."[38] More credible is the allegation of an affair with the film actress Lilyan Tashman, who was feminine, tall, and witty. A former Ziegfeld Follies showgirl under contract to Paramount, Tashman played sophisticated women as well as gold diggers, fast-talking dames, and the heroines' best friend. She was regularly on best-dressed lists. Her marriage to the screen actor Edmund Lowe was celebrated as perfect; they were often interviewed on how they made it work.[39]

But Tashman was primarily lesbian and Lowe primarily homosexual, and their marriage was perhaps "lavender." The actress Mary Brian claimed that Tashman and Lowe "traveled on dual tracks"—in other words, both were bisexual. Tashman had a reputation for seducing women. She had lived in New York with Nita Naldi, another Ziegfeld Follies showgirl, later a Hollywood star. Tashman was bulimic, and Garbo didn't like her attacks of nerves and frequent vomiting. She died in 1934 of a brain tumor, but when Nita Naldi learned of Tashman's death, she exclaimed in anger, "Lil is a martyr to this reducing business!"[40] Garbo met Tashman through Gilbert; Tashman and her husband were regulars at his Sunday brunches. Tashman and Lowe and Garbo and Gilbert went to USC football games together.

Did Gilbert know about Garbo's attraction to women? If he did, he kept it to himself, although in an interview in 1927 he hinted at it: "When she [Garbo] comes into a room, every man stops to look at her. And so does every woman. . . . She is capable of doing a lot of damage."[41] There was also Garbo's comment that she liked the sexual freedom in Hollywood. But Garbo and Gilbert seemed happy during the making of *Love*. The filming went smoothly.

And Garbo seemed comfortable with her "mystery woman" persona. In the summer of 1927, the journalist Malcolm Oettinger interviewed Garbo on the set of *Love*. Gilbert brought him to Garbo for an interview. Oettinger was overwhelmed by her: "She sits back and looks at you through heavy-lidded half-closed eyes, her lips parted in a tempting smile, her slim hands daintily holding a cigarette. She is fully aware of her hypnotic influence, yet she says nothing to bear this out. She is sphinx-like in her silence, cryptic in her comments when she does talk."[42]

In the fall of 1927, after *Love* wrapped, Garbo filmed *The Divine Woman*, based on the life of Sarah Bernhardt. All prints of it have been lost, although still photos and scripts reveal that Garbo, playing Bernhardt, falls in love with an army deserter and goes off with him to a ranch in Central America. That was a fabrication, having nothing to do with Bernhardt's life. Stiller asked Thalberg to let him direct the film, but Victor Seastrom was chosen—and Garbo didn't object. A month later, Stiller, disillusioned and ill, left for Stockholm, as did most Scandinavians in the Hollywood film industry. Sound had entered Hollywood filmmaking with *The Jazz Singer,* made by Warner Brothers in the summer of 1927. Many of the Scandinavians didn't speak English or had a thick accent. They feared for their future in a Hollywood dominated by sound films.

In the spring of 1928 Garbo made *The Mysterious Lady*, playing Tania Federova, a Russian spy in Vienna. Using her charms to steal secret plans from an Austrian official, she gives them to the head of the Russian secret police, another lover of hers. Deciding that she prefers the Austrian, she steals the plans back from the Russian, killing him in the process. In an extraordinary scene, just after she has shot the Russian, as his bodyguard enters the room, she makes spurious love to his dead body so that the bodyguard won't see that his charge is dead. Garbo's cleverness and sexual abandon in *The Mysterious Lady* might make it a "new woman" film, although it doesn't deal with the issue of freedom in marriage, a major concern of 1920s feminists.

Garbo followed *The Mysterious Lady* with *A Woman of Affairs* in the summer of 1928. Gilbert was her co-star. They were still living together in Jack's home, but their romance was strained. Douglas Fairbanks Jr., who played Garbo's younger brother in the film, became their go-between on the set, carrying notes between them. They seemed to him to be angry with each other one day and in love the next. Fairbanks tried to seduce Garbo, but she wasn't interested.[43] She had received a letter from Stiller in Sweden proposing marriage, and it had confused her.

*A Woman of Affairs* was the screen version of *The Green Hat*, by British author Michael Arlen, the smash hit novel of 1922. The censors had placed it on a list of novels that the studios were forbidden to film because of immoral content. Their main issue with the novel was that Iris Storm's new husband commits suicide not because he embezzled money, but because he suffers from syphilis and he doesn't want to infect his new wife. Garbo had seen the play made from the novel when she was in New York in 1925 and she had decided that she wanted to play Iris in a film. After she defeated L. B. Mayer, she told Thalberg that she wanted *The Green Hat* to be her next film. Irving Thalberg was interested; he approached the censors. After a year of negotiations, he persuaded them to allow MGM to film the novel. To get their approval, Thalberg changed the reason for the suicide from syphilis to embezzlement. He changed the title to *A Woman of Affairs*, and he changed the name of the female protagonist from Iris Storm to Diana Merrick. Anyone "in the know,"—in other words, sophisticated moviegoers—would still see its connection to *The Green Hat*, but the average moviegoers wouldn't, and the censors were satisfied. Many of them weren't that discerning or educated.

Iris Storm is a determined woman who lives as she wishes—drinking, dancing, and driving fast in a roadster. Yet, her life is filled with sorrow. Her lover marries a "sweet young thing," who is a replica of Hertha in *Flesh and the Devil*. She spends time in a hospital because she has had either a miscarriage, an abortion, or a nervous breakdown. Her husband commits suicide; her brother is an alcoholic. Taking responsibility for everything negative that has happened, determined to preserve her lover's marriage, acting according to the male code of honor, Iris kills herself by smashing her roadster into a massive tree on the site where she and her lover had pledged undying love to each other.

In November 1928 Garbo made *Wild Orchids*. As in *The Temptress*, *Flesh and the Devil*, and *Love*, her character is married to an older man, in this case an American who imports tea from Java, while she has an affair with a younger man. Lewis Stone, who played supporting roles in six Garbo films, played the older husband. A soldier before becoming an actor, Stone had a military bearing, which translated into strength on the screen. He may seem old to us, but he had been a matinee idol in the early 1920s, and that reputation carried over to his later career.[44] In *Wild*

*Orchids*, Garbo used her child persona; Stone was as much her father as her husband. Her name in the film—Lillie Sterling—implied purity, as did the name of her husband, John Sterling.

She is attracted to the handsome, flirtatious Javanese prince de Gace, who is on the steamship they take to Java and at whose plantation house in Java they stay. Nils Asther, a Swedish actor who resembled John Gilbert, but who had a suave sensuality, played the prince. Garbo had known him in Stockholm; he had attended the Royal Dramatic Academy and had been one of Stiller's "boys." Garbo dated him after she and Gilbert broke up. In his autobiography, Asther contended that they had an affair and that he proposed marriage to her numerous times, but she turned him down. The proposals are probable; the affair is dubious. Garbo's later collection of art included a painting by Asther of a large and a small elephant, with intertwined trunks. Garbo and Asther had ridden elephants together in *Wild Orchids*. The painting by Asther was titled *Platonic Love*.[45]

Asther introduced a central theme of *Wild Orchids* when he asserted that American women are domestic and tame, but Javanese women are wild orchids, wild and unrestrained. Garbo spends much of the movie alternately encouraging and resisting him, since the film hints early on that he won't marry her. In the film, she often uses the Delsarte pose for despair, holding her hair back on the sides of her head with her hands, as she had in the Steichen photo. Early in the filming, she learned of Stiller's death. She finished the film, but she couldn't stop herself from showing her grief.

In the film's penultimate scene, the prince and Lillie's husband, John Sterling, go tiger hunting, even though Sterling finally realizes that the prince is trying to seduce his wife. Terrified that her husband will shoot the prince, Garbo dresses in a safari outfit, with breeches and boots, and goes on the tiger hunt. As they beat the bush to find the tiger, the animal attacks the prince. The husband, motivated by honor, kills the tiger with a gun and saves the prince. In the end, John Sterling is willing to give his wife a divorce. But Lillie has had enough of Java, and she stays with her husband, which seems a wise decision.

Harry Edington persuaded Mayer to let Garbo visit Sweden in late 1928, after she finished *Wild Orchids*. It was nearly three years since she had been there. But rather than finding peace in her native land, she found bedlam, as people demanded autographs and smashed a window in her cab. Her stardom produced the same frenzy in Sweden as in the United States.

Garbo spent time in Sweden with her family and friends and with Stiller's brother Abraham. When he called her his niece, she told him that he should have been able to call her his sister-in-law. Stiller had finally proposed to her in a letter in the spring of 1928, when she was in Hollywood and he was in Sweden. She may have meant to accept his proposal. Stiller had reestablished his career in Sweden, and there was, as Stiller stated in the letter, a "mystical" bond between them. Garbo was twenty-three and Stiller was forty-five, but such age-disparate marriages were not that uncommon. Stiller also told her in the letter that if she refused to marry him, he didn't want to see her again.[46] That was a harsh statement. But before she arrived back in Stockholm, he died from pleurisy, a lung disease; he had chain-smoked for years. Once in Sweden, she had insomnia. Her school friends took turns soothing her at night to help her go to sleep.

There were compensations. On her way to Sweden, she went via New York, and she made a quick trip to Harlem to listen to jazz. Then, on the steamship across the Atlantic, she made new friends—from the heights of Swedish society. Members of the royal family had gone to New York for a wedding, and they were on Garbo's steamship going home. The two sons of the crown prince were on the ship, as were Count and Countess Wachtmeister, who were close to the royal family.

Hörke Wachtmeister was ten years older than Garbo. She was down-to-earth, with a large athletic body. She was also bisexual. She and Garbo walked the deck of the ship together every day for exercise, and Garbo ate dinner with the royal party. Once in Stockholm, she and Mimi Pollak visited the Wachtmeisters at their estate. Called Tistad, it was centered around a sixteenth-century palace with seventy-five rooms. Mimi remembered that Garbo walked around the palace, touching the silver objects that were displayed, showing a desire for expensive things.[47] In her later visits to Sweden, she often visited the Wachtmeisters at Tistad, but there is no evidence that she and Hörke had an affair, except in

1962 when the press found them together in a lesbian night club in Paris. And the Swedish countess replaced Mimi as her primary Swedish correspondent.

The newspapers speculated that Garbo would marry one of the princes, but she quashed the rumors. She did, however, become friends with Wilhelm Sörenson, the son of a wealthy Swedish industrialist. A homosexual interested in filmmaking, Sörenson came to Hollywood in August 1929, staying for a year and becoming Garbo's companion. Their friendship generated many false rumors that they would marry, but Garbo may have wanted that publicity. Sörenson became one of her pseudo-heterosexual male admirers.[48] He functioned for her as a "beard," the slang term for a person who allows their apparent heterosexuality to be used to conceal their date's same-sex desires. Garbo enjoyed Sörenson's company, but after a year, she wasn't displeased when he returned to Sweden. Aside from his first night in Hollywood, she didn't permit him to stay overnight in her home; she feared generating rumors that they were sexually involved.

What happened to Jack Gilbert during Garbo's visit to Sweden: He picked her up at the train station when she returned. On the way home, he proposed to her again. She refused him again. But this time, he found another woman. Ina Claire was a Broadway star who had come to Hollywood to make movies. She was chic, sophisticated, and on the best-dressed lists; soon after meeting her, Gilbert proposed to her, and she accepted. Garbo was upset by that; she called Harry Edington to ask him how to get out, but he retorted only she could do that. Yet she didn't do that; she knew she would only be successful if she married Jack. As she had when her father died, she showed little emotion publicly but she was sorrowful in private.

Gilbert's marriage to Claire didn't last. She turned out to be controlling. She redecorated his house, which still contained Garbo's possessions, and she tried to change his acting style, which he didn't appreciate. After Claire, there would be others: the young Virginia Bruce, who played opposite him in a film and bore him a child. Finally, Marlene Dietrich turned up at his house, playing the redemptive angel, intent on curing him of his alcoholism and saving his career. She almost succeeded before he died of a heart attack.

At his funeral, Marlene swooned and cried, acting like his widow, although she had a husband in Germany. Garbo made no comment, but she must have been angry that Marlene had taken over her lover. She had already done the same with Mercedes de Acosta. But in the Hollywood sexual merry-go-round, jealousy was a forbidden emotion. It was a key element in many films, but in a free-love environment, it wasn't supposed to exist.

Garbo in *The Single Standard*. ARCHIVIO GBB / Alamy Stock Photo

# 7

## *Friends and Lovers;* Anna Christie *and Garbo's Acting*

$\mathscr{A}$FTER GARBO RETURNED to Hollywood from Sweden in March 1929, she made two new woman films. *The Single Standard*, filmed in April, was based on a novel by Adela Rogers St. John. *The Kiss*, filmed in August, was based on a screenplay by Jacques Feyder. Both films dealt with feminist issues concerning marriage. In different ways, each made a case for women's independence.

St. Johns found her title, *The Single Standard*, in the feminist proposal to end the sexual double standard and give women the same sex rights as men. The novel explored whether a woman is justified in having an affair if she is married and has a child. In the movie, Garbo played Arden Stuart, who is "as modern as the radio and bobbed hair."[1] She impetuously goes on a romantic cruise in the South Seas with Packy Cannon, a famous writer-adventurer played by Nils Asther, although they aren't married. After they return to Los Angeles, Packy wants to be independent and goes off on his own. When friends of Arden's who disapprove of her romantic adventure with Packy threaten to ostracize her, Arden marries an old boyfriend and has a child.

After several years, the exciting Packy returns and wants her back. She still loves him, but she bows to convention and remains with her staid husband and adorable child. As in many films of this era, the movie ends on a conventional note, but its exposition suggests that an affair isn't immoral if it is based on love. The movie also suggests that Arden stays with her husband because of their child.

Garbo and Nils Asther in *The Single Standard* (1929). PictureLux / The Hollywood Archive / Alamy Stock Photo

*The Kiss* is set in the 1920s. Garbo played Irene Guarry, who is married to Jacques Guarry, a wealthy older businessman, who emotionally abuses her, but she loves Andé Dubail, a sensitive lawyer who is her age. When a young man with whom she plays tennis passionately kisses her as he leaves her home, Jacques sees the kiss and attacks the young man, dragging him into the study. Irene follows, holding a gun, and we hear a shot. Someone has killed Jacques. Irene is put on trial for murder, and André is her lawyer. She is held not guilty of the crime, which is ruled a suicide, because Jacques lost a lot of money in a bank failure. Once again, as in *A Woman of Affairs*, filmed a year earlier, a man's suicide is blamed on his financial flaws and the code of male honor. Such suicides happened especially during the Great Depression.

In the film's courtroom scene, Garbo wears a modified nun's habit, a reminder of her spirituality. In testifying, she asserts her "new woman" independence, stating that she no longer follows unjust social conventions. A trio of cleaning ladies identifies with her. One of them asserts: "Half of us women would shoot our husbands, if only we had the nerve." In the end, Garbo is reunited with André, the sensitive lawyer. Garbo stated that she liked *The Kiss* because of its "complex femininity and subtle irony."[2] That phrase could be used to describe most of her new woman films.

*The Kiss* resonated to Garbo's famed kisses in *Flesh and the Devil*, while it made a case for free (no-fault) divorce. *The Single Standard* was even more feminist: Garbo dresses in a white cotton shirt and pants during the cruise, attire forbidden to respectable women. *Variety's* reviewer, using that journal's vernacular style, wrote that in the film, "Garbo throws off the cloak of conventionalism for free plunges claimed so common in spots here and on the continent." "Free plunges" referred to free love. *Variety's* reviewer also stated that "the thousands of typing girls and purple-suited office boys will find this film made to their order."[3] "Free plunges" meant free love; "Typing girls" referred to Garbo's many fans among female office workers. "Purple-suited" office boys meant homosexuals.

There is no reference to homosexuality or lesbianism in the film. Did the *Variety* reviewer know that Asther was homosexual, and that Garbo practiced free love? It's probable, given *Variety* was the Hollywood industry's leading trade journal as well as the lesbian and homosexual networks that stretched from coast to coast.

Once Garbo returned to Hollywood from Sweden in March 1929, Harry Edington persuaded her to move from her modest Santa Monica hotel to the elegant Beverly Hills Hotel, more in line with her status as a star. That summer, however, a fan of hers breached the hotel's security, jumped on her car, and was almost killed. Distressed by the incident, Garbo moved to a rented house, with a tall hedge to keep fans out.

In this era stars sometimes moved to new homes to escape fans, who could be relentless. The Garbo-maniacs didn't protect Garbo on the streets, and they were only part of her fan base. Enterprising fans of Garbo and of other stars obtained their home addresses and sometimes appeared at their front doors. They organized bus tours that went by stars' homes, with commentaries delivered by tour guides using megaphones. Garbo hated this practice; because of her acute hearing, she heard the commentaries. But rents were low, and houses—and mansions—were available in Beverly Hills and nearby communities because real estate speculators had overbuilt homes there.[4]

When Garbo went to Sweden for long visits, she gave up her rental house. Given her chronic indecision, she never knew if she would return. She had few possessions in her early Hollywood years; she lived in only several rooms of her rental houses. During her seventeen years in Hollywood, she lived in eleven houses. Not until the 1950s did she establish a permanent home—in New York—but even then, she often took vacations or visited friends in other places.

Harry Edington hired a young Swedish married couple—Gustaf and Sigrid Norin—to cook, clean, drive, and do chores for Garbo, but employing them was a mistake. Gustaf had been a student at the Swedish Royal Dramatic Academy, and he came to Hollywood to act in films. After nine months with Garbo, it was clear that she wouldn't help him, so he and Sigrid quit and sold their impressions of her to journalist Rilla Palmborg. They described her as capricious, stingy, and demanding. She often rang their bell in the middle of the night because of her insomnia or her paranoid fear that a robber was in the house. It's possible that she missed Jack Gilbert's presence or that, given her upbringing, she didn't know how to treat servants. They also noted that Garbo had a closet filled with men's clothing: hats, suits. shirts, trousers, ties, and shoes. In December 1930 they resigned their positions.

Using the Norins' information, Palmborg published two articles on Garbo in *Photoplay* in the fall of 1930 and a book on her in 1931, titled *The Private Life of Greta Garbo*.[5] After that debacle, Garbo hired an eccentric Afro-American man and an elderly German woman as domestics; both were silent. But Garbo was so upset by the breach that she made her friends swear not to talk to journalists about her. If they did, she would drop them.

After the break with Jack Gilbert, Garbo restructured her life. To deal with her insomnia, she went to bed at 8:00 in the evening and read until she dozed off. She didn't like to take sleeping pills, fearing addiction, which was a common Hollywood problem. She got up at five in the morning to swim in the ocean or hike in the hills before the public arrived. When filming, she had to be at the studio at seven in the morning, to do her hair and put on her make-up and costume before filming began at nine. She left the set promptly at five. Garbo functioned best as a creature of habit. No matter how eccentric—or ill—she might be, she liked routine. Always fearing insomnia, she followed her bedtime ritual established in 1929 for much of the rest of her life.

She also made new friends. She left Jack's Sunday brunch circle, remaining friends with Lilyan Tashman and a few others. After Jack Gilbert's capricious behavior, she preferred to socialize with Europeans. Most of the Scandinavians in the Hollywood film industry had left by 1929, so she turned to other European circles. She soon met English actor John Loder and his wife Sophie Kobal and Belgian director Jacques Feyder and his wife Françoise Rosay. Both women were European; both were actresses. Nils Asther and Wilhelm Sörenson soon joined Garbo's group.

They held a brunch every Sunday at the Loders' home in Malibu and parties at the Feyders' home in Hollywood. They sometimes went to the Apex Club to listen to jazz.[6] Garbo occasionally invited this group of friends to her house on the spur of the moment, although she didn't entertain them formally, except for a traditional Swedish Christmas celebration in 1929. It included a decorated Christmas tree, a smorgasbord dinner with many courses, and joke gifts, which was the Swedish custom.

But she often didn't make plans until the last minute; and she sometimes accepted invitations and didn't show up. Because of her phobia about strangers, her friends took care in not inviting anyone to their homes whom she didn't already know. John Loder called Garbo "a law unto herself. She would not meet any of our friends." Like others, Loder found that her times of happiness were followed by days of gloom. But she could be fascinating. Sitting on the floor, she joked like a schoolgirl. And she agreed to star in *The Kiss*, which Feyder was to direct.[7] But Sörenson and Loder talked with a journalist about her, and she dropped them. That doomed the group.

One Saturday evening in the spring of 1930, film magazine writer Harriet Parsons, the lesbian daughter of renowned movie columnist Louella

Parsons, surreptitiously followed Garbo, to obtain information for an article on her. Parsons found Garbo with Jacques Feyder at a restaurant on Olivera Street downtown, the center of the Los Angeles Mexican American community.[8] After they finished dinner, Parsons followed them next door to a puppet theater, which was playing a burlesque of Garbo's *Anna Christie*. After watching the show, Garbo and Feyder went to the other side of the theater, where Adrian had a workshop. After a brief visit, Garbo drove back to her home in Brentwood, with Parsons following her. It was late, so Parsons parked her car in a space hidden by bushes and slept in the car. The next day she followed Garbo by foot on paths through the Santa Monica hills to Salka Viertel's home.

Parsons described what Garbo was wearing during her surveillance. "She was dressed as no other woman in Hollywood would have been dressed," Parsons wrote. She wore "a grey suit, severely tailored, a man's gray shirt, a tie of navy blue with white dots, a heavy grey topcoat, and a dark blue beret, with no hair showing."[9] Garbo wore that clothing as a disguise and because she liked to cross-dress.

In line with her mystery image, Garbo called herself a hermit, but the hermit designation wasn't entirely correct. When making a film, Garbo focused on creating her role before and during filming, and she wouldn't see anyone, fearing that she might lose her concentration. In periods between films, when she wasn't in bed—suffering from a cold, menstrual pain, depression, or some other ailment—she exercised, hiked, swam, and saw friends. She sometimes went to Lake Arrowhead, in the San Bernardino mountains two hours east of Los Angeles; or to La Quinta, a desert resort near Palm Springs. Occasionally she went to Yosemite, the national park in Northern California, which has snow-covered mountain peaks, waterfalls, forests, and hiking trails.

Garbo also had massages and went to a Hollywood spa. And she played tennis, a passion among the movie elite. Their estates usually had a tennis court and a swimming pool. John Gilbert had taught Garbo the game. She played a masculine style, hitting the ball from the baseline and rushing the net. She was welcomed at many Hollywood courts, and she often went to the Saturday tennis parties held by MGM actress Dolores del Rio and her husband, MGM art director Cedric Gibbons. Their marriage was rumored to be "lavender" But the preponderance of evidence indicates it began as a passionate love affair.[10]

In 1932 journalist Dorothy Calhoun wrote: "Everybody who knows anything about her [Garbo] has been interviewed; every source of possible hearsay has been tapped."[11] But Calhoun spoke too soon; she learned so much more that in 1935 she wrote a second article on Garbo. This time she revealed that Garbo went to the movies a lot, especially to the Filmarte Theater in Santa Monica, the only theater in the area to show foreign films. She went fishing with film actor Richard Cromwell. (Cromwell was homosexual and one of her "beards"; he was married briefly to screen star Angela Lansbury.) Garbo sometimes spent a weekend afternoon at the home of cinematographer Willian Daniels, playing with his children, although she refused invitations to meet visiting dignitaries because she found such meetings awkward. But she loved children, who returned her affection because she seemed like a child. Dorothy Calhoun concluded: "Garbo has one of the fullest social lives of any star of the screen."[12]

She remained friendly with Pola Negri, and she walked on the Santa Monica beach with Anita Loos, who lived in a mansion on the "Gold Coast," the stretch of that beach which held a row of mansions, fronting on what is today Pacific Coast Highway, with their backyards open to the beach. Marion Davies and her lover William Randolph Hearst, the newspaper publisher and producer, lived on that beach, as did L. B. Mayer and his family; Irving Thalberg and Norma Shearer, after they married in 1927, and director Ernst Lubitsch. When Edmund Goulding directed Garbo in *Love*, they became friends. She went to his home to discuss "the problems of her profession and her interests in art." But if a stranger appeared, she would suddenly flee.[13]

When she had dinner at the home of Frances Marion, a screenwriter for *Anna Christie* (1930) and *Camille* (1936), she gathered pods from wild roses to make a Swedish soup. Away from the studio, Marion said, Garbo was neither mysterious nor aloof. "With simple tastes, instinctive discrimination between what was real and what was false, she hated the hypocrisy that was evident all around her." She avoided her neighbors, but when the film actress Zazu Pitts lived next door to her, they often chatted. Pitts's three children broke the ice. "When you get to know her," Pitts asserted, "she is one of the friendliest people in the world."[14]

When making films, Garbo always had the same crew. She didn't want to deal with unfamiliar faces. Thoughtful during filming, she gave presents to the crew members. To William Daniels, her cinematographer, she gave gold watches, silver cigarette boxes—and an antique silk Chinese tapestry. "I'm still planning to build a house around it," Daniels joked.[15]

After the break with John Gilbert, Garbo had no acting coach. In April 1930, a year after she and Gilbert parted, she found a new coach at a party at the director Ernst Lubitsch's home, a center for the Hollywood German community, where she met Salka Viertel, a Berlin stage actress.[16] Garbo and Salka spent most of the evening talking on the terrace. Salka, who was sixteen years older than Garbo, found her "hypersensitive, although of a steely resistance," while her opinions about people were "just, sharp, and objective."[17] Garbo was pleased that the only film of hers Salka had seen was *The Saga of Gösta Berling* since, as she told Salka, she found her Hollywood films too similar and too commercial. Detesting her vamp films, she burlesqued sex scenes from them for Salka; she was an excellent mime.

Salka had come to Hollywood in 1928 from Berlin, at the age of thirty-one, with her husband, Berthold, and their three sons, David, Peter, and Christopher.[18] Fox studios had hired Berthold, a writer and director known in Germany. He and Salka were Jewish, although they were part of the early exodus of European artists to Hollywood, who wanted to escape from Europe's postwar inflation and to benefit from the large salaries Hollywood studios paid. The wave of Jewish artists from Germany fleeing Nazism began in 1933, when Hitler took over the government; it became a flood in 1934 when Jews were barred from working in the German film industry. Salka had been a successful actress in Berlin, but she was rarely cast in roles in Hollywood films; she was, she said, "too old" and "not beautiful enough.".[19]

Born and raised in Poland, Salka came from an upper-class family. She was tough and outspoken, but generous and motherly, although she was deeply insecure, a trait she hid behind a façade of irony and competence. She became a counselor to many European émigrés in Hollywood—and to struggling American actors. Actress Betsy Blair found Salka to be a superb friend. When Salka's hair turned prematurely white, she dyed it flaming red. Tall and large-boned, she stood out in a crowd. "I considered her my spiritual mother," Blair wrote.[20]

Salka had a sensual glow. For several years she had an affair with her next-door neighbor, Oliver Garrett, a successful Hollywood screenwriter, who helped her navigate the ebbs and flows of Hollywood. She then had a long affair with Gottfried Reinhardt, the son of Max Reinhardt, the Berlin theatrical impresario. Gottfried was twenty years younger than she, but he was stocky, with a solemn manner, and they didn't seem that different in age. The Viertels had an open marriage, and Berthold was so often in Europe and with other women that Gottfried often lived in her home and functioned as her husband. He worked as an assistant producer at MGM.

In 1929 the Viertels moved to a large house in Santa Monica Canyon, near the beach. Salka held Sunday afternoon get-togethers, with coffee and homemade cake, conversation, ping-pong, and walks on the beach. Her gatherings resembled those held by her mother in Poland and by European intellectuals in Vienna, Berlin, and elsewhere. Salka's "salon" attracted not only European émigrés, like Arnold Schoenberg and Bertholt Brecht, whom she had known in Berlin, but also Americans, ranging from actor Montgomery Clift to Tallulah Bankhead, an eccentric actress from Georgia, who was the daughter of a U.S. Congressman who later became Speaker of the House. Her sexual hi-jinks amused and shocked everyone. She talked openly about her lesbian affairs, salted her conversation with obscenities, and often wore no undergarments. Bankhead tried to seduce Garbo, but her ploys never worked.

Salka was a superb host at her salons, introducing people and making them feel at home. Writer Robert Parrish described the unique blend of talent, fame, and relaxation at one of Salka's salons:

> I walked in the back door and there was a guy with short hair cooking at the stove. In the living room, [classical pianist] Arthur Rubinstein was tinkling on the piano. Greta Garbo was lying on the sofa, and Christopher Isherwood was lounging on a chair. Who's the guy cooking in the kitchen? I asked. Berthold Brecht was the reply.[21]

Garbo didn't always attend Salka's salons, partly because of attacks of shyness, but also because eventually she sometimes went to other

Hollywood gatherings—at Vicki Baum's home in Pacific Palisades, for example, a few miles up the coast from Santa Monica, or at director George Cukor's home in the Hollywood Hills. Baum, from Berlin, wrote the novel on which *Grand Hotel* was based. Cukor, who was homosexual, held luncheons for gender-crossing friends. His home was a showpiece, with six acres of gardens terraced up a hill.

Salka often joined Garbo in hiking in the hills or swimming in the ocean early in the morning. Following Swedish practice, they swam in the nude. When together, they discussed films, the theater, literature, and their lives. Embarrassed by her scanty education, Garbo liked to socialize with educated people; she learned from them. When her insomnia was severe, she read demanding literature: the Russian classics; German writers Johann Wolfgang von Goethe and Thomas Mann.[22] Some of her friends were impressed by her learning: with her photographic memory she could recite verses by many poets. Others thought she was close to illiterate. The truth is probably that she tailored herself to suit her companion, although sometimes she couldn't resist being a child or a clown.

Both Garbo and Salka wanted to return to Europe, but they felt they couldn't. Garbo had her screen career and her drive to be financially independent, while Salka and the boys were dependent on Berthold, still employed by Hollywood studios. Jacques Feyder suggested that Salka play Marthy, the prostitute in *Anna Christie*, in MGM's German version of the film, which he was to direct, and Garbo agreed. She and Salka grew close; Salka was the mother Garbo wanted; Garbo was the daughter in Salka's family of males.

Fred Zinnemann, Berthold's assistant, later an eminent Hollywood director, described Salka as "one of the world's most generous and opinionated women," and she dominated Garbo.[23] At their meetings, Salka was the star and Garbo the audience. She listened as Salka recited lines from the parts she had played on the stage in Berlin, including Penthesilea, in Herman von Kliest's play *Penthesilea*, about the Amazon warrior queen who joined the Trojan forces in The Trojan War. But Salka found Garbo's conversation so elusive that she thought she had no acting training. Garbo was probably speaking in her "baby language."

After reading a biography of Sweden's Queen Christina, Salka suggested to Garbo that she play the queen in a biopic. Garbo agreed—and suggested that Salka write the screenplay. Salka wasn't a writer, but Garbo knew that, at her request, Thalberg would partner Salka with MGM's best writers. Garbo gave Salka a career—as a writer and an acting coach. Salka participated in writing the screenplays for *Queen Christina* and most of Garbo's subsequent films. Deeply impressed by Salka, Garbo developed an abiding love for her. But Salka was never certain how she felt about Garbo.[24]

Garbo and Salka weren't always together, but they often spoke on the phone. In her autobiography, Salka insisted that she wasn't Garbo's teacher. They discussed the movies that she wrote for Garbo, but they lived separate lives. Salka never went with Garbo on her trips to Yosemite, Lake Arrowhead, and La Quinta, and she rarely appeared on Garbo's film sets. They wanted to preserve the belief that Garbo's acting was a "divine gift."[25]

Salka played tennis and swam, but she was no athlete. Unlike many of her friends, she wasn't a Communist. A secular Jew, she led labor, anti-Fascist, and émigré groups, while Garbo hiked, swam, and played tennis—or stayed in bed—in her free time. And Salka had three vigorous boys to raise, while Garbo had no dependents.

In the summer of 1931, while Garbo was making *Susan Lenox: Her Fall and Rise*, Salka was persuaded to introduce Garbo to Mercedes de Acosta, who had come to Hollywood to write a screenplay for Pola Negri—and to seduce Garbo. Mercedes had heard through the lesbian grapevine that Garbo wasn't a lesbian, but she could easily become one. De Acosta, openly lesbian, had a reputation for skill as a lover, and she was on a mission to turn prominent actresses into lesbians. It's not surprising that she wanted to meet Garbo, but Salka was worried about what might happen if that meeting took place.

Mercedes de Acosta, born to parents descended from the Spanish nobility, was raised in a wealthy section of New York's West Side. She met celebrities through her sister Rita Lydig. Eighteen years older than Mercedes, Rita was a fabled beauty, a leader in New York high society,

Mercedes de Acosta, circa 1930. Ronald Grant Archive / Alamy Stock Photo

and a reformer who worked for women's suffrage and birth control, as well as labor rights. The de Acosta family once had money, but Rita's and Mercedes's money came from their wealthy husbands.[26]

Rita introduced Mercedes to her famous friends: the actress Sarah Bernhardt, the sculptor Auguste Rodin, Jack and Ethel Barrymore of the famed Barrymore acting family, and others. Raised a Catholic, Mercedes attended Catholic schools. In 1914 *Vogue* featured her as a New York debutante, and in 1920 she married Abram Poole, a New York society painter.[27] She followed Rita into feminism, working for women's suffrage and then for the Lucy Stone League, formed to persuade women to keep their maiden names after marriage, following the example of Lucy Stone, a leader in the nineteenth-century U.S. women's movement.

Like Rita, Mercedes wore distinctive clothing, but she had her own style. She often wore capes, tricorne hats, and pointed shoes with silver buckles on them, looking like a pirate. She was also known for wearing a dark coat fitted at the waist, with wide lapels and a full skirt, designed by the Paris couturier Paul Poiret. Garbo liked the coat so much that she had a copy of it made for her. Mercedes dyed her hair black, painted her face white, and wore blood-red lipstick—prompting some people to call her "Madame Dracula."

The cultural rebellion of the 1920s fostered individuality, and some stylish women wore offbeat clothing and cosmetics. Mercedes wore only black and white clothes, so Garbo and Salka called her "Black and White." Aldous Huxley described her as "a small but most exquisite woman, both in features and figure, and in the manner of her dress."[28] She was five feet four inches tall. Close to Cecil Beaton, she provided him with information about Garbo to use in his writing about her, until he and Garbo became close friends in the late 1940s.

Mercedes lived a dramatic life, engaging in what Cecil Beaton called "glorious enthusiasms." She also had periods of deep depression. Until she was seven and saw the male sex organ, she thought she was a boy. Discovering her mistake devastated her, until she formed romantic friendships with girls and studied ancient Greek ideas of sex. She interpreted those ideas as suggesting that everyone has a masculine and a feminine side. She took up lesbianism as a cause. Cecil Beaton called her "a furious lesbian."[29]

Matinée idol John Barrymore, a friend of Rita's, introduced Mercedes to Eastern religions when he had her meet Kahlil Gibran, a Hindu poet living in New York. Gibran instructed her in the *Bhagavad Gita*, the major Hindu text, written between 400 B.C.E. and 200 C.E. It proposes that humans and the universe are interconnected and that individuals can find self-realization by overcoming negative drives through study and meditation. Mercedes studied Hindu and Buddhist texts and followed Eastern mystics; her knowledge of Eastern religions was part of her attraction to Garbo, who continually looked for a spiritual path and never seemed to find one. And Mercedes always knew about the latest healers and remedies. She consulted Dr. Henry Bieler, who promoted vegetarianism. Not long after she met Mercedes, Garbo consulted Bieler and became a vegetarian.

Mercedes knew the two great dramatic actresses of the turn of the twentieth century: Sarah Bernhardt and Eleonora Duse. She had had affairs with prominent female performers, including Isadora Duncan, a founder of modern dance, who promoted dress reform; the English actress Eva La Gallienne, with whom she exchanged wedding rings; and the Russian actress Alla Nazimova. When Nazimova came to Hollywood in 1916 to act in films, she formed a Sapphic circle, which some say was called "the sewing circle." Isadora Duncan wrote passionate poems to Mercedes, extolling her sexual ability and writing paeans to her beautiful white hands.[30]

Once Salka introduced Mercedes to Garbo in July 1931, Garbo initially fell for this aristocrat, with her tales of famous friends, knowledge of Eastern religions, and skill at sex. After finishing *Susan Lenox* that summer, Garbo took Mercedes to a cabin on an island in a lake in the High Sierras, where they swam, caught fish, talked, and began an affair. Mercedes was known for her sexual skill and Garbo for "the unbounded freedom of her life."[31]

After her trip to the High Sierras with Mercedes, Garbo displayed deep feelings for Salka, which suggests that the Sierra trip was a failure, that she was comparing Salka and Mercedes as friends and lovers, or that she was forming a triangle with the two of them. On September 18, which was Garbo's birthday, she seduced Salka, who described what happened in a letter to Berthold—her confidante as well as her husband. Greta decorated her house with white gardenias, a symbol of femininity and of secret love. She served Champagne and played Sapphic songs on the gramophone. It was, according to Salka, "a gigantic temptation apparatus." She concluded: "So we were together—it was harmonious and beautiful."[32]

By the late fall, Salka's infatuation with Garbo had dissipated for a time, as Garbo became demanding. She was filming *Mata Hari* and spending time with Mercedes, in the first flush of their romance. Then, looking at Garbo one day, Salka realized that not only did she slouch but she also had a hump on her back. Salka wrote to Berthold, who was in New York, about the hump, but he replied that she should forget it because Garbo had influence in Hollywood and could damage his career. Salka stayed with Garbo as a close friend and mentor but kept her at a distance by having affairs with men, first with Oliver Garrett and then with Gottfried Reinhardt.[33] After the episode of sex in 1931 between Garbo and Salka, there is no further evidence of sexual relations between them.

Hollywood gossips tagged Salka as a lesbian, even though she had married a man and her major affairs were with men. If we apply the Kinsey scale to her, she probably falls into the low range for lesbian desire. Alfred Kinsey, a professor at the University of Indiana, collected 10,000 interviews with men and many interviews with women to determine their sexual preferences. In both instances, he found that sexual orientation existed along a continuum and wasn't either / or. In other words, most men and women in his surveys were heterosexual, but many had experienced homosexual desire and intercourse. He created separate scales for both men and women.[34]

Mercedes's "glorious enthusiasm" led her to exaggerate and mix up chronology when she wrote her memoir, *Here Lies the Heart*. She also must have forgotten that "lies" could mean mistruths as well as location. Salka parodied the title of Mercedes's memoir by adding to it, "and lies and lies." But Salka's parody was too severe; Mercedes exaggerated her importance to Garbo, although the two of them hiked, swam, and played tennis. Mercedes had no family to care for, and her husband lived in

New York. She had time for Garbo, to whom she taught upper-class manners, improved her English, and suggested books to read. She also ran errands for Garbo. In most of Garbo's letters to Mercedes, Garbo discusses her health, gripes about her life, and gives instructions on how to pay her bills or buy her something that she wants. But there is evidence of a continued affair between them, despite ups and downs.

Even before Mercedes appeared in Garbo's life in the summer of 1931, there were references to Garbo's presumed lesbianism in the Hollywood trade journals and in movie magazines. In 1929, *Variety*'s review of Garbo's movie *The Single Standard* slyly referred to Garbo's free love views. In January 1931, in a review of Garbo's movie *Inspiration*, a *Variety* writer called her "one of the strangest personalities of all the freaks or odd ones that have littered Hollywood for years." And Mercedes persuaded Garbo to become more open about her masculinity. *The Hollywood Reporter*, Hollywood's first tabloid, was launched in 1930. On August 21, 1931, a month after Mercedes and Garbo met, the tabloid noted that "Greta Garbo has a new love." On September 23, 1931, the tabloid referred to "an ambidextrous foreign star." ("Ambidextrous" means being able to use either hand for tasks; it was then a common circumlocution for lesbians, homosexuals, and bisexuals.) The tabloid also referred to "the two Garbos."

But Garbo was ambivalent about Mercedes. After Salka, in her subtle, poetic way, informed Garbo that they could be close friends, but not lovers, Garbo turned to Mercedes for sex. That action unleashed Mercedes's obsessive nature, expressed in constant demands for deep expressions of love. After several months, Garbo fled to New York to get away from her. When she returned to Hollywood after a month away, she found Mercedes living in a house near hers. Ever after, when Garbo moved, Mercedes moved to a nearby house. Garbo wrote to Hörke Wachtmeister, a close friend in Sweden, that Mercedes made her nervous.[35] She also disliked Mercedes's love of gossip, and she was incensed when she learned that Mercedes told Cecil Beaton about her doings, which he then used in writing about her.

But the student and the searcher in Garbo kept coming back to Mercedes, who was a master of the arts of seduction and sex. The peasant in Garbo bowed to the aristocrat in Mercedes, while Mercedes considered

Garbo to be her child. Mercedes had a modest reputation as a poet and a playwright, and Garbo recommended her to Thalberg as a screen-writer. Although Mercedes had a modest reputation as a poet and a playwright, none of the scenarios she wrote for Garbo were filmed, while many of Salka's were.

Mercedes and Salka didn't like each other, which isn't surprising. Mercedes didn't attend Salka's salons; she formed one of her own, which may have been a continuation of Alla Nazimova's "sewing circle." She also had an affair with Marlene Dietrich, Garbo's major Hollywood rival. Garbo eventually forgave her this breach of faith; free-love principles permitted it and forbade jealousy. And Mercedes was lavish in spending on Garbo; she once had an elaborate gate built overnight around her mansion when Garbo mentioned a need for it.

Mercedes's husband divorced her in 1935 and married his mistress, but he didn't cut off his large stipend to Mercedes for years. It was her major source of income, financing the mansions she rented and her lar-gesse to Garbo. But she was indomitable. When the stipend ended, she managed to find jobs editing and writing for small magazines, moving between New York and Paris. She became friends with John Lennon and Yoko Ono and was often a guest at their Christmas celebrations. But when she died in 1968, she was destitute.

Garbo didn't permanently break with Mercedes until her autobiog-raphy was published in 1960. Even though Mercedes hid their affair in a cloud of circumlocutions in the memoir, she included a photo she had taken of a topless Garbo on the island in the High Sierras. And her description of her research methods for the autobiography must have alarmed the perfectionist and secretive Garbo. Mercedes's major source, she stated, was her memory. She had kept neither a diary nor a datebook, and when she wrote her appointments down on scraps of paper, she promptly lost them. She did keep letters written to her and other memo-rabilia; they are in her collection in the Rosenbach Museum in Philadelphia. The biographer can figure out a lot about their relationship from that col-lection, but far from all of it.

Sound in films dated from the summer of 1927, but Garbo didn't make her first sound film—*Anna Christie*—until the winter of 1929; she was the last Hollywood actor, except for Chaplin, to make the transition. The change triggered her insecurities, especially since European actors like Vilma Banky, who had a thick German accent, failed in sound films, as did Lillian Gish, who seemed out of date. Audiences laughed at John Gilbert, who was judged a failure because his high voice contradicted his virile image. It's possible, however, that L. B. Mayer, who hated Gilbert, undermined him with weak directors, weak amplification, and negative fan magazine articles.[36]

Garbo's deep alto voice matched her authority as an actress and was a success. Who can forget the moment in *Anna Christie* when she enters a saloon—and the film—and says to the barman, in her low voice, "Gimme a whiskey, with ginger ale on the side. And don't be stingy, baby"? With these words, Garbo established Anna as a tough Swedish American working-class woman. And *Anna Christie* stands with *Queen Christina* as the two most feminist films Garbo made.

In the film, Anna, a former prostitute, has come to New York to seek the help of her father, Chris Christopherson, a coal barge owner, who transports coal between New York and Boston. Early on, we learn that Anna's mother died when she was a child and her father left her with relatives on a farm in Minnesota, who were harsh in raising her. When a cousin raped her, she ran away to St. Paul and ended up in a brothel before going to a hospital, probably to be treated for venereal disease.

The film begins with Chris and his girlfriend Marthy Owen in the waterfront saloon, which is on a wharf on New York's East River where Chris's coal barge is docked. Anna enters the saloon and asks her father if she can stay with him while recuperating from her illness. After a long debate, in which he reveals his weak character, he agrees to take her in. Living in the cabin on the barge, sunning herself on its deck, soothed and stimulated by the water around it, Anna regains her vitality.

Anna rescues a sailor named Mat from the river; his ship has capsized during a fog. Played by Charles Bickford, Mat is large, with rugged features. Working-class to the core, Bickford was an unusual partner for Garbo, whose male co-stars were usually suave and somewhat effete, which emphasized her power. But Anna calls Mat "such a simple guy—a big kid."

Mat proposes marriage to Anna, but she confesses to him that she has been a prostitute, while railing at men who use women for sex and then blame the women for selling their bodies. "It's all men's fault. Men—how I hate men, every mother's son of them," she proclaims. And: "Nobody owns me but myself." Once again, as in all her new woman films, Garbo asserts her independence, rejecting patriarchy in *Anna Christie* in the strongest words she has ever used. Fueling her rage is her knowledge that Mat and her father, like many men, pay prostitutes for sex. One of them is Marthy Owen.

Unable to handle Anna's confession, Mat and Chris get drunk and sign up as crew members on a ship bound for South Africa, telling Anna what they have done. By then, she has become strong and can deal with them. She decides to buy a house while they are gone so that the three of them can live together as a family when the men return. She emerges as the hero of the drama and the strongest character in the film, as she envisions a new life for herself, her father, and Mat. The "Christ" in "Christie" may symbolize her redeemer role.

Frances Marion, the film's screenwriter, stayed close to the playwright Eugene O'Neill's plot, except for adding a scene in which Anna and Mat are on a date at Coney Island, New York's major amusement park. This scene allowed Garbo to use her childish side. Throughout the film, Garbo stresses Anna's masculinity, wearing turtleneck shirts and long, dark, straight skirts, except in the Coney Island scene. With her childish self foremost, wearing a frilly dress, Garbo happily rides a roller coaster with Mat and hangs onto him as he shoots at targets at an arcade booth. Still, her voice is deep and masculine; at base, she is a tough working-class woman.

The film was a smash hit. MGM advertised it with billboards displaying only the words "Garbo Speaks!" in large letters. It was an effective strategy. Garbo's low voice, lower than that of any other Hollywood actress, fascinated audiences.[37] So did her European inflections, slow and languorous, or rising to a peak, like an opera diva making a point and then falling to a point of calm.

Released in 1930, *Anna Christie* had high grosses; they were surpassed only by *Hell's Angels*, a movie about airplanes and pilots starring

Jean Harlow. Signed by MGM in 1932, Harlow, known as the Platinum Blonde because of the dyed color of her hair, was famed for her voluptuous body. She became the studio's number-one siren, but died tragically in 1936. She also added a comedy element to her acting, an approach many actresses of the 1930s followed, employing the traditional connection between beauty and comedy, becoming "fast-talking dames." They exhibited America's energy, the dynamism of urban slang, and female cleverness, implied by "fast talking."

*Anna Christie* ended happily, as did many of Garbo's twenty-four MGM films, contradicting the belief that all her films end tragically. The films include *The Torrent, The Divine Woman, The Mysterious Lady, Love, Wild Orchids, The Kiss, Ninotchka,* and *Two-Faced Woman.* An alternative happy ending was filmed for *The Temptress,* in which Garbo as Elena is neither a drunk nor a prostitute and is united with her lover. The endings of *The Torrent* and *Queen Christina* are more positive than negative, even though Garbo loses her man in them. Stated differently, roughly half of her MGM films had happy endings.

She often suffered in her films; making choices was never easy for her—in her films as in her life. Irving Thalberg decided that she should never initiate major plot action in her films; she should be caught in a dilemma and have to figure it out. In doing that, she would demonstrate a host of emotions. And beginning with *Flesh and the Devil,* in 1926, that dilemma usually involved being married to an older man and in love with a younger man, a variation on the "novel of initiation" motif.

What characterized Garbo's acting? That question is especially interesting for 1929 and 1930, when she had no coach. She and Jack Gilbert had parted before she made *The Single Standard* in 1929, and she met Salka Viertel while making *Romance* in the spring of 1930. She was on her own in *The Single Standard, The Kiss,* the English version of *Anna Christie,* and *Romance.* Her acting in these films is always competent and often outstanding. In fact, she was one of the most highly trained actresses in Hollywood, with several years as a student at the Swedish Royal Dramatic Academy and training by Mauritz Stiller. The German director G. W. Pabst, who directed her in *Joyless Street,* helped her with her acting skills, as did the Hollywood actors Lillian Gish, Pola Negri, and John Gilbert—all close friends versed in film acting. In 1930, she needed a coach only to give her confidence.

In her memoir printed in 1930 in *Lektyr*, the magazine published in Stockholm by her friend Lars Saxon, she described her technique in several sentences: "I live the part I am playing. I am completely under its spell, so that if anyone tries to speak to me or ask me questions, it wakes me up, so to speak." She followed the advice of both Delsarte and Stanislavski that actors should internalize a role until it becomes part of themselves. Mercedes thought that the characters Garbo played possessed her. The acclaimed directors Rouben Mamoulian and George Cukor agreed. Her acting, both said, was intuitive; Mamoulian called it "a divine gift." (Mamoulian directed her in *Queen Christina*; Cukor in *Ninotchka* and *Two-Faced Woman*.)[38]

But she prepared carefully for each role. She read books that provided context. Given her photographic memory, she memorized not only her own lines but also the lines of all the other actors. She practiced movements and gestures to find the ones she wanted to use. The producer Sam Marx saw her walking in the alley behind his office at MGM before filming began on *Grand Hotel*. She was pacing back and forth, varying her steps in speed and rhythm. Marx realized that she was figuring out how the ballerina she was playing in *Grand Hotel* should move.

In describing Garbo's acting, director Clarence Brown stressed the brilliance of her eyes. "She had something behind the eyes that you couldn't see until you photographed her in close-up. If she had to look at one person with jealousy, and another with love, she didn't have to change her expression. No other screen actress has been able to do that on film."[39] The number of close-ups given an actress in her films was considered a measure of her stardom; no other Hollywood actress in Garbo's era reached her total.

Critics of Garbo's acting charged that she was a somnambulist—that she sleepwalked through her films—which was characteristic of actresses in German expressionist films, which often were set in a dream landscape. After watching all of Garbo's films in a seven-day retrospective in New York in 1968, Larry Carr concluded that she was the same in all of them. Françoise Rosay thought that in all her films, Garbo seemed to

be acting in a documentary about herself. Even Salka Viertel told producer David Lewis that Garbo was a "personality" actress, which meant
that her personality dominated her films; in other words, she always
played herself.[40]

Some of this criticism of Garbo for not varying her approach stemmed
from a disagreement over acting styles. Mauritz Stiller had always cautioned her against overacting—to the point that her gestures and her
movements in her films were all small. Basil Rathbone, who played
her husband in *Anna Karenina*, said that he had learned everything he
knew about film acting from her. "She made tiny movements, minute
changes of expression which I actually didn't notice at the time, but when
I saw the scene on the screen, I was amazed."[41] Clarence Brown made a
similar statement, as did many actors in her films. Salka Viertel had been
a stage actress; she didn't entirely understand Garbo's film acting style,
which she had learned from Mauritz Stiller and other film actors and
directors.

Early film acting had been based on stage acting, in which actors'
movements and gestures had to be broad to be seen by an audience.
But the film projector magnified movements, especially when a film
was shown on a large screen. In the 1920s, when the U.S. economy was
booming, Hollywood moguls and other entertainment entrepreneurs
had invested in large, showy movie theaters, "palaces for the people"
with elaborate decorations, sometimes themed to an exotic motif, like
Sid Grauman's Chinese and Egyptians theaters, at two ends of the city
of Hollywood. Some of the large theaters in major cities had as many as
3,000 seats.

Garbo's stride was long and masculine, far from that of a sex goddess.
Both Stiller and John Gilbert worked with her to make it sleek and
slinky. "Panther-like" was the word used to describe the proper walk of
a seductress. Garbo could draw on her training in movement at Dramaten to achieve it, although it wasn't easy for her. When Stiller directed
her in an early photo session for *The Torrent*, he criticized her for "moving like a cart horse" and bellowed, "Good Lord, Greta! Can't we have
some sex?" Then she broke down, and as usual, Stiller comforted
her. But she soon achieved a sensuous walk, as parts of her "square-
shouldered, flat-chested, long-legged body," according to Alexander

Walker, "shifted into sensuous adjustment to each other as she moved and relayed a liberated animal," the panther personified.[42]

She didn't like to rehearse; she always said that her first take was her best take. She didn't want to know the other actors in her films so that she didn't confuse their real lives with their lives in her films. She never watched a day's rushes, the scenes shot during the day that were shown in rough form that evening. A perfectionist, she knew that they wouldn't match what she had wanted to achieve.[43] Yet, given the way films were made, with scenes shot out of chronological order and pauses in filming to correct lights, costumes, or makeup, in addition to delays caused by her own chronic illnesses, Garbo's ability to maintain concentration was impressive.

Her acting was layered. In many of her films, the male protagonist is overcome by her beauty when he first sees her, and she slowly reveals the rest of herself over the course of the film. Using a method technique, she displayed deep emotion toward an object—like the bouquet of flowers that she clutched to her body in the hospital scene in *A Woman of Affairs*, which symbolized her yearning either for a miscarried child or for the lover she has lost. Yet, there is a traditional quality to her acting. As much as she employed a psychological style, her acting was characterized by what Raymond Durgnat and John Kobal called "an older emphasis on artistic intoxication."[44] That description is like the one Harriet Bosse applied to the Swedish actress Tora Teje, whom Garbo had seen playing Anna Christie in a Dramaten production of the play.

Through his creative lighting, William Daniels made her half-lidded eyes seem sexy rather than exhausted, while he converted the fatigue in her face produced by insomnia and pain to romantic agony. According to Parker Tyler, she "got into drag" when she played a glamorous role. Tyler assumed that the real Garbo was more masculine than feminine—although, as Alexander Walker said, "No actress, before or since, has combined the masculine and feminine wills so tightly in one embrace. "[45]

Feeling satisfied after *Anna Christie* wrapped, Garbo held a Swedish Christmas celebration for her group of close friends. Soon after that celebration, she began dating the actress Fifi D'Orsay, publicized as the Girl from Gay Paree, although she was actually Yvonne Lussier from Montreal. D'Orsay looked like Mimi Pollak; she had short brown hair and an infectious laugh. The film magazines covered the relationship; Garbo didn't hide it. In February, a fan magazine declared that Garbo and Fifi had been inseparable "since Garbo and Lilyan Tashman parted company." L. B. Mayer now intervened to end the affair. He had tolerated Garbo's affair with Lilyan Tashman because Tashman was married and renowned as the best-dressed actress in Hollywood, allowing MGM publicists to create the covering story that Tashman was teaching Garbo how to dress. Fifi D'Orsay had no such cachet. Mayer convinced Garbo that Fifi had talked to a journalist about her. Garbo dropped Fifi.[46] But she might have done so anyway; she would soon meet Salka Viertel, and then Mercedes de Acosta, each of whom would take up much of her time.

And she had to face the harsh reality that L. B. Mayer was changing her typecasting again, as he cast her in a film called *Romance*, in which she was to play an opera diva in love with a younger Episcopal priest repeating her "novel of initiation" motif. When she finds out that her priest is no different from any other man, that his sex drive can govern his actions, she repents her sins and enters a nunnery in Switzerland, where she spends the rest of her life in a community of women.

PART IV

# CHOOSING SIDES

Garbo as Diana Merrick, wearing the "Garbo hat." Allstar Picture Library Ltd / Alamy Stock Photo

# Understanding Adrian

## From Flapper to Glamour

*F*ROM 1890 TO 1930, four models of female beauty in turn were hegemonic in the West, beginning with the Gibson girl of 1890. That figure was followed by the "pretty girl" of 1900, the flapper of 1920, and the tall, elegant woman of 1930. Each dominant model was challenged by other models, including its hegemonic predecessor and successor, as the female beauty ideal evolved into new forms. Some contemporary analysts concluded that the tall, elegant ideal of 1930 was based on Garbo; others thought that it was a progression in the cycle of fashion, caused by changes in demographics and cultural styles.

In this chapter I will investigate the "pretty girl," as well as the flapper and its many variations, including the surprising extent to which Garbo played flappers in her films. I will also explore the work of Adrian, MGM's head costume designer in the 1930s, who had an important role in creating Garbo's film persona. I will finish the chapter by focusing on glamour in fashion and in films. I will also take up the subject of height, which is important in the reactions to Garbo and in definitions of ideal beauty in her era.

In the 1900s and 1910s, "pretty girls" drawn by illustrators became ideal models for women's appearance.[1] Descendants of the Gibson girl, the pretty girls were smaller and less aristocratic than Gibson's original. They were coquettish rather than haughty; wholesome, yet appealing. Unlike Gibson's model, set in an upper-class dream world, they were drawn in realistic settings, and they rarely wore tight-laced corsets, unlike Gibson's model. The Gibson girl sometimes played tennis or sat on the beach in a voluminous bathing suit. The pretty girl played a variety of sports, rode in automobiles, was a pal to men, and seemed solidly middle class. She most often looked directly at the viewer in a frank and friendly way, rather than dreamily into space, which was the typical Gibson girl pose. Reflecting a new reality, she was often a college girl. The illustration scholar Mimi Miley credited illustrators Harrison Fisher and Howard Chandler Christy with "turning the demure Victorian girl into an athletic modern woman."[2]

Scores of illustrators in Europe and the United States drew variations on the pretty girl. She was on the covers of magazines and books, in illustrations and advertisements in mass-market magazines like the *Saturday Evening Post* and the *Ladies' Home Journal*, and in Broadway revues. She dated from an era before photography was sufficiently developed to be mass marketed, but the pretty girl was so popular that she continued into the 1920s and 1930s, after photographs had largely taken over her markets.

Like the Gibson girl, the pretty girls were often called by their illustrator's names, such as the Christy girl, drawn by Howard Chandler Christy, and the Fisher girl, drawn by Harrison Fisher. Each illustrator had his or her own style. Norman Rockwell, the most famous of the illustrators, drew a sweet, unsophisticated "girl next door" type. The Christy girl was saucy yet sweet, and James Montgomery Flagg and Cole Phillips drew girls who were vamps. Flagg's girls were posed provocatively, with saucy expressions and bare shoulders and legs. Some of these illustrators, including Gibson, drew tall variations of their girls standing beside tiny men, evoking the male fear that if women became too independent, they might seize power from men.

Women illustrators also drew "pretty girls." Neysa McMein of New York drew *McCall's* covers from 1923 to 1937. Brian Gallagher, her biographer, describes her woman as strikingly pretty, but not beautiful, "and her sweet, casual air was something that young women could attain, even if they weren't pretty." Together with Howard Chandler Christy, McMein judged the "Fame and Fortune" contest held by *Motion Picture*

*Classic* magazine in 1921, which was won by Clara Bow, beginning her career as a motion picture actress.[3]

By 1920 the cycle of fashion had turned away from the "pretty girl" and toward the adolescent flapper. Charles Dana Gibson acknowledged the change when in 1920 he stopped drawing his Gibson girl, bought *Life* magazine, and featured in it drawings by John Held Jr., the best-known flapper illustrator.[4] Held's flappers look like tall, spindly comic-strip characters, representing the satiric mode of the 1920s and reflecting the widespread opinion that the flapper was ridiculous. Held's flappers have bobbed hair, round eyes, plump cheeks, "bee-stung" lips, tubular bodies, and masculine silhouettes, including bound breasts—all flapper features. They also wear short skirts, with a line on their dresses around the hips, not the waist—also part of the flapper style. Yet, according to some recent writers on fashion, many of these features were not in place until 1925.[5]

The hegemony of the flapper represented a turn in fashion's cycle, and it signaled a rebellion of youth against Victorian strictures. It was also a triumph for dress reformers, who had raged against tight-laced corsets for decades, while calling for the adoption of loose shifts and empire-style dresses, with the body line below the bust, making the tight-laced corset irrelevant. Influenced by these reformers, who were sometimes prominent artists, like the Pre-Raphaelites, the eminent Paris dress designer Paul Poiret reintroduced the empire style into dress design in the 1900s.[6]

Held's flapper on the cover of *Life* magazine in February 1926 is dancing the Charleston with a bald man. The Charleston was the 1920s signature dance, emblematic of the huge popularity of African American jazz music and dance in that decade. Beginning as an African folk dance called the Juba, brought to the United States first by slaves and after Emancipation by travelers, it was modified as it moved from dance hall to dance hall in the United States. In the South, it was associated with dock workers in Charleston, South Carolina, from which its name was derived. It became a craze in the United States when it appeared in 1921 on Broadway in the African American musical *Runnin' Wild*.[7] In 1925, Josephine Baker, a standout chorus girl in African American musicals on Broadway, brought the Charleston to Europe, as the lead performer in a troupe of African American singers and dancers who became a sensation in Paris.

Garbo's behavior as Greta Gustafsson in drama school, when she smoked, drank, and went to dance halls and nightclubs, replicated the behavior of the energetic flapper. In the photo of Mauritz Stiller and Garbo on the Swedish steamship docked in New York in June 1925, she is dressed in flapper fashion. Yet, several weeks after that photo was taken, she told journalist Adele Whitely Fletcher that she didn't want to play flapper roles in Hollywood films. She wanted to be a dramatic actress—a Gloria Swanson in fancy clothes—or a comic character, like the bathing beauty she had played in a Petschler movie in Stockholm.[8]

In New York that summer, she saw Katharine Cornell play Iris Storm, the female protagonist in a play adapted from the novel *The Green Hat*, and she decided that she wanted to play Iris in a film adaptation. She achieved that goal in August 1928, when she played Diana Merrick, the film version of Iris Storm, in *A Woman of Affairs*, the film adaptation of *The Green Hat*.[9] When she told Adele Whitely Fletcher that she didn't want to play flappers, she didn't seem to know that Iris Storm was a flapper.

And *A Woman of Affairs* wasn't Garbo's only flapper film. When she played Arden Stuart in *The Single Standard* in the spring of 1929, Hedda Hopper identified her character as a flapper. Hopper was perplexed. She asked, "How could Garbo play a flapper? Since she came to Hollywood, she's always been the industry's major vamp."[10] In fact, most of the characters Garbo played in her new woman films were flappers, if one realizes that the rowdy flapper, having fun at all hours, was only one flapper type.

"Flapper" was originally a slang word for aquatic animals with fins, like dolphins, and for the detumescent male sex organ. By the mid-nineteenth century it was used to describe young prostitutes. By the century's end in England and the United States, "flapper" referred to all vigorous girls, who were known for wearing their hair long and in a single braid down their back, which flapped as they ran. When they graduated from high school, they signaled their maturity by fixing their hair in an adult pompadour atop their heads.

By the late nineteenth century, flapper clothing was marketed in fashion magazines and clothing stores as being for adolescent girls in the awkward period of maturation, when the body assumes its adult shape. That clothing featured a loose dress that skimmed the body and extended to the ankles. It was sometimes called a tubular dress. In the late 1920s, as the flapper style lost popularity and standardization of sizes in women's clothing took hold, the flapper dress became the junior size for smaller women, still sold today.

By the early twentieth century, the number of flappers had increased. In 1913 the *New York World* reported that "the tall aristocrat is out [referring to the Gibson girl], and the flapper, hipless, waistless, boneless, is in."[11] The *World*'s designation of the flapper as the "in" fashion was premature, but it indicates the early appearance of the figure.

Other connections furthered the use of the word "flapper." It was associated with the rubber rain boots called flappers, which adolescent girls wore in the early 1920s. Those boots had closings which, if left unfastened, flapped when the girls walked. In England it was also associated with the girls who rode on the back seat of motorbikes. In France and Germany, however, the word "flapper" was rarely used. In Germany an adolescent girl was called a *backfisch*, meaning a freshly caught, uncooked fish, or a *bubukopf*, meaning short hair.[12]

In France she was called *la garçonne*—a female version of *le garçon*, meaning the boy. The term *la garçonne* came from the title of a 1923 novel by Victor Margueritte, in which the heroine is sexually free. Involved with a Black male dancer from Argentina and a female dance hall performer, she runs a decorating business. The attitudes in the novel were so advanced that it was banned, even in France. But the masculine styles for women designed by the French dress designer Coco Chanel were called Garçonne styles. She based them on her male lovers' attire and on clothing worn by working-class men, like overalls and dungarees.[13]

The Paris dress designer Paul Poiret grumbled in 1920, "Until now, women were beautiful and architectural, like the prow of a ship. Now they all resemble undernourished telephone operators." Hoydens and gamines had replaced the statuesque women of the 1890s and the "pretty girls" of the 1900s and 1910s. Cecil Beaton declared, "Women had developed pert little noses, tiny chins, and goo-goo eyes." He called women a "kewpie doll league." ("Kewpie" is derived from Cupid; a Kewpie doll was a popular androgynous baby doll.) The words "doll" and "baby" gained an additional meaning: they were used as terms of affection by boyfriends for girlfriends. Anita Loos, who was so small that she sometimes bought her clothing in children's shops, suddenly found herself appearing in fashion magazines not only as the author of *Gentlemen Prefer Blondes* but also as a chic model of female appearance. In 1929, the movie magazine writer Joseph Howard noted that flappers were "short of stature as well as of skirt."[14]

When Anita Loos lived in New York in the 1920s, she socialized with Broadway showgirls. She reported that they regarded themselves as freaks. The problem was their height, in an era when small women were in vogue. Hired by revue producers for Amazon choruses, the showgirls had to be at least five feet five inches tall; otherwise, they fit into the smaller chorus girl category. The Hollywood star Nita Naldi, who was five feet eight inches tall, began her career as a Broadway showgirl. In a 1922 interview, she complained about her height: "People are always making fun of me in the streets. They think I'm a strange looking being." Anne Rittenhouse, the fashion editor of the *New York Times*, traced the hegemony of the small woman in the United States in the 1920s to the immigration in the 1900s and 1910s of women from Eastern and Southern Europe, most of whom were small. Rittenhouse wrote: "The small woman of certain European sections influences the clothes worn by millions of us."[15]

The flapper dress was easy to make. It could be shaped from two pieces of fabric sewn together at the shoulders and the sides, leaving room for inset sleeves. Patterns were available in single packets, drawn on heavy tissue paper, and were marketed by women's and fashion magazines, even *Vogue*. Step-in undergarments made of silk and rayon and called cami-knickers replaced tight-laced corsets, although rubber corsets and girdles without stays were popular by the mid-1920s.[16] And the straight silhouette required that women wear a brassiere that flattened the breasts. The Boyishform Company, launched in 1919, specialized in such brassieres. The new tubular dress with its androgynous shape and straight silhouette was often seen as democratic. According to the historian Billie Melman, "Contemporaries regarded the flapper as the sign of a new society—classless, uniform, unisex." Other commentators thought that because of its masculine line, it represented women's new freedoms in taking over men's home-front jobs during the war and in gaining the right to vote in the United States, Germany, and the Scandinavian countries at the end of the war.[17]

Given the long life of the flapper, from before 1900 to after 1930, variations appeared, especially as the flapper absorbed elements of other youthful types—the tomboy, for example, and the baby vamp. Writing in 1915 in *The Smart Set*, the journalist H. L. Mencken and the theater critic George Jean Nathan described the flapper as progressive: "She has read Christabel Pankhurst and Ellen Key and is inclined to think there is something in this new doctrine of free motherhood. She is opposed to the double standard of morality. She has read Strindberg's *Miss Julie* and plans to read Havelock Ellis."

In 1924 *Picture-Play* magazine identified eight types of flappers, including a modern type. That figure "is interested in futuristic art; she knows something about banks, and she professes a great admiration for Gertrude Stein and a great belief in the isms [capitalism, communism, etc.]." The modern flappers in *The Smart Set* and *Picture-Play* differed from the flapper described by Bruce Bliven in *The New Republic* in 1925 as having a "pallor mortis [dead white] complexion, poisonously scarlet lips, richly tinged eyes—looking not so much debauched (which is the intention) as diabetic." Bliven's modern girls resembled prostitutes. Brooke Blower found the same situation in describing young women in Paris in the early 1920s: "It is very difficult to tell who is a prostitute and who is a modern young girl," Blower wrote.[18] There were other types of flappers: baby flappers, "hard-boiled" flappers, "Dumb Dora" flappers, and jazz flappers (called jazz babies).

According to the actress Colleen Moore, who brought the flapper to Hollywood films in *Flaming Youth* (1923), the flapper didn't have to be beautiful. "Any plain Jane could be a flapper," Moore declared.[19] Only energy and the right makeup and clothes were required. Moore also introduced the "Dutch boy" haircut, with hair cut straight and short, with no layering, and bangs over the forehead. For decades, children's

hair had been cut that way; Louise Brooks made that haircut provoca-
tive in *Pandora's Box*, a film she made in Germany in 1929.

There was also a sophisticated flapper, "with a remote, faintly bitter
expression on her face." Called "the flapper deluxe" by novelist F. Scott
Fitzgerald, who often wrote about flappers, she affected the "debutante
slouch" and reflected postwar malaise.[20] Garbo personified "the flapper
deluxe" in her new woman films.

During World War I, as men joined the military, women took over
their home-front jobs and wore male clothing. The astute Coco Chanel
translated this garb into high fashion.[21] Jean Patou, a Parisian couturier
and Chanel's major competitor, used sports attire as a template for his
designs, as women avidly took up golf and tennis after the war. The 1920s
fad for dancing, at its height in 1925, required loose-fitting dresses.[22]

By 1925, most dresses looked like sports clothing—casual, loose fitting, in cotton or rayon. But despair over the deaths in World War I and
the flu pandemic that followed was widespread. So was the "jolie laide"
(beautiful ugly), as many fashionable women scorned flapper frivolity to
adopt a hard-edged chic, wearing sweaters, blazers, and straight skirts.
In *Anna Christie*, Garbo popularized that style, which became a fashion
classic. Or, fashionable women wore fanciful outfits, like the cape, tricorne hat, and buckled shoes worn by Mercedes de Acosta. Cecil Beaton, an astute observer of fashion trends, noted the appearance of a bevy
of fashionable women in the 1920s who designed their own dresses,
prefiguring the reform dress of the 1970s youth rebellion. Bohemians
and even fashionistas wore offbeat clothing.[23] London art students and
Greenwich Village poets and painters favored Indian fabrics and caf-
tans. The New York designer Valentina, Garbo's favorite couturier from
1942 on, favored long gored skirts.

Isadora Duncan and Gertrude Stein introduced sandals; the London
poet Edith Sitwell wore medieval dress, while her brother, the critic
Osbert Sitwell, wrote: "Never before had the ugly woman enjoyed such
a run for her ugliness as in those days after the war." Virginia Nicolson, a
granddaughter of the Bloomsbury artist Vanessa Bell and a grandniece of
Virginia Woolf, stated: "In the twenties and thirties, Bohemia was over-
run with cross-dressing 'Sapphists' in a caricature of male business garb:

double-breasted jackets, severe ties, waistcoats, and shingled hair." Experimentation ruled the arts—in cubism, futurism, and surrealism— and those styles influenced clothing designers, fashion illustrators, and fashionable women.[24]

As early as 1910, female performers in revues became a source for fashions in women's clothing and appearance, and they retained that influence into the 1930s. Revues were popular in New York, Paris, London, and other major cities. They were composed of vignettes on topical subjects, often parodies of those subjects, interpreted by comedians, singers, and dancers—who were mostly female. The star of the revue was the chorus girl, who did tap and toe dancing, kicked her legs high, and blended into a chorus line. She was "a central obsession of American popular culture from the 1900s through the 1920s."[25]

She was also popular in Europe. In Britain, the chorus girl was identified with London's Gaiety Theatre; in Germany with Tiller troupes; in France with the Folies Bergère; in the United States with the Ziegfeld Follies, launched in 1907 by producer Florenz Ziegfeld to "glorify the American girl."[26] Yet, Ziegfeld's chorus girls, no more than five feet, five inches tall and usually shorter, were classified by size as "squabs," "chickens," and "ponies." Ziegfeld wrote that men liked watching "a little girl possessed of a touch of impudence. . . . We feel a good deal like a big dog playing with a kitten."[27]

Many revues included a chorus of tall women, called Amazons, who were at least five feet six inches in height. First appearing in musicals in the mid-nineteenth century, they were derived from ancient tales of Amazon societies and from the legendary tall women called Amazons in the army of the African state of Dahomey. Cross-dressing as soldiers in tights to show off their legs, they did military drills. By 1900 the Amazons in revues had evolved into showgirls as tall as six feet. The showgirls wore sumptuous costumes or the latest fashions, gliding up and down stairs and across the stage. In 1905 the New York World called them "cloak model divinities that are svelte and stately, and wear Paris frocks and are oh so haughty off the stage and on." Like Garbo, they were forerunners of the tall fashion mannequin who became an enduring female beauty ideal by the late 1920s. Ziegfeld stated that Garbo was the only Hollywood actress he would hire as a showgirl.[28] But that preference was partly because most Hollywood actresses were very short.

In the 1910s and 1920s, Hollywood producers hired many Broadway chorus girls for their films.[29] Chorus girl movies were popular, but the fixation with small women in Hollywood went beyond that. The producers rarely recruited showgirls; they wanted small women. The Hollywood actress Mary Astor was five feet five inches tall. In her early career she was given screen tests but was always rejected for film acting as too tall; Hollywood actresses were so petite that she felt like a freak. She broke that barrier when she had a serious romance with John Barrymore, a popular matinee idol, who promoted her career. We know her today from her role as the dangerous female protagonist in *The Maltese Falcon*. Colleen Moore was five feet six inches tall, but because she had small bones, she photographed as much smaller and was acceptable.[30]

In her history of Hollywood beauty, Adela Rogers St. Johns traced the dominance of small women in films to the soubrette on the stage, the chorus girl in Broadway revues, and the small women that film director D. W. Griffith cast in his films. The soubrette on the stage was an energetic adolescent, flirtatious and sexual, pretty, not beautiful, who formed a contrast to the ingenue, often angelic and beautiful. The soubrette led to the chorus girl, often a similar type, although the soubrette was a stand-alone character who didn't appear in a chorus unless she led it. In his films, D. W. Griffith cast small women who resembled the girls he had admired in his childhood in Kentucky. Mary Pickford, Griffith's legendary star, was five feet tall. Pickford was so popular that producers copied Griffith and Pickford in casting small women in major roles in their films. And "as screen beauties became small," St. Johns asserted, "women in general followed the same pattern."[31]

Other analysts traced the vogue for small women in early films to the industry's simple cameras and film stock, which recorded blemishes on faces. Unlike photographs, the film stock couldn't be retouched. Wanting actresses with smooth skin, producers cast adolescents in major roles. It was also believed that the camera added inches and pounds to bodies, giving small females priority in casting. Moreover, Hollywood's many short male producers and directors didn't want actresses to be taller than they were.[32]

Given Hollywood's position on size, 1925 was not a good year for the tall Garbo to appear at MGM. She was five feet seven inches in height, but because she was long-waisted and slim, she often appeared taller in her films than she was in person, while the men who co-starred with her were often shorter than she. Even John Gilbert, who was five feet eight inches tall, had to stand on a box in some of their scenes. Cameras could modify height on the screen, but fans wanted truth. They wrote to the studios for the measurements of stars, and the film magazines published the relevant statistics.[33]

Short women were in vogue in the 1920s, but the tall woman as the cynosure of beauty didn't disappear. In addition to the tall women of art moderne (today called art deco) and the showgirls on the revue stage, she can be seen in the mannequins of dress designers.

The London dress designer Lucile, Lady Duff-Gordon, continued the late nineteenth-century vogue for tall, elegant women, evident in the Gibson girl. When Lucile launched her couturier house in 1904, most mannequins were medium in size because of the belief that medium-sized women didn't compete with the designer clothing they displayed. Lucile disagreed. She realized that clothes show best on tall women.[34] Within a decade, Lucile had salons in London, Paris, and New York, which drew stage and screen stars as well as fashionable women as clients.

Before 1920, respectable people in Britain and the United States considered modeling to be immoral, so Lucile found mannequins among beautiful working-class young women and taught them how to behave like ladies. Her mannequins weighed more than eleven stone (150 pounds), and some were six feet tall. They were, according to Lucile, "big girls with fine figures, gorgeous, goddess-like girls."[35] In 1915, Florenz Ziegfeld attended one of her fashion shows and was so impressed by Lucile's mannequins that he hired all of them as the showgirls in his follies. Lucile collaborated with him on his follies for the next decade.

Lucile's sister, Elinor Glyn, wrote romance novels and Hollywood screenplays, while she advised Hollywood actors and producers on the proper behavior in high society, for the many "high society" movies they made and for the Hollywood high society they were creating. When the film censors interdicted using the term "sex appeal" in films and movie advertising, Glyn suggested the words "it" and "glamour" as replacements. In Glyn's glossary, "it" meant sex appeal with pep; "glamour" meant mystery plus elegance. Glyn first applied "it" to flapper film star Clara Bow and "glamour" to Gloria Swanson. By the late 1920s, MGM's Strickling seized "glamour" and identified it with Garbo.[36]

Lucile's tall models inspired Chanel in the 1920s to hire tall women as mannequins for her Paris salon. She was also influenced by the Russian grand duke Dmitri Pavlovich, a cousin of the dethroned Russian tsar and an impoverished émigré in France after the Bolsheviks won the 1917 Russian Revolution. Pavlovich became Chanel's lover in 1921. She supported him financially and hired his poverty-stricken female relatives as mannequins. They were aristocrats who had also fled Russia as the Bolsheviks took over the country. Chanel came from the peasantry, and she relished having princesses and countesses as employees. Slavic in background, many of her Russian mannequins were tall, with angular features. Chanel herself had angular features.[37]

Many Paris couturiers followed Chanel in hiring émigré Russian aristocrats as mannequins. By 1940 they and their offspring constituted 100 of the 300 mannequins in the city. In her history of modeling, Caroline Evans concluded that mannequins in 1910 were small, no more than five feet five inches tall. By the late 1920s, however, they were at least five feet seven inches tall. A 1925 Paris guidebook described them as being "as tall and slender as cattail leaves."[38]

The tall mannequin was enshrined in 1925 in the wood and wax mannequins at the Paris Exposition internationale des artes décoratifs et industriels modernes. That exposition, featuring recent designs in furniture, fabrics, and dress, mostly from Paris, defined the art moderne style. The expo's traveling show, which toured the United States in 1926, influenced MGM's head art designer, Cedric Gibbons, who used the art moderne style in so many films that it became associated with MGM. Garbo's sets and costumes in her new woman films were largely art deco in style, signaling her modernity at that point in her career.[39]

For the Paris exposition, the sculptor André Vigneau created innovative wax and wood mannequins. Resembling the tall, sculptured figures in fashion magazine illustrations, they were eight feet tall and painted in gold, silver, red, purple, and black—with their clothes the same color as their bodies. Vigneau also based his mannequins on the elongated figures on the façades of late medieval churches. He turned to proportional theory in designing them, using a ratio of eight faces to the body. With their height; sculpted hair; slanted, vacant eyes; and colored skin, Vigneau's mannequins became a sensation. "Paris has gone crazy over the mannequins," wrote one journalist; "they represent a furious kind of modernism."[40] In 1968, the art critic Bevis Hillier renamed the art moderne movement "art deco," taking that name from the phrase *artes decoratifs* in the expo's title. It was a sensible change, since by the 1960s what was defined as modern art was different from the modern art of the 1920s.

Garbo didn't attend the Paris exposition; it was held from May to December of 1925, when she was in Berlin making *Joyless Street* and then in New York and Hollywood pursuing her film career. But publicity about the mannequins was everywhere, while many department stores replaced their existing mannequins with the new figures. Slowly but surely, live mannequins adopted Garbo's style: her bold angularity, her rakishness, her mock insolence, and "the insinuation of an apparently uncontrollable pelvis," as Parker Tyler described it in his essay on Garbo.[41]

By 1925 flapper hegemony reached its height as skirts rose to the knee and the Eton haircut became popular. Fashions then began shifting to a new mode, as Paris designers slowly lengthened the skirt and raised the waistline from the hips to the waist, while Garbo's long bob became the vogue in hairstyles. The change was predictable, given fashion's cyclical nature and a new generation of adolescent girls who wanted to look different from their flapper elders. The *Vogue* editor Edna Woolman Chase sensed in 1925 that the "garçonne" look was losing favor and that it would soon be confined to sports attire, from which it had come.[42] Concurrently, the Paris designer Madeleine Vionnet introduced bias-cut clothes. The bias cut involves cutting diagonally across the warp and woof of a fabric, which makes it cling to the body when made into clothing. Unlike

Chanel, Vionnet based her designs on the female body, not on male garments. But they liberated the body as much as Chanel's designs, while also being sexy. By 1930, Hollywood designers were using the bias cut for many female costumes.

Meanwhile, the concept of streamlining inspired a new curved shape for women. Streamlining was based on the aerodynamic principle that air moves faster around oblong objects than straight ones; designers of airplanes and automobiles adopted that shape for their vehicles to reduce air resistance and increase their speed. As sometimes occurs in the history of design, mechanical design influenced the design of buildings, furniture, and even the shape of the female body. All these entities developed curves.[43]

According to the *Vogue* editor Marge Garland, a "new look" in the design of clothing for women appeared in 1930. It included longer skirts cut on the bias in sections, with an indented waistline and a rounded bosom. *Vogue* proclaimed: "For the first time in many of our lives, we are to have waists."[44] The magazine could have made the same claim about breasts. In 1919 the Boyishform Company made brassieres that flattened women's breasts to achieve the straight silhouette fashionable in the 1920s, but full-breasted women found such brassieres painful to wear. The Maidenform Company, founded in 1924, made bras for all shapes and sizes of breasts. It soon put Boyishform out of business.

The new look of 1930 was both romantic and sensual. Mildred Adams wrote in the *New York Times*: "The siren has replaced the flapper; impish and gamine impertinence have given way to slow, seductive languor." She referred to the fashion cycle in noting that the siren was "perilously close" to replicating the elegant woman of the 1890s. In the summer of 1929, she watched the siren figure spread from Europe to the United States before the stock market crash in October. Her observations contradict the theory that major changes in fashion always follow major economic changes.[45]

Hollywood films contributed to creating the new look, since the advent of sound in 1927 plus the onset of the Depression brought an emphasis on sex to films, initiating the so-called pre-Code era. In 1927 the moguls decided that their actresses should abandon the prevailing flat silhouette. Aware that "men hated the fashion scene without breasts," the moguls decreed that their designers use Vionnet's bias cut to create a curvy "Hollywood line."[46] Even Garbo, without much of a bust, was publicized as curvy. Glamour was on its way.

Meanwhile, by the late 1920s, tall and narrow "spike heels" came into fashion in women's shoes. They were lower than today's spikes, but they made legs appear longer, in line with a fashion for long legs, resulting from the post–World War I vogue of sports for women. The fashion historian James Laver, a shrewd observer of fashion trends, contended that before women's sports took hold, short female legs were preferred.[47] That preference may seem strange to us; even Laver was surprised by it. But it can be seen in the photos in the early 1920s of female athletes and chorus girls in the *Police Gazette*, a widely read semipornographic magazine. The legs of these women are short and round.

When spikes came into vogue, Garbo refused to wear them, realizing the damage they could do to feet and to leg muscles. She wore only shoes appropriate for walking. She was firm, even with the famous shoe designer Salvatore Ferragamo, who was known for his spike heels. When she insisted that he make comfortable shoes for her, he based them on male shoe styles.

Beginning with *A Woman of Affairs*, Adrian designed most of Garbo's costumes for her films.[48] He had studied dress design at the Parsons Schools of Design in both New York and Paris, and he had designed costumes for Broadway revues. Tall and elegant, Adrian was homosexual, although in 1939 he married petite star Janet Gaynor in what may have been a "lavender" marriage. But they lived together for twenty years and had a son.[49]

Adrian rejected the work of previous designers of Garbo's clothing in her films. To hide her bulky body and broad shoulders, they had dressed her in the traditional vamp costume of a long slinky gown with an Elizabethan stand-up collar. Instead, Adrian stressed her masculine features. He viewed her as "a sturdy tree, with her feet planted firmly on the ground."[50] He designed sports clothing for her to wear in *A Woman of Affairs*, especially a belted trench coat with a pink plaid lining and padded shoulders. It was based on the coats British officers wore in the

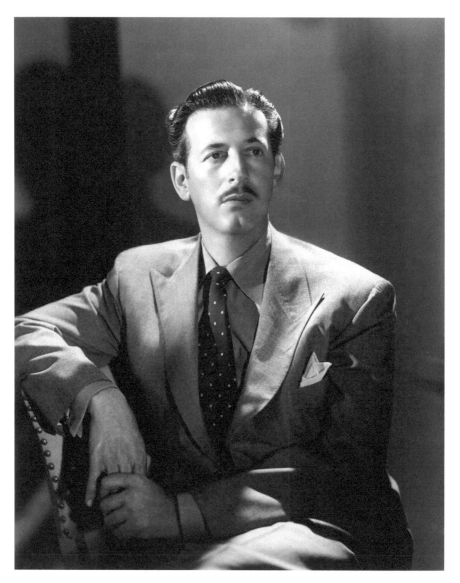

Costume designer Gilbert Adrian. Masheter Movie Archive / Alamy Stock Photo

trenches in World War I. L. B. Mayer and Clarence Brown, the director of *A Woman of Affairs*, were both certain that Garbo would lose her audience if she "came down to earth" and dressed in modern styles. But Adrian prevailed, and he was right. The movie was a hit, and the coat was a fashion sensation.[51]

He also used padded shoulders in *Wild Orchids* in a Javanese ceremonial dress that Garbo wears. The Paris designer Elsa Schiaparelli claimed that she had originated the broad shoulders, but in the United States they were called "the Adrian look."[52] Adrian stated that he designed them first for Garbo and then for Joan Crawford. They remained in style on and off for decades.

Adrian also designed a cloche hat with a broad brim for Garbo in *A Woman of Affairs*. Known as the "Garbo hat," it initiated a fascination with the headgear she wore in her films. Adrian stoked that interest by designing unusual head coverings for her—cloches, berets, turbans, and skullcaps, all meant to draw attention to her face. He also designed the rakish Eugenie hat, with feathers drooping over its side, that Garbo wears in *Romance*. Copies of Garbo's hats were marketed at hat shops or in the cinema departments of department stores.[53] The cinema department was a feature of department stores from the 1920s to the 1950s that no longer exists today. Hats went out of style in the 1970s, except to keep heads warm in the winter and to shade faces from the sun.

The movie magazine writer Helen Louise Walker praised Adrian's designs for Garbo. Without Adrian's genius, according to Walker, Garbo might have "gone the way of all vamps, into an early demise."[54] Adrian saw beyond this "bizarre" creature, as Walker called the vamp, to a modern Garbo. She was publicized as a sex goddess, but she didn't like to show her body in public, unless she was swimming or sunning—accepted female nude activities in Sweden. And her large, angular body didn't look sensual in a bathing suit, as is evident in *The Single Standard* and *Two-Faced Woman*. She didn't like décolleté clothing, which Adrian called one of her eccentricities. He created high-necked evening gowns for her, often with bare backs, which became fashionable. "She had a knack for wearing the most astonishing things with a total lack of self-consciousness," Adrian said. "She turned the unconventional into a part of herself."[55] Adrian disagreed with the frequent assumption that Garbo had no interest in clothes, because she dressed for everyday in sports attire or masculine styles. He stated that she helped him create her costumes.[56] After all, in Stockholm she had been a fashion mannequin and a saleswoman at an elite department store.

Yet, in her period films, beginning in 1930 with *Romance,* she wore Victorian dresses over tight-laced corsets, or high-waisted empire gowns. This bifurcation in style, which fascinated her fans, was maintained. In 1930, the *New York Evening World* reported: "As her rivals become more and more feminine, with ankle length frocks, the Norse mystery goes to the other extreme. Her severe bathrobes, her unrelenting use of a navy-blue beret, her adherence to the roughneck sweater and tailored skirt of flannel, her simple belted tweed coats and mannish felt hats are characteristic of her waking hours."[57]

The Garbomaniacs wore this attire. Margaret Reid noted in the *Los Angeles Times* in 1931: "Despite the fact that Garbo appears on the screen in clinging velvets and silks, so much is known of her private taste that her followers signify their intent by affecting the rough tweeds which constitute the garb of the Garbo in private life."[58]

Modern versions of Garbo's costumes were marketed in department stores, and they influenced designers in Paris and New York. According to the fashion writer Stefania Ricci, the masculine shirt and trousers Garbo wore in *The Single Standard* in 1929 "allowed men's clothing to burst on the [female] fashion scene even more than the creations of Chanel." In *Anna Christie,* Garbo introduced laced shoes, leather jackets, and heavy tweed outfits. Even costumes from her period films were influential in creating fashions, like the Eugenie hat in *Romance.* Her masculine clothes in *Queen Christina,* made in the fall of 1933, brought heavy velvet jackets and broad linen collars into fashion. In 1936 *Vogue* devoted an entire issue to *Camille* (1936), the story of a mid-nineteenth-century Parisian courtesan, in which Garbo wore clothes from the 1850s.[59]

As the vogue of the flapper faded by the late 1920s, the realm of glamour took hold. Sophisticated, mature, and sensual, it suggested a fantasy world of luxury and money, whose inhabitants drank exotic cocktails, went to nightclubs, and sailed the ocean in luxury liners. That world was appealing to women in nations mired in the Great Depression; it offered a fantasy escape from their financial woes. The fan magazine journalist Elsie Qui thought that Garbo was responsible for this change "to some degree." But, she concluded, "we were simply sick of gin-guzzling, nicotine redolent cute kids. The jazz mood dictated our clothing, home furnishings, backyards, and bird cages." And, she wondered, "Will the style dictators take us back to the stuffy, drab, severities of the Victorian era?"[60] The answer is a resounding no, as designers used mirrors, silks and satins, silver and gold, and marble and ebony to create a streamline moderne dreamworld. But that style, in its turn, would generate new dreams, and fashion would turn to the past for reassurance.

By the early 1930s, even as fashions for women became more feminine, the popularity of trousers and masculine suits for women soared. Such clothing was a response to the dislocations of the Great Depression and an extension of the 1920s female vogue of wearing sailor pants for day and pajamas for the beach, home entertaining, and evening wear.[61] Marlene Dietrich stated that she wore trousers because they were more comfortable than skirts; Garbo stated that she liked them because she could put her possessions into her pockets and didn't have to carry a handbag on her long walks. As conservatism increased in the 1930s in tandem with the Great Depression, lesbianism was even more stigmatized, but trousers for women lost some of their association with gender nonconformity.

Meanwhile, Garbo featured her masculine side in playing Anna in *Anna Christie*, her first sound film, in late 1929. She followed it with a series of feminine roles, beginning with *Romance*, made in the spring of 1930. After *Anna Christie* was screened, the movie magazines began hinting that she was both masculine and lesbian. Something had to be done to make her seem feminine again.

Garbo as Susan Lenox. Photo 12 / Alamy Stock Photo

# 9

# *The Pre-Code Era*

*T*HROUGHOUT HER HOLLYWOOD career, Garbo encountered city and state censorship codes and enforcement boards, which censored the content of movies shown in their jurisdictions. The U.S. Supreme Court validated the codes in 1915, ruling that movies were a commercial product—not an art form—and thus were not covered by the free speech protection clause of the First Amendment of the U.S. Constitution. In 1922, sex and drug scandals involving Hollywood stars and directors shocked the nation and brought widespread calls for federal censorship. In response, the moguls formed the Motion Picture Producers and Distributors Association of America (MPPDA), to monitor the morality of films and to constrain the censorship boards. It was often called the Hays Commission, after William B. Hays, a former postmaster general who became its director. Hays added a clause to actors' contracts forbidding immoral behavior, and in 1926 he established the Studio Relations Committee (SRC), with power over films in production.[1]

Many producers resisted the censors. In 1927 the introduction of sound into Hollywood films brought a greater realism to them, as well as urban slang, fast-talking dames, hard-boiled criminals and gangsters, and increased sex. In response, representatives of the MPPDA and the pro-censorship groups met in Hollywood in March 1930 to write a code for the entire industry. The city and state boards, each with their own agenda, were impeding movie making.

The group that met in Hollywood wrote a conservative code for the industry. It banned sex perversion (homosexuality) in films, as well as miscegenation (mixed-race marriage), profanity, vulgarity, overly sexual scenes, adultery, the words "sex" or "sexuality," and any mention of venereal disease. Premarital sex had to be condemned; crime punished; and authority figures and the nuclear family respected. But the code gave a major decision on a movie's morality to an ad hoc committee of three producers, who had to submit their conclusions to the MPPDA for their seal of approval.

Some producers kept making racy movies, especially with the onset of the Great Depression, a decline in movie attendance, and a weak enforcement of the 1930 code. Not until 1934, when Joseph Breen, a devout Catholic, became head of the MPPDA, was the code rigidly enforced. Film historians call the four years between 1930, when the censorship code was written, and 1934, when it was strictly enforced, the "pre-Code era." Pre-Code films featured adulterous spouses, sexually free unmarried individuals, larcenous public figures, and hard-boiled gangsters, criminals, and prostitutes.

The pre-Code era had an impact on Garbo's career. So did the increasing hints in the media after the release of *Anna Christie* that her baritone voice and masculine interpretation of *Anna* indicated that she was masculine and perhaps androgynous. She didn't conceal her relationships with Lilyan Tashman and Fifi D'Orsay. L. B. Mayer disciplined Garbo by casting her in *Romance*, about a romance between an older opera diva and a young male Episcopal priest. A typical "novel of initiation" theme, the film also marked a return to her spiritual / siren typecasting. Other motives for casting Garbo in this film were related to her position in the MGM roster of female stars, as Joan Crawford and Norma Shearer vigorously challenged her.

In line with the sexuality of the pre-Code era, Garbo played a prostitute or a courtesan in seven of the eight films she made from *The Kiss* in 1929 to *Queen Christina* in 1933. *Anna Christie* was both a new woman film, in which she railed against men, and a pre-Code film, because she had been a prostitute. In *Romance, Inspiration,* and *Mata Hari* she was a courtesan. In *Susan Lenox: Her Fall and Rise,* she was first a prostitute and then a courtesan. In *As You Desire Me* she played a nightclub torch singer who is controlled by a sadistic manager, until she becomes a countess in the last reels. *Grand Hotel*, in which she played Grusinskaya, an aging Russian prima ballerina, seems far removed from this theme, although she has a romance with a jewel thief, played by John Barrymore.

These films drew large audiences, even though some movie critics accused the languorous Garbo of sleepwalking through them. But languor can be sensual, and William Daniels was able to photograph her fatigue as sensual. Her European markets remained strong, and the Garbomaniacs were still there, ready to copy her clothing, hairstyles, and behavior, and to attend her films multiple times. Nor did the powerful Garbo disappear in these films; that persona had become central to her acting. In fact, some male actors refused to play opposite her, fearful that her forwardness would compromise their virility.[2]

Even Clark Gable, who played Garbo's lover in *Susan Lenox*, never again appeared opposite her in a film. His star ascended rapidly; he starred in five films in 1931 in addition to *Susan Lenox*, including two with Joan Crawford, his longtime lover. Tall and muscular, he had a handsome face with dimples. He could turn his face from hard to soft in an instant. He replaced the feminized Rudolph Valentino and the energetic John Gilbert as Hollywood's top male star and women's ideal male.

Beginning with *Grand Hotel*, Garbo was listed as "Garbo" in her movie credits; her given name, Greta, was dropped. It was a testimony to her iconic status, to her success in her pre-Code films, and to her dislike of the feminine name Greta. Only great opera and stage stars were called by their last names.

Although Garbo complained about all her pre-Code films, *Romance* was the only film she refused—before giving in. She might have launched a strike, as she had in 1926 and 1927 to end her earlier typecasting as a vamp, but she had neither the energy nor the backers to do that again. By 1930, even her manager, Harry Edington, who was paid by MGM, was no longer entirely on her side. He had, for example, accepted Marlene Dietrich, Garbo's major European rival in Hollywood films, as a client, and he backed all of Thalberg's and Mayer's choices for her. Nor did Garbo's 1927 contract give her control over her films. Under its terms she had a large salary and guarantees that she did not have to appear in commercials and that she had to make only two films a year (a concession to her chronic illnesses). But she didn't have control over the directors, co-stars, and sources on which her films would be based. Raymond Daum contended that when the studio gave Garbo a choice among screenplays in her pre-Code period, she always chose the easiest one.[3]

Her health remained an issue. The press continually reported on her insomnia and anemia, which were cited as the reasons for her fatigue. Clarence Brown, who directed her in seven films, including *Flesh and the Devil*, *A Woman of Affairs*, *Anna Christie*, *Romance*, and *Inspiration*, said that by 1930 she had recovered from her 1927 breakdown, but she was never a strong woman. "She has not the physical strength many players have for the long hours in the studio."[4] She had been a success in *Anna Christie* as a working-class working woman. But Joan Crawford, who had become a star through playing dancing flappers, and Jean Harlow, whom MGM hired in 1932, took over MGM's working-class, working woman roles. Both had advantageous marriages: Crawford to Douglas Fairbanks Jr., the son of Douglas Fairbanks and the stepson of Mary Pickford, who were Hollywood royalty, and Harlow to Paul Bern, an MGM executive.[5] Crawford's marriage to Fairbanks ended in divorce, but she then married Franchot Tone, a Broadway actor, plus she had her ongoing affair with Clark Gable, which was never entirely a secret. Harlow's husband died tragically months after they married, but the studio covered up what was a probable suicide.

Norma Shearer did even better: in 1927 she married MGM chief producer Irving Thalberg.[6] He had been looking for a wife for some time. As he reached his late twenties, he worried about the prediction of his doctor when he was a child that he would live a short life. He wanted to marry an actor who could be MGM royalty along with him and was willing to have children.

Shearer came from a middle-class family in Montreal, Canada; she had gone to high school before her father went bankrupt. Needing to support herself, she went to New York to become an actress. She was ambitious, a sly schemer, tough and resilient, and five feet two inches tall, a good height for a film actress. She slimmed down her body, and did exercises to get control over a "lazy eye," which had made her cross-eyed. She became a "pretty girl" model for James Montgomery Flagg, while making movies for independent film companies near New York. In 1923 L. B. Mayer hired her as an ingenue in his new film production company in Hollywood.

Shearer was not a great beauty, but she was pleasant and industrious, chic and trim, and passionately devoted to her career and the movie business, with perfect manners and a perfectly modulated voice. Thalberg had dated beautiful showgirls and several film actresses, including Norma. Through luck and shrewdness, she maneuvered Thalberg into proposing.

Always an actress, always adept at manipulating without seeming to do so, Shearer was the perfect wife. She took care of Irving's health, calling doctors, nursing him herself, holding dinner parties, and bearing two children because Irving wanted them. She also converted to Judaism to please his mother. Even before Mary Pickford and Douglas Fairbanks divorced in 1936, Pickfair had ceased to be the center of Hollywood high society, and the Thalbergs' home on the Santa Monica beach replaced it, while Irving and Norma became Hollywood's new king and queen. Mercedes de Acosta and Marlene Dietrich met at one of Shearer's parties.

As Thalberg's wife, Shearer could have any role she wanted, if he agreed. It turned out that she wanted to be a "sexy" dramatic actress with a feminist bent; in other words, she wanted to take over Garbo's slot. She carried out a brilliant scheme. Thalberg wanted to make his adored wife the top actress in Hollywood, but he didn't think she was sexy enough to be a siren. To convince Thalberg that she could be a siren, Shearer had George Hurrell, then a private photographer, shoot her as a vixen, with hair askew, eyes half-lidded, dress half-open, and bare legs. As a vamp, Garbo didn't reveal much of her body; she projected sensuality through her eyes, movements, and voice. Shearer outdistanced her. The Hurrell photos changed Thalberg's mind.

Determined to make his beloved wife MGM's top female star, Thalberg cast her in a series of films—*The Divorcee, A Free Soul, Strange Interlude*—which made her "the torchbearer for the Single Standard." (*A Free Soul* was adapted from a novel by Adela Rogers St. Johns, and *Strange Interlude* from a play by Eugene O'Neill—an eerie repeat of Garbo's casting in *The Single Standard*, based on a novel by St. Johns, and

*Anna Christie*, adapted from a play by O'Neill.) Shearer was publicized as the first American film actress to show that an unmarried respectable woman could have affairs with impunity.[7] Garbo's new woman films, which had the same message, seem to have been forgotten. In 1930, Shearer was awarded the Oscar for best actress in *The Divorcee*, winning over Garbo, who was nominated for *Anna Christie*. After Delight Evans saw *The Divorcee*, she wrote in *Screenland* that Shearer had turned into another Greta Garbo.[8]

Given Garbo's European background and her Swedish accent, the logical move was to return her to her typecasting as a siren given that she wasn't sufficiently proficient in English to portray the very American character of a fast-talking dame. Ironically, Marlene Dietrich's hiring at Paramount in 1930 to rival Garbo, in addition to the many other European actresses who were hired at other studios for the same purpose, increased the pressure on Thalberg to return Garbo to the siren slot. Since most of these actresses were publicized as sirens who would outdistance Garbo, Thalberg needed her to rise above them. Between January and May 1933, for example, twenty-one overseas actresses arrived in Hollywood. Several, like Lily Damita, who starred in many American films and married the handsome and swashbuckling actor Errol Flynn, became featured players, but most made a film or two and then left Hollywood, either because they didn't like the United States or because they didn't make the grade as a Hollywood actress.[9]

Both to discipline and shelter Garbo and to return her to her typecasting as a siren, Edward Sheldon's play, *Romance*, was chosen as her first film after *Anna Christie*. Sheldon had written *Romance* in 1914; it had been a hit on the stages of both London and New York. By the 1930s, however, when plays by Eugene O'Neill and Maxwell Anderson were being performed, it was badly out of date. Set in the 1860s in New York, it revolved around the romance between a young Episcopal priest named Tom Armstrong and a famed opera diva, Rita Cavallini, who is akin to La Brunna, the opera singer that Garbo had played in *The Torrent*, her first MGM film. Cavallini has an older lover, Cornelius Van Tuyl, played in the movie by Lewis Stone.

Gavin Gordon, who played Armstrong, effectively portrayed his physical strength and his religiosity, all simpering smiles and awkward sighs. Thalberg wanted to get rid of him, but Garbo insisted that he stay, perhaps because he was homosexual. She was also sympathetic to him. Soon after they began filming, he broke his shoulder, and he was in pain throughout the filming. He refused to have it put in a cast. He had long dreamed of acting opposite Garbo, and he refused to give up his dream. Garbo was convinced that her fans would make the film a success.

Garbo has a cynical side in *Romance*, since her opera diva is a woman of the world. She calls love "a beast that you feed all through the night and when morning comes—love flees." When her clergyman learns that she has been a courtesan, he assumes that she no longer practices that vocation, and he forgives her. But when he discovers that she is involved with Van Tuyl, who is one of his major parishioners and a close friend, he rejects her. She renounces her opera career, becomes a nun, joins an order in Switzerland, and renounces her new woman persona.

Even Garbo's costuming in *Romance* seems a repudiation of the independent person she had played in *Anna Christie* and her other new woman films. In *Romance*, which was set in the 1860s and for which Adrian was the designer, Garbo wears the tight-laced corsets and hoop skirts which were characteristic of women's dress in that era. Her hair is arranged in sausage curls, reminiscent of Mary Pickford's hairstyle when she played a child. The Eugenie hat Adrian designed for her for *Romance*, with feathers provocatively hanging over one edge, became a fashion fad. Adrian had modeled that hat after one worn by the empress Eugenie, the stylish wife of the French emperor Napoleon III, in the 1860s. It is reminiscent of costumes he had designed for Broadway revues.

Adrian had overruled L. B. Mayer in dressing Garbo as a modern woman in her new woman films, but he now acceded to Mayer. Not only had femininity for women become fashionable in 1930, but also Adrian was homosexual, and homophobia was rampant in the 1930s. He married screen star Janet Gaynor, who was reputed to be lesbian, and they had one child. The rumor in Hollywood was that it was a "lavender" marriage, although Garbo told Cecil Beaton that she was amazed by the great love Adrian showed for his wife.

To justify casting Garbo as a siren again, Mayer had press releases sent to the media stating that she had lost her "glamour" in *Anna Christie*, but in *Romance* she would regain it. By 1930, "glamour" had become a Hollywood watchword, partly because the 1930 Code forbade any use of the word "sex." To persuade Garbo to do the film, Mayer sent Bess Meredyth, a top MGM screenwriter, to talk to her.[10] Meredyth had written the screenplays for *The Mysterious Lady* and *A Woman of Affairs*, and she was slated to write the screenplay for *Romance*. She had written powerful roles for Garbo in those previous films—the clever spy Tania Federova in *The Mysterious Lady* and the dashing flapper Diana Merrick in *A Woman of Affairs*. There was no reason to assume that Meredyth would not do the same for Garbo in *Romance*, and indeed, Rita Cavallini has a tough, self-assured side.

Why did Mayer send Bess Meredyth to see Garbo? It's probable that he wanted Meredyth to discreetly point out to Garbo that she needed to establish her femininity after the hints in the movie magazines about her "male voice" in *Anna Christie*. Meredyth was feminine; Salka Viertel, who worked with her on the screenplay for *Queen Christina*, described her as "a jolly blonde, pink-faced, all dimples and curves," and one of the most highly paid writers at MGM.[11] Like many women in the Hollywood movie industry, she was an iron butterfly, sweet on the surface but tough underneath. She was married to Michael Curtiz, a prominent director at Warner Brothers who had immigrated from Hungary to Hollywood, making him one of Garbo's favored Europeans.

Meredyth probably alluded to the morals clause in acting contracts, which could be applied to Garbo because of her lesbian behavior with Lilyan Tashman and Fifi D'Orsay. Meredyth could also describe *Romance* in ways that would please Garbo's feminist side. She could point out that Armstrong is to blame for Rita's retreat to a nunnery, because at their last meeting he tries to persuade her to spend the night with him. Rita is appalled. Clasping her hands together as though praying, she pleads with Armstrong not to treat her as a sex object, as all other men have. Influenced by his religiosity, she becomes a nun. Whatever Meredyth said, she persuaded Garbo to do *Romance*, although Garbo called Harry Edington the next day and tried to get out of it.

Shearer expanded her new power. Her brother Douglas Shearer became head of MGM's sound department, and George Hurrell became chief of portrait photography. Garbo didn't like the outlandish persona he assumed to motivate his sitters, jumping up and down, acting like a great ape. He did her portrait photographs only for *Romance*. After that, Garbo returned to Clarence Bull as her MGM photographer. He was quiet and unassuming, but he took brilliant photos. That's what Garbo liked.

After Garbo finished filming *Romance* in the spring of 1930, she filmed the German version of *Anna Christie*, with Salka playing the prostitute, Marthy Owen. In the fall, she played an artist's model in *Inspiration*, based on a novel titled *Sapho* by the French author Alphonse Daudet, about artists and their models in Paris, especially a model named Sapho, renamed Yvonne Valbret and played by Garbo in the film. (This Sapho bears no relationship to Sappho, the ancient Greek lesbian poet on the island of Lesbos.) Valbret is beloved by the Paris artists, all of whom want to paint her. As in *Romance*, Garbo is involved with a younger man, but as is standard in Garbo's older woman–younger man films, the actors were about the same age off the screen. In this film, she rejects the younger artist so that he can marry a young woman acceptable to his parents, while she is left with an older male lover, who seems much more interesting than the young man. At this point, Garbo complained that her roles were all the same.[12]

In the summer of 1931, she played Susan Lenox in *Susan Lenox: Her Fall and Rise*, an adaptation of a novel by David Graham Phillips. Lenox goes down and up the social scale, beginning as a dancer in a circus troupe, rising to be an elegant New York courtesan, and then finding the man who deserted her early in the film, who is her "one true love." Clark Gable, the new heartthrob, played her lover. But by the time twenty writers had contributed to the screenplay and the script, partly because the SRC kept requiring changes, the film had become confused. Garbo walked off the set six times, and writers each time had to fix the problem. Walking off the set was Garbo's way of complaining.

Garbo spends much of the film running away from men who are trying to force her to marry a man she doesn't love, or trying to find Gable, who thinks she has deserted him. Especially surprising is that Gable, with

his dimples, looks feminine, while Garbo's masculine body is emphasized. When Garbo catches Gable at the end of the film, they speak
some unexpected lines. Garbo says to Gable: "We are two cripples. Only
together can we become straight." Gable replies: "You have a queer way
of looking at things." In 1930s homosexual slang, "queer" meant homosexual and "straight" meant heterosexual, as they still do today. As
Andrea Weiss suggested, such homosexual hints—which were common in
pre-Code films—were partly addressed to men's voyeuristic interest
in lesbians.[13]

But those hints also suggest that Mayer and Thalberg knew that
Garbo's audiences were largely female but also included many lesbian
women and young homosexual men. Several fan magazine writers
alleged that men were afraid of Garbo once she stopped playing vamp
roles, while women were drawn to her power. According to Mercedes de
Acosta, the average man didn't find Garbo "cute" enough for his taste.
When Dorothy Manners read a selection of Garbo's fan mail from men,
she found that the letters were mostly written by young men.[14]

Garbo met Mercedes de Acosta during the filming of *Susan Lenox*,
and they went to the cabin in the High Sierras after filming ended. In
fact, Garbo succumbed so easily to Mercedes that one suspects Garbo
knew about her before they met. Garbo, like Mercedes, had access to
lesbian networks, and she wanted to find someone to write a screenplay
for her in which she would either cross dress or play a man. Mercedes
had been involved with several Broadway actresses, and Bessie Marbury,
a renowned agent who represented George Bernard Shaw and Somerset
Maugham, was Mercedes's agent. Bessie was also a leader among New
York lesbians, and she and Mercedes were close.

Mercedes found her title, "Desperate," in Nietzsche's advice in *Thus
Spake Zarathustra* to live one's life desperately—to find one's best self.
Mercedes's screenplay tells the story of a young and dashing girl called
Erik who turns herself into a "beautiful" young man and ends up as a
cowboy taming wild stallions in Wyoming. Mercedes saw Thalberg
then; Garbo must have arranged the meeting. But Thalberg didn't like
Mercedes, who put on her aristocratic air in his presence. He thundered
at her: "We have been trying to build Garbo up as a great glamorous

actress and you come along and try to put her into pants and make a monkey out of her.... Do you want to put all America and all the women's clubs against her?" But Garbo didn't give up on Mercedes. Learning of Thalberg's rejection, she suggested to Mercedes that she write a screenplay of Oscar Wilde's *Picture of Dorian Gray*.[15]

Mercedes refused, and Garbo then turned to Salka Viertel. Before she left for Sweden in June 1932, she had Salka meet Thalberg. In 1930, Salka had suggested to Garbo that she play *Queen Christina* in a biopic of the monarch; she now persuaded Thalberg to assign Salka to write the screenplay, with Bess Meredyth assisting her. Salka knew how to charm the difficult producer.

Garbo played a spy in *Mati Hari* in the fall of 1931, a fading prima ballerina in *Grand Hotel* in early 1932, and an amnesiac in *As You Desire Me* soon after. In both *Mata Hari* and *As You Desire Me*, she burlesqued Marlene Dietrich, who burlesqued Garbo in several films. And the costumes Adrian designed for Garbo in *Mata Hari*, including a shimmering black body stocking that made her look like a snake, were so fantastic that they toured the United States on their own.

*Mata Hari* contains many cross-gendered touches, especially in the casting of the feminine—and homosexual—Ramon Novarro as a soldier obsessed with Mata Hari. Convicted of spying and sentenced to death, Mati Hari, played by Garbo, walks to her execution by a firing squad wearing what looks like a nun's habit, displaying her spirituality. Showing her independence, another Garbo feature, she proclaims: "I am Mata Hari! I am my own master." Garbo found *Mata Hari* silly, as she spoke louche lines, moved in a serpentine manner, and danced around a huge statue of Shiva, the Hindu deity with arms like an octopus. June Knight, a professional dancer, did most of the dance; Knight later realized that Garbo had tried to seduce her while learning the dance with her.[16]

One of Mercedes's relatives had known Mata Hari, and Mercedes served as an unofficial adviser on the film. It's not surprising that the film has homosexual touches, which mirror the early relationship between Garbo and Mercedes. Garbo's remaining films show little influence from Mercedes, although she encouraged Garbo to make *Queen*

*Christina*, and she wrote a screenplay for her on the life of Joan of Arc, which Garbo never filmed.

In early 1932, Garbo played a fading ballerina in an episode of *Grand Hotel*. It was the first Hollywood film with several stars in the same movie, each with a different story, all staying at Berlin's Grand Hotel. It launched a popular film genre—the all-star movie. Garbo is surprisingly persuasive as the ballerina. She wears a tutu, although she doesn't dance *en pointe*, and her love scenes with the aging John Barrymore are campy. But she pronounced her famous line "I want to be alone" in the film. Producers often had stars refer to their off-screen lives in their films to promote interest in them as personalities, encouraging audience members to identify with their favorite stars, whose lives were detailed in the movie fan magazines. In *Grand Hotel*, Joan Crawford played a secretary, but she and Garbo weren't in a scene together, and they rarely met on the set. But Crawford had copied Garbo's appearance.

At the Hollywood premiere of *Grand Hotel*, the worst satire of Garbo ever conceived was performed. When the film ended, Wallace Beery, an MGM star who played a businessman in *Grand Hotel* and who was known for crude behavior, came on stage, wearing the grotesque costume he had worn as Sweedie, a Swedish maid he had burlesqued in a series of silent films. Will Rogers, the eminent comic cowboy, played the announcer; he was a friend of Beery's and was in on the joke. After Rogers proclaimed that Beery was Garbo, Beery repeated some Garboisms in a high falsetto voice. He expected "I t'ink I go home" to bring down the house, but the audience booed him and many people walked out. Garbo wasn't there; she often didn't attend the premieres of her films, preferring to view them after they had been released. Beery and Rogers both apologized publicly for the prank, but Garbo didn't respond.[17]

Garbo finished the films required by her 1927 contract with *As You Desire Me*, adapted from a play by Luigi Pirandello. She begins the film as Zara, a torch singer in a nightclub in Budapest, wearing a platinum blonde wig and looking like Marlene Dietrich. She is suffering from amnesia because of horrible experiences during World War II; gang rape is implied, since German and then Russian soldiers occupied Hungary during the war. She is controlled by a sadistic manager, played

Garbo in *Mata Hari* (1931). colaimages / Alamy Stock Photo

Garbo in a sheer gown for *Mata Hari*. Collection Christophel / Alamy Stock Photo

by Erich von Stroheim, who found her exhausted, with no memory, and nursed her back to health and made her the sexual woman he desired her to be. After one of her nightclub performances as Zara, a man she doesn't recognize approaches her and tells her that she is Countess Maria Varelli, who disappeared at the end of the war. He has been searching for years for Maria, and the trail led to Zara. Zara eagerly goes with him to Count Varelli's estate, and she quickly turns herself into a facsimile of the soft and radiant Maria. She is persuaded that she was—and still is—the wife of the Italian count Bruno Varelli, played by Melvyn Douglas. Garbo is now a soft woman, like the peasant girl she played in the first half of *The Torrent*.

Then Garbo's sadistic manager appears at the Varelli estate, accompanied by a middle-aged, unattractive woman who claims to be the Countess Varelli. But the Count refuses to accept her; he and the bogus/authentic Maria have fallen in love. Von Stroheim had a long history in Hollywood. He is remembered today as the visionary director of movies like *Greed*. But Mayer and Thalberg detested him because when he directed *The Merry Widow* for them in 1925, he ran over budget and wouldn't obey them. They tried to fire him, but the entire crew refused to continue with the film unless von Stroheim was retained. They were outmaneuvered; they kept von Stroheim. Garbo honored his talent, and she wanted the manager / lover in *As You Desire Me* to show a sadistic streak, in contrast to Melvyn Douglas, gentle and undemanding, who played Count Varelli. With a low, raspy voice and little expression on his face, von Stroheim looks like a stern Prussian official, capable of anything.

Garbo wanted to help von Stroheim, who was old and chronically ill. She covered for him, while she spent much of her free time during the filming listening to his stories of acting in Vienna and in early Hollywood. She was known for helping struggling actors; she had backed Gavin Gordon as her lover in *Romance*. In *Queen Christina*, she would try to revive John Gilbert's failing career by insisting that he be cast as Don Antonio, her lover in the film.

*As You Desire Me* subtly asks several questions: Is the real Garbo a tough performer, like the nightclub singer Zara? Or is she a soft woman, like Countess Maria? Will Garbo remain in Hollywood as a performer or return to her homeland in Sweden? That last question was often asked about Garbo, who was confirmed as a woman of mystery in *As You Desire Me*, since the issue of whether she is Maria is never resolved. But there is more to this film than the issue of Garbo's past and future. Based on a play by Pirandello, a master of modern drama, *As You Desire Me* questions the nature of reality. It asks if we are ever truly independent, or only the person we see reflected in the eyes of others. Do we all make ourselves into the person that others want us to be?

During the making of *As You Desire Me*, Garbo moved into Mercedes's house. This time, Mercedes's contention that Garbo lived with her during her films seems to have been accurate. Garbo had lost a good deal of money in the failure of a Beverly Hills bank, but she didn't want L. B. Mayer to find out about it, since he might use it to reduce his salary offer in the upcoming negotiations over her contract. Mercedes had Garbo move into her house, which Garbo had supposedly purchased. But Garbo wasn't happy during the filming; Mercedes stated that Garbo would come home after a day of filming and sit at the top of the basement stairs, staying there for several hours, saying nothing. Perhaps it was Mercedes who suggested that she finally meet Cecil Beaton, who might be able to cheer her up with his fey personality and his witticisms. Photographing Hollywood stars for a new book, he was staying with the director Edmund Goulding and his wife, the dancer Marjorie Moss. Goulding was mostly homosexual, but he married Moss, a former Broadway dancer, to give her an income and take care of her because she suffered from an illness.

Garbo was friends with Goulding, who had directed her in *Love* and *Grand Hotel*. At Beaton's request, Goulding asked Garbo if she would come to his house to meet Beaton, but she refused because "he [Beaton] talks to newspapers." Yet, several hours later, when Beaton looked out a window of his room in Goulding's house, he saw Garbo in the garden with Goulding and Moss. "If a unicorn had suddenly appeared in the late afternoon light," he wrote in his diary, "I could have been neither more surprised nor more amazed than by the beauty of this exotic creature."[18]

Then they all went to the living room. Garbo was in a playful mood. She hopped around the room, impersonating grand actresses, quoting snatches of poetry. They ate lobster americaine (lobster in a tomato sauce, flambéed with cognac) and drank Bellinis (champagne and peach juice). They played charades and did improvisations, while they played Strauss waltzes and Rachmaninoff symphonies on a gramophone. "The lights were turned out and our bacchanalia became wilder in the firelight"— Beaton wrote that in his diary, implying that something sexual had occurred, but it was probably nothing more than a kiss between Garbo and him, although Goulding was known in Hollywood for hosting sex orgies.

The four of them—Garbo, Beaton, Goulding, and Moss—interacted until the early morning of the next day. Garbo had an early studio call, and Beaton was leaving Hollywood that day to return to England. After Garbo left, Beaton surreptitiously put in his pocket a yellow rose that Garbo had earlier picked out of a large bouquet of roses in a vase "and fingered with a variety of caresses," as Beaton wrote in his diary. He pressed the yellow rose in his diary, took it with him to his country home in England, framed it, and hung the picture over his bed. He didn't see Garbo again for fourteen years.

Harry Edington now negotiated an extraordinary new contract for Garbo. Mayer agreed to pay her $250,000 for each of two films and to let her produce and star in *Queen Christina*. The contract continued the rights she had been given under her 1927 contract, while giving her control over the plays or novels on which her films would be based.

Garbo had won her second conflict with Mayer. And she had the highest salary of any woman in the United States, as her friend Cole Porter implied in his song "You're the Top":

You're the National Gallery
You're the top!
You're Garbo's salary . . .

During the pre-Code era, Garbo had made more money for MGM than any other star, largely due to the European revenues from her films. Mayer feared that she might move to Sweden and make films on the Continent, cutting off a major MGM revenue stream. He considered Garbo's high salary necessary to keep her at MGM.

After signing her new contract, Garbo left Hollywood for one of her periodic visits to Sweden. Mercedes followed her to New York, where they had a quarrel that Anita Loos called "too amazing."[19] Mercedes had wanted Garbo to select her to write *Queen Christina*, but Garbo had already given the assignment to Salka Viertel, and she wouldn't change her mind. Then Mercedes demanded to go to Sweden with Garbo, who adamantly refused. This refusal led to the quarrel. Garbo usually refused to quarrel with anyone; she was known in Hollywood for her self-control. But she didn't follow that rule in her relationship with the impetuous Mercedes, who had her own ways of trying to control her Swedish friend, which often didn't work. Mercedes flew back to Hollywood, while Garbo went on to Stockholm.

Garbo was exhausted when she left for Sweden in 1932. To meet the April deadline on her 1927 contract, she had rushed from *Grand Hotel* into *As You Desire Me* with almost no break. This was the first film in which Melvyn Douglas co-starred with her. It's not surprising that Douglas was annoyed with her for taking many breaks because of her gynecological condition, or that Mercedes found her sitting at the top of the cellar stairs, staring into space.

When she was finally on the steamship to Sweden, Garbo had a brief encounter of a friendly kind. Philip Cummings, a young New England schoolteacher and poet, was on the ship. Garbo was twenty-seven; he was twenty-six. She had a first-class cabin; he was in third class. He had a knack for cultivating celebrities. Sneaking up to the first-class deck, he saw Garbo playing shuffleboard with another passenger. In a break in the game, he introduced himself to her, speaking in German and Swedish, which she enjoyed, and he asked her to play a game of shuffleboard with him. She did so, and they established a connection, playing shuffleboard every day for the next eight days of the trip. An attendant tried to remove Cummings from first class, but Garbo intervened, and he stayed.[20]

A ship across the ocean creates its own universe. Away from normal lives, people on ships often establish warm bonds—which may seem strong during the voyage but often disappear once land is reached. On the steamship from New York to Sweden in early 1929, she had met Wilhelm Sörenson, who became her companion for nearly a year.

Sörenson was homosexual. And so was Philip Cummings. Regarding herself as a young man with a homosexual bent, Garbo liked to socialize with homosexual young men.

One hopes that they walked the deck and sat in deck chairs, talking about poetry and their lives. Garbo needed a break from Mercedes and her fans, a band of whom crowded her as she got on the ship and pulled a piece of fabric off her coat. She and Cummings didn't have an affair. When the boat docked in Gothenburg, Garbo gave Cummings a friendly kiss and told him that she considered him her friend. There is no evidence that they met again. He went on to have a serious affair with the Spanish poet Federico García Lorca. Garbo stayed in Sweden for ten months, and when she returned to Hollywood, she began working on *Queen Christina*.

Once in Sweden, Garbo went hiking and swimming in the summer and skiing and skating in the winter. She spent time with her family and friends, including Mimi Pollak, Max Gumpel, and the Wachtmeisters. She researched the life of Queen Christina in Swedish archives, bringing back with her a suitcase filled with her notes. Harry Edington issued a press release in her name. It stated that she had taken over Stockholm's Theatre Intima, associated with Strindberg and Stiller, and that she intended to turn it into a repertory theater, with a permanent company of actors. From such contact, the press release stated, "springs the genuine daemonic force, the creative energy which infects everyone engaged in the production." She hoped that the success of *Grand Hotel*, which had inspired her, would persuade other studios to form groups of "star power players."[21]

But she never followed up on the press release, which may have been a ploy in her campaign to make L. B. Mayer believe that she would return to Sweden if he didn't give her what she wanted. In a later statement to Cecil Beaton, she expressed her preference for film, which she called "vaster" than the stage. Thousands of people can be seen in one shot; the rhythm of a whole city can be displayed in a few inches of film. Garbo added that she had often wished to become a director and put on the screen "some of the things that impressed her."[22]

In fact, given Garbo's careful preparation for her roles, planning her emotions and movements beforehand and practicing them until they became second nature, she directed herself in many of her films. Her official directors, especially Clarence Brown and George Cukor, mostly maintained a supportive environment for her during filming, while they often gave her signals through the hole in the black flats that surrounded her, beginning with the movie *Love* in the summer of 1927. She had issues with Ernst Lubitsch, the director of *Ninotchka*, because he acted out scenes before she played them and expected her to copy his interpretation. She had a similar issue with Rouben Mamoulian, the director of *Queen Christina*, but they negotiated a truce—and became romantically involved for a short time. Mauritz Stiller had acted out her scenes for her before she had played them, but that was years before, and Stiller, who had trained her as a film actress, was special.

While Garbo was in Sweden, Mercedes became seriously involved with Marlene Dietrich. Garbo didn't react publicly to what was a betrayal on Mercedes's part, but she must have been upset. Mercedes and Marlene met at a party at Irving Thalberg's home. Soon after the party, Marlene wrote to Rudy Sieber, her husband / confidante, still living in Germany, that Mercedes was very attractive, but she had looked miserable at the Thalberg party.[23] The next day, Marlene appeared at Mercedes's home, offering to nurse her back to health. Dietrich was a vixen, but she was also a German hausfrau. She prepared sumptuous meals— for her family, her friends, and her lovers. And she had a daughter—a perfect foil for her sexy self.

But Dietrich became annoyed by Mercedes's constant adulation of Garbo. In response, Mercedes tried to please Dietrich by promising to bring to her bed any woman she wanted. And she dismissed Garbo: "I do know that I have built up in my emotions a person that does not exist. My mind sees the real person—a Swedish servant girl with a face touched by God—only interested in money, her health, sex, food, and sleep."[24] As was Dietrich's way, however, she paused her relationship with Mercedes in the late spring of 1933, returning to Europe just as Garbo returned to Hollywood from Sweden. Once back, Garbo stayed at Salka's house, but she didn't give Mercedes up. Within six months, she had Mercedes find her a house to rent. Within a year, photographers shot

Garbo and Mercedes walking down Hollywood Boulevard, both of them wearing men's pants.

Two months after she returned from Sweden in June 1933, Garbo began filming *Queen Christina*. Once again, she had to face the recurrence of her chronic gynecological ailments. And by the spring of 1934, a combination of Catholic and Protestant pro-censorship groups put teeth into the harsh censorship code in 1930. The clause in the 1930 code giving producers major input over its enforcement was abrogated, and Garbo's career was threatened.

Garbo as Queen Christina. Moviestore Collection Ltd / Alamy Stock Photo

# 10

## *Breaking Free*

### *Queen Christina*

*I*N THE SPRING of 1928, while filming *The Mysterious Lady*, Garbo told Fred Niblo, the film's director, that she wanted to play male roles. Niblo was so shocked by her statement that he chastised her in an article he wrote titled "Masculinity Menaces Movie Maidens," which was published in the movie magazine *Hollywood*. "Feminine fans, as well as the masculine majority," Niblo stated, "have little sympathy for the so-called heroine exploiting her boyish figure and her usurped masculine ideas. Women are refreshing in business and in films chiefly for their femininity."[1]

Garbo paid little attention to Niblo. A year later, while in New York on her way from Stockholm to Hollywood, she told a *New York Times* reporter that she wanted to play innovative roles, ones different from what other actresses were playing. And she didn't want to play a silly siren, getting dressed up to seduce men.[2] In her own way, she was trying to continue Mauritz Stiller's innovative approach to films. Her new woman films were an initial success in that endeavor. She next tried to play cross-dressing women and even men, with much less success.

In April 1929, soon after returning to Hollywood, Garbo wore a white male shirt and pants in *The Single Standard* for her cruise in the South Seas with Packy Cannon. That same month, she again made her desire to cross-dress public when she attended a Hollywood masquerade ball dressed as Hamlet, the sixteenth-century Danish prince made famous by Shakespeare's play. For the masquerade ball, Adrian made Garbo a standard Hamlet costume: black tights, high black boots, and a black velvet doublet. He added a black mask over her upper face, since it was a masquerade ball. The Hamlet costume had multiple meanings. Hamlet in Shakespeare's play is depressed and often unable to act on his resolve to revenge his father's murder. As Hamlet, Garbo mocked her own melancholy. She also drew from the theatrical tradition that a woman who successfully played a major male part was a genius. Hamlet was the favorite cross-dressed role of stage actresses. From the eighteenth century to the mid-twentieth century, over 200 actresses played the part, including the esteemed English actress Sarah Siddons in the late eighteenth century and the famed French actress Sarah Bernhardt a century later.[3]

The Danish actress Asta Nielsen, who had played a starving woman in *Joyless Street* and often starred in German movies, filmed a version of *Hamlet* in which she played the Danish prince as female, cross-dressed as male, changing the relationships in the play. Hamlet and Ophelia are both in love with Horatio, Hamlet's friend. Only Queen Gertrude, Hamlet's mother, knows that her son is female, since she gave birth to him. Nielsen's Hamlet was acclaimed as a tour de force. At one of Salka Viertel's salons, Garbo explained to émigré director Max Reinhardt how she would play the Danish prince, although there is no record of what she said.[4] Reinhardt had been a major Berlin theater impresario; he staged a version of *Hamlet* in contemporary dress. His son Gottfried was Salka Viertel's lover.

In the summer of 1932, Mercedes de Acosta and Cecil Beaton took Garbo to Alice B. Toklas's apartment in Paris to see the many Picassos on the walls collected by Gertrude Stein, Toklas's life partner. Garbo looked at the pictures without saying anything and then left. There is no explanation for why she committed such a social faux pas, although her shyness and her paranoia could attack her without warning. Toklas, who was offended, called Garbo "Mademoiselle Hamlet." It was a criticism of Garbo for being, like the Danish prince, overly self-involved.

Crossed-dressed women appeared in the circus and in burlesque from the early days of these forms of entertainment. In the premodern era, such women were considered magical because they were able to cross gender lines so completely. They later appeared on the stage, playing Hamlet and other important male roles, which were called "breeches roles." They were ubiquitous in popular musicals, like the Amazon choruses in revues, and they later appeared in pantomime as the principal boy when the use of child actors on the stage was restricted. On the stage, a small woman usually plays Peter Pan.

In her study of cross-dressed women in silent films, Laura Horak found such women in nearly 400 films—from the start of the movies in 1879 to 1929, the year that Garbo starred in *The Kiss*, one of Hollywood's last silent films. Mary Pickford cross-dressed in four films; Anna Q. Nilsson and Joan Crawford each in one; and Marion Davies in four.[5]

Yet, these actresses weren't defined as lesbian when they cross-dressed. Madeleine Mahlon praised the Swedish actress Anna Q. Nilsson, who freelanced in the Hollywood film industry, for portraying a man without using "cute tricks" in *Panjola* (1923), an adventure film set in the gold mines of Rhodesia. "The mystery," Mahlon continued, "is how a woman as feminine as Anna Q. can so skillfully submerge her femininity on the screen."[6]

By the time Garbo's career took off in 1927 with *Flesh and the Devil*, cross-dressing in films was declining, and by the 1930s, with the onset of a conservative mood in the United States fostered by the Great Depression, cross-dressing had largely disappeared from Hollywood films. Garbo cross-dressed in scenes in four films: *Wild Orchids, The Single Standard, The Kiss*, and *Queen Christina*.

Garbo told her gay friend David Diamond, an American composer whom she met at one of Salka's salons, that she had proposed to L. B. Mayer that she play Joan of Arc, but he had turned her down. Joan was a French peasant girl in the sixteenth century who heard the voices of saints telling her to lead the French army and drive the English out of France. Dressing like a soldier and putting on male armor, Joan successfully completed this mission, but she was burned at the stake for cross-dressing—a useful excuse to get rid of her. Garbo later proposed that she play the nineteenth-century novelist George Sand, a woman who cross-dressed, adopted a male name, and supported the rights of women and workers. She also wanted to play Dorian Gray, the protagonist in Oscar Wilde's 1890 novel *The Picture of Dorian Gray*.

Following a decadent impulse, Dorian Gray explores his society's forbidden pleasures, with devastating results. Wilde's novel raises questions about beauty, morality, gender, and self-fulfillment. The lives of these three individuals—Joan of Arc, George Sand, and the fictional Dorian Gray—were discussed throughout Garbo's Hollywood career as possible subjects for her films, but none was ever put into production. As she grew older, she proposed that she play Henry Wooton, the instigator of Dorian Gray's decadent behavior—and that Marilyn Monroe play the actress who commits suicide when Gray rejects her.

Homosexuality and bisexuality gained attention in the 1920s, due to the sexual revolution of the decade and to the popularity of the theories of Sigmund Freud. Freud concluded that all humans are bisexual at birth and that becoming oriented to one's own gender may be unfortunate, but it is natural, not perverse. In 1926, Edouard Bourdet's play *The Captive*, about a married woman who leaves her husband for her lesbian lover, opened in New York to large audiences, but the New York censors closed it down as obscene, causing a sensation. *The Captive* was then produced in many U.S. cities, and it was shut down only in Los Angeles. Many reviewers praised Bourdet for depicting a woman who acts according to her true self, while the language in those reviews educated the public about non-heteronormative sexualities.[7] Garbo treasured a copy of the script from *The Captive* she owned, signed by Helen Menken, the actress who played the married woman in the New York production.[8]

The sexual rebellion of the 1920s brought the publication of many novels about lesbians and bisexuals; Sarah Waters called it "an explosion."[9] Many of these novels are positive about their subjects, and some were bestsellers. In 1927 Rosamond Lehmann's *Dusty Answer* and Marcel Proust's *Cities of the Plain* appeared. The next year saw the publication of Virginia Woolf's *Orlando*; Wanda Neff's *We Sing Diana*; Djuna Barnes's *Ladies' Almanac*; and Hall's *Well of Loneliness*.

*Ladies' Almanac*, by Djuna Barnes, focused on the free-love salon in Paris of the American heiress Natalie Barney, who had moved to Paris because homosexual acts weren't illegal in France, as they were in the United States. Cross-dressing was illegal in France, although a cross-dressed woman wouldn't be prosecuted if she registered with the police. Many artists and writers, predominantly lesbian, attended Barney's Friday evening celebrations. Several writers assert that Garbo was a symbol to these women of their aspirations and that Mercedes de Acosta brought Garbo to one of Barney's events, although there is no record of what happened there.[10]

In *The Well of Loneliness*, Radclyffe Hall set several scenes in Barney's salon, although Hall's work is mostly about a fictional woman named Stephen Gordon who is confused about her sexual identity. To explain Gordon's confusion, Hall used the theory of inversion, devised by male sexologists. It proposed that the internal—and true—self of lesbian women is male. In the process of maturing, their anatomy becomes female, but internally they remain male. Living a false self, they can't be happy. According to inversion theory, homosexuals also were psychologically damaged, because their internal selves remained female while their outer selves became male. Hall's novel became a bestseller after being prosecuted as obscene in both Britain and the United States.

In Virginia Woolf's feminist treatise, *A Room of One's Own* (1929), Woolf proposed that humans are naturally androgynous and that they are most in balance when they acknowledge both the male and female sides of their selves. Based on her studies of sex in ancient Greece, Mercedes de Acosta wrote in a draft of her autobiography that the Greeks "accepted homo-sexuality and bi-sexuality, whose impulse they regarded as just another stream toward the same great sea—the eternal source of love." She couldn't understand the so-called "normal people, who believe that a man should only love a woman and a woman a man." Many great artists and philosophers, Mercedes continued, lived contented lives in a "half-tone" state—as bisexual or homosexual.[11]

Marlene Dietrich expressed a simple version of Freud's theory that object choice, not personal orientation, determines sex drive, when she stated that "in Europe it doesn't matter if you're a man or a woman. We make love with anyone we find attractive."[12] In a letter to Mimi Pollak in 1930, after Mimi had married a man, Garbo puzzled over Mimi's sexual orientation as well as her own. She knew she would never marry a man; it was against her nature. And she had often thought that she and Mimi belonged to each other.[13]

Garbo was deeply sensual. Sam Green, a close friend of hers in her later years, stated that she was "downright seductive, always grabbing one's hand, putting her hand on one's knee." But she was ambivalent about lesbianism, even though she often saw herself as male and took the masculine name Gurra in her relationship with Mimi. In her affair with the actor Gilbert Roland in 1943, she thought of herself as bisexual. She called her female self "Eleanor." Her male self, whom she described as gentle and sentimental, she called "Mountain Boy."[14]

She told Cecil Beaton that she was intrigued by "fantastic [sexual] paths." But she was sometimes critical of homosexuality, saying to Beaton that it didn't fit life's natural pattern. The well-to-do, who live sheltered lives, she said, can handle its stigma, but the lives of the poor are so difficult that they can't deal with the animosity they may incite. Beaton thought that in making this statement, Garbo was referring to herself.[15] If she was the subject of her statement, she was adding another layer of cruelty to her childhood, in addition to poverty and sexual assault. In fact, the novelist and critic Gore Vidal, who became close to Garbo in her later years, said that she had told him that she had had sex with her sister.[16] If her parents had discovered them, the consequences would probably have been dire.

Like Marlene Dietrich, Garbo had many lovers. Some were female, but many were male. According to the Hollywood director George Cukor, who directed her in *Camille* and *Two-Faced Woman* and became a close friend, she would "do anything, pick up any man, go to bed with him." Salka Viertel called her a sexual adventurer. Five years after Garbo died, Raymond Daum, a close friend of George Schlee, published a letter in the *New York Times* on May 7, 1995, stating that producer Walter Wanger had told him that Garbo was the most sexually alive woman he had ever known: "There is nothing she doesn't know about sex." Wanger also thought that she preferred women to men.[17]

Garbo's friends included many homosexual and bisexual men and lesbian and bisexual women. They sometimes separated into groups defined by sexual orientation, as at George Cukor's lunches for his gender-crossing friends. They formed informal networks linked through letters and phone calls. In Weimar Berlin, homosexuals and lesbians formed their own political groups, but they didn't form such groups yet in Britain or the United States, where sodomy was illegal and the mainstream population defined oral sex as perverse. Sam Green, a New York art dealer close to Garbo in the 1960s and 1970s, stated that "everyone had to be a lesbian in the '30s, even if they didn't want to be. They dressed up and went to lesbian bars. It was the thing to do."[18]

Green must have been referring to the avant-garde, since in the United States individuals identified as homosexual in the 1930s could be arrested, sent to prison, and subjected to electroshock treatments to try to change their sexual orientation—a dubious and brutal procedure. Before the 1930s the laws against homosexuality focused on acts, but by the 1930s, homosexuality was defined as an identity, broadening its scope.[19]

The film star Katharine Hepburn, who resembled Garbo, identified with straight men, was called Jimmy by her close friends, and thought of herself as a tomboy. Because she blamed herself for her brother's suicide when they were young, she was drawn to men who, like Spencer Tracy, were emotionally damaged. But her primary sexual relationships were with women, especially with Constance Collier and Phyllis Wilbourn. Collier had been a star of the Edwardian stage; in her later life she became an acting coach in New York and Los Angeles, and she sometimes acted in films. Wilbourn was Hepburn's secretary for many years. She told the Hepburn biographer Scott Berg that "Miss Garbo wanted me to look after her, but then Miss Hepburn stepped in and swept me away." Hepburn said that in the 1920s and 1930s "homosexuality was in the air."[20] Hepburn and Garbo were friends, not lovers.

The 1920s was an era of sexual experimentation, but in the 1930s lesbians and homosexual men were stigmatized as perverts. The conservative reaction to the sexual revolution of the 1920s reached a height in the 1930s, as the Great Depression brought fear and alienation and a search for scapegoats to blame for society's ills. In novels published in the 1930s, lesbians were often portrayed as vampires. Publishers feared censorship from groups such as the New England Watch and Ward Society, established in the nineteenth century, and the National Organization for Decent Literature, founded in 1930. Moreover, censorship of films came to a climax in 1934 with the strict enforcement of the 1930 draconian moral code.

Early in 1933, L. B. Mayer reorganized MGM's production branch after Irving Thalberg suffered a heart attack on Christmas Day 1932, at the age of thirty-three. Shortly after the attack, he went to Europe to recuperate, and he stayed away from Hollywood for nine months. The prediction of his physicians when he was a child that he wouldn't live beyond the age of thirty was not far off the mark: he died in 1937, at the age of thirty-eight.

Mayer had long been jealous of Thalberg's genius at film production, and he disliked Thalberg's demands for salary increases. Mayer used Thalberg's illness as an excuse to take control of MGM's production branch. He appointed four production assistants equal to Thalberg, each of whom was given his own production unit, reporting directly to Mayer. Among the new producers were Walter Wanger and David O. Selznick, the husband of Mayer's daughter Irene. Wanger became the producer for *Queen Christina*, while Selznick was assigned *Anna Karenina*, which Garbo filmed in the spring of 1934.

It was disheartening for Garbo to lose Thalberg, who had guided her career thus far, overseeing production on all her films. And Thalberg's assistant Paul Bern, who often worked on Garbo's films, died mysteriously of a probable suicide in the fall of 1932, inciting a scandal over his sexuality, since he had married Jean Harlow, MGM's sex queen, only several months before. Mayer fired the male homosexuals passing as heterosexual on his roster of actors, including Nils Asther and Ramon Novarro, by refusing to renew their contracts when they came due.[21] This changing of the guard partly explains why L. B. Mayer often intervened in the filming of *Queen Christina*, which he had approved only because of his fear that Garbo might desert MGM and return to Sweden. It also provides a context for Mayer's periodic attempts to discipline Garbo.

When Salka Viertel first met with Thalberg to discuss the screenplay for *Queen Christina*, he told her to pay attention to the relationship between Christina and her lady-in-waiting, Ebba Sparre, because of the surprising success in 1931 in the United States of the German film *Mäd-chen in Uniform*, about homoerotic relationships in a German girls' school. But Mayer didn't share Thalberg's interest in non-heteronormative sexuality; he was homophobic and sympathetic to the conservatives. And the tide was turning away from the free sexuality of the 1920s toward a more conservative stance, which would peak with the anti-communism of the post–World War II years. That movement was especially directed against Hollywood and against homosexuals.

As Garbo began filming *Queen Christina*, she seemed in good spirits.[22] She had returned from her visit to Sweden with a good deal of information about Queen Christina from the Swedish royal archives. She had toured the palaces in which Christina had lived and the places important in her life. Garbo's official MGM biography for 1933 concluded: "The actress showed an enthusiasm [for *Queen Christina*] that she had seldom displayed toward any film project." To reach her dressing room and the sets where she was filming, she strode down MGM's paths, rather than being chauffeured on its roads or walking through the bushes to hide, which were her usual practices. She went over the drafts of the screenplay with Salka Viertel and the other writers assigned to the movie; she spent hours with the set designers and with Adrian, *Queen Christina*'s costume designer.[23]

Garbo's facial features resembled those of Queen Christina, although the monarch was five feet tall and had a hook nose and a shoulder at a strange angle from having been dropped as an infant. Garbo was so determined to make an accurate movie of the queen for the Swedish nation that she wanted to undergo cosmetic surgery on her face to look more like the queen. But her suggestion was quickly rejected, becoming the first of many disappointments for her in making the film. Garbo had the most powerful contract of any Hollywood actor, but L. B. Mayer still intervened. He was a master of disingenuous manipulation and making his position sound like the right one.

Queen Christina was fascinating in her own right.[24] Born in 1626, she was the only child of Gustavus Adolphus, Sweden's sixteenth-century warrior king, to survive past birth. She became queen at the age of six, when her father was killed in battle, although a privy council ruled the country until she assumed the throne at the age of eighteen, in 1644. She was given the classical education reserved for boys, and she was schooled in the arts of kingship. She loved her studies, wanting to master everything known in her day. As an adult, she walked and talked like a man, swore like a soldier, and told off-color jokes.

And she never liked her mother, Maria Eleonora of Brandenburg, where Berlin is located. Maria Eleonora was egocentric, uneducated, and not an affectionate mother. Her mother's deficiencies help explain Christina's identification with men. She had no respect for femininity or female tasks. Her clothing was eccentric: she wore male attire for riding and hunting, and in other situations she mixed male and female garb. Some biographers conclude that she was transgender.

Christina didn't like most women, but she loved Ebba Sparre, one of her ladies-in-waiting, whom she called Belle, the French word for beautiful. She made certain that Sparre was cast as Venus, the goddess of love, in masques and spectacles staged at her court. As an adolescent, Christina was pressured to marry a man—especially her cousin Karl Gustav, to carry on the Vasa line, which passed through her father and then through her as his only direct descendant. But she refused to give up her independence, saying about heterosexual intercourse that she didn't want to be plowed, like the fields of a peasant. In Salka Viertel's screenplay, Christina's privy counselor is appalled by her desire to remain an "old maid," but Christina retorts: "No, I shall remain an unmarried bachelor." "Bachelor" originally meant a wandering knight.

Highly educated for her day, Christina was famed as the "Minerva of the North." She sympathized with *les précieuses*, a group of female French intellectuals who championed women's dignity and deplored male tyranny. Christina wrote to scholars throughout Europe inviting them to come to Sweden to form a Swedish academy akin to the one in France. She had some success. The French philosopher René Descartes joined her group, but he died from pneumonia soon after arriving in Stockholm in the winter. That put a damper on the academy.

Christina was not a democrat, although she sometimes identified with the peasants. She disliked having to obey Sweden's privy council and to deal with the four parliamentary estates (nobles, clerics, merchants, and peasants); she thought of herself as divinely ordained. She was extravagant in funding her academy, in bringing theater and opera troops to Sweden, and in commissioning paintings and other art works. When ruling Sweden, she sold crown lands and created many noble titles to raise money for what her councilors considered extravagances. Those actions of hers angered Swedes so much that after Christina abdicated the throne, a law was passed prohibiting a woman from ruling the country. The law wasn't overturned until the twentieth century.

Salka's screenplay for *Queen Christina* begins with the death of Gustavus Adolphus in battle, and it continues to Christina's abdication in 1654, at the age of twenty-eight, which was Garbo's age when she made the film. Salka's screenplay captured the queen's toughness and majesty and her flirtation and joking, although Salka downplayed Christina's crudeness and caprice.

The Hollywood censors shortened the intimate scene between Christina and Belle written by Salka. In instigating a kiss, Garbo cups Ebba's face in her hands as if to drink from it—a gesture that had become a signature of hers in her love scenes. However, in a private conversation, which Christina overhears, Belle expresses her desire to marry a courtier. Christina, looking sad, tells Belle that she will permit the marriage. In real life, Belle married a nobleman.

Salka overlooked Christina's conversion to Catholicism, which was the major reason for her abdication. Lutheranism in the seventeenth century was harsh; Christina never forgot her childhood terror at hearing a sermon on the Last Judgment. As told in the Bible, on the day the earth ends, Christ will bring all humanity together and send believers to heaven and unbelievers to hell. The sermon was replete with demons and the fires of hell. After this, Christina was attracted to a free-thought sect within Catholicism that stressed rationality and free will. Her conversion allowed her to live in Rome, an imperial city, at the center of baroque culture. When she left Stockholm after abdicating, Christina didn't go to Spain, as the movie implies; she went to Rome.

In Rome, as in Stockholm, the real Christina supported artists and musicians—especially Alessandro Scarlatti, a major baroque composer. She founded an academy in Rome as well as the first opera house in the city. The pope was so enthused by the conversion of a major Protestant monarch to Catholicism that he allowed Christina to live in a palace inside the walls of the Vatican. When she died, he approved her burial in the Holy City.

Salka also omitted from her screenplay Christina's friendship with Cardinal Azzolino, the Vatican secretary of state. Some writers claim that she and Azzolino were lovers. But this was the era of the Catholic Counter-Reformation, when many priests kept their vows of chastity to show the purity of the Catholic faith. Prelates living in luxury had been one of the causes of the Protestant Reformation of the sixteenth century, and the Catholic Church was now trying to bring apostates back to the faith.

Christina's supposed romance with the Spanish grandee Antonio Pimentel de Prado is at the center of Salka's version of Christina's life. L. B. Mayer had demanded that Christina have a heterosexual lover, to conform to the heterosexual plot line that governed Hollywood films. Antonio did exist. The king of Spain sent him as a special envoy to Christina's court, to encourage her to convert to Catholicism. He stayed in Sweden for some time, although there is no evidence of a romance between Christina and him beyond flirtation.

Salka brilliantly constructed the character of Don Antonio, played by John Gilbert in the film. Racism is a subtheme of the movie, as the Swedish nobles insist that Christina marry her cousin, Karl Gustav, blonde and blue-eyed, to preserve the purity of her Swedish blood. With black hair and dark skin, Gilbert represented the Spaniards who had intermarried with Moors from North Africa over the centuries of Moorish occupation of parts of Spain. Having Don Antonio convince Christina that Spain was a place of great artists and writers, with a warm and sunny clime and governed by romance and pleasure, carried an antiracist message at a time of Hitler's growing power in Europe.

The English actor Laurence Olivier, then young and unseasoned, was offered the role of Don Antonio. He came to Hollywood, where he put on a Spanish costume to rehearse a love scene with Garbo. But she didn't warm up to him. She was cold and distant throughout the rehearsal, and he was given his salary and sent home. In fact, he was too young to impersonate Don Antonio, he didn't look Spanish, and he couldn't match Garbo's power. He commented later that he was "nervous and scared of [his] leading lady. I knew that I was lightweight for her and nowhere near her stature."[25]

The English actor Leslie Howard was offered the role of Antonio, but he turned it down because he knew that Garbo had overwhelmed most of her male co-stars and he didn't want that to happen to him. It's probable, as some individuals involved with the making of *Queen Christina* contended, that Garbo had wanted Gilbert from the beginning, and that L. B. Mayer had refused.[26] Bringing Olivier from England and then failing to warm up to him sounds like a complex Garbo maneuver to get her way.

In the film, Garbo is vibrant. Contemporary observers noted that her usual sorrow was absent from her face. The movie magazine writer Larry Reid opined, "She has lost her languorousness and her secret sorrows and is less an exotic automaton."[27] John Gilbert matched Garbo's power with his own brand of confident sensuality, while the sound engineers, aware of his problems with a high-pitched voice, took care to deepen that pitch. He could elicit a romantic response from Garbo, although in the film there is no precise physical love scene between them. By then, Gilbert had married Virginia Bruce, his third wife, and had a newborn baby. Garbo complained to Rouben Mamoulian, the film's director, when Jack became overly romantic. Mamoulian rebuked him, and Gilbert replied to him with a Shakespearean turn of phrase: "Backward, turn backward, O Time, in your flight."

Rouben Mamoulian was the third or fourth choice for director of *Queen Christina*, but his input was crucial to the movie's success. Persuading him to direct the film was a coup; he was one of Hollywood's most innovative directors. Armenian in background, he had studied Konstantin Stanislavski's techniques at the Moscow Art Theatre. As with many individuals in Garbo's life, the Bolshevik Revolution of 1917 lay behind his decision to immigrate to the United States. Coming to the country in 1923, he had soared to fame as a director of operas and Broadway musicals.[28]

Toward the end of filming *Queen Christina*, L. B. Mayer insisted that the movie have a happy ending, with the lovers united. Mamoulian changed Mayer's opinion by persuading him that the greatest romances in Western literature, like *Romeo and Juliet*, end in tragedy. When Mayer

A cross-dressed Christina, with John Gilbert. United Archives GmbH / Alamy Stock Photo

saw the final close-up that ends *Queen Christina*, with its mixture of triumph and sadness, he let Mamoulian's decision stand. Garbo stated that, as always, Salka "worked on the script to a saturation point."[29]

Christina is as tough as the men in the film. She delivers speeches about wanting to be independent, to end the country's warfare, and to live her life on her own terms, not as a symbol of national power. Salka and Garbo believed in these ideas; they made Christina a modern woman. Garbo eliminated the half-lidded eyes, come-hither looks, and hip-swinging gait she had affected to look like a siren in earlier films. In *Queen Christina* she projected her real self: her awkward gait and masculine stride; her bulky, big-boned body.

Much of the movie takes place in the interior of Christina's castle, which is dark and gloomy. But the bedroom in an inn, where Christina and Antonio spend three days and nights together because a raging snowstorm prevents travel, is white and bright. A famous scene in *Queen Christina* occurs in that bedroom after it is made clear that Christina and Antonio have spent their three days and nights together engaged in lovemaking. The sex is implied in the film. That scene, brilliant in conception, is more sensual than actual lovemaking would have been.

The scene begins with Christina eating grapes on the floor, lying on her back, holding the grapes sensually above her head. She then rises and slowly walks around the room, touching objects—a pillow on the bed; a bedpost, which she strokes like a lover; a spinning wheel; the mantel of the fireplace. At the same time, she delivers a monologue about needing to engrave these objects in her memory, to be able to relive in retrospect her time in that room. During her monologue, Gilbert as Antonio lounges on the floor, watching her, looking sensual and satiated.

In a classic exercise in method acting in which an actor shows emotion in terms of an object, Garbo does the touching and talking, reaching a climax when she states that she feels like God must have felt after creating the world and its creatures. Some scholars have argued that this scene has a lesbian subtext because Garbo is in control, but I think that Christina is ecstatic about the sex she has had with Antonio and that she talks about her need to remember the objects in the room because at that point in the film she expects that she will return to the throne and marry her cousin. Her abdication is a possibility throughout much of the film, but she doesn't make the final decision to renounce the throne and go off with Antonio until near the end of the movie.

In the seventeenth century it was customary for male travelers, even if strangers, to sleep in the same bed. The verbal byplay between Christina and Antonio while undressing before getting into bed is a gender-crossing tease, playing with the reality that only Garbo and the audience know that she is a woman. Gilbert brilliantly portrays a seventeenth-century nobleman. He looks like the portraits of such individuals in museums; he has a feminine, sensual air associated with southern European men at the time. The Swedish nobles in the movie are highly masculine, even warlike. But in his walk, talk, and movements, Antonio has feminine qualities, and that is central to his appeal.

The film scholar Jane Gaines brilliantly evaluated Garbo's costumes in *Queen Christina* as revealing "the unstable nature of gender and sexual

identity." Adrian designed them. In the film, Garbo wears male clothing when posing as a courtier or riding a horse. In ritual scenes in the
throne room, her clothes are more feminine, and they become even
more so after she and Antonio declare their love for each other. Like the
real Christina, at her abdication, she wears a white gown and, again like
Christina, she takes the crown off her head herself—a symbol of her
authority even as her reign ends. She wears male clothing to ride on
horseback to the port where she is to meet Antonio to sail to Spain.

But on his way to the ship, Antonio is wounded in a duel with a Swedish courtier who had been a lover of Christina's, and he dies in her arms
as he lies on the deck of the ship. She is now wearing a female version of
a male cloak, as she had expected to go with Antonio to Spain. Stunned
that Antonio is dead, Garbo as Christina grieves for a few minutes,
deeply affected, but she controls herself and moves on.

She is Christina, always the queen, but now free from patriarchal control. She is headed for Spain, anticipating the adventures that lie ahead.
She gets up and moves to the front of the ship, with the wind blowing
through her hair and her eyes fixed on the horizon. She stands there, leaning on the carved bow of the ship, looking like the ship's figurehead, the
female figure carved out of wood and placed at the bow of ships, a goddess to keep the ships, their crews, and their passengers from harm.

Rouben Mamoulian ended the film with one of the most celebrated
close-ups in films. When Garbo asked him what expression she should
show on her face as she stands at the bow of the ship, he told her to keep
her face blank, so that audience members themselves could decide what
she was feeling. She does not blink as the camera begins at a distance
and slowly moves close to her face. But as in so many of her close-ups, as
well as the 1928 photo of her taken by Edward Steichen, I think that she
registers subtle expressions on her face: elegance and earthiness, sadness and spirituality, and male and female.

The writer Ida Zeitland proposed that Garbo's face in the close-up that
ends *Queen Christina* embodied ideal beauty. Her face transcended her
own era to become "the face that poets sing about, the face of Helen and
Iseult and the Blessed Damozel . . . the face of all fabled beauty." Helen in
Zeitland's tribute referred to Helen of Troy; Iseult dies for love in the
medieval romance Tristan and Iseult (or Isolde). The Blessed Damozel

is the central figure in Dante Gabriel Rossetti's poem "The Blessed Damozel." Looking down from heaven, the Damozel promises both spiritual redemption and sexual freedom to the lover she addresses.[30]

But Zeitland was not the only writer to see eternity in Garbo's face. By 1933, when *Queen Christina* was filmed, writers throughout Europe and the United States were proclaiming that Garbo was the world's most beautiful woman. Yet, Garbo's ever-present demon, the demon of depression, was lying in wait, ready to strike, at the first sign of unhappiness on Garbo's part. Behind it were the chronic illnesses from which Garbo suffered, and which, in a supreme effort of will, she kept under control.

Garbo close up. PictureLux / The Hollywood Archive / Alamy Stock Photo

# 11

## *Denouement*

$B$ Y 1930, GARBO was widely acclaimed as the world's most beautiful woman. During that year, the British fashion expert James Laver saw many Garbo imitators on the streets of London, Paris, and New York. "No one who studies the fashion magazines or even takes a walk in the streets could fail to recognize her influence," Laver asserted. "She has imposed her look with extraordinary completeness." The fan magazine journalist Mary Alcorn wrote in 1932, "A large crop of today's stars are imitations of Greta Garbo. You have to read the captions to tell one from another."[1]

That year, *Vanity Fair* published "before Garbo" and "after Garbo" portraits of the major Hollywood stars Joan Crawford, Marlene Dietrich, Katharine Hepburn, and others. In the "before" photos they are heavily made up and look coquettish, while in the "after" photos they have high cheekbones, sunken cheeks, and less makeup, looking like Garbo. "Even their expressions [in the *Vanity Fair* photos]," wrote Garbo biographer John Bainbridge, "are uniformly languorous and inscrutable, as if they are brooding over some secret sorrow."[2] That melancholy expression was derived from Garbo; it would become a standard feature of the Hollywood glamour portraits of the 1930s

Was Garbo the source of the tall, elegant woman who by 1930 had become the female beauty ideal? She contributed to its genesis, but the looks of other female figures played a role—like the tall art deco woman and the tall mannequin. In addition, young women of a new generation wanted to look different from their flapper elders. As flapper skirts became ever shorter, women finally had to cover their knees when they sat down, because their short skirts would ride up, embarrassing them.[3] They wanted a change.

Many couturiers had never liked the flapper style because it was easily copied, decreasing their sales, and they preferred to design for older women, their traditional clients, not for adolescents.[4] The Great Depression, which reached an early peak in 1932, also encouraged a mature look for women, now regarded by many as defenders of the home in a time of despair. In 1920 the tall, elegant woman of the 1890s, embodied by the Gibson girl, was antique, but by 1930 she had become interesting again. The wheel of fashion was slowly turning, combining a fashion from the past with an impulse from the present.

How did Garbo react to her position as the world's most beautiful woman? She read the movie magazines, and she was close to Adrian, who kept contemporary fashions in mind when he designed costumes. She must have known about her position. But she still suffered from her chronic ailments: a lack of hydrochloric acid, anemia and anorexia, bipolarity, and frequent bronchial complaints related to her chain-smoking. And her ovarian inflammation flared up during the making of both *Queen Christina* and *Camille*. She showed great self-control in keeping to the production schedules for her films. The writers of those production schedules now took Garbo's physical problems into account in creating them.[5]

The tough female protagonist in Hollywood pre-Code films paralleled the "new woman" of fashion. The fan magazine journalist Ruth Biery called the new film heroine a "shady dame" with "a mysterious allure," which Biery called "glamour," using a word now associated with Garbo. According to Biery, the "shady dame" also had the hard-headed attributes of men and some of their physical characteristics—such as tall, narrow-hipped, broad-shouldered bodies. "The shady dame can take care of herself," wrote Biery. "She has a man's viewpoint and a man's ability to deal with brutal situations." Biery contended that the figure was a new sex and that Garbo had originated it.[6]

Articles on "shady dames" segued into articles on Garbo's influence on women, especially during the filming and distribution of *Queen Christina*. It wasn't hard to figure out that the movie was as much about Garbo as about the queen, given the monarch's cross-dressing, dislike of being an object, and desire to be independent—all characteristic of Garbo, who told screenwriter Sam Behrman that Christina was closer to her own persona than any other character she had played in films.[7]

In May 1934 the journalist Gretchen Colnik wrote that Garbo had appeared when women were looking for a liberated woman with whom to identify—after women's suffrage had been achieved and the sexual revolution was underway. "For almost ten years she [Garbo] has dominated the female sex," stated Colnik. "She set the hair styles for the long bob, the beret, and pill box hats—and showed women how to wear mannish styles." The reporter Ruth Rankin regarded *Queen Christina* as the culmination of the feminist movement in the United States. Women, she wrote, had achieved a gender revolution. "They talked about 'the single standard,' organized clubs, battled their way into the professions and politics." Now Garbo was impersonating the reformist queen of a major nation, honoring women's triumph in making their voices heard.[8]

During the filming of *Queen Christina*, Garbo retained the enthusiasm in her acting that she had shown at the beginning, but she lost it in her private life. Her emotions began to go up and down. When Ruby Neely, her hairdresser, was killed in an automobile accident, Garbo broke down and cried. Garbo and Neely, called Billie by her friends, had been close; together they had created Garbo's hairstyles for many of her films.

To succeed Billie, Garbo chose Sydney Guilaroff, who had recently joined MGM's hairdressing staff, eventually designing hairstyles for most of MGM's female stars.[9] Guilaroff was a closeted homosexual who never married but did adopt two children, whom he raised. He became another "beard" for Garbo. In his autobiography he claimed that they had been lovers, but as with Wilhelm Sörenson and Nils Asther, that was unlikely.[10]

During the late summer of 1933, as filming began on *Queen Christina*, Mercedes de Acosta's face was badly damaged in an automobile accident, although she underwent cosmetic surgery to repair it. By late fall, Garbo again had Mercedes do odd jobs for her, including finding a house for her to rent. Mercedes wrote to Marlene Dietrich, now a friend, not a lover, that Garbo was treating her with loving kindness again.[11]

But Mercedes became angry when she learned that Garbo was dating Rouben Mamoulian, *Queen Christina*'s director. Mercedes paced in front of Garbo's house on one occasion when Mamoulian appeared with his car to pick up Garbo. After Garbo got into the car, she crouched on the floor by the front seat so that Mercedes wouldn't see her as they drove out the driveway. Mamoulian found Garbo's behavior ridiculous; he made her sit on the seat. Mercedes seemed to regard Mamoulian as a rival for Garbo's affection. Now back in Garbo's good graces, Mercedes tried to take control.[12]

Garbo wrote depressed letters to Hörke Wachtmeister, now her best friend in Sweden. At the end of August, she wrote that she was suffering from severe insomnia. Several weeks later, she wrote that everything had gone wrong in the filming of *Queen Christina*. She decided that it was impossible to achieve anything beyond the ordinary in Hollywood, and that making *Queen Christina* was the last time she was going to try.[13] She kept to this decision during her remaining years at MGM.

In January 1934, several weeks after *Queen Christina* was released, Garbo wrote to Hörke that she had been in bed for three weeks. She complained about John Gilbert, calling him "a little Spaniard." For a long time, she had believed that Christina abdicated the throne because she was tired of performing the ceremonial duties of a queen and wanted to be free; she couldn't believe that Christina had abdicated because she loved "a little Spaniard." But now she decided that Christina's love for Antonio was, in fact, the reason for her abdication. Because of Gilbert's drinking, he missed filming sessions, and Garbo had to cover for him, which she resented. Her complaints about the film broadened into discontent with her life. In her January letter to Hörke she expressed a standard grievance: because she was living in exile from Sweden to make money, she was a prostitute.[14]

Garbo's acting in *Queen Christina* is impressive, especially given the pain from her ovarian and pelvic inflammations that she endured during its filming. But Garbo was indomitable. As always, she was kind and patient with the film's crew and the other cast members. But critics realized that Garbo was a different person in this film. In the 1930s, Mary Cass Canfield had criticized Garbo for sleepwalking through her films. But Canfield was entranced by Garbo's acting in *Queen Christina*. She wrote an open letter of congratulations to Garbo, which was published in *Theatre Arts Magazine*. Garbo's performance as the queen conveyed, according to Canfield, "a symbolism touched with poetry, which had never before appeared in your work." Garbo "had soared into the blue like some liberated bird." Canfield concluded, "It seems that any producer would have been inspired to use you in historical, poetic, or legendary plays. Why not cast you as Lady Macbeth or Joan of Arc?"[15]

Reactions to the film weren't all positive. Sales of feminine versions of Garbo's masculine clothing in the film, marketed in the cinema shops of department stores, were weak. After that, MGM marketed only Garbo's headgear from her films, which were modest in price due to technical innovations in the making of hats.[16] Garbo's standing in the polls conducted by movie theater owners of their audiences dropped from fifteen in 1933 to thirty-four in 1934. This negative standing helped L. B. Mayer convince Salka and Garbo that *Queen Christina* had been a failure—and to emphasize the point, he changed the books on the film, reducing its financial grosses.

The Studio Relations Committee (SRC) objected to two scenes in *Queen Christina*. The first was the scene in which Christina kisses Ebba Sparrow on the lips; the second was the scene in which Garbo and Gilbert are in the bedroom in the inn and Garbo walks around the room sensually touching objects in the room. The censorship board wanted these scenes cut from the film.

But Walter Wanger, *Queen Christina*'s producer, paid no attention to the SRC's ruling. Instead, he invoked the clause in the 1930 production code which assigned a final decision on a film's morality to an ad hoc committee of three producers. Wanger assembled such a committee and, predictably, its members approved *Queen Christina*. Then, without obtaining the required seal of approval from the SRC, he released the film. That action angered the censors. The film—and Wanger's insolence—gave them a reason to end the three-person appeals committee and to enforce the draconian 1930 code.[17]

As a desire for stricter morality appeared among Catholics and swept other constituencies, in January 1934 Catholic leaders founded the Legion of Decency to mobilize boycotts of the movies they judged immoral. By the summer, ticket sales in the Midwest for movies the Legion denounced were plummeting. The SRC was turned into the Production Code Committee (PCC), with a majority of Catholic members and with the devout Joseph Breen as its head. Garbo's older films were still playing in theaters around the United States, but Breen withdrew them from circulation, except for *Grand Hotel* and *Mata Hari*, which was reedited and severely cut. Even *Queen Christina* was no longer shown.[18] It was a blow for Garbo, whose sense of failure was always strong.

Rejecting the lives of Isadora Duncan and Joan of Arc as subjects for her next film, Garbo returned to her old formula of sex and spirituality, choosing *The Painted Veil*, a W. Somerset Maugham novel, as the basis for her next film, even though it resembled *Wild Orchids*, which Garbo had made in late 1928. The "veil" in the title referred to peoples' tendency to disregard reality and view life through a veil of illusions. As in many of her films, Garbo would be involved in a triangle with two men; the process of choosing between them would allow her to show indecision and suffering.

In *The Painted Veil*, Garbo plays Katrina, a young Austrian woman craving adventure. She marries an idealistic older scientist who is going to China to fight a cholera epidemic, and she accompanies him there. In pursuit of his ideals, the doctor neglects his new wife, just as Lewis Stone, the older husband in *Wild Orchids*, neglected his young wife. Falling for a dashing (and untrustworthy) diplomat, Garbo / Katrina has an affair with him. When the diplomat refuses to marry her, she travels with her husband to the Chinese interior, where the epidemic is raging. Once there, she realizes the value of her husband's work and joins a group of nuns who are nursing sick children, rekindling her love for her spouse. As so often in her films, she wears a dress that looks like a nun's habit. When her husband is badly hurt by a villager angry that the scientist has torched his village to stop the epidemic from spreading, Garbo nurses him. And she rejects the diplomat who now wants to marry her.

Why Garbo approved of *The Painted Veil* as the basis for a film of hers is perplexing, but she knew it wouldn't demand much innovative acting from her, and after *Queen Christina*, she was no longer interested in innovation. She was also in a rush to leave Hollywood and go to Sweden, partly because she always felt better in Sweden and also because she hoped to have an operation there to relieve her ovarian inflammation. Such procedures were easier to hide in Sweden than in Los Angeles, where journalists had informants in hospitals.

*The Painted Veil* was a failure. Audiences laughed at some of Adrian's costumes with Asian touches. The SRC forbade any physical contact in the romantic scenes, making them implausible. Salka Viertel, a writer on the film, chiefly remembered that the producer had insisted that a scene contain a statue of Confucius, the Chinese sage, while mistakenly calling him Vesuvius—the name of the deadly volcano near Naples in Italy responsible for the destruction of the Roman city of Pompei. In a letter to Berthold she claimed that Garbo was responsible for the film's failure: "The mystery image just isn't working any more," she added. Garbo called the movie a "mess."[19]

Garbo spent her time off screen with actor George Brent, who played the diplomat in the film. Like many of Garbo's companions in real life, he was offbeat. A native of Ireland, he had played roles in productions at Dublin's famed Abbey Theatre, and he had fought for Irish independence from Britain as a member of the Irish Republican Army. Threatened with arrest, he fled to the United States and went to Hollywood, where he reestablished his acting career. Like Garbo, he was a loner who went to bed early and didn't attend parties, although he was a womanizer who liked to be married. His five wives included the featured film actresses Ruth Chatterton and Ann Sheridan. He owned a secluded home in the San Fernando Valley, which at that time contained mostly orange groves and chicken farms, unlike the crowded suburban metropolis of today. Garbo and he hiked, swam, played tennis, and, it is alleged, boxed against each other. Brent told friends that he and Garbo were going to be married, but as with her other male companions who thought she was going to marry them, that never happened.[20]

During the making of *Queen Christina* her ovarian inflammation flared up. Hörke Wachtmeister's daughter Gunnila, who was also close to Garbo, told the journalist Sven Broman that when Garbo complained of fatigue in her letters to her mother, which she often did, the fatigue was caused by her ovarian inflammation. Gunnila had known Garbo since her childhood; she considered the Swedish star to be part of her family. Garbo had played with her when she was a child, and she had gone swimming and skiing with Gunnila and her parents. Gunnila called Garbo "Auntie Greta."

Gunnila trusted Sven Broman, who was a well-known Stockholm journalist. When he decided to write about Garbo, he interviewed people who had known her, and he found primary sources about her. From that research, he wrote *The Divine Garbo*, a very positive biography. When Garbo became angry with him for writing that book, in the summers of 1957 and 1958 he went to Klosters, in Switzerland, where Garbo spent the summers, and he secured an introduction to her. He spoke Swedish, which she enjoyed, and he flattered her, which she also liked. Learning that she suffered from chronic bronchitis, he recommended an inhaler to her, which no doctor had yet suggested. She secured one, and it improved her breathing. He became a walking companion of hers, which was Garbo's sign that she trusted him. During the next twenty years, he saw her in New York and in Europe

After Garbo died, Gunnila wanted the letters Garbo had written to her mother to be published, to show Garbo's dedication to Sweden, her ambivalent feelings about Hollywood, the extent of her illnesses, and the role the Wachtmeister family had played in her life. Broman published the letters in his two later books on Garbo, *Conversations with Garbo* and *Garbo on Garbo*. Without Gunnila Wachtmeister and Sven Broman, the full extent of Garbo's illnesses and her courage in dealing with them would never have been known.

Another proof of Garbo's internal problem, which she tried to conceal, can be found in a letter she wrote in November 1935 to Salka Viertel, still her acting coach and close friend. Garbo was in Sweden at the time. She told Viertel that her ovarian inflammation had returned. But she had no lover, so she supposed her trouble stemmed from wrongs done to her in the past—which I read as a guarded reference to her internal inflammations, the result of gonorrhea contracted during sex. That explains her curious reference to having no lover.[21] MGM publicists countered rumors that she was gravely ill by issuing a press release stating that she had a bad cold. While in Sweden that winter, she had a gynecological operation, probably to try to relieve the inflammation.

In the early 1930s, Mae West appeared in Hollywood. Playing a comic voluptuous sex queen from the 1890s, with large breasts and hips, she had a gift for double entendres and suggestive language. She was signed by Paramount in 1932, and her popularity saved the studio from bankruptcy. The journalist Brian Jay Chapman thought that she posed a threat to Garbo because West's type of comedy signaled a change in public taste. Chapman compared West to President Franklin Roosevelt. Like Roosevelt, according to Chapman, West was warm and earthy. The public was coping with the Great Depression, and that's what they wanted, not Garbo's melancholy. Chapman maintained that MGM received many letters declaring that Garbo should become livelier and less gloomy.[22]

Chapman was probably correct, but by 1933, the SRC was censoring West's subtle sexy humor. Moreover, Jean Harlow, MGM's new sex icon, went beyond Garbo in showing her body, while adding a comic element to her characterizations, as did the many actresses who played "fast-talking dames."[23] Shirley Temple, who was eight years old when she rose to stardom in 1935, was able to solve adult problems in her films when adults gave up. She personified American innocence in contrast to European decadence—an old trope in comparisons of the two continents. Temple was followed by L. B. Mayer's many child actors, including Judy Garland and Mickey Rooney. They added another challenge for Garbo.

The Depression brought a celebration of America's mythic past, rooted in innocence and virtue in conquering a continent and establishing a democracy, and forgetting the devastation to the Native American populations in that conquest. The all-American girl and the "girl next door" rose to prominence, a backdrop to the rise of Marilyn Monroe in the 1950s. Audiences could be fickle, always looking for new faces. Garbo's turn to comedy didn't occur for four more years, since she still brought large receipts to MGM, ranking below only Clark Gable in the amount of money she generated for the studio—which was a strong argument against changing her screen image. Most of her box office receipts, however, came from Europe.

From *Queen Christina* on, Garbo gave Salka Viertel control over her career. She had abandoned her dreams of reforming Hollywood or even herself, and she trusted Salka completely, which may have been unwise. Salka helped Garbo cope with her shyness, but her choices for Garbo's films and the acting style she promoted are questionable. Salka was still frustrated at having to give up her acting career to support her family, and she was still jealous of Garbo, although she showed these feelings only in her diary and in her letters to her husband, Berthold.

Once *The Painted Veil* wrapped, Salka decided that Garbo should play Anna Karenina in a sound film version of Tolstoy's novel *Anna Karenina*—a role Garbo had played seven years earlier in the silent movie *Love*. Salka preferred romantic dramas for Garbo, and she wanted to keep Garbo away from Mercedes de Acosta. Thalberg and Garbo had liked Mercedes's script for *Joan of Arc*, but according to Garbo, L. B. Mayer rejected it.

David O. Selznick, Irene Mayer's husband, was slated to produce *Anna Karenina*, but he was ambivalent about the project; he thought that Garbo had played too many heavy dramatic roles and she shouldn't do another one. In early January, he sent Salka Viertel to La Quinta, the resort near Palm Springs where Garbo was resting, with a letter from him to Garbo, arguing against her playing Anna Karenina. Viertel delivered the letter, but she may have argued against Selznick's proposal. Gifted at debate, Viertel was able to produce a winning argument in almost any situation. Selznick's letter to Garbo read: "We have lost our enthusiasm for a production of *Anna Karenina*. I personally am waiting to see you in a smart, modern picture, and to do a heavy Russian drama on the heels of so many ponderous, similar films . . . would prove to be a mistake."[24]

Selznick continued by suggesting that Garbo star in a film version of Philip Barry's play *Dark Victory*, the story of a woman's struggle with despair as she goes blind from a brain tumor. The play is a female tear-jerker, but its setting is contemporary, and its female protagonist is a modern woman. Bette Davis, under contract to Warner Brothers, played the role in a film version several years later, to great acclaim. Such films wallow in women's supposed masochism, but the women in them often exhibit power and determination.

Salka's argument against scrapping *Anna Karenina* prevailed. She had already begun writing its screenplay, and, like Garbo, she needed money. Moreover, Salka wanted to write films for European audiences. In her autobiography, she called Europe "her longed-for holy ground."[25] Her husband moved to Germany in 1931, but she remained in Hollywood to provide an income for them and their poverty-stricken relatives in Europe. Berthold periodically visited Salka and their family in Santa Monica, and their marriage managed to survive, although both had other partners. They didn't divorce until 1947. Salka's fame in Europe increased exponentially with her portrayal of the prostitute Marthy Owen in the German version of *Anna Christie* in 1930 and with participating in writing Garbo's screenplays.

Given her influence over Garbo, Salka chose several historical dramas as the bases for her next films. Through Garbo, she could play the sorts of roles she had once played in Berlin.[26] Only in letters to Berthold did she reveal her anger at Garbo's selfishness and her own difficulties with MGM. She rarely appeared on a Garbo set, which obfuscated her relationship with the Swedish star. As Stiller often had, Salka coached Garbo before filming began. But it's incorrect to see Salka as a version of Marilyn Monroe's coach Paula Strasberg, who was often on the set with Monroe. Both Salka and Garbo were devoted to promoting the idea that Garbo's acting was divinely inspired.

As early as 1934, Salka stated that she didn't want to be a "Garbo specialist" any longer. But she needed the large salary she was paid by MGM, and she had been typecast in that category. Salka remained a Garbo specialist throughout her career at MGM. Salka's letters to Berthold suggest that she wanted to be known for her humanitarian drive to help others. That worthy motive is evident in her salon, her leadership of refugee and anti-Nazi organizations, her support for struggling young actors, and her ability to make and sustain friendships. She created the legend that she was a secular saint—whether on purpose or as a byproduct of her activities. The legend is true, except for her treatment of Garbo and Mercedes.

Mercedes argued that Garbo shouldn't be cast in roles as a grand dame but rather in ones in which she was close to nature and didn't wear glitzy costumes.[27] Mercedes was obsessed with Garbo's spirituality and her love of nature, and she wanted her to play saints like Joan of Arc and even Francis of Assisi. In the end, Garbo didn't play such roles, although Salka and Garbo re-created her as a secular goddess. The film critic Alastair Cooke thought that Garbo played her last historical figures—Anna Karenina, Camille, and Marie Walewska—"with a sort of amused grandeur." The plots were "high hokum," according to Cooke, but Garbo was "a tolerant goddess" who "wraps everybody in the film in a protective tenderness."[28]

Garbo's 1934 *Anna Karenina* followed the Tolstoy novel more closely than did *Love*, her silent film version of the novel. Whereas *Love* had been set in contemporary times, the remake was set in the 1870s, which was Tolstoy's original setting. Adrian dressed the female characters in late Victorian style, with straight fronts on long dresses, tight-laced corsets, and long bustles on their buttocks. The Production Code Committee heavily censored the film, requiring Garbo to be gloomy throughout it, foreshadowing her suicide at its end when her lover deserts her and demonstrating without a doubt that adultery, like crime, doesn't pay.

Basil Rathbone played Anna's husband in the film. Tall and stern, with a stylized English accent, he later became renowned for playing Sherlock Holmes, the famous British fictional detective. Fredric March, reputed to be one of the most versatile actors in Hollywood, played Vronsky, Anna's lover, although he had to be ordered to play the role; he was tired of playing in period dramas. As Anna's husband, Rathbone was menacing and dull, and as Vronsky March was unconvincing. Their acting was so weak that Garbo spent most of her time when not filming in her dressing room, talking with Constance Collier, the famed Edwardian actress, who played a supporting role in the film. Collier was a regular at Salka's salon and Cukor's parties.

Garbo followed *Anna Karenina* with two more melodramas, in a repeat of having followed *Anna Christie* with a series of melodramas. The ones after *Anna Karenina* began with *Camille*, which was based on the Alexandre Dumas *fils* play of 1850, *La Dame aux camélias*, about a courtesan suffering from tuberculosis who dies in the arms of her lover. After *Camille* came *Conquest*, about the romance between Napoleon Bonaparte and the Polish countess Marie Walewska. This film was released in Europe as *Marie Walewska*, but in the United States it was called *Conquest*

Garbo in *Anna Karenina* (1935). Mashester Movie Archive / Alamy Stock Photo

because its producers feared that Americans had never heard of the Polish countess.

Garbo played the same character in all three films: a woman involved in an ill-fated love who either dies or is deserted by her lover. In *Anna Karenina*, she kills herself when she sees her lover with another woman.

In *Camille* she dies from tuberculosis. In *Conquest*, Napoleon deserts Marie Walewska to marry an Austrian princess, even though Marie has borne him a child.

*Anna Karenina* and *Camille* were both successes. Garbo won the award for best actress given by the New York Film Critics for her performances in both films, and the Venice Film Festival judged *Anna Karenina* the best film of 1936. But *Marie Walewska* was a failure; it's surprising that Garbo agreed to make it. Salka probably chose it because she identified with Poland as her homeland. But when Garbo was in Paris, she often visited Les Invalides, the huge complex that contains Napoleon's tomb. Born to a working-class family, he had risen through the ranks of the army to conquer Europe. Garbo identified with him.

Camille had long been a favorite role of dramatic actresses. Both Sarah Bernhardt and Eleonora Duse, the great tragediennes of the late nineteenth and early twentieth centuries, had played the role, but Garbo's acting in the role was judged to be superior to both of theirs. George Cukor directed the film. He was homosexual and considered a "woman's director," largely because actresses felt safe with him. Unlike many directors, he wouldn't try to seduce them.[29] When he first met Garbo, he wrote to the screenwriter Hugh Walpole that he didn't like her; he found her "arty and rather pretentious." He continued, "I think lesbians—real lesbians—are a little heavy in the hand. . . . They are so god-damned noble, simple, and splendid."[30] He thought that Garbo was lesbian; he must not have known yet about her involvements with men. To have elicited such a negative reaction from Cukor, Garbo must have assumed her diva persona, haughty and regal. But he and Garbo soon became friends. He included her in his Sunday brunches, along with Katharine Hepburn, Constance Collier, Lilyan Tashman, and other homosexual and bisexual actors.

Garbo's acting in *Camille* isn't notably different from her acting in her previous films, although it is amplified and modulated because she liked the role and gave it added depth. Still, the journalist Don Herold of *Commonwealth* charged that in the film, she magnified love "to a pathological importance. She is sex on a high horse."[31] Moreover, *Camille* seems like a remake of *Inspiration*, Garbo's 1931 silent movie about a Paris courtesan who gives up her young male lover to a younger woman. Hollywood jokesters had called *Inspiration* "*Camille* without a cough," referring to the similarity between the two dramas, except that in *Camille* the heroine suffers from tuberculosis and coughs a lot.

Both movies contain scenes in which an older male relative of the young male lover persuades Garbo's courtesan character to acknowledge the burden she will be on her young lover and to give him up. In both films, the actor who plays the young lover isn't especially attractive; in *Camille*, Robert Taylor, who plays Armand, has a beautiful face, but he looks and acts like a tailor's dummy. In both films, an older male friend of Garbo's is more interesting than the younger man. And in both movies, Garbo's courtesan has a circle of friends who are boisterous and crude, providing a backdrop that makes her seem charming and virtuous, covering the reality that she is engaged in selling her body—thereby satisfying the censors.

Garbo felt revived by the success of *Camille*, and she managed to get through *Conquest*, her next film. After two years of development, involving seventeen screenwriters, the script for *Conquest* still wasn't finished when production began on the film. Filming lasted for over six months and exhausted everyone involved in it. Garbo was absent during eighteen days of filming; the pain from her ovarian and pelvic inflammations had reappeared. Several million dollars were spent on *Conquest*; it was the most expensive MGM film since *Ben Hur* in 1925.

The French actor Charles Boyer, suave and slightly feminine, with a sensual voice, often played French lovers in American films. He was short, which was a requirement for playing Napoleon, famed for his short stature. But Boyer played Napoleon in *Conquest* as egocentric, curt, and dismissive, another weak lover for the cool but emotional Garbo. Why she remains obsessed with him after he has deserted her to marry an Austrian princess is hard to comprehend.

*Conquest* was a critical and commercial failure. Part of the problem was that Irving Thalberg wasn't there, with his ability at reediting films; he had died from his heart ailment at the age of thirty-seven during the last month of filming *Camille*, in September 1936. At this point, Cecil Beaton was both harsh and insightful about Garbo's career: "She believed in the part of Queen Christina and was roused from her apathy with the result that we saw Garbo not as a phantom but as a real and noble character. [But] during the years that followed we began to wonder why this enigma with her romantic ideas and spiritual thoughts had made no more efforts to break the fetters she professed to despise."[32]

In using the word "fetters," Beaton expressed Garbo's belief that MGM had imprisoned her in roles as a prostitute and an adulteress. Beaton knew that she made these films because she needed money to be financially independent, and after *Queen Christina* she was convinced that innovative films couldn't be made in Hollywood. Despite her contractual control over her films, she did what Salka and the studio wanted. She rarely again mustered the strength she had shown in fighting for her new woman films and for *Queen Christina*.

The feminist literary scholar Betsy Erkkila concluded that Garbo's four films after *Queen Christina*—*The Painted Veil*, *Anna Karenina*, *Camille*, and *Conquest*—"all re-inscribe the patriarchal myth of female self-sacrifice in the service of a man."[33] Yet, her power as an actress undergirds all of them; many critics praised her acting in *Camille* as a tour de force.

In her 1935 to 1936 visit to Sweden after finishing *Anna Karenina*, the "frail" Garbo, to use Sven Broman's description of that part of her persona, spent much time in bed, suffering from gynecological complaints. It's possible that she had an operation to try to end her internal inflammation, which had flared up during the making of *Queen Christina*, causing her the pain she wrote about in her letters to Hörke Wachtmeister. On the other hand, Broman's "strong" Garbo hiked, swam, and played tennis during the summer and skated and skiied during the winter.

In October 1935, Mercedes de Acosta appeared in Stockholm, after Garbo jokingly invited her to visit her there. Baffled by what to do with Mercedes, Greta took her to the Stockholm Zoo. They also went to a special Christmas celebration at Tistad with the Wachtmeisters. There was a decorated tree, gifts, candles, and a typical Swedish Christmas smorgasbord dinner. Even though it was several months until Christmas, Garbo had so often described the Swedish Christmas celebration to Mercedes that she wanted to participate in one. At the end of this visit, Garbo told Mercedes not to write her again which Mercedes disregarded. She was a clever manipulator, obsessed with Garbo, while Garbo needed her to run errands.

In December 1935, she and Noël Coward, who was in Stockholm, played a joke on the press by fabricating a romance between the two of them. There was no romance, only a friendship, but Coward made Garbo go to restaurants, plays, and parties with him. Such coercion was typical of Garbo's friends, many of whom were baffled by her refusal to go to public places that seemed safe to them.

In January 1936 John Gilbert died at the age of thirty-nine. Garbo mourned his death, but she didn't break down. She hadn't seen him since they had co-starred in *Queen Christina* three years previously, and since then, Marlene Dietrich had taken him over, both as a dependent and a lover. Dietrich nobly tried to stop his drinking and revive his career, but she was too late. He died of a heart attack. To the end, he mourned losing Garbo.

On her visit to Sweden in 1935 to 1936, Garbo looked for an isolated estate to buy within driving distance of Stockholm and Tistad. She wanted to realize her dream of living like the Wachtmeisters. She found a property with a thousand acres of land, a working farm, stands of forest, several small lakes, and a sixteenth-century manor house.[34] She bought it in September 1936, with the Wachtmeisters serving as intermediaries. At the time, she was making *Camille* in Hollywood and working on preproduction for *Conquest*, but she went ahead with buying her estate, called Härby Gar. She installed her brother, Sven, as the estate's manager and persuaded her mother to move there. But Sven was a weak manager; he failed at this task, as he had at others, including acting in the movies under the name "Sven Garbo." Yet, he redeemed himself when he moved to Santa Fe with his family and became a successful landscape and portrait painter. Garbo visited him in Santa Fe on her trips between New York and Hollywood.

The failure of *Conquest* didn't defeat Garbo. During its filming and for six months after its completion, she was involved with Leopold Stokowski, the renowned conductor of the Philadelphia Philharmonic Orchestra. Stokowski played a major role in making classical music popular in the United States. With a shock of white hair, a sculpted face, and a dramatic style, both in conducting and in his life, Stokowski was attractive to women. His biographer calls him "a male sex symbol." Self-centered, with a veneer of European sophistication, he had intense, brief affairs with women. A showman, like several of Garbo's lovers, he made himself into a celebrity, sometimes expanding on the truth of his life, such as calling himself a Hapsburg when actually he came from a poor family in East London.

He also believed in free love. His second wife, Evangeline, an airplane pilot, asserted that both she and Stoki (his nickname) believed that "true love expresses itself through one's concern for the other's happiness—not one's own. That's how individual love merges with universal love." [35] That was a free love principle. Stoki was devoted to health foods, exercising, yoga, nudity, and Eastern religions—all Garbo interests—and he had decided to seduce Garbo before he met her.

Stokowski began their affair when he came to Hollywood to make a movie. He persuaded Anita Loos, an old friend, to hold a lunch at her house, to which he, Garbo, and several others were invited. He wasted no time in courting Garbo, taking her aside after the lunch and telling her that the gods had decreed that they were to have an epic romance. "It was written in the stars," he said. She was charmed by his intensity; she easily fell for magnetic older men who could guide her and had no obvious reason to exploit her. When they met, he was fifty-four and she was thirty-one, but neither minded the age difference. During their relationship, Garbo called him "Stoki" and "boyfriend."

They were inseparable for nearly a year. Gottfried Reinhardt, Salka Viertel's young lover, remembered Garbo kneeling in front of Stokowski at Salka's home and listening, enraptured, to his tales of his spiritual adventures, such as spending a day—from sunrise to sunset—with a mystic on the top of a mountain in India.[36] He and Garbo made the rounds of Hollywood nightspots. They joined the circle of Europeans around Vicki Baum, the author of the novel that was the basis of *Grand Hotel*, which met at her house in Pacific Palisades. Garbo later told the actor David Niven, who had purchased Baum's house and whose wife, Hjordis, was Swedish, that she had spent some of her happiest days at Baum's home.[37]

When Stoki offered to guide Garbo through Europe, which she had never seen, aside from Sweden and Germany, she eagerly accepted. They stayed for a month in a villa in Italy and then motored to Sweden by way of North Africa, France, and Germany, arriving at Härby Gar, Garbo's estate, where they spent several weeks. Except at Garbo's estate, which had stone walls and gates to keep strangers out, the international press corps didn't let them alone. During their stay in Italy, a crowd of journalists and photographers camped outside the gates of their villa, climbed nearby trees to see what was happening inside, and bribed the villa's staff for information. Even then, Italy was known for its many paparazzi, photographers who relentlessly stalk celebrities. The gaggle of journalists was reduced in size in France, Germany, and Sweden, but they didn't entirely disappear.

Garbo and Stoki had a disconcerting time in France and Germany, since the European powers were preparing for war. In March 1938 Hitler annexed Austria, and France called up its military reserves. Then in May, the *Hollywood Reporter* published an article accusing Garbo, Joan Crawford, Marlene Dietrich, and other stars of being "box-office poison." The article was part of a campaign by small-town theater owners to end the studios' practice of forcing them to exhibit films they didn't want, in order to show movies that they did want. In brief, the small theater owners wanted more control over their bookings. Most of the stars listed in the ad continued their careers, although the studio producers used "the box-office poison" charge as a ploy to reduce salaries.

Garbo and Stoki went on their planned visit to the Wachtmeisters at Tistad. While they were there, Hörke Wachtmeister thought that the two of them acted as though they were in love, but she suspected that nothing would come of it, given Garbo's characteristic indecision.[38] Indeed, after a year together, Garbo and Stoki were bored with each other. And although he claimed to detest press coverage, he made a fuss if anyone they encountered on their journey didn't know who he was. Garbo suspected that he called press outlets during their journey and revealed where they were.[39]

Stoki and Garbo traveled to New York separately; Garbo arrived in October. Their affair was over. Stoki continued his conducting career, becoming ever more famous, and he married Gloria Vanderbilt, an heiress to a huge Vanderbilt fortune, who was much younger than he. Garbo continued her career, but she now turned to comedy to invigorate it.

# PART V

# CELEBRITY

# 12

## *Success and Failure*

*A*s a child, Garbo had dreamed of becoming not only a great actress but also a celebrity, as a member of international high society. In a game she played with her childhood friend Elizabeth Malcolm on the roof of the outhouses behind her family's apartment, they pretended that they were on a beach on the Riviera, "lying near aristocrats and millionaires who are vacationing here." The backyard was a windswept ocean; the children playing there were swimmers in the ocean; the gramophone music drifting through the open window of an apartment was "sweet melodies from a fashionable casino orchestra."[1]

Just as Greta's dream of becoming a great actress came true, so did her dream of becoming a celebrity, as a member of international high society. In 1943 she met the famed New York couturier Valentina and became involved with her husband, George Schlee, in a relationship that lasted until Schlee died in 1964. By 1955, when she was fifty, she and Schlee were part of the set led by Aristotle Onassis, the Greek shipping magnate known today for marrying Jacqueline Kennedy, the widow of John F. Kennedy, the assassinated U.S. president. Along the way, she had on and off relationships, especially with the British photographer Cecil Beaton. In the 1960s she joined the group around Cécile de Rothschild, a lesbian member of the Rothschild family and one of the world's wealthiest women.

Garbo had a magnificent condo in New York, property in Beverly Hills, and a collection of fine art and antiques. Her mesmeric beauty drew everyone she met to her; she could pick and choose her friends. She played major games of love and adventure. And her search for a spiritual path she could follow became more intense as she aged.

Garbo's 1939 film *Conquest* (titled *Marie Walewski* in Europe) was a critical failure, but her next film—a comedy titled *Ninotchka*—was a huge success. World War II had destroyed her overseas markets, and even Salka Viertel realized that Garbo's best chance for success in films at this point was to play comedy, which would show her versatility as an actress and which U.S. audiences seemed to want. Garbo had played comic roles in Stockholm in a short film advertising Bergstrom's department store and in a slapstick film for Peter Petschler about a fireman, a tramp, and three bathing beauties. She was funny with her friends in private, telling jokes and playing pranks. She was often fey and childlike, with "a pixie sense of humor, mixed with a dead-pan sense of the ridiculous"—a trait of Mauritz Stiller's that she had internalized.[2] She used her childish self in her acting in *Wild Orchids*, *Anna Christie*, and other films.

Looking for a comedy for Garbo, Salka came across a spoof of Russian Communism. Three daffy Comintern agents, who resemble the irreverent Marx Brothers of Hollywood films, have been sent to Paris to sell the jewels confiscated by the Soviet government from the Russian Grand Duchess Swana, played by Ina Claire. When they send ambiguous reports to their superiors in Moscow, the Comintern sends the agent Ninotchka to Paris to find out what they are doing. Garbo played Ninotchka.

In Paris she meets Count Léon d'Algoult, a suave boulevardier played by Melvyn Douglas, who is the lover of Grand Duchess Swana. Another spoof was intended, since John Gilbert had married Ina Claire after breaking up with Garbo. But she and Claire became friends; they both liked healthy living, and Gilbert had moved on to yet another wife. (Claire told Hugo Vickers that one day at lunch, Garbo propositioned her.)[3]

In the film, Douglas as Count Léon romances Ninotchka, turning her from a communist into to a capitalist by showing her the freedom and frivolity of the West in contrast to Soviet rigidity. Garbo was often identified with her hats in her films; in *Ninotchka* she sees a silly cone hat in a store window. She buys it and wears it, symbolizing her turn from communism to capitalism and from a stern Communist functionary into a frivolous woman in love. Such hats were in fashion in the West; they were designed by the Paris couturier Elsa Schiaparelli, who was influenced by the surrealists.

At the end of the film, the three zany Comintern agents are in Budapest, where they have opened a Russian restaurant. Ninotchka travels there from Moscow and the count from Paris, and they reunite with each other as well as with the three stooges, who have become their friends. In the plot's tomfoolery, the jewels are forgotten, and no one seems to care. The movie was advertised with the slogan: "Garbo laughs." In fact, Garbo laughs uproariously when Douglas as the count falls off a chair in a bistro. Throughout the movie, she also mocks her image as a goddess. Until Ninotchka falls in love, Garbo plays her as a comic deadpan character with a stern monotone voice and a robotlike demeanor.

As Garbo prepared for *Ninotchka* in the spring of 1939, she began losing weight. Ever since 1927, when she collapsed while making the first *Anna Karenina*, which was scrapped and remade as *Love*, she had watched her weight, often weighing herself on a bathroom scale, which she always had nearby. But the *Conquest* disaster and the discussions over the choice of her next film made her anxious. By then, MGM had purchased nearly a hundred novels and screenplays that could serve as the bases of films for her. When a major star was involved, MGM never scrimped on spending money; choosing from among the trove was daunting. She was close to developing anemia and anorexia again. Louella Parsons mentioned the problem in a column in which she worried about Garbo's health. "Alarming is the health of Greta Garbo," Parsons opined. "She has no appetite, and her friends are worried about her inability to put on weight."[4]

Garbo went for several months to a psychologist for talk therapy. A consultant hired by MGM, Dr. Eric Drimmer, who was Swedish, had treated Clark Gable and Robert Taylor, as well as members of the Swedish royal family. Garbo liked him; his advice was like that of her friends— she should face her demons, conquer them, and forge a life for herself. He concluded that Hollywood had caused many of her problems, hardly a startling insight, but he also concluded that her mystery image had taken her over, becoming an unhealthy obsession. Drimmer also revealed that they spent a lot of time during her sessions discussing Eastern religions, a subject on which Garbo seemed to be an expert.[5]

Drimmer helped Garbo, but she didn't calm down until, just before making *Ninotchka*, she met Gayelord Hauser, a leader of the natural foods movement in the United States. Born in Germany, Hauser had recovered as a young man from a bout of tuberculosis through exercise and a strict diet recommended by a naturopath—a medical practitioner who used natural food and exercises for healing. Impressed by the procedure, Hauser opened a natural foods store in Chicago, one of the first in the United States. He created his own system, stressing proteins, vitamins, and exercise, introducing vegetable juices, yogurt, wheat germ, and other protein-rich foods to Americans.[6] A natural showman, tall, dark, handsome, and impeccably dressed, he lectured in Europe and the United States on his system. Frey Brown, an art student with a flair for promotion, was his personal and business partner.

Hauser developed a clientele among female movie stars, including Gloria Swanson and Marlene Dietrich. He was irresistible to older women, including many in New York high society. He wrote cookbooks and had his own radio show, while his system of "becoming beautiful through eating" was adopted at the beauty retreats established by Elizabeth Arden, the titan of a cosmetics empire.[7] As Hauser's clientele increased, he moved to Hollywood and bought a house in the Hollywood Hills.

Mercedes de Acosta, who used natural remedies, recommended Hauser to Garbo, as did Leopold Stokowski, another devotee of natural foods. Hauser was ten years older than Garbo, and, like Mauritz Stiller, he dominated her, which she liked. He became another companion and father figure to her. He invited her to dinner, beginning their friendship, which lasted until he died in 1985. He recommended that she eat foods high in protein and iron, including meat. Unlike Dr. Henry Bieler, whom Garbo still consulted, he wasn't a vegetarian. She followed Hauser's advice and gained weight.

Hauser didn't let her give in to melancholy. When she became depressed, he took her on long walks or out to dinner to lift her spirits. He, Garbo, Frey Brown, and Mercedes de Acosta went on picnics. They went to Reno to see a rodeo and to Jamaica to relax. Hauser owned homes in Palm Springs and Sicily, and Garbo visited them with him.[8] A shrewd investor, he gave her financial advice; they jointly invested in Beverly Hills real estate, eventually owning the most lucrative block on Rodeo Drive, the commercial center of Beverly Hills. Along the way, Mercedes was dropped; in her autobiography she praised Dr. Henry Bieler for helping Garbo, but she never mentioned Hauser.

Hauser told his friend Nancy Cooke de Herrera, a yoga teacher, that he left Frey Brown for several years to live with Garbo. No other source, aside from Herrera, mentions this episode. The film critic Richard Schickel, who knew a close friend of Hauser's, called the natural foods leader a homosexual whom Garbo "enticed into a heterosexual fling." This possibility seems more likely. Or the friendship may have been platonic, like most of Garbo's friendships with homosexual men.[9]

Filming on *Ninotchka* ended in November 1939, and the next month, Garbo went with Hauser to New York, where he gave lectures and dealt with business matters. They went to plays and socialized with his society friends. Hauser introduced Garbo to Jessica Dragonette, a New York celebrity, and her husband, Nicholas Turner. Dragonette is unknown today, but she was famous in the 1940s and 1950s; she had her own weekly radio show on which she sang songs from operettas and musical comedies, attracting 50,000 listeners. She also gave concerts across the nation. Because she was tall and blonde and concealed her private life, she was called "radio's Greta Garbo."

Dragonette held a salon on Saturdays, attended by celebrities in the arts and the theater, and Garbo sometimes went to it when she was in New York. Like most of her New York friends, Jessica and Turner had an apartment on the Upper East Side, not far from the hotels and apartments where Garbo lived. In her autobiography, Dragonette reflected on Garbo's clothes at their first meeting, noting Garbo's reputation for wearing inexpensive clothing from army-navy stores in public. "How can they say she's badly dressed?" Dragonette wrote. Wearing a dark blue outfit and a peach scarf, Garbo looked to Dragonette like "the quintessence of chic."[10] Hauser, with his elegant attire and control over Garbo, probably was responsible for the clothing upgrade. Dragonette and Turner remained Garbo's friends for many years. Nikki, much younger than Jessica, was very good-looking. They both liked to flirt with Garbo; they both had a zany streak like hers. When she adopted an outlandish character in their presence, they played along with her, expanding on the situations and people she created. They were also both devout Catholics, and that became important to her. There was a piano in their apartment, and Garbo sometimes sang along with Jessica. Or she came over to lie in the sun on their large roof terrace.

After leaving New York in 1940, Garbo and Hauser, along with Frey Brown, flew to Nassau in the Bahamas to join Axel Wenner-Gren on his yacht. Wenner-Gren was a wealthy Swedish businessman who collected celebrities as friends, including Garbo. The four of them spent several weeks cruising the West Indies. Some authors claim that the British film director Alexander Korda, who was a liaison between the film industry and the British secret service, recruited Garbo to spy for the Allies and assigned her to monitor Wenner-Gren. Yet, much scholarship has been devoted to proving that Wenner-Gren's spying was an effort to persuade Hitler against going to war. He later established the Wenner-Gren Foundation, supporting anthropological research.[11]

Through Hauser, Garbo met celebrities who became close friends, including Dragonette and the author Erich Maria Remarque, who was at a New Year's Eve party in 1939 that Hauser and Garbo attended. Remarque was the author of *All Quiet on the Western Front*, a blockbuster novel about World War I. Anita Loos described him as "handsome, elegant, and a connoisseur of every amenity—art, women, jewels, food and wine." Remarque was attracted to Garbo by her "beautiful dark voice."[12] Garbo contacted him after returning to New York from the West Indies, and for the next several months they walked in Central Park and went to art galleries, plays, and elegant offbeat restaurants—all favorite Garbo activities. For her New York pied à terre, Garbo rented a suite in the Ritz Tower, an elegant uptown apartment hotel on Park Avenue.

When Garbo and Remarque returned separately to Los Angeles the next summer, they continued their affair, with walks on the beach during which Garbo charmed Remarque by doing handstands. Remarque felt that the relationship might have become serious; she was open and caring, and she made love with "the absence of any form of sentimentality, or melodrama, and yet full of warmth."[13] But Garbo could be distant, and Remarque was obsessed with Marlene Dietrich, who was momentarily chasing the French actor Jean Gabin. When Dietrich found out about Remarque and Garbo, she became nasty, spreading the news that Garbo had gonorrhea, which may have been true. Remarque went back to Dietrich. Perhaps Garbo seduced Remarque to get back at Dietrich, who hadn't hesitated in seducing Mercedes de Acosta when Garbo went on her trip to Sweden in 1932.

Garbo followed *Ninotchka* with *Two-Faced Woman*, a farce about a grim female ski instructor named Karin Borg, set at a winter resort in upstate New York and in New York City. Garbo played Karin. Melvyn Douglas again played opposite her—this time as Larry Blake, a vacationing New York publisher. His cynical suavity played well against Garbo's coolness and emotionalism. After a whirlwind courtship, they marry, but Douglas returns to New York alone after he discovers that Karin intends to continue her independent life. To win him back, Garbo moves to the city and poses as Karin's twin sister, Katharine, an amoral modern woman, who fascinates Larry and lures him back through playful spoofs. MGM was now openly using Garbo's reputation as two different women in a film plot. They had implied that split throughout her films, most recently in *As You Desire Me*, in which Garbo played Zara the nightclub singer and Maria, her kind alter ego.

The production of *Two-Faced Woman* ran into many problems—a weak script rewritten too many times and a director (George Cukor) who disliked the film, while Gottfried Reinhardt, Salka Viertel's lover and the producer on the film, didn't like Garbo and wasn't sympathetic to her during filming. The plot itself was an old saw; it had been made into a movie several times before. Moreover, Constance Bennett played the publisher's former lover, and she tried to undermine Garbo, upstaging her and giving her bad advice on her appearance and her costumes. Bennett, chic and sophisticated, was a major star. Garbo unfortunately followed her advice; in her own acting, she never upstaged or tried to undermine another actor, and she never suspected that Bennet was giving her bad advice.

Given Garbo's disappearing foreign markets during World War II, L. B. Mayer decided to turn her into an all-American oomph girl, dispensing with her glamour. He was convinced that this change would increase her popularity in the United States. Adrian had designed an elegant wardrobe for Garbo to wear, but Mayer dispensed with it and had her clothing chosen from the racks of a department store. Her hair was cut, curled, and upswept in an unflattering hairdo that made her look older than she was. Adrian disliked the new costumes so much that he resigned from MGM, saying that "when the glamour ends for Garbo, it ends for me."

In a swimming pool scene in the film, Garbo wears a bathing suit and shows off her body, even though it is athletic, with muscular lines, not sinuous, like a bathing beauty's. She had been unattractive in a similar suit in *The Single Standard*; perhaps Gottfried Reinhardt was trying to undermine her—he had never liked her. And although she wasn't much of a dancer, he had her dance a "chica-choca," a modified rhumba. When the dance instructor hired to teach Garbo the dance came to her house to begin her lessons, he found her hiding in a tree, engaging in characteristic bizarre behavior. He coaxed her down and taught her the dance. When George Cukor was asked what he thought of the decision to change Garbo's image, he replied, "It was a shitty decision."[14]

No one at MGM seemed to realize that the term "two-faced' could mean a liar, as well as someone who literally had two faces. Thus, Karin / Garbo's morality was directly attacked. The final indignity was that after the Production Code Board approved *Two-Faced Woman*, the Catholic Legion of Decency condemned it on the grounds that having Garbo play her own sister, with both involved with the same man, was incestuous. Cardinal Spellman of New York, a moral crusader, launched a one-man campaign against the film, preaching sermons and writing articles condemning it. He was friendly with L. B. Mayer, and the two of them reached a compromise on the film favorable to the League. Mayer pulled the film from circulation and had it reedited, adding a scene in which Larry Blake learns early in the film that the twin is Karin / Garbo playing her sister. Although the film made a decent profit, the intervention upset Garbo, who felt humiliated. She was especially hurt by the many letters she received from women's organizations condemning the film.

*Time* magazine called the Catholic campaign against *Two-Faced Woman* an attempt to increase the membership of the Legion of Decency by attacking a major star. Garbo claimed that the studio "had dug her grave" and "was trying to kill her."[15] But *Two-Faced Woman* didn't end Garbo's career. In 1942 she signed a contract with MGM for a film called *The Girl from Leningrad*, about a love affair between a nurse and a soldier during the Russo-Finnish conflict of World War II. After several months, however, MGM cancelled the film. They then discussed having her star in *The Paradine Case* as a wife charged with murdering her husband, although by this point in her career, Garbo avoided films containing violence, and she turned down the role. Alfred Hitchcock later directed it, with Italian star Alida Valli.

Talks were held about other films she might make, including one based on Oscar Wilde's *Picture of Dorian Gray*, but nothing materialized. Salka Viertel wrote a script based on the true story of a Norwegian female skipper, with a crew of men, who ran the German blockade of the North Sea, but despite Salka's pleading, Garbo also turned that film down. By 1940 L. B. Mayer was concentrating on younger actresses— Greer Garson, Lana Turner, Hedy Lamarr—all glamorous, all able to play Garbo roles.[16] Garbo lost a brilliant negotiator that year when Harry Edington gave up managing actors and became production head at RKO.

Salka Viertel lost her influence at MGM, in line with Garbo's falling fortunes and the anti-communist attacks on the film industry. Salka was a humanist, not a communist, but she had friends who belonged to communist groups. She was guilty by association. L. B. Mayer fired her, infuriating Garbo, who remembered only too well Mayer's firing of Mauritz Stiller during the filming of *The Temptress*. But Garbo refused to fight for Salka, telling her that she had already done enough for her. That only made Salka angry; she saw herself as the linchpin in Garbo's career. The two women were annoyed with each other, and their friendship cooled.

After *The Girl from Leningrad* was dropped, Garbo had no MGM contract, only vague promises from Mayer, who had her possessions removed from her dressing room at the studio and taken to her home. Garbo had the hairstylist Sidney Guilaroff find out why Mayer had done this, which she considered an insult. Guilaroff learned that Mayer had given Garbo's dressing room to Lana Turner. Guilaroff found the action a "degrading way to let a great star go."[17] Garbo again felt humiliated.

By the early 1940s the Swedish star Ingrid Bergman, who was ten years younger than Garbo, was rising to the top of the polls. David Selznick had brought her to MGM. Like Garbo, Bergman had attended the Swedish Royal Dramatic Academy on a scholarship, and, again like Garbo, she had begun her acting career in Swedish and German films. She was tall and large-boned. But she had her German mother's round cheeks and was more cheerful than sad.

In 1942 she starred in *Casablanca*, which won the Academy Award for best picture that year and was the most popular movie made during the 1940s. It brought Bergman to the top of the polls.[18] As a type, Bergman was a cross between an exotic woman and a girl next door. That combination was popular in the early 1940s, as World War II brought the glamorous female spy into favor, as well as the pin-up girl, who was a voluptuous descendant of the girl next door. Bergman was more sweet than sexy, but the pin-up girl, with large breasts, was a favorite of American servicemen, who pinned up photos of voluptuous film actresses in their mess halls and bunk rooms to firm up their morale.

The film historian Mark Vieira called 1942 the "Twilight of the Screen Goddesses," because Norma Shearer and Joan Crawford—in addition to Garbo—left MGM that year.[19] Youth was a consideration in casting major roles, and these actresses were all well past thirty; Garbo was thirty-six. She might have become a character actress, playing older women, a move made by Marlene Dietrich that revived her career. But Garbo rejected that possibility. Indeed, she was ambivalent about acting, even in films, as she shaped the next part of her life.

In early 1942, after the disappointment of *Two-Faced Woman*, Gayelord Hauser took Garbo to New York again. Gayelord had played a role in upgrading Garbo's wardrobe, and he would continue to do so. This time, he brought her to the couturier salon of Valentina, a rising dress designer with clients from the avant-garde in the theater and among the wealthy elite. Once again, Hauser took charge of Garbo's clothes. He was convinced that Garbo and Valentina would like each other and that Valentina's designs were perfect for Garbo.

Valentina was a White Russian émigré to the United States, one of those who fled Russia as the Bolshevik forces took control of the country. Devoutly Russian Orthodox, she was deeply superstitious. She was shorter than Garbo, but she had a bony face and body and long red hair, and she resembled the Swedish star. Enjoying jokes, they sometimes exchanged identities. Valentina, playing Garbo, signed Garbo autographs, writing "tricked you" in Russian after the false signature.

Despite Garbo's friendship with Valentina, she became involved with George Schlee, Valentina's husband.[20] Schlee was a businessman, a lawyer, and a man of the world. He was born in St. Petersburg to a wealthy family that owned considerable farmland in the Crimea, as well as the major hotel in Sevastopol, a Crimean port on the Black Sea. At the age of twenty-one he was appointed a general in the White Russian army. Fleeing the Bolsheviks, so the story goes, he came across the fourteen-year-old Valentina Sanina sitting in the Sevastopol train station, with neither family nor possessions except the family jewels, not knowing what to do.

He took her under his wing, and they fled the Bolshevik army, following an émigré path to Athens, then to Constantinople, then to Paris, and finally to New York. Along the way, they married, although Valentina is supposed to have said, "I can't give you love because I don't know how to do it, but if you want friendship, then I'll marry you." He said, "If you marry me, I'll take care of you for the rest of your life."[21] He kept that promise for the next twenty-two years, until he died in 1964. During their hegira from Sebastopol to New York, at times they had money; mostly they were broke. When asked how they managed, Schlee supposedly said, "We ate our jewels." Schlee was known for his witticisms.

Valentina had studied ballet and acting, and both she and Schlee became involved in the theater in Paris and New York, making influential friends. Valentina didn't sew, but she designed her own clothes, eschewing the flapper style. Her skirts and dresses were cut on the bias, long and flowing, topped by jackets and capes. At theater intermissions, women admired Valentina's clothes and asked her where they could buy them. Seeing a future for Valentina as a designer, Schlee organized shows of her designs at society resorts, with Valentina the mannequin. In 1923 they opened a shop in New York; by 1942 they had three dozen employees. Valentina became New York's leading designer, while Schlee managed the business. She charged at least $500 for a dress.

Valentina was fitting a dress on a nude Garbo when Schlee entered the fitting room. It is said that he and Garbo fell in love on the spot, as Schlee gazed at her naked body. What is known is that Garbo became close to Valentina and Schlee, sometimes serving as a model at Valentina's salon, often going out socially with them. At first it was thought that Valentina and Garbo were lovers, but Garbo and Schlee were the couple. People were shocked by the arrangement, as George took out Valentina one night and Garbo the next. Schlee soon told Valentina that he was in love with Garbo, but he was certain she wouldn't marry him; she didn't want to be married.

Garbo wasn't Schlee's only extramarital involvement, and Valentina had her own long-term lover in Karl Barnett, president of the Bollingen Foundation, which promoted the theories of Carl Jung. Garbo claimed that the physical part of the Valentina-Schlee marriage lasted only seven years, which justified her taking over Schlee.[22]

Schlee was far from handsome; some people found him ugly. Others thought that he looked like Mauritz Stiller, and that was why Garbo was attracted to him. He was as domineering as Stiller: "He had Stiller's self-possessed abruptness, a manner of bidding others to do his will."[23] He also had entrée to New York high society. During his relationship with Garbo, he took over many tasks that she disliked: paying bills, getting plane tickets, calling for taxis. He also owned a limousine and had a chauffeur on call. And he could be Garbo's greatest supporter, confident that she would make more films. He said that she reminded him of Eleonora Duse, who had been in retirement for eleven years and returned to greater triumph than before.

Schlee soon took over managing Garbo's career, which may not have been wise. Eventually, he made all the decisions regarding their life. As time went by, he became jealous of her flirtations with other men. In praising her, he focused on her hardness, not her sensuality or femininity. He called her "a flawlessly cut gemstone in the show-window of womanhood—hard and cool on the surface yet forged in fire and everlasting."[24]

Garbo's friends were divided about Schlee. Salka Viertel and her circle didn't like him; they thought he had little aesthetic taste and was hopeless as a producer. They disagreed with his conservative politics. But David Niven, a charming and sophisticated Hollywood actor from Great Britain, thought that he was perfect for Garbo. Schlee was, according to Niven, "a cosmopolite of immense knowledge, charm, kindness, and understanding. She seemed completely happy in his company."[25] Schlee was Jewish, and he was masterful at telling funny stories, especially Jewish jokes. He indulged in cornball humor, which Garbo liked. Garbo deferred to Schlee, although he told Hollywood photographer Jean Howard that taking care of her was like taking care of a two-year-old child. Garbo complained to Salka that he would sometimes meet her requests with a cold-blooded stare, which she detested.[26]

As usual, Garbo spent the summer after she met Valentina and Schlee in Hollywood. Erich Remarque and Gayelord Hauser were there, as was Salka Viertel. Realizing that her Hollywood career had failed, Mercedes moved back to New York, where she saw Garbo from time to time; she was still a major source of knowledge about alternative doctors and medicines. At the end of World War II, she settled in Paris. She and Garbo saw each other occasionally, but both had other partners, and Mercedes was involved with the Hindu faith and with friends who were shamans. She was obsessed with Garbo, but she always had her own friends.

Under Hauser's aegis, Garbo gave up her peripatetic Hollywood life and bought a home, where she displayed a love of gardening. She planted flowers, herbs, and shrubs, and did the weeding and pruning herself, as she had at her family's garden plot in Stockholm when she was a child. And she decorated her new home, using the salmons, pinks, and greens that were her favorite colors. She even hired Barbara Barondess MacLean to help her. A sometime actress, MacLean had played a flirtatious peasant girl in Queen Christina, but she had subsequently given up acting and had become an interior designer and a broker of fine arts and antiques.

Garbo made new friends, including the actor Clifton Webb, another homosexual, who had been a dancer on the Broadway stage. Webb described Garbo as a "person of wondrous beauty," with "the most delicious wit and sense of humor." According to Webb, she went to many parties when in Hollywood in the summers, and she did exercises at George Cukor's home two or three mornings a week, along with Cukor,

Webb, Constance Collier, and Somerset Maugham—all were bisexual or homosexual.[27] It seems that a more joyous Garbo was trying to break through.

The Second World War, which was underway, affected Garbo's life. She brought her mother, her brother, and her brother's wife and children to the United States to save them from a possible German invasion of Sweden. She didn't visit Sweden again until 1946, after the war had ended. None of these relatives liked the United States, but they stayed. Garbo's mother Anna died in 1944, and she was buried in the family plot at Woodlawn Cemetery, in Stockholm. Garbo hadn't visited Anna much; Salka Viertel had become the mother figure in Garbo's life. Sven and his family settled in Santa Fe, New Mexico, where Garbo bought him a home. He became a painter of landscapes and figures and was finally successful. Garbo often visited him on her trips between New York and Hollywood. After Sven died in 1967, she considered his daughter Gray and her husband and children to be her family.

Sweden was neutral in this war, as in World War I, although its government allowed Germans free access to the country, and its iron and steel industries sold materiel to Germany. The film historian Charles Higham contended that Garbo helped the Allies track down Swedes who were spying for Germany, using her contacts in Sweden to identify them. According to Higham, the London film executive William Stephenson persuaded her to join the British Security Co-ordination, set up in 1940. Higham concluded that she was a "great heroine" who was involved in the rescue of Jews from Denmark, as she put pressure on King Gustav of Sweden to allow the Danish Jews to enter Sweden and facilitated the escape of the atomic scientist Niels Bohr from occupied Denmark. That conclusion has been disputed, although after the war ended, Stephenson, film liaison to the British Security Co-ordination, bought an apartment in Garbo's building on East 52nd Street, one floor up from Garbo's apartment.[28]

There was also her curious relationship with Dag Hammarskjöld, the Swedish diplomat and secretary-general of the United Nations, who knew the details of Allied intelligence operations in Scandinavia. After the war ended, he and Garbo met in New York. She told Raymond Daum that she wanted to discuss with Hammarskjöld "things that had happened a long time ago." She also expressed a desire to meet the Danish ambassador to the United States to thank him for the help the Danish government had given to the Jews during World War II. Did those matters involve her own intelligence work during that war? Laila Nylund, the daughter of Max Gumpel, told Karen Swenson that her father had been involved in intelligence work. Did Max recruit Garbo to assist him? Gumpel remained Garbo's close friend until he died in 1965.[29]

Garbo gave $10,000 to the Finnish War Relief Fund—perhaps thinking of Stiller, who was born and raised in Helsinki. She also gave Salka money for her organization to assist the Jews who had escaped from Hitler's persecution. Some say that she gave a large sum of money to the aid organization established in the name of screen star Carole Lombard, who had tragically died in a plane crash while traveling across the country selling war bonds. But Garbo didn't participate in the activities that Hollywood stars organized to help with the war effort, including war bond drives and the Hollywood Canteen. The Canteen was launched by Bette Davis and other film actors to provide food and entertainment to soldiers going overseas to war. Garbo was criticized by the press for not participating in these efforts. Salka Viertel defended her, maintaining that Garbo bought bonds privately and helped her in aiding émigrés from Hitler's Germany to the West Coast. But Garbo kept her participation secret. She was still afraid of strangers and unwilling to appear in public.[30]

In 1939, Garbo joined a group of film people assembled by Anita Loos. The group included Charlie Chaplin and Paulette Goddard, then Chaplin's wife, as well as Salka Viertel, Mercedes de Acosta, and the novelists Christopher Isherwood and Aldous Huxley and Huxley's wife, Maria. Huxley and Isherwood had recently come to Hollywood, hoping to write for the movies, and Loos, a prominent Hollywood screenwriter, was helping them. They all lived within walking distance of Loos's home on the Santa Monica beach, so it wasn't difficult for them to get together. Isherwood was homosexual; he was living with his partner in the apartment above Salka's garage. Huxley's wife was mostly lesbian, and she procured women for her husband. Becoming friendly with Mercedes de

Acosta, Maria was rumored to have joined Hollywood's so-called lesbian sewing circle.[31]

Garbo was interested in the Hinduism that both Huxley and Isherwood professed. They belonged to a Hindu sect called Vedanta, which holds that the material world is an illusion. Because humans are ignorant of their unity with a larger spirit, called Brahman, they are condemned to a cycle of death and rebirth. By realizing Brahman through meditation and prayer, humans can leave the cycle and reach Samadhi, which is a more rigorous version of the Buddhist Nirvana. Garbo occasionally attended services at the Vedanta temple in Hollywood, and she told her psychologist Eric Drimmer that she went to Glendale to hear the talks of a swami. According to Drimmer, in their sessions they often discussed Eastern religions; he found her to be expert on them.[32] She had studied them ever since she met Mercedes de Acosta. Garbo's library, auctioned off after her death, contained many books on spirituality and on Eastern religions. She often told friends that she wanted to go to India, as Mercedes had, but she never carried out that fantasy.

The new group had lunch on the weekends at Anita Loos's home on the Santa Monica beach, after which they walked on the beach. Or they went on picnics—the Europeans in the group loved picnics. A picnic they held in 1939 is legendary. It is important in the story of Garbo's life because it gives an indication of her involvement with Hinduism. Anita Loos often wrote about that picnic in her many brief memoirs; it had a comic element that she found amusing.

According to Loos, its participants were so fantastic that they might have come from *Alice in Wonderland*. There were several Theosophists from India, representing the belief system originated in the late nineteenth century by Helena Blavatsky, a Russian immigrant to the United States. Blavatsky claimed that a group of spiritual adepts had schooled her in a doctrine combining religion, philosophy, and science, which she named Theosophy. That belief system spread throughout the world. In an age filled with wars and the rise of dictators like Mussolini in Italy, Franco in Spain, and Hitler in Germany, the dogmas of all religions were being questioned, and Theosophy held great appeal.

At the picnic, the Indian women wore elegant saris, but the rest of the group wore old sports clothes. Garbo was disguised in a pair of men's trousers and a battered hat with a floppy brim; Paulette wore a Mexican outfit. Charlie Chaplin, Christopher Isherwood, and the English philosopher Bertrand Russell, who was then teaching at UCLA, all looked like pixies on a spree.[33]

The picnic gear was as unusual as the cast of characters. The Indians, following their vegetarian beliefs, couldn't cook or eat their food in vessels contaminated by food derived from animals, so they were weighted down with new crockery and new pots and pans. Greta, then a strict vegetarian, was on a diet of raw carrots, and she had attached bunches of carrots to her belt. The Indians ate vegetables, but the Americans ate sliced ham and potato salad, except for the always elegant Paulette Godard, who had brought along several bottles of champagne and jars of caviar in a cooler.

The group set up their picnic on public land along a path in the Santa Monica Mountains, but a forest ranger walking by admonished them for picnicking in a restricted area. They looked so disheveled to him that he wouldn't believe that they were the famous writers and actors they said they were. He gave them a citation and told them to move on.

In the summer of 1943, Garbo had another brief sexual encounter with a well-known individual. Gilbert Roland was a film star who had been a Latin lover in the 1920s and after, and he resembled Jack Gilbert. In his diary, he detailed his affair with Garbo. They had met years before, and ever since that meeting, he had dreamed about her. Recently, they had passed each other on a street in Beverly Hills. He was about to join the army, and he decided to take a chance. Knowing that Salka Viertel was close to Garbo, he gave her a note for Garbo with his address on it. The next night, Garbo appeared at his home. They had a romantic dinner and spent the night together. The next day, he left to join the army.[34]

According to his diary, the affair continued over the next months. He was stationed in North Carolina, and he visited her in New York, staying at her apartment. They participated in the activities Garbo liked best: walking in Central Park, and going to galleries, movies, and elegant, offbeat restaurants. In early December she wrote him a "Dear John" letter, saying that she didn't have the strength to continue the affair. That was a standard excuse of hers to end a relationship, but it may have been the truth, given her chronic illnesses. Besides, by then, she was involved with Valentina and George Schlee. In a letter to Roland, she called her wistful, feminine self "Eleanor" and her gentle, masculine self "Mountain Boy."

Roland was at the time married to Constance Bennett, the actress who had sabotaged Garbo in *Two-Faced Woman*. Was this affair with Roland a payback on Garbo's part? It was difficult to navigate the social and sexual worlds of Hollywood, replete with subversion and intrigue and a free-love attitude toward sex, which could be used to justify almost any behavior. Garbo couldn't avoid being influenced by it, and Salka Viertel, who played the role of go-between in this instance, was a linchpin of Hollywood's liberals, as well as a presence at the Hollywood studios. Like many others in the Hollywood film industry, she believed in free love, and she was pleased to deliver the note from Gilbert Roland to Garbo. By 1943, however, Garbo and Salka's relationship had cooled considerably, but both wanted to reconstruct it. Salka's delivering Gilbert Roland's note to Garbo was a start.

# 13

## *New York*

I N 1946, AFTER World War II had ended, Garbo visited Sweden again. This time, she took George Schlee with her—a testimony to his importance in her life. But the trip wasn't a success. During the war, she had sold her Swedish estate, Härby Gar, loosening her ties to her home country. On the 1946 trip, Garbo and Schlee visited her friends in Stockholm, and they spent three weeks at the estate near Stockholm of Max Gumpel, her former lover and longtime friend. Max's daughter Laila was there, along with Max's other children. Garbo played games with them and told them stories about trolls. But reporters and photographers wouldn't let Garbo alone. Laila remembered that they seemed to be everywhere: "There were newspaper photographers and reporters hiding in the bushes and trees [on the Gumpel estate] across eleven acres of land."[1] After this tumult, Garbo concluded that the Swedish press was worse in bothering her than the U.S. press.

Schlee didn't like Sweden. He didn't speak Swedish, and Swedes didn't like Russians, an old hostility made worse by the threat of a Russian invasion of Sweden during World War II. Moreover, Schlee didn't like watching Garbo flirt with Max Gumpel, even though she was an inveterate flirt. Garbo and Schlee were together for the next eighteen years, but they didn't visit Sweden again.

Garbo didn't see Hörke Wachtmeister on this 1946 visit. They had corresponded during most of the war, but Hörke cut back on her letters, and Garbo began to worry that something was wrong. Before the war ended, Hörke stopped writing. Sven Broman told Karen Swenson that he thought that Hörke had dropped Garbo because she had shown too much interest in Nils Wachtmeister, Hörke's husband.[2] One can imagine Hörke's concern, even if it was only a case of flirting. Garbo was, after all, the world's most beautiful woman. It's also possible that something in their relationship estranged them. Garbo told Cecil Beaton that during her 1946 visit to Sweden she felt uprooted, as though she was American and not Swedish.[3] She went to Sweden twice more, in 1962 and 1968, but that was the end of her visits to her native land.

Garbo often said that she yearned to be two people: the public movie star Greta Garbo, and a private person who was not famous and not interesting to the public. When she left MGM in 1942, she gave up her association with Garbo and acted on the latter desire. She had already used the name Harriet Brown as a pseudonym; she now adopted it as her real name. Creating a fictional character named Harriet Brown, who was as ordinary as her name, Garbo traveled as Harriet Brown, registered in hotels under that name, and answered only if called Miss Brown or Harriet. She had matchbooks made with the name Harriet Brown printed on their covers. Most of her mail was addressed to Harriet Brown. Her close friends called her Miss G, GG, or an affectionate term like "Grushka" or "Toscar." Toscar was the name Garbo gave Mercedes to call her when they first met at Salka Viertel's home. Toscar is a Russian word used to describe the state of yearning and despair, which some consider fundamental to the Russian identity. The Swedish equivalent is "Grushka." Mercedes was the first person to use that affectionate name; Salka and others eagerly called her that as well.

She never talked about her life as Garbo, and she never used the pronouns "I," "me," or "mine," substituting the royal "we" or "one" for them, further confusing who she was. She often assumed the expression of one of her film characters, as though her career had taken her over, making her the Frankenstein monster that she had feared. Or she may have been clowning, a strong part of her persona. Christopher Isherwood described her use of expressions from her films as irreverent: "If you watch her for a quarter of an hour, you see every one of her famous expressions. She repeats them, quite irreverently. There is the iron sternness of Ninotchka, the languorous open-lipped surrender of Camille, Mata Hari's wicked laugh, Christina's boyish toss of the head, Anna Christie's grimace of disgust."[4]

Other friends of hers remarked on that behavior. Gore Vidal, who often lived in Klosters when Garbo was there, thought that her assumption of her film characters was mischievous: "She had about six poses.... If you had been brought up on her movies you kept finding yourself suddenly in the midst of *Conquest* or *Camille*.... She knew she had this effect.... She was rather mischievous."[5]

She could be intelligent in conversations. Even after she and Schlee were a couple, she went to Valentina's parties at the Schlee-Valentina apartment, which Schlee maintained as his official residence. He and Valentina were too intertwined—in business, in New York high society, in party giving—for them to split up. The playwright and screenwriter Sam Behrman, who had worked on scenarios and scripts for several of Garbo's films, stated that Garbo loved to talk about "large subjects." At one of Valentina's parties, she and Robert Sherwood retreated to Valentina's bedroom and talked about world peace for two hours.[6]

Yet, discarding both "Garbo" and "Harriet Brown," she often became an adolescent girl—or boy. At a party at the Valentina-Schlee apartment, she was seated next to the the English actor John Gielgud. He found her to be "extraordinary." According to him, she had "a little girl face and short hair tied with an Alice ribbon; hideously cut dress ... to her calves and then huge feet in heel-less black pumps." He continued, "Lovely childlike expression—never stopped talking but to absolutely no purpose. But I couldn't make out if her whole attitude was perhaps a terrific pose."[7] Gielgud, a well-known actor, was the elegant nephew of the famed actress Ellen Terry. He had an eye for clothing design, but the Garbo dress he disliked was probably created by Valentina, whose designs hadn't yet reached London. Garbo liked to trick people. It was part of her childlike, comic self.

She sometimes dressed as a teenage boy. When Aldous Huxley came to Garbo's Hollywood house to discuss writing a screenplay for her, she was wearing boy's clothing. Mercedes de Acosta was there. They talked about screenplays Huxley might write for Garbo, including one on St. Francis of Assisi. Huxley quipped, "Including his beard?" He wrote a screenplay for Garbo on Marie Curie, who with her husband discovered radium. Salka Viertel took over the project, but when World War II began, her screenplay was scrapped. It was later made with Greer Garson as Marie Curie.

The director Joshua Logan, who had directed *South Pacific* on Broadway to great acclaim, met Garbo and Schlee in the spring of 1949 in a town square outside Paris to discuss having him direct a Garbo film. The three were already in Europe; Garbo chose the location to avoid reporters. At first, Logan didn't recognize her, until he realized that she was dressed as an adolescent boy, in short pants, looking about fourteen. He found her clothing and attitude strange. "That day I never felt I was talking with a grown person. She had a child's laugh, and the things that amused her were childish things. Here was doomed Camille and noble Queen Christina and tragic Anna Karenina transformed into Huck Finn." To the actor David Niven, a close friend of Garbo's, she seemed to be a child, "living in her own secret world." Like a child, Niven stated, "she came and went as she wished."[8] Posing as a child or as an adolescent was part of the act she performed for her own amusement and that of others.

One might regard the last part of Garbo's life, from leaving MGM in 1942 to her death in 1990, as a play that she created, directed, and starred in. Her friend the singer Jessica Dragonette said, "It was her spontaneous ability to act every scene in life, as well as on the screen, that makes her so fascinating."[9] Jessica and her husband Nicholas Turner often joined Garbo in her fanciful conversations, playing along with the scenario she established. Garbo had directed herself in many of her films; she had briefly considered becoming a director. And she took a large role in directing her relationships, even when she played a subordinate part—from her long association with George Schlee through shorter ones with Cecil Beaton, Erich von Goldschmidt-Rothschild, and Cécile Rothschild.

She also continued to form triangles, with herself in the middle, subtly controlling the two other people involved. In this scenario, Schlee, Beaton, and the two Rothschilds might be viewed as extensions of Mauritz Stiller, John Gilbert, Mercedes de Acosta, and Salka Viertel, who had been earlier mentors and subordinates. Garbo was shy, but she knew how to use her shyness to control others. That had been apparent as early as her adolescence, when she landed a job as a saleswoman at Bergstrom's department store in Stockholm.

After the end of World War II, Garbo increasingly regarded New York as her home. She had many friends there, and a rich social life. By the early 1940s, after her trips there with Gayelord Hauser, she became close to Hauser's friends Jessica Dragonette and her husband Nicholas Turner. She chose her friends for their sophistication, playfulness, and learning. They included Katharine Hepburn; Allen Porter, curator of photography at the Museum of Modern Art; and Brian Aherne and his wife Eleanor, even though Aherne had been a longtime lover of Marlene Dietrich's.

She occasionally saw Mercedes de Acosta. Several years after the war ended, Mercedes established a residence in Paris, and Garbo spent time with her there.[10] Some Garbo friends claimed that she and Mercedes went to lesbian bars in New York in the 1950s, which is possible. Valeska Gert, who had played the madam in *Joyless Street*, had moved to New York and opened a lesbian bar in Greenwich Village. In her study of lesbians in the United States in the 1920s and after, Lillian Faderman identified Beatrice Lillie, Tallulah Bankhead, Jeanne Eagles, and Joan Crawford as frequenting lesbian nightclubs in Harlem. Garbo was friendly with several of these women, and she had always loved Harlem and its jazz clubs.[11] She might be included in Faderman's group, as might Mercedes de Acosta and Anita Loos, both of whom often went to Harlem.

Garbo continued to call herself a "hermit," but an individual who met her at three New York parties within two weeks described her as a "hermit about town."[12] Never holding a party, she kept her friends separate, fearing that they might gossip about her if they met. She maintained her taboo: if any friend spoke to the press about her, she would drop them.

The growing sophistication of New Yorkers, especially those on the wealthy East Side, where Garbo usually stayed, made its residents less apt to bother her, especially as her film career faded into the past. With New York's theaters, art galleries, museums, restaurants, and Harlem jazz clubs, it was the cultural center of the United States. Not until the 1980s did Los Angeles challenge it. And its inhabitants had a reputation for leaving celebrities alone.

New York had appealing places for walking—still one of Garbo's favorite activities. She always lived near Central Park, with its meadows, forests, bodies of water, species of birds, and proximity to the Metropolitan Museum of Art. She loved window-shopping, and there were many stores displaying merchandise behind plateglass windows on Fifth Avenue and the avenues on the East Side. To look for antiques, she had only to walk to Third Avenue, which was lined with antique shops. Small markets, specialty shops, fruit stands, drug stores, and small restaurants were on almost every block. She could take long hikes, swim, and play tennis in New York suburbs like Greenwich, Connecticut. Her friends Fleur and Gardner Cowles and Maud and Eustace Seligman had second homes there, each with a tennis court and a swimming pool and miles of forests and trails for walking. Cowles was the publisher of *Life* and *Look*; Seligman was a renowned New York lawyer.

She sometimes visited Allen Porter in his country house in Edgewater, in upstate New York. He was a small, humorous man who always laughed at his own jokes. He and his friends with country homes nearby, including the decorator Billy Baldwin, were mostly homosexual. They formed a group they called "the sewing circle," borrowing the name of the Hollywood group of lesbians and bisexual women that Alla Nazimova formed in the 1910s.[13] Garbo became friends with them, but once George Schlee took over her life, she rarely saw them, because Schlee preferred to socialize with people in high society. Like Mauritz Stiller, Schlee decided what they would do.

In 1951 Garbo became a U.S. citizen. She sold her house in Brentwood that year and leased a four-room apartment in the Hampshire House, on Central Park South. She moved her possessions to New York. But she still went to Hollywood in the summers; she still disliked New York's humid summer weather. And she still had friends in Hollywood, including Salka Viertel, George Cukor, and her tennis friends.

Until well into her seventies, Garbo traveled a lot—to the West Coast, to the West Indies, to Europe. Traveling had been a part of her life ever since Mauritz Stiller had taken her to Berlin, Constantinople, and Hollywood when she was in her early twenties. She became famous for her walks around New York, although it is less well known that she usually had a friend along with her, or she stopped at a friend's apartment for drinks or coffee. Coffee, not tea, is the favored Swedish drink.

Before Schlee died, Garbo dressed simply but elegantly when she went to lunch or dinner with a friend, or to a party or a museum, in clothes designed by Valentina or another major designer. Ferragamo still made her shoes—flat, styled after men's shoes. She had multiple pairs of trousers made to order by one of New York's best tailors. To disguise herself, she wore sunglasses and hats with large brims, but that disguise became so familiar that some of her friends thought that she wanted strangers to identify her, that on some level she liked the attention. Given the large salary MGM had paid her, plus her frugality and investment advice from Max Gumpel in Sweden and Gayelord Hauser and George Schlee in the United States, she became very wealthy. She was worth many millions of dollars when she died.

George Schlee remained her major companion until his death in 1964. During her years with Schlee, she had a short relationship with Baron Erich von Goldschmidt-Rothschild and a long relationship with Cecil Beaton. The baron introduced her to his cousin, Cécile Rothschild, who took over Schlee's role in Garbo's life after he died. Garbo never married, although Beaton often proposed to her, and when she decided that she wanted to marry Schlee, he wouldn't divorce Valentina. Given Valentina's Russian Orthodox faith, she didn't believe in divorce, and Schlee refused to initiate proceedings. He also wouldn't break with Garbo. He said he had to deal with two "crazy" women, and he didn't want to make things worse.[14]

When Garbo left MGM, independent producers offered her many films, and she was interested. She was also worried; always superstitious, she remembered the Hollywood adage that you are only as good as your last picture, and in her eyes, her last picture, *Two-Faced Woman*, had been a flop. *The Painted Veil* and *Conquest* hadn't done much better, and she incorrectly thought that even *Queen Christina* had been a failure. They were redeemed by *Ninotchka*, which was universally praised. She also remembered her mother's adages: "If you let the devil on board, you must row him to the shore," and "If you start by having too much faith in it, it will end by going to hell." She had many taboos. When Sven Broman finished a nighttime telephone conversation with her with the words "sleep well," she admonished him never to say that to her. "I'm full of taboos," she told Broman. "Now I'll lie awake all night and think about having to sleep well."[15]

In 1943, a consortium was formed for her to star in George Bernard Shaw's *St. Joan*, about Joan of Arc. J. Arthur Rank was to produce the film, Salka Viertel to write the screenplay and script, and George Cukor to direct. But Shaw regarded Garbo as a sex goddess past her prime, and Joan was seventeen when she heard voices telling her that she was destined to lead a French army to drive the English out of France. Garbo was thirty-eight; Shaw didn't want to cast her as Saint Joan.[16]

That summer, Garbo was preparing to journey by ship to London to meet Shaw, persuade him to support casting her as St. Joan, and begin shooting the film. But World War II was ongoing, and crossing the ocean was dangerous. And, given Britain's precarious position in the war, its government didn't want a historical war between England and France featured on the screen, potentially damaging Britain's World War II alliance with France. The production was cancelled, upsetting Garbo, who called it "a blow of disappointment to my career—a hefty blow."[17]

Screenplays and scripts were continually submitted to her, but none was filmed. Either she rejected them, the funding fell through, or some other problem arose. Tennessee Williams wanted her to play Blanche DuBois, the fading southern belle, in a film based on his play *A Streetcar Named Desire*, but Garbo turned him down, telling him that she wanted to play androgynous characters like Oscar Wilde's Dorian Gray. Regarding Blanche DuBois, she said to Williams, disingenuously, "I could never be an involved or complicated person. I'm too direct and masculine. I could never tell lies, and see things around the corner, like that girl in the play."[18]

By 1947 she was ready to play George Sand, a nineteenth-century French novelist, memoirist, and journalist who gained notoriety for wearing men's clothing in public, but Schlee intervened. He didn't like Sand. He persuaded Garbo to give up the project, even though Salka Viertel had written a treatment and a script. Schlee talked Garbo into agreeing to play the duchess in a screen adaptation of Balzac's 1834 novel

*La Duchesse de Langeais,* about a frivolous Paris socialite who is kidnapped by a secret fraternal order and imprisoned in a convent, where she dies. Garbo even did a screen test to prove that she could play the part.

In the summer of 1949 Garbo was in Rome with Schlee, waiting to start filming the Balzac novel and fending off paparazzi, when funding for the project fell through. Garbo felt humiliated. She finally realized that her name was no longer strong enough to carry a film by herself. In 1952 George Cukor contacted her to play Rachel in a film version of Daphne du Maurier's *My Cousin Rachel.* After reading the novel, Garbo agreed to do the film, but the next day, she changed her mind. "I'm sorry," she told Cukor, "I can't go through with it. I don't have the courage." There were many subsequent offers. Cecil Beaton wanted Garbo to star in a film for which he would design the costumes, and even G. W. Pabst, who had directed her in *Joyless Street,* approached her, with a version of Homer's *Odyssey* in which he wanted her to play the roles of both Penelope, the loyal wife, and Circe, the temptress. But neither of these suggestions nor any others reached the production stage.

Billy Wilder and Walter Reisch, who were the writers on *Ninotchka,* asked Garbo, in exasperation, what comeback role she wanted to play. Her answer floored them. A male clown, she replied. She explained why: "Under the make-up and the silk pants, the clown is a woman. And all the admiring girls in the audience who write him letters are wondering why he does not respond."[19] Wilder thought that she was attracted by a clown's white makeup, which would hide her age. Was she putting them on? Probably, although Garbo often called herself a clown, hiding her true self, engaging in comedy and fantasy.

Salka Viertel blamed the producers for Garbo's failure to return to films, especially Walter Wanger, who had been the producer on *Queen Christina* and now had his own production company. Wanger at first intended to film Garbo in the life of George Sand, but he changed the film to *La Duchesse de Langeais.* Playing George Sand, Garbo could have explored issues relating to gender and sexuality, but Sand wasn't glamorous, and Wanger came to fear that a film about the French novelist and cross-dresser wouldn't succeed at the box office. Salka Viertel wrote, "The display of dilettantism, inflated egos, incompetence, and a hypocritical, indecent disregard for the sensibilities of a great actress [by producers] has been unsurpassed."[20] On one level, Salka remained devoted to Garbo, and she was sometimes included in the film offers.

But Garbo was often indecisive. She seriously considered only a few of the many scenarios and scripts sent to her. Her indecision increased as she aged, especially since she was wealthy and didn't need to make money. Both George Cukor and Salka Viertel, her close friends, believed that Garbo would have found some excuse to end any chance of resuming her career. "Garbo is impatient to work and on the other side she is afraid of it," wrote Viertel to Cukor. "I understand very well after all these years of idleness. Work is a habit, and she has lost it."[21]

In 1942 Garbo began collecting antiques and fine paintings. Her love of antiques dated to her quest with Mauritz Stiller in 1924 to find antique furniture for *The Saga of Gösta Berling*. Her favorite style was eighteenth-century provincial, the style of furniture used in the two manor houses in that film. The source of her love for fine art is more complicated. Wealthy people often buy fine art for its aesthetic appeal and as a financial investment; that was as true of the wealthy in Garbo's day as it is today. During her years in Hollywood, Garbo saw important paintings in the homes of film actors. Erich Maria Remarque, a lover of hers in 1942, had a collection of fine art, including masterpieces by Renoir, Degas, and Cezanne.[22] He talked about his collections with Garbo; soon after that, she began investing in fine art.

The major galleries for antiques and fine art in the United States were then in New York, and Garbo was often there. In November 1942 she went with Barbara Barondess MacLean to an auction in New York that featured works by Auguste Renoir, the famed impressionist painter of figures and landscapes. When she had asked MacLean to take her along, MacLean replied, "This is not for your temperament—you take six months to decide to buy a piece of furniture that costs $300." Despite her hesitation, MacLean took Garbo with her, and according to MacLean, Garbo "almost had a heart attack when I bid $14,500 for one Renoir and then $18,500 for the other." But Garbo decided to buy the paintings, and she wrote a check to pay for them. It was the first check MacLean had ever seen her sign. That way, she didn't have to pay MacLean a commission.[23] But Garbo didn't like to write checks. With her signature on them, they might never be cashed.

During the week that she bought the two Renoirs, she also bought Renoir's *Enfant assis en robe bleue*, his portrait of his nephew Edmond, in which Edmond looks like a beautiful long-haired girl, like Garbo when she was a child. She also bought a Georges Rouault painting of the head of a woman who looked like a man. After Schlee died in 1963, she bought six works by Alexej Jawlensky, the Russian painter who painted what he called "mystic faces"—portraits of androgynous individuals in dark glowing colors with immense dark eyes, resembling religious icons. Jawlensky believed that "art is the desire for God." Garbo, who researched the art she bought as carefully as she had researched her films, liked that sentiment, which appealed to her sense of spirituality.[24]

Garbo's collection reflected her interests as well as her complex personality. Harlequins from the commedia dell'arte were the subjects in some of the paintings she bought, and she also bought abstract paintings, cross-gendered paintings, and realistic paintings of flowers. Her collection included Nils Asther's *Platonic Love*, paintings by her brother Sven, and a drawing of Cecil Beaton by Bebé Berard that Beaton had given her. According to Garbo's niece Gray Reisfield, "She was always finding a spot for seductive little anonymous painted bouquets she came across in her travels."[25] Her collection eventually filled the walls of her New York apartment. They recapitulated the history of modern art, constituted a group of friends she could always depend on, and were a tribute to her intelligence, her sensitivity, and her fame.

Garbo was especially motivated to move to New York when in July 1944 a burglar appeared in the hall outside the bedroom door in her Brentwood home, making real her fear of burglars. The door was open; she saw a shadowy figure in the corridor outside her bedroom, and, panicked, she climbed out a window and slid down a drainpipe to the ground. The burglar didn't manage to steal much, but after the burglary, any noise outside her house brought her to a window, peering through the blinds.[26] In some ways, Manhattan was safer than Hollywood. It was full of tall apartment buildings, with doormen monitoring anyone wanting entry and elevator boys scrutinizing whoever tried to get on the elevator. At that time, few such arrangements existed in Hollywood. She would have to hire her own guards there.

During the year after the burglary, Garbo lived at the Ritz Tower in New York. She went back to Hollywood, but she sold her house there in 1951 and bought her Hampshire House apartment. After she sold her Brentwood home, she sometimes stayed with Salka Viertel in Santa Monica when she went to the West Coast. She often used Salka's address as her address. But Salka, who wasn't good with money and was burdened with debt, sold that house in 1953. She was angry that the wealthy Garbo didn't offer her the money to keep her house, but Salka, who was proud, didn't ask her for it. She and Salka often replayed their initial strong bond when they met and their subsequent disengagement. When Garbo became involved with George Schlee and then with the group around Aristotle Onassis, Salka didn't approve. She felt that these people were self-absorbed, with no concern for others or for the radical politics that she espoused. Salka and Garbo both were stubborn; once again, they had reached an impasse.

In March 1946, Cecil Beaton again appeared in Garbo's life when he came to New York on a photographic assignment. Fourteen years had passed since their last meeting, at Edmund Goulding's home. This time, they met at a party given by a *Vogue* editor. Beaton approached Garbo, and she responded to him; they began walking in Central Park and nearby. Within three weeks, he asked her to marry him, and he would do so regularly for the next several years. She treated his proposals as both serious and a joke. She was still committed to George Schlee, although she sometimes felt caged in by him, and then she had to break free for a while and spend time with someone else.

Beaton lived nearby, staying in the Plaza Hotel on Fifth Avenue near Central Park in a suite that he had decorated. Garbo wouldn't see him on weekends; they were reserved for Schlee, who didn't complain about the presence of Beaton in Garbo's life for several years. The British photographer was known to be a homosexual; Schlee may have thought that he was one of Garbo's homosexual friends.

But Schlee was wrong. Beaton primarily had sex with men, but there had been women in his life. Adele Astaire, Fred Astaire's sister and his dance partner on the stage, had initiated Beaton to heterosexual sex in an experience he enjoyed. Jean Howard, a Hollywood blonde and a successful photographer, went with him to see a suite he had decorated in a New York hotel. Once they were in the bedroom of the suite, he threw her on the bed and pounced on her. She released herself and left, with Beaton yelling after her, "Don't you like male bodies?" Howard found the episode amusing.[27]

Given Garbo's androgynous appearance and her identification with masculinity, Beaton may have considered her more male than female. Although he dressed immaculately in male clothing and was often on men's best-dressed lists, he had cross-dressed since his school days, and he loved to wear makeup. And Garbo had been a central figure in his fantasies for over twenty years.

Beaton was well known. His acting skills were considerable, and like Garbo, he was self-made. The son of an executive in a timber company, he had taught himself photography. Witty, satirical, and charming, a student at Cambridge University, he promoted himself into the highest ranks of England's artistic bohemia. At first, he photographed debutantes and social climbers looking for publicity; then members of the haute bourgeois; and finally, the royal family, especially Queen Elizabeth and Princess Margaret. He also designed costumes and sets for plays and movies. Becoming tired of this glamorous milieu, during World War II he became a war photographer, traveling to far-flung cities and battlefronts to photograph the horrors and strange beauty of war. There was depth to his persona.

He was charismatic and kind, tall and reedlike, a Peter Pan who deferred to Garbo, consoled her when she was down, and played the games she invented. It's not surprising that she confided in him. But she never completely trusted him; she was aware of the venom of some of his early writing on her, and he kept making mistakes, as when she finally allowed him to photograph her, restricting what he could publish from that sitting to one photograph, and he published the entire results.

Garbo spent three months with Beaton in his country home in England, traveling by car to see cathedrals and castles, roaming by foot over the English countryside, allowing Beaton to call her "wife." He introduced her to his famous friends: Princess Margaret; writers and artists with country homes near his; and Anthony Eden, the British prime minister, with whom he and Garbo had lunch at 10 Downing Street. Beaton gave her a new world of British elites to charm with her beauty and her offbeat behavior. But she was overwhelmed by his energy; he never seemed to sit still, and she couldn't keep up with him. She paused her relationship with Beaton when she received a distressed letter from Schlee, who wanted her back, since the newspapers were proclaiming that she was going to marry Beaton.

Despite long periods in limbo, the relationship between Beaton and Garbo survived until 1961, when the first volume of his diary, *The Wandering Years*, was published. It contained a description of their hijinks at Edmund Goulding's home, when they drank Bellinis and frolicked all night. She hadn't known about the diary, or that more volumes were forthcoming, with detailed descriptions of their affair. She had cut Mercedes de Acosta off in 1960 when her autobiography, *Here Lies the Heart*, had appeared, even though Mercedes had mostly hidden their affair. She would do the same to Beaton in 1961, although she reconciled with him some years later.

George Schlee introduced Garbo to Baron Erich von Goldschmidt-Rothschild in the early 1950s. Silver-haired and courtly, with impeccable manners, he was fifteen years older than Garbo. When he lived in Berlin, the baron had owned an important collection of paintings until the Nazis seized it; the Rothschilds were Jewish. The baron escaped to New York, where he advised wealthy people on investing in fine art. He often accompanied Garbo to galleries and auction houses. Like most of Garbo's friends, he found her fascinating, "a woman of every contradiction. One moment she was a serious-minded bluestocking, the next moment a Nordic gypsy dancing on top of the world." He was also entranced by her beauty.[28]

George Schlee was overburdened by running the business end of Valentina's salon, which included supervising the sixty women she employed. In a letter to the screenwriter Sam Behrman, he called the salon a "volcano," with constant phone calls to him and blow-ups on the part of the staff—and Valentina.[29] Knowing that Garbo liked to have a companion on her walks, he introduced her to the baron, who knew fine art and had time on his hands. It's surprising that Schlee allowed Garbo to associate with such handsome, cultured, and wealthy men. Salka Viertel, never friendly with Schlee, speculated that he needed to take breaks from Garbo and that he used her to gain entrée to the circle around the Greek shipping mogul Aristotle Onassis.[30]

The baron accompanied Garbo to auctions at the elegant Parke-Bernet auction house, as well as on walks, and to restaurants for lunch or dinner. In the summer of 1952, she accompanied the baron and his ex-wife on a driving tour of Austria. At the end of the tour, they dropped Garbo off at a hotel in Cannes, on the Riviera, where Schlee was waiting for her to spend the rest of the summer with her. She and Schlee then rented a yacht and sailed to Portofino in Italy, to visit Lilli Palmer and Rex Harrison, well-known actors who owned a villa in Portofino. In her memoir, Lilli Palmer described a chance meeting there between Garbo and the duchess of Windsor, for whom the British king Edward III had given up his throne. Palmer mused, "The woman for whom a man would be willing to give up his throne should obviously have been Greta Garbo, forever the world's most beautiful woman, unique and unattainable.... But there she sat in old blue slacks and a faded blouse, a lonely woman."[31] She might have added that Wallis Warfield Simpson, the duchess of Windsor, was considered by many to be chic, not beautiful, a "jolie laide" with a winning personality.

In 1953 Schlee cemented his relationship with Garbo when he persuaded her to buy a seven-room apartment on the fifth floor of the building where he and Valentina lived on the ninth floor. Schlee convinced her that it was an excellent investment. She was charmed by the building, which was on a cul-de-sac that ended at the East River. The apartment she bought had a large living room with huge glass windows that overlooked FDR Drive and the river. Resembling apartments that she had visited in Stockholm on that city's waterways, she could watch the boats passing by on the East River and think of her time in Stockholm. Or she could reminisce about her role as Anna Christie, since Anna had lived on a coal barge docked on the East River, not far from her apartment.

Once she bought the apartment in 1953, Garbo considered it her home for thirty-seven years, until she passed. Its only disadvantage—which turned out to be considerable—was that Valentina was furious when Garbo moved into it; she almost left George Schlee over what she considered a serious breach of faith. But the three of them lived in uneasy harmony until Schlee died in 1964, still living with Valentina. He was Garbo's perfect father. He was always ready to give her financial advice; to arrange their traveling; to keep photographers and fans away from her.

In 1955 he bought Le Roc, a mansion in the South of France on a large rock outcropping in a tiny village called Cap d'Ail (Cape Garlic), three miles south of Monte Carlo, a town on the Riviera with casinos, expensive restaurants, and a harbor for yachts. It was a playground for the super wealthy. Le Roc was isolated and hard to reach; no stranger could find Garbo there. Until Schlee died in 1964, Garbo spent part of every summer there with him. Schlee and Garbo rarely had guests there, although they occasionally entertained Prince Rainier and Princess Grace of Monaco.

They also met Aristotle Onassis and his crowd on the Riviera, and they sailed with him and other guests on his huge yacht, a former frigate, outfitted with a swimming pool, a screening room, a collection of fine paintings, many bedrooms, and as many as fifty servants. Onassis was a womanizer, and he courted Garbo, even with Schlee present, until he finally proposed marriage to her. When Schlee heard about the proposal, he made a public scene, although Garbo had turned down Onassis. Because of his outburst, Schlee was barred from the yacht. Garbo went with Schlee, and Onassis courted Italian opera singer Maria Callas, before marrying Jackie Kennedy.

In the fall of 1964, Garbo's relationship with Schlee suddenly ended when he died of a heart attack in Paris, on their return to New York from Le Roc. He had been ill for several years. The night he died, they had gone out to dinner with Cécile de Rothschild. Garbo had then gone back to their hotel room and to bed. Taking a walk, Schlee was hit by the heart attack and collapsed. The proprietor of a restaurant found him and called an ambulance, in which he died. Rothschild was contacted, and she took Garbo over. She spirited her from her hotel, waited until she calmed down, and put her on a private plane to New York.

Villa Le Roc in Monte Carlo. *Süddeutsche Zeitung* Photo / Alamy Stock Photo

Valentina came to Paris to claim Schlee's body. She had it brought to New York, and she arranged for a funeral. She barred Garbo from the funeral, from their apartment, and from Le Roc, which she inherited and soon sold. Playing the bereaved widow, even though she had spent summers for years in Venice with her lover, Valentina had a Greek Orthodox priest cleanse Le Roc and her New York apartment of Garbo's spirit. Valentina was very superstitious.

For the next twenty-five years, until Valentina died in 1989, seven months before Garbo passed, they didn't speak to each other. Valentina called Garbo "the vamp" or "the fifth floor," the floor where Garbo's apartment was. They managed to reach an unspoken agreement under which Garbo had the rights to the lobby during the day, but at seven o'clock she had to return to her apartment, and then Valentina could go out. The elevator boys knew that if they picked up Valentina on the ninth floor, they mustn't stop at the fifth floor, because Garbo might be there.

Garbo's friends were surprised by her grief over Schlee's death. She was disconsolate for months. During her 1962 visit to Stockholm, when she received a telegram from Schlee saying that they couldn't marry because Valentina was Greek Orthodox and she didn't believe in divorce, Garbo had confessed to her school friends that her failure to marry had been a great mistake, as great as her failure to get over her shyness. She envied people who were growing old with a partner. But she didn't say that she had figured out how to use her lack of self-confidence to further her own ends. In essence, it was the shy Garbo that no one could resist.

Given Cécile de Rothschild's aid in spiriting Garbo away from Paris after George Schlee's death, Cécile moved to the center of Garbo's life. In photos, Cécile looks mannish and dignified, with white hair and a bulky body. But she was wealthy, collected fine art, and liked to garden.

In the summer of 1965, Garbo and Cecil Beaton toured the Greek islands on Cécile Rothschild's yacht, with Cécile and several of her friends. Beaton was miserable on the cruise. Garbo behaved like a child, using expressions he hated, like "I won't tell you that," and "You guess." But Beaton liked Cécile. Open and friendly, Cécile didn't hide her lesbianism; she was among the wealthy group that Garbo had once said could indulge in any sexual behavior with impunity. But Beaton thought that Cécile was mesmerized by Garbo, acting "like a kid [goat] hypnotized by a cobra." On the other hand, when Cécile met Salka Viertel several years later, she told Salka that Garbo was "exhausting and overbearing."[32]

Cécile was very wealthy, and she loved adventure—traveling to a distant land, seeing a new play, touring a new museum. Like Gayelord Hauser, she relieved Garbo's melancholy through activity. Garbo didn't live with her, but most summers, she went on a long cruise with Cécile on her yacht, and most winters, Cécile visited Garbo in New York. They sometimes met in Paris. Like George Schlee, Cécile took over the tasks that Garbo hated: booking hotels and restaurants; securing tickets for airplanes, plays, and museums. Cécile had assistants who took care of these matters, and she had access to a car and driver in most cities, through Rothschild connections.

Both Cécile and Erich von Goldschmidt-Rothschild were members of the fabulously wealthy Rothschild family, which was Jewish. Centuries before, Christian church law forbade Christian merchants in many lands from engaging in "usury," or charging interest on loans, but Jewish law contained no such prohibition. Subject to discrimination in many careers and businesses, some Jews became bankers, moving into a business that was open to them.

In the late eighteenth century, Mayer Amschel, the founder of the Rothschild banking dynasty, lived in a red house in the Jewish ghetto in Frankfurt, Germany. He turned his business changing money into a bank and adopted the historic name Rothschild as his surname, drawn from his red house. He had five sons, and when they were adults he established each of them in a major city—Paris, London, Berlin, Vienna, and Genoa—where each one founded a bank. The rulers of the many small German states, which were independent until Germany was unified in 1871, had difficulty securing loans. They turned to the Rothschild bankers, who could draw on intra-European resources. The most spectacular Rothschild loan financed the English army in the Napoleonic wars, making a sizable profit in the end, since they chose the winning side. They also financed the French government in building the Suez Canal, and Cecil Rhodes in founding Rhodesia and exploiting the diamond mines in South Africa. They provided loans for building many railroads, a new form of transportation.[33]

The Rothschild brothers and their families socialized and vacationed together, and they supported each other's banks. The first Rothschild generations married cousins; the later ones married the offspring of other wealthy families, often Jewish. They became vintners, racehorse breeders, collectors of fine art, and philanthropists. The rulers of the Austro-Hungarian Empire gave them titles, as did Queen Victoria of England; that's why the Rothschilds in Garbo's orbit were called "baron" and had a "de" (French) or a "von" (German) in their surnames. Cécile de Rothschild was a member of the French Rothschilds and a direct descendant of Mayer Amschel.

Cécile didn't take over Garbo's life, as George Schlee had. Garbo reconnected with friends she hadn't seen for a while. Those friends included the radio singer Jessica Dragonette and her husband, Nicholas Turner, who said that Garbo now came to their apartment for drinks several evenings a week, while he became one of her walking companions. With their own brand of humor, Turner and Dragonette entered into Garbo's fantasy games. said that after Schlee passed in 1964 and Jessica in 1980, Garbo asked him to take over Schlee's place in her life, eventually marrying her, but Turner refused her. He knew how she had manipulated Schlee, and he didn't want that to happen to him.[34] According to Phyllis Wilbourn, Garbo had offered her that position before Katharine Hepburn "swept her away."

Reconnecting with Dragonette and Turner led Garbo to Gayelord Hauser, who had introduced her to them in the first place. She now visited Hauser at his estate in the Hollywood Hills and at the mansion he owned in Sicily, near Palermo. Indicating their closeness, Gayelord called her "girl-friend." His guest house was available to Garbo for free, and she liked that. Despite her wealth, she was still frugal. Every Sunday, no matter where she was, Gayelord called her, although he didn't always enjoy their conversations. "That woman is so pessimistic," he told a friend. "I talk about everything I can think of, but she always brings it back to her own gloom and doom."[35] Hauser died in 1984, ending another one of Garbo's major friendships.

She also reconnected with her niece Gray Horan, Sven Gustafsson's daughter. Sven died in 1967. Gray was now married and living with her husband and children in New Jersey. Exhibiting a strong and renewed sense of family, Garbo visited them there, and they spent time with her in New York. She played games with her nephews; in her sixties, she taught them how to do somersaults, and they adored her.[36] Under a sofa in her New York apartment, they found a group of tiny plastic trolls—painted in vivid colors, with bushy hair and spooky faces. They often played fantasy games with the trolls. Garbo's friend Sam Green also found the trolls. He concluded that Garbo played with them, especially on nights when she couldn't sleep.

Gray and her family were among the few individuals Garbo entertained in her apartment; she wouldn't bring her friends together because she still feared that they would exchange stories about her or talk to journalists. Several times, she took Gray with her to Antigua, an island in the West Indies, to swim and soak up the sun. Gray was impressed that on these occasions her aunt read serious literature, while she read popular novels. Gray was intelligent and well educated; her husband was a dentist. They now constituted Garbo's official family, although Garbo also reconnected with Salka Viertel when Salka moved to New York to help raise her granddaughter Christine.

Salka found Christmas Eve 1958 to be symbolic of the love they shared, which may have lessened from time to time, but which never ended. On that Christmas Eve, Salka was staying at a friend's apartment, and she was alone. Suddenly, there was an unexpected knock on the door. Salka opened the door to find Garbo there, with a small, decorated Christmas tree and a bottle of vodka. They greeted each other warmly, and Salka found glasses for the vodka. They toasted each other, with both saying "Skol." In her memoir, Salka wrote that on that Christmas Eve she found Garbo "compassionate, unchanged, and very dear."[37]

Garbo later told Salka that she had spent Christmas Day with the Schlees and that she had found that day to be to be "sheer torment."

# 14

## Summing Up

W HEN GARBO RESIGNED from MGM in 1942, she had achieved her childhood dream of becoming a great actress. She had shown authority and humanity in playing the title role in *Queen Christina*; because of that film, she had become an inspiration to women and men worldwide. When Winston Churchill was on Aristotle Onassis's yacht along with Garbo, cruising the Mediterranean, he told her that when he was in his air-raid shelter in London during the German bombings of London in World War II, he had watched *Queen Christina* to firm up his resolve. Svetlana Alliluyeva, Josef Stalin's daughter, saw *Queen Christina* as an adolescent in Moscow. Identifying with Christina, she realized that she was the rebellious daughter of an autocrat. Jiang Qing, the wife of Mao Zedong, the totalitarian ruler of China during the twentieth century, identified with Garbo in *Camille*. She wrote to Garbo that she had watched *Camille* so often that the tape on which it was recorded had broken and couldn't be fixed.[1]

Garbo had triumphed twice over the powerful and crafty Louis B. Mayer—in 1927, when he agreed to cast her in dramatic roles, not just vamp parts, and in 1933, when production began on *Queen Christina*. Among her last experiences with him was during the filming of *Camille*, when he asked the producer David Lewis to bring her to his office alone. Garbo had never been in this office. Mayer closed the door behind her. She came out several minutes later with a strange expression on her face. Lewis was certain that Mayer had tried to seduce her.[2]

The journalist Rilla Page Palmborg had paid Garbo's domestic staff to expose flaws in her character, and she had then used what they told her to write an article and a book critical of Garbo. At the end of the book, however, she praised Garbo for having successfully challenged the popular stereotype of Swedes as country yokels, stupid and too tall. Through Garbo's photographs and films, Palmborg implied, she had replaced that negative stereotype with an image of the Swedish woman as the epitome of beauty—an image that persisted throughout the twentieth century. Palmborg might have added that by making sloe eyes and high cheekbone fashionable, Garbo had challenged the racism then directed at Slavic women. These features can be found today on models on fashion runways throughout the world.

Given Garbo's insecurities, apparent in her attacks of anxiety, depression, and paranoia, plus the threatening way the public often treated her, she can hardly be faulted for turning for security to wealthy individuals with the money to protect her, becoming a celebrity in the process. She must have felt a sense of triumph as a female Don Juan, whom no man or woman could resist. She achieved the vaunted American dream of rising from poverty to wealth by turning herself from the daughter of indigent parents who had raised her in a "slum" into the world's most beautiful woman and its greatest actress. She was a female Napoleon or a reconfigured Cleopatra for the twentieth century. In Plutarch's *Lives of the Noble Greeks and Romans*, written while his subjects were still alive, Plutarch described Cleopatra as plain looking but mesmeric in personality.

Once the definition of ideal female beauty had shifted from chubby to svelte, and from round eyes and cheeks to sloe eyes and high cheekbones, Garbo became the world's ideal female beauty. Her ability to ignore the criticisms of her appearance and her acting and to follow her star to its ultimate destination is worthy of praise, even though, as others have pointed out, she often seemed unable to choose a novel or a play that was worthy of her acting ability. But it must not be forgotten that Garbo thought she was a failure in *Queen Christina* and that Salka

Viertel, always jealous of her, was ambivalent about Garbo's acting ability.

Her greatest triumph may have been her assertion of her will to keep her chronic illnesses under control and pain and depression at bay. We know today that the adage "mind over matter" works, as we turn to yoga, biofeedback, Pilates, acupuncture, and Chinese tai chi to calm ourselves and gain control over pain. All these systems existed when Garbo was alive, but until recently they were considered foolish fads. It was Mercedes de Acosta who persuaded Garbo to turn to them. Garbo's chronic illnesses didn't disappear, although after 1957, when she had an attack of pain from her ovarian and pelvic inflammations, there is no further mention of these ailments in newspapers or in the archival material on her. I suspect that she finally took a sulfa drug or penicillin to end it.

But she didn't avoid the ailments of aging; as she aged, she developed arthritis, diabetes, and what she called lumbago, or severe back pain. Due to her chain-smoking, often of cigarillos (small, thin cigars), she developed what we today call COPD (chronic obstructive pulmonary disease). None of these illnesses killed her; she finally developed kidney disease, from which her father had died. But she was brave; she underwent kidney dialysis two days a week in the year before she died.

Moreover, as she aged, her physical beauty diminished—in terms of definitions of ideal beauty in the mid-twentieth century. Because of the large amount of time she had spent sunning herself during her life, she developed wrinkles, a natural product of aging, which were considered ugly during her lifetime and are still considered ugly today, as we fixate on youth as the ideal. Sunblock lotion didn't exist during Garbo's lifetime; only suntan oil was available. It aided tanning, but it didn't prevent wrinkles. Many of her friends unexpectedly found her staring at her face in a mirror to see if she had developed wrinkles. It wasn't a futile gesture; her mother had become wrinkled at a relatively young age, and Garbo seemed to know that wrinkles are hereditary. She worried about being dropped from MGM because of them.

She was especially concerned about the transverse wrinkles between her nose and her mouth. Ingmar Bergman, the famed Swedish film director, discussed them in his autobiography, *The Magic Lantern*. When

Garbo was in Stockholm in 1962, she visited Bergman in his office at SFI. She was then fifty-seven. At first, he found her beauty "imperishable." "If she had been an angel from one of the gospels, I would have said that her beauty floated above her." When Bergman turned on a desk lamp, however, the light illuminated Garbo's face, and Bergman was startled. "Her mouth was ugly," he wrote, "a pale slit surrounded by transverse wrinkles. It was strange and disturbing. All that beauty and in the middle of the beauty a shrill discord."[3]

Was Bergman's statement misogynistic? Or was he identifying Garbo as a "tragi-sexual goddess"? Peter Bradshaw used that term to characterize the many beautiful Swedish women in Bergman's films who are emotionally and sometimes physically wracked with pain.[4]

Gayelord Hauser thought Garbo's transverse lines had been caused by her continual puffing on cigarettes, but despite her extraordinary willpower, she was unable to give up smoking. In 1935, when Salka Viertel was in her late thirties, Salka went to a London clinic for a face-lift, but Garbo wouldn't undergo surgery on her face; she was afraid of the knives that would be used. She went to Erno Laszlo, the New York cosmetologist, for facial treatments, but this Svengali of the Face, as he was called, told her that he couldn't do anything about the lines. She wore the popular "frownies," small adhesive strips which were supposed to stop wrinkling, but they didn't have much of an effect.

She often talked about loving alcohol, calling whiskey "mother's milk," but that was a common conversational gambit in the 1970s and 1980s, when many sophisticated people drank a lot. She may have been a pattern drinker—she limited herself to two shots a day of either vodka or scotch, and her friends say that she kept to that limit. But she wasn't an alcoholic; if she stumbled during her last years, that was probably a result of the heart attack she had in Klosters in 1988, when her niece, plus a doctor, went to the Swiss village to bring her back to New York. Karen Swenson did considerable research on the issue of Garbo's drinking, and I agree with her conclusions that Garbo wasn't an alcoholic.[5]

Throughout her career, Garbo was honored for her acting. She never won an Oscar, but she was nominated for the award four times: for *Anna Christie* and *Romance* in 1930; for *Anna Karenina* in 1936; and for *Camille* in 1937. Among her films, only *Grand Hotel* won the Oscar for best picture. Realizing her greatness as an actress, the executive board of the Academy of Motion Picture Arts and Sciences awarded her a special Oscar in 1955 for "luminous and unforgettable screen performances." She didn't go to Hollywood to receive the award; she still wouldn't appear in public. Nor would she put her foot into cement outside Grauman's Chinese Theater in Hollywood, another tribute to stardom.

Sweden also honored her. She was awarded the blue ribbon of Litteris et Artibus, Sweden's highest artistic award; she was the first actress to be so honored. In 1981 she was named a commander of the Royal Order of the North Star, First Class. That same year, Sweden issued a stamp honoring her, with a scene from *The Saga of Gösta Berling* on it. She didn't go to Sweden to receive these awards; special ceremonies were held in New York.

Garbo wasn't a philanthropist, but she gave money to the Finnish War Relief Fund and to Salka Viertel's fund for the Jewish refugees from Hitler's tyranny who came Los Angeles. It's said that she gave a large sum to the foundation established in the name of Carole Lombard, a Hollywood film star, who was killed in a plane crash on the way home from a tour selling war bonds for World War II. Garbo had a reputation for visiting Hollywood people who were in mourning or very ill; she made such visits to Elizabeth Taylor after her husband Mike Todd died in a plane crash, and to Montgomery Clift after he suffered the terrible accident that disfigured his beautiful face. She cared for Harry Crocker, a Hollywood journalist who had been a close friend, during his final illness.

She did the same for George Schlee and Salka Viertel. It was in memory of her father, for whom she had cared as he died from kidney disease when she was a teenager. She generously helped John Gilbert and Erich von Stroheim when their careers were failing, and she helped Gavin Gordon, her co-star in *Romance*, when he broke his shoulder in a car accident while filming. But she was always frugal, and in her will she left her estate, nearly intact, to her niece.

In 1968, Garbo finally finished decorating her seven-room apartment in New York. Given her perfectionism and indecision, that task took her fifteen years to complete. She adopted a grand European design. The living room contained Louis XV and Regency sofas and chairs. There were damask curtains at the windows, and a huge eighteenth-century Aubusson carpet on the floor. The paneled fireplace wall contained bookshelves with sets of leatherbound classics on them, surrounding a sedate fireplace. They were for show; Garbo once said that she hadn't read any of them. But such a display of leatherbound books was common in decorating schemes in the mid-twentieth century.

Garbo's bedroom contained eighteenth-century painted Swedish furniture. The dining room was furnished with a large table and twelve chairs with needlepoint seats, as though Garbo had meant to hold large dinner parties. But, like so much in her life, it was just for show; it was an appropriate setting for a screen goddess in her later years. The upholstery on the furniture was in shades of green, pink, rose, and salmon—her favorite colors. She used little white in her decorating scheme; she found it dull. She seems to have been planning this decorative scheme for years. She had the decorator Billy Baldwin match in paint the off-pink color of a swatch of fabric she had taken from a lampshade on the first Swedish train on which she had ridden. She used the paint Baldwin produced to paint all the walls in her apartment.

There were expensive knickknacks on the tables, reminiscent of the objects she had touched in the visit she and Mimi Pollak made to the Wachtmeisters' mansion outside Stockholm in 1929. Her art collection covered the walls of most of the rooms in her apartment, sometimes from floor to ceiling. Cecil Beaton, who discerned the influence of George Schlee in her decorative scheme, disliked it. He called it "a hodgepodge of colors." Others found it warm and bright. Reflecting her sense of humor, she placed a blow-up plastic snowman, dressed in a vest and a hat, on a chair in her living room.

Was Garbo lesbian? I have addressed this question throughout this book, and I will review some of my conclusions here. The evidence is compelling for affairs with Mimi Pollak, Mercedes de Acosta, and Salka Viertel—even if intercourse was infrequent. The evidence for affairs with Louise Brooks, Lilyan Tashman, and Fifi D'Orsay is less substantial, although it exists. I stand in the camp of those who conclude that Garbo and Cecil Beaton had an affair, and I can't believe that George Schlee would have left Valentina for Garbo if she didn't offer him sex, although Garbo may have pursued him because of his ability to manage her financial affairs. He became angry when she flirted with other men, and he became apoplectic when he discovered that her relationship with Cecil Beaton went beyond friendship. In the case of Cécile de Rothschild, the individuals who knew Garbo and Cécile are split. Betty Spiegel, the wife of the producer Sam Spiegel, and the photographer Jean Howard are certain that they were physically involved, while Sam Green is adamant that they weren't.

Garbo never called herself a lesbian, although she had friends who used that word, especially Mercedes de Acosta. Garbo may have realized that male children and men were treated better than female children and women, so she adopted what men wore. Or was it a masquerade on her part, like her pretense in her thirties that she was a young girl—or a young boy? But she often called herself a "young boy" or a "man," and many of her friends stated that she looked like a man. She loved to cross-dress, but that alone does not mean she was a lesbian.

Like Marlene Dietrich, Garbo had many lovers. Some were female, but many were male. According to the Hollywood director George Cukor, she would "do anything, pick up any man, go to bed with him."[6] Salka Viertel called her "a sexual adventurer," but evidence exists for only one sexual encounter between the two of them. Raymond Daum stated in a 1995 letter to the New York Times that producer Walter Wanger told him Garbo was the most sexually alive woman he had ever known and that Garbo was more attracted to women than to men. Marlene Dietrich simplified the matter by saying that European women had sex with anyone they found attractive. By and large, Garbo didn't hide her affairs with men, but she kept her affairs with women secret. Both Elizabeth Bergner, a star of the German stage, and Ina Claire, a Broadway star and one of John Gilbert's wives, who had played a Russian countess in Ninotchka, disclosed that she had tried to seduce them, but they had refused her.

Three themes in Garbo's later years stand out. The first is her friendship with Salka Viertel, after Salka moved to Klosters, an Alpine village in Switzerland, to be with her son Peter and his family. The second is her association with art broker Sam Green, whom Cécile de Rothschild recruited to watch out for Garbo as she aged. The third is her successful completion of her search to find a religion that satisfied her. That success grew out of her friendship with Jessica Dragonette and her husband, Nicholas Turner, which lasted from 1940, when Gayelord Hauser introduced them, until 1980, when Jessica died. Nikki, as he was called, was much younger than Jessica, and he remained friends with Garbo until her death in 1990. Jessica expressed the core of that friendship in her description in her autobiography of their interactions at their first meeting. Both were also devout Catholics, and that faith became important to Garbo.

In the early spring of 1960, when Salka Viertel moved to Klosters, her son Peter, a successful writer, supported her financially. He had moved there several years earlier because of its excellent skiing and because, as a writer, he liked its quiet. Located in a large valley between two mountain peaks, Klosters had remained a traditional Alpine village. Its architecture was dominated by Swiss chalets, which are built like log cabins, with the logs piled up and held together with cement. They have decorated balconies and large plateglass windows, to generate heat from the sun's rays and to afford a panoramic view of the forests and mountains that surround Klosters. Their gabled metal roofs are pitched at a steep angle so that snow will slide off. Their exteriors are often decorated with signs and symbols; the architects who originally designed them were influenced by the Romantic movement and by farmhouses in Sweden and Germany. The name "Klosters" was derived from a cloister that had been built there in the thirteenth century.[7]

Davos, a modernized village, is roughly seven miles from Klosters. It is accessible by a scenic ride on a narrow-gauge train that traverses a somewhat-harrowing mountain track. In the early twentieth century, Davos had a large sanitarium for sufferers from bronchial and lung diseases, who benefited from the fresh mountain air there. Thomas Mann wrote his epic novel *The Magic Mountain* while staying there. He was a regular at Salka's salon in Santa Monica after he left Germany for the West Coast; he may have told her about these Swiss mountain villages.

Peter Viertel loved Klosters, calling it in his memoir *Dangerous Friends* "a Shangri-La that often lay above the clouds in brilliant sunshine." But Salka didn't like Klosters. After a life full of people, noise, and confusion, while raising three boys, working at a noisy Hollywood movie studio, advising refugees and Hollywood actors, running organizations, and holding a salon, Klosters was too quiet for her. She didn't like its climate of long, cold winters and brief warm summers, and she didn't like the snow. She didn't know how to ski, and she was too old to learn. Soon after she arrived, Peter married actress Deborah Kerr; they spent half the year in Spain, and Peter sent his daughter, Salka's beloved grandchild, to a private school in England. Salka felt abandoned. She was destitute, living on Peter's largesse, while her two other sons were in the United States, with neither the money nor the time to visit her, and she didn't have the funds to visit them. She hosted a tea many afternoons, but she spent much of her time in Klosters reading and eventually writing her autobiography, *The Kindness of Strangers*.

In typical Salka fashion, in that memoir she hid her deep discontent with her life, making her autobiography nearly as false as Mercedes de Acosta's. Given Salka's involvement with family and friends throughout most of her life, her title doesn't jibe with reality. "I have always depended on the kindness of strangers" is among the last lines in Tennessee Williams's play *A Streetcar Named Desire*. It is spoken by Blanche DuBois to the doctor who will take her to a mental institution. A fading Southern belle, she mourns the loss of her beauty, but she still expects a man to save her, even though her brother-in-law, Stanley Kowalski, has raped her. The line is deeply ironic. Spoken by a madwoman, it has no meaning at all. Perhaps in her title Salka refers to the many individuals she didn't know who gave money to fund her attempts to save Jews in Eastern Europe from Hitler's Holocaust. Or she may have been chastising her sons—and Garbo—for not helping her more. In Klosters, when she wrote her autobiography, she felt abandoned.

Salka titled the German version of her memoir *Das unbelehbare Herz*, a phrase which translates into English as the irredeemable heart. That phrase seems to mean that her emotions always motivated her actions, especially her extraordinary efforts to save the Jews in Europe threatened by Hitler's holocaust, and that nothing could stop her from following where her emotions led her.

Soon after Salka arrived in Klosters, she received a letter from Garbo saying that her Swedish friend wanted to visit her. Garbo wrote: "You would never know that I love you when you never hear anything from me, but I do, and forever. I would give anything to be back in the days when I could take my buggy and drive to Mabery Road and see you—the vibrant, wonderful person that is you."[8] It's not surprising that Garbo wanted to visit Salka in Klosters. What Salka disliked about Klosters—the cold, the silence, the small population—appealed to Garbo. The dry air would help her breathing; the Swiss ethic of privacy meant that the local people would accept her as Harriet Brown and not bother her, even if they knew that she was Garbo. The Klosters population was used to celebrities in their midst; Britain's then-Prince Charles and his family came there every year for skiing, as did Hollywood notables like Audrey Hepburn, Yul Brynner, Orson Welles, and Gene Kelly. In some circles, Klosters was known as "Hollywood on the Rocks."[9]

Garbo mostly went there in the summer. Wandering around the town and sometimes walking to Davos, she discovered the small local cemeteries, which gave her a feeling of peace and a sense of eternity. "It's not morbid walking around cemeteries," she said, "it's rewarding and uplifting." She left New York in July and returned around September 15, which was her birthday, when she could assume that New York had cooled down and that air conditioners, which bothered her breathing, weren't being used.

Some of Peter's close friends moved to Klosters, like the novelist Irwin Shaw, known for his novel *The Young Lions*, about soldiers in World War II. He and his wife liked the snow, the skiing, and the quiet, which was conducive to writing. Gore Vidal soon appeared—some say it was because as a homosexual who wrote about homosexuality, he was fascinated by Garbo and he wanted to know her better. He wrote in his memoir *Palimpsest* that Garbo liked to dress up in his clothes and pretend that she was a homosexual boy.[10] She loved to flirt with all of them: Peter, Irwin Shaw, Gore Vidal. She sometimes recruited them to walk with her to the train station, where she bought movie fan magazines; her favorite, according to Vidal, was *Silver Screen*. As always, she liked to be one of the boys.

Salka agreed to Garbo's visit with enthusiasm. It was like a daughter coming home to her mother. And she knew that if she arranged a visit that Garbo really liked, she might come back again. She also knew that Cécile de Rothschild had a villa in St. Moritz, Brian and Eleanor Aherne a house on Lake Geneva, and Noël Coward a retreat at Les Avants. She also knew that Garbo, who had difficulty making decisions, often took no action.

For Garbo's first visit to Klosters, Salka organized shopping expeditions and mountain hikes for the two of them, providing a schedule of activities for Garbo. She had a taxi pick up Garbo at the Zurich airport and drive her to Klosters. She, not Peter's cook, prepared Garbo's meals, following Garbo's limited diet. She found a place for Garbo to rent, and she filled it with necessities so that everything Garbo needed would be there when she arrived. With time on her hands, Salka was, ironically, acting like Mercedes de Acosta.

Salka's scheme worked. Garbo came back almost every year for the next thirty years. Even though Garbo grumbled and complained, she still preserved her affection for Salka. They were both powerhouses, and they sometimes fought for control, but as always, Salka expressed her ambivalence about Garbo only in her diary. On October 7, 1967, she wrote that Garbo was increasingly lonely, but she treated Cécile terribly. November 21, 1967: "I am still attached to Greta. But her narcissism is exasperating. She cannot stop mourning the loss of her beauty." July 21, 1968: "Her letters have been the same for forty years." August 17, 1968: "No one bores me as much as Greta."[11]

Garbo told her New York friends that she lived the same boring life in Klosters that she lived in New York: up early with exercises in the morning; shopping in the village; lunch; an afternoon nap; a long hike; dinner; early to bed. But there were compensations: friends she made in Klosters; the same climate as in Sweden, without the crowds of journalists and photographers that followed her in her home country; the beauty of the mountains and forests. At first, Salka found Garbo a chalet to rent, but later she stayed in two rooms in the top floor of the village hotel, with spectacular views of the mountains and the forests.

And Klosters offered her a place to practice her humanitarian instincts. It was hard to realize that Salka was slowly declining, but the tough Polish woman who dyed her white hair red and had been a Hollywood powerhouse was slowly succumbing to the paralysis of Parkinson's disease, to deafness, and to severe arthritis. Eventually, Salka was confined to a wheelchair, and she had to be fed, dressed, and bathed, as she slowly lost her sight and her hearing. In the 1970s, Garbo's friend Sam Green came to Klosters with Garbo, shortly before Salka died. He wrote of the experience, giving the only extant glimpse into the relationship between Garbo and Salka as Salka slowly passed: "We walked about half mile up the road to a little chalet and, without knocking, went in through the side door. I followed her up to a second-floor balcony, where a wizened lady with flowing white hair was sitting, wrapped up in a lap robe. She couldn't speak, and I don't think she could comprehend, either, but Garbo made small talk with her, and there was a sense of communication between them."[12]

Salka died in 1978, at the age of eighty-nine. She was buried in the Klosters cemetery. Garbo continued to go to Klosters in the summers for the next twenty years, until she had a mild stroke, and her niece Gray Horan, along with a doctor, flew to Zurich, took a car to Klosters, picked up Garbo, and then reversed the journey to bring her back to New York by plane.

The second theme concerns Sam Green, who became important in Garbo's life in 1970, when Cécile de Rothschild recruited him to watch over Garbo for her. As Garbo reached her mid-sixties, Cécile worried that she spent too much time alone in her apartment, with only an elderly Swiss woman to care for her, as well as the apartment. Sam was thirty; he lived only a few blocks from Garbo, and he carried on his business as an art broker from his home.

When he and Garbo met, they liked each other so much that he became one of her walking companions. When they were both in New York, they talked on the phone several mornings each week, planning their walks and discussing their lives. As he had with other famous friends, he recorded their conversations for posterity.

On their walks Garbo and Sam played childish games like Kick the Can and Imitate the Passerby, and Sam kept strangers away from Garbo. Garbo suspected that many of them wanted her autograph because it was worth a lot of money; she called them "customers."

Garbo allowed him to enter her apartment where, like a beloved son, he repaired leaky faucets and replaced light bulbs. She didn't permit strangers in her home, and she considered repairmen to be strangers.

Sam even cut her hair after she decided that the beauticians in salons sold what she told them to journalists.

Garbo and Sam took trips together. She sometimes went with him on weekends to his beach house on Fire Island, off the New York coast, a favorite vacation spot for New Yorkers.

Sam took her to London, where he talked her into making a last visit to Cecil Beaton at his country home. Beaton was paralyzed from a stroke he had suffered several years earlier. Sam called their meeting a real "tear-jerker." Before they ate lunch, Garbo sat on Beaton's lap, kissing and hugging him.

The childish behavior of Garbo and Sam—as well as of Cécile—can be seen in a prank that the three of them played when they had brunch at The Regency Hotel on Park Avenue, where Cécile stayed when she visited New York. Garbo always wore a large trench coat with many pockets to the brunches, and when they were seated, she kept it on. They then hid much of the flatware on the table in the pockets of her coat, to see if the hotel manager would have the nerve to search a celebrity like Garbo. In fact, they were never caught.

Garbo's adventures with Sam weren't always happy. On her eightieth birthday, in 1985, the Rothschilds held a birthday party for her at one of their wineries near Paris. She was told that it would be small and intimate. Neither Garbo nor Sam knew that the Rothschilds intended to play a prank on her. But when she and San arrived at the winery, there were over a hundred guests, including journalists and photographers. The menu was composed of foods that Garbo couldn't eat, like shellfish. She tolerated the party, but she was seething inside. Garbo had often teased Cécile for her large body and solemn air, and Cécile may have been paying her back. After the party, Garbo dropped the Rothschilds, including Cécile. She felt humiliated, and she couldn't stand that emotion.

Garbo soon dropped Sam after a tabloid reporter contacted his assistant, who talked about his relationship with Garbo. The tabloid then ran a feature story claiming that Garbo and Sam were going to be married. That was untrue; Garbo and he were just good friends. Sam made the publisher print a retraction; he tried to convince Garbo that the story was a simple mistake, but she wouldn't listen. Once Garbo made up her mind, she rarely backed down.

The third theme that dominated her final years was religion, which had always been important to her. She had abandoned the Lutheranism in which she had been raised, but she remembered the ecstasy of belief in an all-powerful God and his promise to bring believers to heaven once they died. She discovered Hinduism and Buddhism through Mercedes de Acosta, but she was never entirely able to accept them, although she was intrigued by the doctrine that man and the universe are one and that negative emotions like jealousy and envy can be eliminated through meditation and prayer. Through Christopher Isherwood and Aldous Huxley, she met Krishnamurti, the great Hindu teacher, but even he didn't convert her. She took her friend Jean Norman with her to a revival meeting held by Billy Graham, the Christian evangelist preacher, in New York's Madison Square Garden. She was impressed by him and the crowds he drew, but not enough to come forward at the end of the service for his laying on of hands to bring the spirit of God into the congregant and the cry of "I believe!"[13]

She often expressed a desire to go to India with Mercedes to meet swamis there, but that never happened; Mercedes probably became too insistent about her beliefs. In 1936, however, Garbo wrote with great excitement to Hörke Wachtmeister, denying the Lutheran belief in a triune god and original sin and proclaiming that "there is only one God and he created everything out of one spirit. And God is love." A month later, she wrote to Hörke that "I would like to travel to India and become wise. If I did that, perhaps I could find some way to master my body."[14]

Her personal library, sold at an auction after she died, contained many books on religion and spirituality; she had studied those subjects for years. Her therapist Eric Drimmer found her to be expert on Eastern religions, which they often discussed in her therapy sessions. She and Sam Green discussed reincarnation—a tenet of Hinduism—but her practical side took over, and she had many objections. "They go to another form [after death]? Are they flowers or stars or horses? That means there would be another world. Everybody you see around—idiots, sickly children, all kinds of things. You change on this earth so that you can prepare for the next coming?"[15] She had great difficulty meditating—"The same bloody thoughts were still there." She told those thoughts to go away, but they kept coming back.

In many ways, acting had become Garbo's religion and Mauritz Stiller her god; he had taken her over at the beginning of her acting career and re-created her, sending her into a trancelike glow in front of the camera, in which she created movements and expressions that had become second nature to her when she practiced them for hours before performing for the camera. That mesmeric glow made her into an idol worshipped by millions of fans who wanted to touch her, like the gods carried through the streets in India who are revered by people who want to touch them to receive their divine blessing. Could the worship of her fans bring Garbo into a belief system? Or did secular idolatry and her fans' sometimes frightening obsession with her get in the way of her attempt to find a religious faith? Deep inside, she was cynical and practical, but there was spiritualism within her as well.

Her New York walking partners—Nikki Turner and Raymond Daum in particular—have said that on their walks with her she wanted to go into every church they went by, including Jewish synagogues and Quaker meetinghouses, and pray in them, hoping to be hit over the head by faith.[16] She envied people who were religious; they seemed so certain about life and death. She had once shared in that certainty, but she was now terrified of both.

Jessica Dragonette, influenced her more on religion than anyone else. Garbo remained close to Jessica from their meeting in 1940 until Jessica's death in 1980. A devout Catholic, Jessica had been raised in an orphanage near Philadelphia by the Sisters of Charity. Garbo was in awe of her because of her great fame and her spirituality, evident in her calm, glowing demeanor, and because she was supposed to have cured a dying girl in a hospital in Toronto by singing "Ave Maria" to her over the telephone. Dragonette called her autobiography *Faith Is a Song*; she felt that through her singing, she was professing her faith and spreading the Christian gospel.[17]

Garbo never identified Jessica's brand of Catholicism with the prelates who led the conservative film censorship movement. In 1934 they had all her films still showing in the United States put into storage. They had tried to cut out important scenes in *Queen Christina*, and they had been on the set of her remaining films. Then-Bishop Francis J. Spellman of Boston had launched a one-man campaign against her movie *Two-Faced Woman* on the grounds that it was immoral for her to play two sisters in love with the same man.

Garbo asked Jessica Dragonette to describe her Catholic faith. That request launched a conversation on Catholicism and on religion in general that lasted for many months, and for several years, Nikki took Garbo to Catholic Mass most Sundays at St. Patrick's Cathedral. Just before Jessica died in 1980, she was certain that she was close to converting Garbo to Catholicism. She was going to turn Garbo over to Bishop Fulton J. Sheen of New York for the final steps. Given her fame, Jessica knew most of the senior Catholic clergy in the United States; she often attended and sang at their conventions.[18]

Sheen was an interesting choice. He was among the most liberal Catholic prelates in the United States, and he was its most effective and popular preacher. A professor at Catholic University in Washington, D.C., where he taught theology, he appeared regularly on radio and television, and he counseled many individuals. He emphasized the grace of God and the need to address world poverty; he was not an anti-communist crusader, as were many Catholic prelates in the era of McCarthyism. Sheen was an adversary of the conservative Francis J. Spellman.[19]

Jessica had a deep impact on Garbo, but so did Nikki, in taking her to St. Patrick's Cathedral. There was a statue of St. Bridget of Sweden there, and Garbo was drawn to it. St. Bridget, or Brigitta, lived in Sweden in the fourteenth century. A married woman with six children who grew to adulthood, she became a nun after her husband died. She founded the Bridgettine Order which still exists today. She was canonized because she had multiple visions of Christ in which he gave her very specific messages. She is today one of the six patron saints of Europe, and many Lutheran churches honor her on her birthday. Jessica and Nikki would have known about her; it's possible that Garbo was introduced to her when she was a devout Lutheran as a child in Sweden.

Garbo wrote to Salka about her new interest in religion: "I am going to a church where there is a saint called Jude, and I stand and stare at him and ask him to remember me. There is a guardian there and since I don't cross myself or do anything but stare and ask without words, I am sure he thinks I am some sort of lunatic."[20]

Who is St. Jude? And what is the connection to Brigitta? Who is the guardian? St. Jude was one of Jesus's twelve apostles, known as the saint of hopeless causes, to whom many desperate people pray. He is not well known, because he's easily confused with Judas Iscariot, the apostle who betrayed Jesus to the Roman authorities and is one of Christianity's great villains. A statue of him is in the old St. Patrick's Cathedral, on Mulberry Street on the Lower East Side—not the newer one on Fifth Avenue. And in one of Brigitta's visions, Christ told her to pay attention to St. Jude. Descriptions of St. Brigitta's visions were written down soon after they occurred; those descriptions are still extant today.

I thought at first that "the guardian" must have been the guardian angel, a familiar figure in Christianity who watches over believers. But Garbo would have said "guardian angel" if that's what she meant. I then realized that Garbo must have gone to the Old St. Patrick's on one of her long walks, when it was open for prayers, and no one else was there except a literal guardian who was guarding it. The saint of hopeless causes, to whom desperate people pray—St. Jude sounds perfect for Garbo. In fact, she had a small figure of St. Jude on her key chain and a larger statue of him in her bedroom. Her housekeeper recalled that if the figure wasn't there on the keychain when Garbo went out of the apartment, she would come back and get it.[21]

Garbo began to go downhill after she tripped over a vacuum cleaner in her apartment in 1987 and twisted her ankle. She now had to walk with a cane, which interfered with her taking long walks. Then came the stroke she suffered in Klosters in 1988, soon followed by a worsening of her kidney disease, which sent her kidney dialysis twice a week.

She died in her apartment on Easter Sunday, April 15, 1990. Her niece, Gray Horan, was with her. According to Nicholas Turner, Garbo was calm in her final months because she practiced what Jessica had told her, derived from her Catholic faith: "You have to take the pain. You have to take the punishment. That's the way it is." Turner said that Garbo was praying to St. Jude when she died.[22] She was eighty-four years old.

As was standard Swedish custom, Garbo was cremated, but her ashes were not buried for a number of years, because her niece feared that her grave would be looted, as Charlie Chaplin's had been. In the end, her ashes were placed in an urn and buried in the Woodland Cemetery in Stockholm, in Södermalm, at the end of the trolley line from downtown, where her mother, father, and Alva had been buried years before. The Woodland Cemetery was designed in the 1920s by the eminent Swedish architects Gunnar Asplund and Sigurd Lewerentz. It is in an ancient Nordic forest, with the graves between the trees, marked by small standing gravestones, and a wandering path through it. Statues and chapels designed by famous Swedish architects are discreetly placed in it. Reflecting Sweden's communitarian ethic, it contains no private mausoleums. A huge granite cross in an open space beyond the forest dominates the landscape. A place of somber and romantic beauty, it is meant for walking and for meditation. It has been designated a UNESCO World Heritage site.

But Garbo lies alone. A simple large headstone made of a pinkish marble stands above the grave, with only her name, Greta Garbo, written on it, in her handwriting, in large letters. A grove of trees surrounds it; it is not too far from a chapel that is built in the form of a large, round peasant farmhouse with a peaked roof. It is a fitting tribute to a woman who lived a courageous life, maintaining a difficult career even when in great pain and becoming a world icon of acting and of female beauty.[23]

# ACKNOWLEDGMENTS

WRITING ABOUT GRETA Garbo has been an adventure for me, linking my favorite subjects: beauty, biography, and film history. Ten years ago, I discussed writing about Garbo with her niece, Gray Horan, and we agreed that Garbo's appearance had never been deeply contextualized. A decade later, I have the finished book.

Aware of superb writing on Garbo in languages other than English—French, German, and Swedish—I decided to use European sources as well as American sources in writing this book, which no Garbo scholar writing in English has yet done. I also decided to push the traditional limits of biography, by making contextualization as important as chronology. I learned to read Swedish. I especially thank Kim LaPalm for helping me with Swedish translations and Doug Kremer for translating German texts for me, and for serving as my editorial consultant. To Karen Swenson I owe a special debt of gratitude for sharing with me her research notes from her superb biography of Garbo, and to the outstanding film scholar Mark Vieira for doing the same. To Nicole Solano at Rutgers University Press I owe much gratitude for her fine editorial work, her constant encouragement, and her attention to detail—in particular when sourcing hard-to-obtain images nearly 100 years old.

I was awarded several grants for researching and writing this book, including the Fulbright Chair in American Studies at Uppsala University in Sweden and a Berlin Prize at the American Academy in Berlin.

My research was also supported by a grant from the Retired Faculty and Staff Association at the University of Southern California.

I owe special thanks to the staffs at the scholarly institutes and libraries whose collections I consulted. These include: the Margaret Herrick Library of the American Motion Picture Academy of Arts and Sciences; the British Film Institute; the Swedish Film Institute: the German Literary Archives at Marbach, Germany; the Swedish Royal Library in Stockholm; the film archive at the U.S. Library of Congress; the New York Public Library, especially the Billy Rose Collection; the Oral History Collection at Columbia University; Joan Miller of the Reid Cinema Archives at Wesleyan; the collections of film magazines in the special collections of the Cinema Library at the University of Southern California; Rebecca A. Baugnon of the Karen Swenson Collection at UNCW; and the microform collections at the University of California–Los Angeles. My thanks, as always, to my agent William Clark, for his sound advice and encouragement.

Additional special thanks with much gratitude to Hugo Vickers and Dr. A. Crothers for their gracious assistance and invaluable insights as well as allowing reproduction of Cecil Beaton writings ©The Literary Executor of the late Sir Cecil Beaton, by permission of the Master and Fellows of St John's College, Cambridge.

A new era in film scholarship on microfilm has been opened up by the superb collection of film magazines on the Digital History Fan Magazine Collection. I also refer to Wikipedia for general information and The Internet Archive for books.

Thanks to individuals who aided me in my research and writing: Elinor Accampo; Alice Echols; Virginia Wexman; Jane Gaines; Hilary Hallett; Boze Hadleigh; Dag Blanck; Arne Lunde; Anthony Slide; Craig Loftin; Karin Huebner; Hugo Vickers; Dolores Janiewski; Hilary Hallett; Shelley Stamp; Ned Comstock of the Cinematics Arts Library at USC; and the members of the history department and the women's studies program at Uppsala University. Finally, I want to acknowledge the help of my daughter, Professor Olivia Banner, a superb scholar in her own right, and also the support of my husband John Laslett, during trying times of illness.

# NOTES

**Prologue**

Epigraph 1: Gray Horan, "Garbo at Home," in *The Greta Garbo Collection: Auction November 15, 1990* (New York: Sotheby's, 1990), n.p.
Epigraph 2: Sven Broman, *Conversations with Garbo* (New York: Viking, 1992).

1. Some Hollywood studios reported to an executive branch in New York, near the Wall Street banks that by 1920 were financing films. At MGM, Louis B. Mayer in Hollywood reported to Nicholas Schenk in New York.

2. Clipping, Greta Garbo file, Margaret Herrick Library, American Motion Picture Academy of Arts and Sciences (hereafter cited as AMPAAS).

3. The two new biographies of Garbo are Robert Dance, *The Sexy Sphinx: How Garbo Conquered Hollywood* (Jackson: University Press of Mississippi, 2021), and Robert Gottlieb, *Garbo* (New York: Farrar, Straus and Giroux, 2021). The most thoroughly researched biographies remain Karen Swenson, *Greta Garbo: A Life Apart* (New York: Scribner's, 1997), and Barry Paris, *Garbo* (1994; Minneapolis: University of Minnesota Press, 2002), although I disagree with Paris's conclusion that Garbo was asexual. But his devastating critique of Antonin Gronowicz, *Garbo: Her Story* (New York: Simon & Schuster, 1990), persuaded me not to use Gronowicz. I have also used David Brett, *Greta Garbo* (London: Bobson, 2012), with care, because my research findings often differ from his. On Garbo's films see Mark A. Vieira, *Greta Garbo: A Cinematic Legacy* (New York: Harry N. Abrams, 2005).

4. European Garbo scholars have not found the harsh criticism of Garbo in the European movie fan magazines that I found in U.S. magazines. Author's conversations with Maria Adorno, University of Cologne, and Daniel Weigand, University of Zurich, at the conference "Les Visage de Garbo," University of Lyon, March 12, 2020.

5. See Anthony Slide, *Inside the Hollywood Fan Magazines: A History of Star Makers, Fabricators, and Gossip Mongers* (Jackson: University Press of Mississippi, 2010).

6. Joan Jacobs Brumberg, *Fasting Girls: The History of Anorexia Nervosa* (New York: Vintage, 2003).

7. Raymond Daum, *Walking with Garbo: Conversations and Recollections*, ed. Vance Muse (New York: HarperCollins, 1991), 148.

8. Ruth Harriet Louise, unsourced clipping, Greta Garbo file, Billy Rose Theatre Collection, New York Public Library, Lincoln Center (hereafter cited as BRTC); Jane Gunther, "A Friendship," in *Greta Garbo Collection*, n.p.; Mercedes de Acosta, *Here Lies the Heart: A Tale of My Life* (1960; Mansfield Center, CT: Martino, 2016), 319; Eleanor Boardman, quoted in Kevin Brownlow, *Hollywood: The Pioneers* (London: Collins, 1970), 193.

9. Cecelia Parker, "What Garbo Taught Me," in *The Legend of Garbo*, ed. Peter Haining (London: W. H. Allen, 1990), 205–206; Ruth Biery, "The Story of Greta Garbo," *Photoplay*, May 1928.

10. Tallulah Bankhead, "Some Secrets of 'Moscow,'" in Haining, *Legend of Garbo*, 21; Sven Broman, *Garbo on Garbo* (London: Bloomsbury, 1990), 190. See also the interview with Lionel Barrymore, Greta Garbo mss., "Will Garbo Return to the Screen?," 1955, Hedda Hopper Papers, AMPAAS. See also Jean Negulesco, *Things I Did and Things I Think I Did* (New York: Simon & Schuster, 1984), 207–209; Billy Baldwin, *Billy Baldwin Remembers* (New York: Harcourt Brace Jovanovich, 1974), 172.

11. Virginia Vincent, "Famous Figures," *Screenland*, October 1930; Cecil Beaton, *Memoirs of the 40's* (New York: McGraw-Hill, 1972), 105; Pola Negri, "I Was the First 'Exclusive' Star," in Haining, *Legend of Garbo*, 134.

12. On free love, see Lois W. Banner, *Intertwined Lives: Margaret Mead, Ruth Benedict, and Their Circle* (New York: Alfred A. Knopf, 1984).

13. On feminism in the 1920s and 1930s, see Nancy L. Cott, *The Grounding of Modern Feminism* (New Haven, CT: Yale University Press, 1987); Karen Offen, "Defining Feminism: A Comparative Historical Approach," *Signs: Journal of Women in Culture and Society* 14, no. 1 (Autumn 1988), 119–157.

14. Lewis Jacobs, quoted in Haining, *Legend of Garbo*, 231.

15. Cari Beauchamp, *Without Lying Down: Frances Marion and the Powerful Women of Hollywood* (Berkeley: University of California Press, 1997), 193. See also Hillary Hallett, *Go West, Young Women! The Rise of Early Hollywood* (Berkeley: University of California Press, 2013), passim.

16. See Dorothy Manners, "Even Hollywood Heroes Can't Resist Them," *Movie Classic*, October 1931.

17. Paris, *Garbo*, 307–308. According to Paris, *Queen Christina*'s profit was greater than that of all other Garbo films except *Mata Hari* and *Grand Hotel*.

18. Bonding in saloons and athletic clubs, they took over well-paid occupations like directing and screenwriting. Karen Ward Mahar, *Women Filmmakers in Early Hollywood* (Baltimore: Johns Hopkins University Press, 2006); Hilary A. Hallett, *Inventing the It Girl* (New York: Liveright, 2022), 377; Marilyn Monroe, *My Story* (New York: Stein and Day, 1974), 41. For a discussion of women's victimization in Hollywood, as well as a defense of the perpetrators by one of them, see Michael Selsman, *Sex Games in Hollywood* (Los Angeles: Troike, 2018).

19. On the history of beauty, I have used the books I have written on the subject—*American Beauty* (New York: Alfred A. Knopf, 1983); *In Full Flower* (New York: Alfred A. Knopf, 1992); and *Marilyn: The Passion and the Paradox* (London: Bloomsbury, 2012)—and the research I have recently done. I have profited from reading Valerie Steele, *Fashion and Eroticism: Idols of Beauty from the Victorian Age to the Present* (New York: Oxford University Press, 1985), and Arthur Marwick, *Beauty in History: Society, Politics, and Personal Appearance c. 1500 to the Present* (London: Thames & Hudson, 1988), although I often disagree with their conclusions. Other works on the history of beauty I have used are cited in the endnotes.

20. On proportional theory, see Lynn Gamwell, *Mathematics in Art* (Princeton, NJ: Princeton University Press, 2016), as well as Umberto Eco, *History of Beauty*, trans. Alastair McEwen (New York: Rizzoli, 2004), on proportional theory, and Francette Pacteau, *The Symptom of Beauty* (Cambridge, MA: Harvard University Press, 1994).

21. Kate de Castelbajac, *The Face of the Century: 100 Years of Makeup and Style*, ed. Nan Richardson and Catherine Chermayeff (New York: Rizzoli, 1995), 68; Mary Lee, "Gadgets of Beauty," *Silver Screen*, February 1926; Carol Ockman, "Was She Magnificent? Sarah Bernhardt's Reach," in *Sarah Bernhardt and the Art of High Drama*, ed. Carol Ockman and Kenneth Silver (New Haven, CT: Yale University Press, 2005), 25; and Angela Della Vacca, *Diva: Defiance and Passion in Early Italian Cinema* (Austin: University of Texas Press, 2006).

22. Edmund Burke, *A Philosophical Inquiry into the Origin of Our Ideas of the Sublime and Beautiful* (London: R. and J. Dodsley, 1757); William Hogarth, *The Analysis of Beauty, Written with a View of Fixing the Fluctuating Ideas of Taste* (London: J. Reeves, 1753). Because of the Christian belief that in the Garden of Eden, Eve took the apple of knowledge from the devil in the form of a snake, snakes play a major role in Western art that deals with female beauty. Hogarth justified his use of snakes by stating that there was hardly an ancient statue that did not include a snake—which is an overstatement of the actual situation.

23. Joan Dejean, *The Essence of Style: How the French Invented High Fashion, Fine Food, Chic Cafes, Style, Sophistication, and Glamour* (New York: Free Press, 1995); Cecil Beaton, *The Glass of Fashion* (Garden City, NY: Doubleday, 1994), 166–191.

24. Gloria Swanson, *Swanson on Swanson* (New York: Random House, 1980), 244. For designers in general, see Julian Robinson, *The Golden Age of Style: Art Deco Fashion Illustration* (New York: Harcourt Brace Jovanovich, 1974), 93.

25. Georgina Howell, *Vogue Women* (London: Pavilion, 2000), 107. On Strickling and glamour, see Arthur H. Lewis, *It Was Fun While It Lasted* (New York: Trident, 197), 171.

26. Adrian, "Setting Styles through the Stars," *Ladies Home Journal*, December 1933, Adrian Collection, AMPAAS; Carolyn Van Wyck, "Any Woman Can Be Beautiful," *Photoplay*, March 1932. Van Wyck was *Photoplay*'s beauty editor. *Photoplay* was the most important movie fan magazine. Sarah Berry, *Screen Style: Fashion and Femininity in 1930s Hollywood* (Minneapolis: University of Minnesota Press, 2006).

27. Edna Woolman Chase and Ilka Chase, *Always in Vogue* (Garden City, NY: Doubleday, 1954), 168.

28. On Steichen, see William A. Ewing and Todd Brandon, *Edward Steichen: In High Fashion: The Condé Nast Years* (New York: W. W. Norton, 2008), and Penelope Niven, *Edward Steichen: A Biography* (New York: Clarkson Potter, 1997).

29. Barbara Haskell, *Steichen* (New York: Whitney Museum of Art, 2000), 29.

30. Christian A. Petersen, *Edward Steichen: The Portraits* (San Francisco: Art Museum Association of America, 1984), 12.

31. Leonard Hall, "Garbo-maniacs," *Photoplay*, January 1930; James M. Fidler, "Are They Making a Goddess Out of Garbo?" *Motion Picture*, March 1934.

## Chapter 1   Garbo Glorified and Demonized

1. I disagree with the conclusion reached by the French philosopher Roland Barthes in *Mythologies* and by Judith Brown that Garbo shows no expression on her face in her photographs and film close-ups. See Judith Brown, *Glamour in Six Dimensions: Modernism and the Radiance of Form* (Ithaca, NY: Cornell University Press, 2009), 97–110. Brown references the scholars who hold this position. In finding subtle expressions on Garbo's face, I follow Robin Muir, *The World's Most Photographed* (London: National Portrait Gallery, 2005), 72–87, and Robert Dance and Bruce Robertson, *Ruth Harriet Louise and Hollywood Glamour Photography* (Berkeley: University of California Press, 2002).

2. I discuss the Delsarte system at length in chapter 3.

3. Glenda Young, *Clarence Brown: Hollywood's Forgotten Master* (Lexington: University Press of Kentucky, 2018), 94.

4. Frederick Lewis Allen popularized the 1920s as "the roaring decade" and "the age of the flapper." See Allen, *Only Yesterday: An Informal History of the 1920s* (1931; New York: HarperCollins, 1964). On the flapper, see chapter 8, below.

5. Philippe Blom, *Fracture: Life and Culture in the West, 1918–1938* (New York: Basic Books, 2015); Paul Fussell, *The Great War and Modern Memory* (New York: Oxford University Press, 2000); Samuel Hynes, *A War Imagined: World War I and English Culture* (New York: Atheneum, 1991).

6. Leslie Baily, *Scrapbook for the Twenties* (London: F. Muller, 1959), 40; Hans Belting, *Face and Mask: A Double History*, trans. Thomas S. Hansen (Princeton, NJ: Princeton University Press, 2017); Caroline Alexander, "Faces of War," *Smithsonian Magazine*, February 2017.

7. Unsourced clipping, Bernarr McFadden Publications, Greta Garbo file, BRTC; James M. Fidler, "Are They Making a Goddess Out of Garbo?" *Motion Picture*, March 1934; Helen Dale, "Two Queens Were Born in Sweden," *Photoplay*, October 1932: "For the last eight years Garbo has been the subject of criticism and praise more than any other star in Hollywood."

8. Rose Reilley, "Greta Garbo: Gracious and Glorious," 1926, unsourced clipping, Garbo Family Scrapbooks, author's collection (hereafter cited as GFS); Robert Sherwood, *Life Magazine*, 1928, reprinted in Michael Conway, Dion McGregor, and Mark Ricci, eds., *The Films of Greta Garbo* (New York: Cadillac, 1963); "Snow or Rain," *Photoplay*, November 1927; Natalie Neff, "Garbo's Way," *Silver Screen*, November 1923; James Oppenheim, "Garbo Psychoanalyzed," *Screenland*, November 1929; Gordon Hillman, "Greta Garbo Triumphs in a New State Film," *Boston Daily*, January 22, 1929, GFS.

9. *Screen Book Magazine*, December 1932, quoted in Haining, *Legend of Garbo*, 22–23.

10. "Why Is Garbo the World's Love Ideal?," *Silver Screen*, May 1930; Ramon Romero, "Roaring 40s," *Motion Picture*, December 1928; Ruth Vasey, *The World According to Hollywood, 1918–1939* (Madison: University of Wisconsin Press, 1997), 217–218.

11. Kenneth E. Silver, *Chaos and Classicism: Art in France, Italy, and Germany, 1918–1930* (New York: Guggenheim Museum, 2004), 32–51.

12. Patricia Mears, "The Arc of Modernity," in *Elegance in an Age of Crisis: Fashions of the 1930s*, ed. Patricia Mears and G. Bruce Boyer (New York: Fashion Institute of Technology, 2014), 61–123; Nancy Hall-Duncan, *The History of Fashion Photography* (New York: Alpine, 1979), 363–364; Ruth Waterbury, "Olympus Comes to Hollywood," *Photoplay*, April 1924.

13. See Michael Williams, *Film Stardom, Myth and Classicism: The Rise of Hollywood Gods* (London: Palgrave Macmillan, 2013).

14. Helen Parde, "Artificial Exotics," *Picture Play*, October 1932; Frances Marion, "Hollywood," unpublished manuscript, special collections, University of Southern California Cinema Library, 363 (hereafter cited as USC).

15. Margery Wilson, "The Soul of Garbo," *Screenland*, December 1931. For a similar and more recent discussion of ethnic crossing in Russian history, see Orlando Figes, *Natasha's Dance: A Cultural History of Russia* (New York: Metropolitan, 2002), 861–867.

16. De Acosta, *Here Lies the Heart*, 143; Alexandre Vassiliev, *Beauty in Exile: The Artists, Models, and Nobility Who Fled the Russian Revolution and Influenced the*

*World of Fashion,* trans. Antonina W. Bouis and Anya Kuckarev (New York: Harry N. Abrams, 1998), 423.

17. Harry Lang, "Have Foreign Women More Sex Appeal than American Girls?," *Movie Mirror,* July 1932; Vasey, *World According to Hollywood,* 217–218.

18. William Rubin, *Primitivism in Twentieth Century Art: Affinity of the Tribal and the Modern* (New York: Museum of Modern Art, 1984), 2–3; Ghislaine Wood, "The Exotic," in *Art Deco, 1910–1939,* ed. Charlotte Benton, Tim Benton, and Ghislaine Wood (2003; London: Victoria and Albert Museum, 2015), 120.

19. Banner, *Intertwined Lives*), 177–190; Brunette Jules-Rosette, *Josephine Baker in Art and Life: The Icon and the Image* (Urbana: University of Illinois Press, 2007), 184–199.

20. Arne Lunde, *Nordic Exposures: Scandinavian Identities in Classical Hollywood Cinema* (Seattle: University of Washington Press, 2010), 20–30.

21. I discuss theories of "whiteness" in film studies in Lois Banner, "The Creature from the Black Lagoon: Marilyn Monroe and Whiteness," *Cinema Journal* 47, no. 4 (Summer 2008): 4–29.

22. Ann Sylvester, "There Are Styles in Stars, Too," *New Movie Magazine,* September 1928.

23. On Garbo's freckles, see Dorothy Hensley, "The Inside Story of Garbo's Great Success," *Motion Picture,* June 1932.

24. Clare Booth Brokaw, "The Great Garbo," *Vanity Fair,* February 1932.

25. The name "Nefertiti" translates into English as "beauty has arrived."

26. Walter H. Pater, *Studies in the History of the Renaissance* (London: Macmillan, 1873), 118–119.

27. Rana Kabanni, *Imperial Fictions: Europe's Myths of Orient* (Bloomington: Indiana University Press, 1988), 68; Deborah N. Mancoff, *Jane Morris, The Pre-Raphaelite Model of Beauty* (San Francisco: Pomegranate, 2000), 78, 89, 103. "Her face did not conform to the favored doll-like beauty. Her strongly configured bones and hollowed cheeks were considered signs of ill health."

28. On art deco and the art deco woman, I have used Benton, Benton, and Wood, *Art Deco,* and Lucy Fischer, *Designing Women: Cinema, Art Deco, and the Human Form* (New York: Columbia University Press, 2003).

29. David Robb, introduction, and Faye Ryan, "Modern Tragicomedy and the Fool," in *Clowns, Fools, and Picaros: Popular Forms of the Clown,* ed. David Robb (Amsterdam: Rodopi, 2007), 1–5.

30. Martin Green and John Swain, *The Triumph of Pierrot: The Commedia dell'arte and the Modern Imagination* (New York: Macmillan, 1986).

31. Cecil Beaton in "The Sketch," 1934, reprinted in Hugo Vickers, *Loving Garbo: The Story of Greta Garbo, Cecil Beaton and Mercedes de Acosta* (New York: Random House, 1994), 50–51. Lillian Faderman and Stuart Timmins note that the word "gay" for homosexuals was first used in the 1930s. Faderman and Timmins,

*Gay L. A.: A History of Sexual Outlaws, Power Politics, and Lipstick Lesbians* (2006; Berkeley: University of California Press, 2009), 5.

32. Wendy Wick Reaves, *Celebrity Caricature in America* (Washington, DC: Smithsonian Institution, 1988), 22.

33. On Garbo's white eyelashes, see Nils Asther, "Garbo," in Nathaniel Benchley, "This Is Garbo," *Collier's*, March 1, 1952, 13, and Beaton, *Memoirs of the 40's*, 235.

34. Fred E. Basten, *Max Factor's Hollywood: Glamour, Movies, Make-up* (Los Angeles: General, 1995), 53.

35. Charles Higham, *Hollywood Cameramen: Sources of Light* (Bloomington: University of Indiana Press, 1970), 67–70; Frances Marion, *Off With Their Heads: A Serio-Comic Tale of Hollywood* (New York: Macmillan, 1972), 197; Daum, *Walking with Garbo*, 136; Cecil Beaton, Diary, 1947, Cecil Beaton Papers, St. John's College Library Special Collections, Cambridge University (hereafter cited as Beaton-Cam.).

36. Basten, *Max Factor's Hollywood*, 90–95.

37. Conway, McGregor, and Ricci, *Films of Greta Garbo*, 68.

38. Ruth Lyman, ed., *Couture: An Illustrated History of the Great Paris Designers and Their Creations* (Garden City, NY: Doubleday, 1972), 83; Martin Battersby, *The Decorative Twenties* (New York: Macmillan, 1969), 108.

39. "Adrian Answers Twenty Questions on Garbo," *Photoplay*, September 1935.

40. See, for example, Myrtle Gebhart, "Their Dual Personalities," *Picture Play*, June 1930.

41. See Marjorie Garber, *Vice Versa: Bisexuality and the Eroticism of Everyday Life* (New York: Simon & Schuster, 1995).

42. Herbert Cruikshank, "Garbo: Myth of the Movies," *Talking Screen*, July 1930; Roland Wild, *Greta Garbo* (London: Hazell, Watson & Viney, 1933); Maddy Vogtel, "Blonde Venus and Swedish Sphinx," *Vanity Fair*, November 1934; "Who Is the Most Beautiful Star in Hollywood?," *Photoplay*, March 1930.

43. Cruikshank, "Myth of the Movies"; Frederick L. Collins, "Ziegfeld Would Have Said, 'Throw Her Out!,'" *Photoplay*, April 1935; Lois Shirley, "The Enemy of Beauty—Over-Exercise," *Photoplay*, August 1931 ("No woman athlete is beautiful. Physical exercise shouldn't be overdone"); Heather Addison, *Hollywood and the Rise of Physical Culture* (New York: Routledge, 2003), 108.

44. *Philadelphia Inquirer*, April 18, 2000, clipping, Mercedes de Acosta Papers, Rosenbach Museum, Philadelphia (hereafter cited as Rosen.).

45. See Jim Tully, "Jim Tully Dissects Garbo," *New Movie Magazine*, January 1932; Robert Sherwood, "Miss Garbo and the Microphone," unsourced clipping, n.d., GFS.

46. Erika K. Jackson, *Scandinavians in Chicago: The Origins of White Privilege in Modern America* (Urbana: University of Illinois Press, 2019), 58–59; Rilla Palmborg, *The Private Life of Greta Garbo* (New York: Doubleday, 1934), 279.

47. Ruth Biery, "Hollywood's Cruelty to Greta Garbo," *Photoplay*, January 1932.

48. Louella Parsons, syndicated column, *Los Angeles Times*, August 10, 1933; Jimmy Starr, *Los Angeles Evening Herald Examiner*, reprinted in G. D. Hamann, *Greta Garbo in the '30s* (Los Angeles: Filming Today, 1996), 72; *Los Angeles Times*, July 6, 1946: "I t'ink I go home became a household word." That phrase, and "I want to be alone," became standard lines for radio comics. See James Harvey, *Watching Them Be: Star Presence on the Screen from Garbo to Balthazar* (New York: Faber and Faber, 2014), 22–23.

49. Henry T. Finck, *Romantic Love and Personal Beauty* (New York: Macmillan, 1925), 325–328; M. O. Stanton, *Encyclopedia of Face and Figure* (1839; Philadelphia: F. A. Davis, 1919), 850–851; Alexander Walker, *Beauty in Women: Analyzed and Classified* (Glasgow: T. D. Morrison, 1892), 239–241; Sharrona Pearl, *About Faces: Physiognomy in Nineteenth-Century Britain* (Cambridge, MA: Harvard University Press, 1984), 29: "Pick-pockets—beggars—prostitutes—sailors, coachmen, and such like, have high cheekbones and protruding jaws."

50. Michael Bruni, *Venus in Hollywood: The Continental Enchantress from Garbo to Loren* (New York: Lyle Stuart, 1970), 25–27.

51. Edwin Schallert, "Foreign Accent Fails as Means of Getting a Job," *Los Angeles Times*, September 4, 1932; Oppenheim, "Garbo Psychoanalyzed."

52. Larry Carr, *More Fabulous Faces* (Garden City, NY: Doubleday, 1979), 2.

53. Reaves, *Celebrity Caricature*, 158–181, 234.

54. Clarence Brown, interview with Kevin Brownlow, in Brownlow, *The Parade's Gone By* (Berkeley: University of California Press, 1975), 146–147.

55. Daum, *Walking with Garbo*, 113.

56. Helen Ludlum, "Bob or Grow?" *Screenland*, May 1930.

57. Faderman and Timmons, *Gay L. A.*; Daum, *Walking with Garbo*, 111; Hubert Blumer, *Movies and Conduct* (New York: Macmillan, 1933), 45; Henry James Foreman, *Our Movie-Made Children* (New York: Macmillan, 1933), 145. See also Samantha Barbas, *Movie Crazy: Fans, Stars, and the Cult of Celebrity* (New York: Palgrave Macmillan, 2001).

58. Negulesco, *Things I Did*, 207–209; interview with Lionel Barrymore, "Will Garbo Return to the Screen?," AMPAAS; Barbara Barondess, in Benchley, "This Is Garbo"; Baldwin, *Billy Baldwin Remembers*, 172.

59. Broman, *Garbo on Garbo*, 100; Anita Loos, *Fate Keeps on Happening* (New York: Dodd, Mead, 1989), 90; Adela Rogers St. Johns, "Garbo: The Mystery of Hollywood," *Liberty Magazine*, July 27, 1929. See also Beaton, *Memoirs of the 40's*, 275; Cecil Beaton, unpublished Diary, Beaton-Cam.; Hugo Vickers, *Cecil Beaton, Greta Garbo, and Mercedes de Acosta* (New York: Random House, 1940), 182.

60. Leonard Stanley, *Adrian: A Lifetime of Movie Glamour, Art, and High Fashion*, text by Mark Vieira (New York: Rizzoli, 2018), 134; St. Johns, "Mystery of Hollywood"; Faith Service, "Garbo Never Sleeps," *Movie Classic*, September 1931;

Katherine Albert, "How Garbo's Fear of People Started," *Photoplay*, March 1932: "When I took an interviewer to see Garbo, she came back and said, 'That girl has been badly hurt—deeply, terribly hurt.'"

## Chapter 2  Childhood

1. Elizabeth Malcolm, as told to Rakel Erikson, "The Garbo You've Never Heard About," *Movie Mirror*, August 1935; "Greta Garbo Wanted To Be a Tight Rope Walker," *Photoplay*, May 1934.

2. Kaj Gynt, as told to Adela Rogers St. Johns, "An Unknown Chapter in Greta Garbo's Life," *Liberty*, August 18, 1934; Greta Garbo letters to Eva Blomqvist, Greta Garbo Archive, Swedish Film Institute, Stockholm (hereafter cited as SFI).

3. Federation of Swedish Genealogical Societies, *24 Famous Swedish Americans and Their Ancestors* (Stockholm: Federation of Swedish Genealogical Societies, 1996). I purchased this book at an auction of Garbo's possessions at Julien's Auctions in Beverly Hills in December 2012. No previous Garbo biographer has used it.

4. Hans Norman and Harald Runblom, *Transatlantic Connections: Nordic Migrations to the New World after 1800* (Oslo: Norwegian University Press, 1988).

5. "Eliminate the TB Scourge," *New York Times*, May 19, 2016.

6. Gynt in St. Johns, "Unknown Chapter."

7. Gynt in St. Johns.

8. Becky Ohlsen, *Pocket Stockholm* (Oakland, CA: Lonely Planet, 2015); Henry Albert Phillips, "Where Garbo Learned Her Trade," *New York Herald Tribune*, December 20, 1936; Fritiof Billqvist, *Garbo: A Biography* (New York: G. P. Putnam's Sons, 1960), 9.

9. Henry Albert Phillips, "Greta Garbo—Home-Town Girl," *Screenland*, March 1935; Broman, *Garbo on Garbo*, 36.

10. Gynt in St. Johns, "Unknown Chapter."

11. Thomas Hall, *Stockholm: The Making of a Metropolis* (London: Routledge, 2009); Agnes Rothberg, *Sweden: The Land and the People* (New York: Viking, 1934), 112–120; Gustav Sundborg, ed., *Sweden: Its People and Its Industry* (Stockholm: Government Printing Office, 1904), 106.

12. Per Anders Fogelström, *Remember the City* (Iowa City, IA: Penfield, 2015), 1–5; John Lewis Austin, "Intima Teatern and the Formation of Theatrical Modernity in Sweden" (PhD diss., University of Illinois–Urbana, 1997), 82–86.

13. Frederick Sands and Sven Broman, *The Divine Garbo* (New York: Grosset & Dunlop, 1979), 12.

14. Sven Broman, "I Proposed to Garbo Three Times," in *Det Handlar om kärlek: Minnen från ett liv i tidningsvärlden* (Stockholm: Wahlstrom & Widsrand, 1993). Swedish Lutheranism retained elements from Catholicism, such as High Mass.

15. Greta Garbo, "My Life as an Artist," *Lekytr*, 1930, in Haining, *Legend of Garbo*, 40.

16. Broman, *Garbo on Garbo*, 186.

17. John Lindow, *Trolls: An Unnatural History* (London: Reaktion, 2014); Gynt in St. Johns, "Unknown Chapter." On Garbo's belief in Mara, see Paris, *Garbo*, 471.

18. Beaton, Diary, December 3, 1947, Beaton-Cam.; Laila Nylund, interview with Karen Swenson, March 2, 1995, Karen Swenson Collection, University of North Carolina Special Collections, Wilmington, NC (hereafter cited as UNCW).

19. Malcolm in Erikson, "Garbo You've Never Heard About."

20. Garbo, "My Life as an Artist," 40.

21. Peter Joel, "The First True Story of Garbo's Childhood," *Screenbook*, reprinted in Martin Levin, *Hollywood and the Great Fan Magazines* (New York: Arbor House, 1979), 14–15, 172.

22. Ruth Biery, "The Story of Greta Garbo," *Photoplay*, April 1928.

23. Broman, *Garbo on Garbo*, 234–235.

24. Greta Garbo letters to Eva Blomqvist, Greta Garbo Archive, SFI.

25. Ellen Key, *Love and Marriage*, trans. Arthur G. Chater (New York: G. P. Putnam's Sons, 1911), 74–75. In *Surpassing the Love of Men: Romantic Friendship and Love between Women from the Renaissance to the Present* (New York: William Morrow, 1981), Lillian Faderman discusses these relationships in European and American history. In *Intertwined Lives*, I point out that such relationships extended to cross-sex as well as same-sex desire; in other words, many were bisexual in nature. Like Mead and Benedict, Garbo had serious relationships with both boys and girls as an adolescent, and like Mead, as an adult she was bisexual. After being rejected by several men, the adult Benedict was involved only with women.

26. Ake Sundberg, "That Gustafson Girl," *Photoplay*, April 1930.

27. John Bainbridge, *Garbo* (1958; New York: Holt, Rinehart, and Winston, 1971), 25; Broman, *Garbo on Garbo*, 190; Alexander Walker, *Garbo: A Portrait* (New York: Macmillan, 1980), 26.

28. Mona Mendes, *Extraordinary Women in Support of Music* (Metuchen, NJ: Scarecrow, 1997), 29–35.

29. Frederick J. Marker and Lise-Love Marker, *A History of Scandinavian Theatre* (Cambridge: Cambridge University Press, 1996); G. Brocket and Franklin J. Hildy, *History of the Theatre* (Boston: Beacon Press, 2008); Gary J. Williams, ed., *Theatre Histories: An Introduction* (New York: Routledge, 2006).

30. Elza Schallert, "Carl Brisson, Garbo's Old Friend," *Los Angeles Times*, January 21, 1934.

31. Garbo, "My Life as an Artist," 37–91.

32. Austin, "Intima Teatern," 87.

33. On Garbo's fascination with Pickford, see *Garbo,* written and directed by Christopher Bird and Kevin Brownlow, narrated by Julie Christie (Burbank, CA: Turner Entertainment, 2005), DVD.

34. Biery, "The Story of Greta Garbo." *Photoplay,* April 1928.

35. See Kay Redfield Jamison, *Touched with Fire: Manic-Depressive Illness and the Artistic Temperament* (New York: Free Press, 1993).

36. Daum, *Walking with Garbo,* 113; Haining, *Legend of Garbo,* 41.

37. Beaton, *Memoirs of the 40's,* 285.

38. See Dana Becker, *Through the Looking Glass: Women and Borderline Personality Disorder* (Boulder, CO: Westview, 1997); Janet Leibman Jacobs, *Victimized Daughters: Incest and the Development of the Female Self* (New York: Routledge, 1994); Elizabeth Wales, *Trauma and Survival: Post-traumatic and Dissociative Disorders in Women* (New York: Norton, 1993); Lenore Terri, *Too Scared to Cry: Psychic Trauma in Childhood* (New York: Harper & Row, 1990).

39. Ramon Novarro, in *London Daily Mail,* January 1930, reprinted in Haining, *Legend of Garbo,* 26; Nicholas Turner, interview with Karen Swenson, February 8, 1993, Swenson Collection, UNCW; Linda B. Hall, *Dolores del Rio: Beauty in Light and Shade* (Palo Alto, CA: Stanford University Press, 2013), 152–153.

40. Beaton, *Memoirs of the 40's,* 203.

41. Malcolm in Erikson, "Garbo You've Never Heard About." On the Swedish temperance movement, see Jackson, *Scandinavians in Chicago,* 68.

42. Sally Eckengren, "Greta the Barber Shop Girl," *Everybody's Magazine,* December 1933, reprinted in Haining, *Legend of Garbo,* 65–66.

43. Sands and Broman, *Divine Garbo,* 12.

44. Phillips, "Greta Garbo—Home-Town Girl," 78; Eckengren, "Greta the Barber Shop Girl."

45. Daum, *Walking with Garbo,* 68.

46. Scott Reisfield, "A Portrait of Garbo," in *Garbo: Portraits from Her Private Collection,* ed. Scott Reisfield and Robert Dance (New York: Rizzoli, 2003), 26.

47. On the Salvation Army, see Diane Winston, *Red-Hot and Righteous: The Urban Religion of the Salvation Army* (Cambridge, MA: Harvard University Press, 1999).

48. Lizbeth Stenberg, "A Star in a Constellation," in *Re-mapping Lagerlöf: Performance, Intermediality, and European Transmissions,* ed. Helena Forsås-Scott, Lizbeth Sternberg, and Bjarne Thorup Thomsen (Lund, Sweden: Nordic Academic Press, 2014), 24–38.

49. Regulation involved inspecting women thought to be prostitutes for venereal disease. Because women who weren't prostitutes were sometimes apprehended and inspected, the Swedish women's organizations secured the repeal of regulation. On

prostitution in turn-of-the-twentieth-century Stockholm, see Yvonne Svanström, *Policing Public Women: The Regulation of Prostitution in Stockholm, 1812–1880* (Stockholm: Atlas, 2000).

50. Bergitta Ney, "The Woman Reporter Goes Street Haunting," *Media History*, June 2001.

51. Beaton, *Memoirs of the 40's*, 2.

52. Sands and Broman, *Divine Garbo*, 224.

53. Jack Larson, "Garbo: Outtakes of a Life," unpublished ms., Swenson Collection, UNCW.

## Chapter 3   PUB, Dramaten, and Mimi Pollak

1. Sands and Broman, *Divine Garbo*, 25, from an interview with Garbo in *Lektyr* magazine.

2. Geoffrey Crossick and Serge Jaumain, *Cathedrals of Consumption: The European Department Stores, 1850–1930* (London: Ashgate, 1999); Shelley Stamp, *Movie-Struck Girls: Women and Motion Picture Culture after the Nickelodeon* (Princeton, NJ: Princeton University Press, 2000), 18–19.

3. See, for example, Thérèse Andersson, *Beauty Box: åFilmstjärnor och skönhets* (Stockholm: University of Stockholm Press, 2006).

4. Andersson, 70.

5. Sands and Broman, *Divine Garbo*, 25–26.

6. Broman, *Garbo on Garbo*, 41.

7. Broman, 31. Greta told her acting school classmate and friend Vera Schmiterlöw about her affair with Gumpel, and Vera told Sven Broman about it. Schmiterlöw later became a star in German films.

8. Eugene Nifford, "I Gave Garbo Her First Chance in Films," reprinted in Haining, *Legend of Garbo*, 79.

9. Billquist, *Garbo: A Biography*, 35.

10. Robert Payne, *The Great Garbo* (New York: Rowman & Littlefield, 1976), 42; Sands and Broman, *Divine Garbo*, from interview with Hellberg,

11. Austin, "Teatern Intima," 83–87.

12. Austin, "Teatern Intima," 83–87.

13. Austin, "Teatern Intima," 87; Carla Waal, *Harriet Bosse: Strindberg's Muse and Interpreter* (Carbondale: Southern Illinois University Press, 1990), 69.

14. Swenson, *Greta Garbo*, 45.

15. Karl Martin, "If You Knew Greta Garbo," *Redbook*, August 19, 1933.

16. On Delsarte, I have used George Taylor and Rose Whyman, "François Delsarte, Prince Serge Volkonsky, and Mikhail Chekhov," *Mime Journal*, April 2015; Rose Whyman, *The Stanislavsky System of Acting: Legacy and Influence in Modern Performance* (Cambridge: Cambridge University Press, 2008); and

James M. McTeague, *Before Stanislavsky: American Professional Acting Schools and Acting Theory, 1875–1925* (Metuchen, NJ: Scarecrow, 1993).

17. The Delsarte system slowly lost favor among actors when it was rigidly applied in classes on oratory for women, which were popular in the nineteenth century, especially in the United States.

18. In writing about the acting school, I have relied on Mimi Pollak's memoir, *Teaterlink: Memoarer* (Stockholm: Askild & Karnekull, 1977).

19. Pollak, *Teaterlink.*

20. Payne, *The Great Garbo*, 54. On Garbo's photographic memory, see the Clarence Bull interview in Norman Zierold, *Garbo* (New York: Stein and Day, 1969), 81. Garbo was renowned in Hollywood for memorizing not only her own lines in her films but also the lines of all the other actors.

21. Mimi's speculations on why Greta was attracted to her are contained in an interview in *Svenska Dagbladet*, April 22, 1990, Swenson Collection, UNCW. On Mimi's background, I have used her autobiography, *Teaterlink.*

22. For George Funkvist's statement about Greta's lesbianism, see Göran Söderström, "Privatpersonen Stiller och hans Krets," in Frederik Silverstolpe and Gregor Eman, *Sympatiens hemlighet fulla makt: Stockholm's Homosexuella, 1860–1960* (Stockholm: Stockholmia, 1999).

23. Pollak, *Teaterlink*, 72–73.

24. In analyzing Greta's letters to Mimi, I have used three sources: 1. letters contained on the website of the Garbo fan club, Garbo Forever, http://www .garboforever.com; 2. letters sold at Sotheby's London auction house in 1993, read and translated by Tony Fletcher for Karen Swenson, Swenson Collection, UNCW; 3. a compilation of the letters Greta wrote to Mimi by Tin Andersén Axell, published in 2005. Andersén identifies himself as a close friend of Mimi's. Tin Andersén Axell, *Djävla älskade unge!* (Rimbo, Sweden: Fischer, 2005). In Garbo's letters to Mimi, she is often vague about dates and spelling. It's standard practice for letters sold at public auction to be put on public view before being auctioned, when they will probably disappear into private collections. They can be copied during the public viewing period. Garbo's March 1925 comments to Mimi are in "Sweet Little Beloved Mimmi [*sic*]," March 9, 1925, in Andersén Axell, *Djävla älskade unge!*

25. Waal, *Harriet Bosse*, 161.

26. On changes in the theater, I have relied on Kenneth MacGowan and William Melnitz, *The Living Stage: A History of the World Stage* (New York: Prentice Hall, 1955), and de Acosta, *Here Lies the Heart*, 67.

27. "Damn Beloved Child!," 1924, in Andersén Axell, *Djävla älskade unge!*; Greta to Mimi, 1923, Sotheby's; Garbo Forever.

28. "Damn Beloved Child!"; "Immer und Immer mein Liebling."

29. Lillian Faderman, *Odd Girls and Twilight Lovers: A History of Lesbian Life in Twentieth Century America* (New York: Columbia University Press, 1991), 62–92.

30. See Söderstrom, "Privatpersonen Stiller och hans Krets."

31. Nifford, "I Gave Garbo Her First Chance," 80; "Dear Little Misse," June 6, 1923, in Andersén Axell, *Djävla älskade unge!*; Sotheby's, 1923.

32. Nils Asther, *Narrens väg: Ingen gudasagt memoarer* (Stockholm: Carlssons, 1988).

## Chapter 4    Beauty and the Beast

1. Broman, *Conversations with Garbo*, 52–53.

2. Daum, *Walking with Garbo*, 42–43.

3. Nifford, "I Gave Garbo Her First Chance," 82.

4. On Stiller and the Swedish film industry, I have used Jacques Garreau, "Mauritz Stiller, ou L'insolent génie d'un cinéaste de Suède" (PhD diss., Université Rennes, Haute-Bretagne, France); Peter Cowie, *Swedish Cinema: From Ingeborg Holm to Fanny and Alexander* (Stockholm: Swedish Institute, 1985); Hans Axel Pensel, *Seastrom and Stiller in Hollywood: Two Swedish Directors in Silent American Films, 1923–1930* (New York: Vantage, 1969); Gösta Werner, *Mauritz Stiller och Hans Filmer, 1912–1916* (Stockholm: Norstedt, 1969); and Bengt Idestam-Almquist, *Mauritz Stiller: 1886–1928* (Paris: Anthologie du Cinéma, 1967). In 1919 Svenska Biografteatern merged with Filmindustri to become Svensk Filmindustri (SFI).

5. Pensel, *Seastrom and Stiller*, 18.

6. Charles Brackett interview, Columbia University, Oral History Project (CU-Oral).

7. Interview with Abraham Stiller in *Hupvud Stabladet*, March 10, 1971, Swenson Collection, UNCW.

8. Nils Asther in Benchley, "This Is Garbo."

9. Victor Seastrom, "The Man Who Found Garbo," *Biografbladet*, December 1950, reprinted in Haining, *Legend of Garbo*, 85–93.

10. Marguerite Engberg, "The Erotic Melodrama in Danish Silent Films, 1910–1918," *Film History* 5 (March 1993): 63–67.

11. Bram Dijkstra, *Idols of Perversity: Fantasies of Feminine Evil in Fin-de-Siècle Culture* (New York: Oxford University Press, 1988), 334–335.

12. Nina Auerbach, *Woman and the Demon: The Life of a Victorian Myth* (Cambridge, MA: Harvard University Press, 1989).

13. See Angela Dalle Vacche, *Diva: Defiance and Passion in Early Italian Cinema* (Austin: University of Texas Press, 2008). On German vamps, see Valerie Weinstein, "Henrik Galeen's *Alraune* (1927): The Vamp and the Roots of Horror," in *The Many Faces of Weimar Cinema: Rediscovering Germany's Film Legacy*, ed. Christian Rogowski (Rochester, NY: Camden, 2010), 198–210.

14. My analysis of Stiller's films is based on the sources listed in note 4 of this chapter and on my viewings of fifteen Stiller films. *Sir Arne's Treasure, Erotikon,*

and *The Saga of Gösta Berling* are available on YouTube and Netflix in the United States. At the Royal National Library in Stockholm in the spring of 2017 I watched *Madame de Thèbes, Kärlek och journalistik, Ballet primadonna, Thomas Graal's bästa film, Thomas Graal's bästa barn, Song of the Scarlet Flower, The Avenger, Johan, Vingarne,* and *GunnarHedes Saga (The Blizzard)*. Most of Stiller's films before 1916 were lost in a fire at the warehouse where they were stored. Garreau and Werner reconstructed the plots and characters of these films from film stills and notes taken during their productions, which are held by the Swedish Film Institute.

15. Selma Lagerlöf, *The Saga of Gösta Berling*, trans. Lillie Tudeer (1918; Mineola, NY: Dover, 2004), 32.

16. Sue Prideaux, *Strindberg: A Life* (New Haven, CT: Yale University Press, 2012), 114–120.

17. Marker and Marker, *History of Scandinavian Theatre*, 231.

18. Garreau, "Mauritz Stiller," 69–76. On women in Stiller's films, see Laura Horak, "Sex, Politics, and Swedish Silent Film: Mauritz Stiller's Feminism Comedies of the 1910s," *Journal of Scandinavian Cinema* 4 (2003): 193–208; Louise Wallenberg, "Stilleristic Women: Gender as Masque and Ambivalence in the Work of Mauritz Stiller," *Aura: Film Studies Journal* 6 (2000): 36–46; and Werner, *Mauritz Stiller,* 238–248.

19. Werner, *Mauritz Stiller,* 238.

20. Daum, *Walking with Garbo,* 4; Ragner Hyltén-Cavallius, "How Stiller Discovered Greta Garbo," *Gefle Dagblad,* October 27, 1933; Broman, *Garbo on Garbo,* 65.

21. Gail Marshall, *Actresses on the Victorian Stage: Feminine Performances and the Galatea Myth* (Cambridge: Cambridge University Press, 1998).

22. Sven-Hugo Borg, "The Only True Story of Greta Garbo's Private Life," 1933, supplement to *Film Pictorial,* https://www.greta-garbo.de/private-life-of-greta-garbo-by-sven-hugo-borg/02-greta-garbo-private-life-by-sven-hugo-borg.htm; Victor Seastrom, "As I Remember," in Bengt Idestam-Almquist, *Classics of the Swedish Theater* (Stockholm: Swedish Institute, 1952).

23. Seastrom, "Man Who Found Garbo," 88.

24. Asther, *Narrens väg,* 74; David Robinson, *Hollywood in the Twenties* (New York: A. S. Barnes, 1968), 83.

25. Garbo to Mimi, December 16, 1925, in Andersén Axell, *Djävla älskade unge!,* 262.

26. Brumberg, *Fasting Girls.*

27. Beaton, Diary, n.d., Beaton-Cam.

28. Borg, "Only True Story"; Seastrom, "As I Remember"; Edgar Sirmont to Mauritz Stiller, June 12, 1924, Mauritz Stiller Papers, SFI.

29. Payne, *Great Garbo,* 59.

30. Joseph Garncanz, "Art and Industry: German Cinema of the 1920s," in *The Silent Film Reader*, ed. Lee Grieveson and Peter Krämar (New York: Routledge, 2004), 292.

31. Irene Mayer Selznick, *A Private View* (New York: Alfred A. Knopf, 1983), 60; Agnes Smith, "Up Speaks a Gallant Loser," *Photoplay*, February 1927; Daum, *Walking with Garbo*, 48.

32. Interview with Barry Selznick (L. B. Mayer's grandson), Turner Classic Movies, 2005; Broman, *Garbo on Garbo*, 48.

33. Patrice Petro, *Joyless Street: Women and Melodramatic Representation in Weimar Germany* (Princeton, NJ: Princeton University Press, 1989); Eric Rentschler, "An Auteur Directed by History," in *G. W. Pabst: An Extraterritorial Cinema*, ed. Eric Rentschler (New Brunswick, NJ: Rutgers University Press, 1990).

34. Olaf Peters, ed., *Berlin Metropolis, 1918–1933* (New York: Prested, 2016); Otto Friedrich, *Before the Deluge: A Portrait of Berlin in the 1920s* (New York: Harper Perennial, 1972).

35. Joseph von Sternberg, *Fun in a Chinese Laundry* (New York: Macmillan, 1965), 229; Anita Loos, *A Girl Like I* (New York: Viking, 1956), 249–263.

36. Salka Viertel, *The Kindness of Strangers* (1969; New York: New York Review of Books, 2019), 101–103.

37. Katie Sutton, *The Masculine Woman in Weimar Germany* (New York: Berghahn, 2011), 7.

38. Lisa Appignanesi, *The Cabaret* (1976; New York: Universe, 2004). Some writers mistakenly maintain that during the filming of *Joyless Street*, Garbo had an affair with Marlene Dietrich, presumably a featured player in the film. The program for *Joyless Street*, in GFS, lists Herta von Walther, a German film actress, as playing the role under contention.

39. Edgar Sirmont to Mauritz Stiller, June 12, 1924, Mauritz Stiller Papers, SFI.

40. Broman, *Garbo on Garbo*, 68, 252; Rilla Page Palmborg, "The Private Life of Greta Garbo," *Photoplay*, September 1930.

## Chapter 5   Hollywood

1. John Baxter, *The Hollywood Exiles* (New York: Taplinger, 1976), 115.

2. Daum, *Walking with Garbo*, 20; Pola Negri, *Memoirs of a Star* (Garden City, NY: Doubleday, 1970), 198–201; Jesse L. Lasky Jr., *Whatever Happened to Hollywood?* (New York: Funk & Wagnalls, 1973), 42.

3. Hubert Voight, as told to Gurdi Haworth in "I Loved Garbo," *New Movie Magazine*, February 1934. Relevant material can be found in the entry on Kaj Gynt on Wikipedia.

4. Hubert Voight, with Larry Englemann, *Saturday Review*, March / April 1945, Swenson Collection, UNCW; interview with Hubert Voight, in Sylvia Shorris and

Marion Abbott Bundy, *Talking Pictures with the People Who Made Them* (New York: New Press, 1994).

5. "Garbo, the Mysterious," undated and unsourced clipping, Greta Garbo file, BRTC; Dorothy Calhoun, "What Women Learned from Her," *Motion Picture Classic*, August 1927. See also Sydney Valentine, "Miracles of Makeup," *Screenland*, October 1930; *Film Pictorial*, July 1, 1933.

6. Selznick, *Private View*, 61.

7. Hubert Voight, "When No One Wanted Garbo," *Los Angeles Times*, October 6, 1935.

8. Voight.

9. "Garbo's Untold Story," *Screen Play*, August 1933.

10. Loos, *Girl Like I*, 105–106.

11. Adele Whitely Fletcher, "Why Is Garbo Love's Stepchild?," *Silver Screen*, July 1930.

12. Daum, *Walking with Garbo*, 27.

13. Greta Montabel, "The Man Who Saved Greta Garbo's Career," *Screen Book*, July 1934.

14. Sands and Broman, *Divine Garbo*, 55–57; Arnold Genthe, *As I Remember* (New York: Reynal & Hitchcock, 1936), 166; Samuel Marx, *Mayer and Thalberg: The Make-Believe Saints* (New York: Random House, 1975), 66.

15. Cal York, *Photoplay*, March 1932; A. L. Wooldridge, "Hollywood Makes Them Over," *Picture Play*, February 1930. "Cal York" was a made-up name derived from "California" and "New York"—various *Photoplay* writers wrote the column.

16. Beaton, *Memoirs of the 40's*, 210. In a letter to Mimi Pollak dated late 1925, Garbo stated that she had written to Mimi that she was going to be married, but she decided not to.

17. Elza Schallert, "Famed of Europe Frolic," *Los Angeles Times*, November 22, 1931.

18. Katherine Albert, "The Unknown Hollywood I Knew," *Photoplay*, January 1932.

19. Calhoun, "Inside Story of Garbo's Great Success"; *Motion Picture*, May 1932; Monk, "Why Stars Are Stars."

20. Sven-Hugo Borg, "Heart-Breaking Days in Hollywood," *Motion Picture*, May 1932; Borg, *Hollywood Studio Magazine*, November 1971; Beauchamp, *Without Lying Down*, 146.

21. Broman, *Det Handlar*, 310.

22. Alice L. Tildsley, "The Screen's Newest Meteor Is a Moody Daughter of Sweden," *Motion Picture Classic*, May 1926, reprinted in Shane Brown, ed., *Silent Voices: Vintage Interviews with Silent Film Personalities* (Los Angeles: Createspace, 2017), 151–156.

23. Beth Day, *This Was Hollywood: An Affectionate History of Filmland's Golden Years* (New York: Doubleday, 1960), 36; St. Johns, "Mystery of Hollywood"; Marion, *Off with Their Heads*, 146; Joan Crawford, *A Portrait of Joan: The Autobiography of Joan Crawford* (Garden City, NY: Doubleday, 1962), 12; Teet Carle, "The Young Swedish Girl Was Scared," *Hollywood Studio Magazine*, November 1974.

24. Negri, "I Was the First 'Exclusive' Star," 134–137; Biery, "Hollywood's Cruelty to Greta Garbo."

25. Michaela Krützen, *The Most Beautiful Woman on the Screen: The Fabrication of the Star Greta Garbo* (New York: Peter Lang, 1994). The large collection of photos of Garbo in the Margaret Herrick Library shows no extensive changes in Garbo's face. Nor do the photos used by Krützen. Garbo denied that she had undergone any cosmetic surgery, except for a small bump removed from her forehead. See Broman, *Garbo on Garbo*, 2.

26. Valentine, "Miracles of Makeup"; Val Lewton, "Greta Garbo's Road to Stardom," *Film Weekly*, January 1932, reprinted in Haining, *Legend of Garbo*, 97–99.

27. A second version of Garbo's casting in *The Torrent* relates that portions of a Garbo screen test were included by mistake in scenes of floods that director Monta Bell looked at for potential use in *The Torrent*. He was so taken by Garbo that he insisted that Thalberg and Mayer cast her as the female lead in the film. See Marion, *Off with Their Heads*, 131–135.

28. Howard Gutner, *Gowns by Adrian The MGM Years, 1928–1941* (New York: Harry A. Abrams, 2001), 37.

29. "Queen of Hearts—Aileen Pringle," *Motion Picture Classic*, May 1925. According to *Screenland*, Garbo in *The Torrent* played "one of our old movie friends: the girl who conquers Paris overnight." *Screenland*, July 1926.

30. Campbell McCullough, "What Makes Them Stars?," *Photoplay*, October 1928.

31. Daum, *Walking with Garbo*, 95.

32. Adela Rogers St. Johns, "At Last—the Blonde Vampire," *Photoplay*, March 1935.

33. Sands and Broman, *Divine Garbo*, 64.

34. Charles Higham, *Merchant of Dreams: Louis B. Mayer, M.G.M., and the Secret Hollywood* (New York: Donald I. Fine, 1993), 93.

35. The 1925 documentary of the MGM lot is available at "1925 Tour of MGM Studios," YouTube video, https://www.youtube.com/watch?v=Trni2JBzDaE. Garbo isn't in it because she hadn't yet arrived in Hollywood. Joan Crawford appears in it, but she is called Lucille LeSeuer, her original name. Norma Shearer and Marion Davies appear in the documentary. E. J. Fleming provides a detailed description of the MGM lot in *The Fixers: Eddie Mannix, Howard Strickling, and the MGM Publicity Machine* (Jefferson, NC: MacFarland, 2005), 18–52.

36. Christopher Isherwood, *Prater Violet* (New York: Farrar, Straus and Giroux, 1987), 30–31, 60.

37. Adela Rogers St. Johns, "The Great Garbo," *Silver Screen*, November 1933.

38. "Dearest Sweet Mimi," March 6, 1927, in Andersén Axell, *Djävla älskade unge!*

39. Herbert Moulton, "A Reluctant Siren," *Picture-Play*, October 1926.

40. Gary Carey, *All the Stars in Heaven: Louis B. Mayer's MGM* (New York: E. P. Dutton, 1981), 18.

41. Voight, "I Loved Garbo."

42. For biographies of Mayer, see Higham, *Merchant of Dreams*, and Carey, *All the Stars in Heaven*. Given charges that Higham fabricated sources, his work needs to be treated with caution. Those charges can be found in a Wikipedia article about him at https://en.wikipedia.org/wiki/Charles_Higham_(biographer). Recent Mayer biographies, especially Scott Eyman, *The Life and Legend of Louis B. Mayer* (New York: Simon & Schuster, 2005), focus favorably on his role in founding and heading a major studio. I prefer Samuel Marx, *Mayer and Thalberg*. Marx, an MGM story editor, knew the people and the events he chronicles.

43. Marx, *Mayer and Thalberg*, 24, 72, 74; Leatrice Gilbert Fountain, with John Maxim, *Dark Star* (New York: St. Martin's, 1985), 31.

44. On Thalberg, I have especially used Roland Flamini, *Thalberg: The Last Tycoon and the World of M-G-M* (New York: Crown, 1994).

45. Donald Ogden Stewart, *By a Stroke of Luck! An Autobiography* (New York: Paddington, 1975), 196. Samuel Marx, *A Gaudy Spree, The Literary Life of Hollywood in the 1930s: When the West Was Fun* (New York: F. Watts, 1987), 31.

46. Nancy Lynn Schwartz, *The Hollywood Writers Wars* (New York: Alfred A. Knopf, 1982), 24.

47. Cecil Beaton, *The Wandering Years: Diaries, 1922–1939* (London: Weidenfeld and Nicolson, 1961), 254.

48. Julie Shawnell, "Garbo or Dietrich?" *Pictorial Review*, July 1932; Larry Carr, *Four Fabulous Faces: The Evolution and Metamorphosis of Garbo, Swanson, Crawford, and Dietrich* (New Rochelle, NY: Arlington House, 1970), 141.

49. "Dear Little Mimosa," in Andersén Axell, *Djävla älskade unge!*, nr. 18.

## Chapter 6   The Agony and the Ecstasy

1. Fountain, *Dark Star*, 116. I have relied on the memoir of Leatrice Gilbert Fountain, Gilbert's daughter, on the early life of her father. I have also used Eve Golden, *John Gilbert: The Last of the Silent Film Stars* (Lexington: University Press of Kentucky, 2013). Rowland Lee's discussion of the dinner is contained in Rowland V. Lee, "Adventures of a Movie Director," unpublished manuscript (Los Angeles: American Film Institute, 1971).

2. Gurra to Min Lilla Mimosa, December 16, 1925, Andersén Axell, *Djävla älskade unge!*, 160. When he became a Hollywood actor, Einar Hanson changed his surname to Hansen. He died tragically in a car accident on June 3, 1927.

3. Fountain, *Dark Star*, 7.

4. Ben Hecht, *A Child of the Century* (New York: Simon & Schuster, 1954), 498; Patsy Ruth Miller, *My Hollywood: When Both of Us Were Young: The Memories of Patsy Ruth Miller* (New York: O'Raghailigh, 1988), 15.

5. Fountain, *Dark Star*, 172. Gilbert's wives included Olivia Burwell, a contract player he met at the boardinghouse where they both lived early in his Hollywood career. He subsequently married the screen star Leatrice Joy, who divorced him because of his drinking. His next wife was Ina Claire. His last wife was Virginia Bruce.

6. Katherine Lipke, "Greta Garbo Most Alluring," *Los Angeles Times*, October 17, 1926; Jack Larson, interview with the author, January 23, 2014. Larson was best known for playing Jimmy Olson, the young reporter in the Superman series on TV. Genial and friendly, he was well liked in Hollywood. He was also close to Salka Viertel.

7. Ruth Biery, "The Story of Greta Garbo," *Photoplay*, June 1928; Sundberg, "That Gustafsson Girl"; Rilla Page Palmborg, "Greta Has Her Say about American Men," unsourced clipping, GFS.

8. Flamini, *Thalberg*, 97.

9. Dorothy Calhoun, "They Learned about Women from Her," *Motion Picture Classic*, August, 1927, 36–37.

10. Smith, "Up Speaks a Gallant Loser."

11. Fountain, *Dark Star*, 125.

12. *Variety* review, excerpted in Conway, McGregor, and Ricci, *Films of Greta Garbo*, 59; Delight Evans, "The Editor's Page," *Screenland*, March 1930; Evans, "How Does Sex Appeal Sound?," *Screenland*, September 1928; Evans, "Kisses Have as Much Individuality as Faces—Observe John Gilbert," *Screenland*, January 1928.

13. Shorris and Bundy, *Talking Pictures*, 354.

14. Malcolm H. Oettinger, "Once Seen, Never Forgotten," *Picture Play*, April 1928.

15. Richard Meryman, *Mank: The Wit, World, and Life of Herman Mankiewicz* (New York: Morrow, 1978), 210.

16. Carey Wilson, "Stars Are Human After All," *Photoplay*, September 1936; Bainbridge, *Garbo*, 124–125.

17. Nicholas M. Turner, interview with Karen Swenson, February 8, 1962, Swenson Collection, UNCW.

18. Fountain, *Dark Star*, 130–131. Most Garbo biographers contend that King Vidor never commented on the wedding, although I found an interview in which he confirmed Garbo's failure to attend the wedding and Gilbert's attack on Mayer,

in Charlotte Chandler, *The Ultimate Seduction* (Garden City, NY: Doubleday, 1984), 206. No previous Garbo biographer has used this source.

19. St. Johns, "Mystery of Hollywood." According to Leatrice Fountain, St. Johns was "a clever woman with a keen sense of humor and a son who looked a lot like Jack, who left him a large bequest in his will." *Dark Star*, 217.

20. Salka Viertel, Diary, October 6, 1960, Salka Viertel Papers, Deutsches Literaturarchiv (German National Literary Archive), Marbach, Germany (hereafter cited as DLAM); Beaton, *Memoirs of the 40's*, 112.

21. Biery, "Story of Greta Garbo."

22. Ezra Goodman, *The Fifty-Year Decline and Fall of Hollywood* (New York: Simon & Schuster, 1961), 75.

23. On the mobbing of Garbo at the L. A. premier of *Flesh and the Devil*, see Katherine Albert, "Don't Envy the Stars," *Photoplay*, March 1929, and Harrison Carroll, "Who Remembers the Premiere When Greta Garbo and John Gilbert Were Almost Mobbed?," *Los Angeles Evening Herald Examiner*, January 29, 1937. Mark Vieira mistakenly claims that this episode never happened. See Vieira, *Greta Garbo: A Cinematic Legacy* (New York: Harry A. Abrams, 2005), 48. Marx, in *Mayer and Thalberg*, 130, includes a picture of Garbo at the premiere, along with John Gilbert and M.G.M. studio executives Howard Strickling and Paul Bern.

24. Cal York, "What's the Matter with Greta Garbo?," *Photoplay*, April 1927; Louise Brooks, "Garbo and Gish: The Executive War on the Stars," *Sight and Sound*, January 1959; Monk, "Why Stars Are Stars"; Calhoun, "They Learned About Women"; Ruth Biery, "Misinformation," *Photoplay*, June 1928.

25. Broman, *Conversations with Garbo*, 111; "Before and After Using," *Photoplay*, September 1927, 42. "Using" refers to taking cod liver oil. Anemia and pernicious anemia are genetically linked to individuals of Scandinavian descent. Garbo's breakdown and the deaths of Barbara LaMarr in 1926 and Lilyan Tashman in 1934 were linked to anorexia and bulimia. Garbo's breakdown occasioned a campaign against dieting in the fan magazines. See Catherine Brody, "Wholesale Murder and Suicide," *Photoplay*, July 1926, 105; Edward Churchill, "Is Garbo Doomed?," *Silver Screen*, June 1931; Rakel Ericson, "Why Garbo Is Tired," *Picture Play*, July 1934; Dorothy Calhoun, "Taking the Die Out of Diet," *Motion Picture*, July 1932.

26. I can find no evidence for Mark Vieira's contention that Garbo may have had a child during her strike against MGM. She was photographed in January 1927 at the Hollywood premiere of *Flesh and the Devil*, with no sign of pregnancy. Vieira seems unaware of Garbo's fatigue and her dieting. See Vieira, *Greta Garbo*, 45–47.

27. David Lewis, *The Creative Producer: A Memoir of the Studio System*, ed. James Curtis (Metuchen, NJ: Scarecrow, 1995), 93.

28. For a definition of ovarian inflammation, which often accompanies pelvic inflammatory disease, see the Mayo Clinic website. For a definition by clinicians that includes its connection to gonorrhea, see Maryam Shahi, Emily Amaroja, and

Christopher Crum, "The Fallopian Tube and Broad Ligament," in *Diagnostic Gynecologic and Obstetric Pathology*, ed. Christopher Crum et al. (Philadelphia: Elsevier, 2018), 716–760. For its history, see Simon Szreter, ed., *The Hidden Affliction: Sexually Transmitted Diseases and Infertility in History* (Rochester, NY: University of Rochester Press, 2019); Kevin Brown, *The Pox: The History of a Very Social Disease* (New York: Sutton, 2008); and John Lesch, *The Miracle Drugs: How the Sulfa Drugs Transformed Medicine* (Oxford: Oxford University Press, 2007). My thanks to King Reilly, M.D., for recommending sources on ovarian inflammation.

29. Maria Riva, *Marlene Dietrich: The Life* (New York: Pegasus, 1992), 164–166.

30. Melvyn Douglas and Tom Arthur, *See You at the Movies: The Autobiography of Melvyn Douglas* (Lanham MD: University Press of America, 1986), 88–89; Melvyn Douglas interview, CUOHP, 1958.

31. De Acosta, *Here Lies the Heart*, 217.

32. Alexander Walker, *Garbo: A Portrait* (New York: Macmillan, 1980), 79–83, notes that there was a seven-month hiatus between the end of filming *The Divine Woman* in November 1927 and beginning *The Mysterious Lady* in May 1928.

33. For a discussion of sex addiction in Hollywood during these years, see Selsman, *Sex Games in Hollywood*.

34. Matthew Kennedy, *Edmund Goulding's Dark Victory: Hollywood's Genius Bad Boy* (Madison: University of Wisconsin Press, 2004).

35. Patrick McGilligan, *George Cukor: A Double Life* (New York: St. Martin's, 1991), 109.

36. "Dear Mimi," November 1926, Sotheby's 1993; Patsy Ruth Miller, interview with Karen Swenson, December 11, 1994, Swenson Collection, UNCW; Adela Rogers St. Johns, *The Honeycomb* (Garden City, NY: Doubleday, 1969), 179.

37. "Darling Mim! [*sic*]," September 15, 1927, in Andersén Axell, *Djävla älskade unge!*; Sotheby's, November 26, 1927.

38. John Kobal, *People Will Talk: Conversations with Hollywood Legends* (New York: Alfred A. Knopf, 1985), 79; Brooks letter to Kevin Brownlow, October 19, 1968, quoted by Paris, *Garbo*, 266.

39. Malcolm H. Oettinger, "Lacquered Lily," *Picture Play*, April 1932; William J. Mann, *Behind the Screen: How Gays and Lesbians Shaped Hollywood, 1910–1969* (New York: Viking, 2001), 112–119. I have used Mann to identify the gay men and lesbian women whom Garbo knew.

40. Harry N. Lair, "Lilyan Tashman's Last Interview," *Hollywood*, June 1934. Meryman, *Mank*, 210–211, mentions Tashman's bulimia.

41. Smith, "Up Speaks a Gallant Loser"; David Niven, *Bring on the Empty Horses* (New York: G. P. Putnam's Sons, 1975), 25.

42. Oetinger, "Once Seen, Never Forgotten."

43. Douglas Fairbanks Jr., *The Salad Days* (New York: Doubleday, 1988), 129–130.

44. Frances Marion, "Hollywood," 11–19; Clara Beranger, "Famous Types and Why They Appeal," *Picture Play*, September 1926; "Lewis Stone: Imperturbable Gallant of the Cinema," *Motion Picture Classic*, May 1924. Off screen, Stone was comforting and calm.

45. Nils Asther, *Platonic Love*, small oil painting reproduced in a photograph in Sotheby's auction catalogue of *The Greta Garbo Collection*.

46. A copy of the letter is in the Swenson Collection, UNCW.

47. Broman, *Conversations with Garbo*, 111.

48. Broman, 191; Rilla Palmborg, "The Man Who Tried to Elope with Garbo," *Photoplay*, September 1931.

## Chapter 7    Friends and Lovers; *Anna Christie* and Garbo's Acting

1. Adela Rogers St. Johns, *The Single Standard* (New York: Cosmopolitan, 1928), 2.

2. Garbo, "My Life as an Artist," 63.

3. *Variety*, quoted in Conway, McGregor, and Ricci, *Films of Greta Garbo*, 81.

4. Baxter, *Hollywood Exiles*, 119.

5. Palmborg, "Private Life of Greta Garbo," 158. *Photoplay*, September 1930, October 1930; Palmborg, *Private Life of Greta Garbo*.

6. John Loder, "A Year in the Life of Greta of Greta Garbo," *Film Weekly*, March 23, 1932, in Haining, *Legend of Garbo*, 147–153.

7. John Loder, *Hollywood Hussar* (London: H. Baker, 1977).

8. Harriet Parsons, "Twenty-Four Hours with Garbo," *Silver Screen*, January 1931.

9. Parsons.

10. On homosexuals in Hollywood, I have relied on Mann, *Behind the Screen*; Mann, *Wisecracker: The Life and Times of William Haines, Hollywood's First Openly Gay Star* (New York: Viking, 1988); and Faderman and Timmons, *Gay L. A.*

11. Calhoun, "Inside Story of Garbo's Great Success."

12. Dorothy Calhoun, "Why Garbo's Friends Dare Not Talk," *Motion Picture*, July 1935.

13. Mollie Merrick, "Hollywood in Person," *Hollywood Citizen News*, in Hamann, *Garbo in the 30s*, 49.

14. Marion, *Off with Their Heads*, 152; Zazu Pitts, "My Children Love Greta Garbo," *Film Pictorial*, May 27, 1933.

15. William Daniels interview, Mark A. Vieira files, unpublished source material for his book *Greta Garbo: A Cinematic Legacy* (New York: Harry N. Abrams, 2005).

16. Writers on Garbo give different dates for the Lubitsch party, ranging from February 1929 to April 1930. Salka Viertel states that the party was given for "a visiting German star." Garbo and the Viertels were at a going-away party for Emil

Jannings in 1929, but the room was so crowded that Garbo left before the Viertels reached her. If Dietrich was the visiting star, as is probable, the party would have been in April 1930, when Dietrich arrived in Hollywood. The date of the party helps in determining the length of Salka's involvement with Garbo.

17. Viertel, *Kindness of Strangers*, 142.

18. On Salka Viertel, I have used Donna Rifkind, *The Sun and Her Stars: Salka Viertel and Hitler's Exiles in the Golden Age of Hollywood* (New York: Other Press, 2018); Katharina Prager, *"Ich bin nicht gone Hollywood!": Salka Viertel—ein Leben in Theater und Film* (Vienna: Braumüller, 2007); Viertel, *Kindness of Strangers*; and the German version of her autobiography, *Das unbelehrbare Herz: Ein Leben in Der Welt, des Theaters, und der Literatur and des Films* (Hamburg: Classen Verlag, 1970). On the relationship between Viertel and Garbo, I have been especially influenced by Nicole Nottelmann, *Ich liebe dich für immer: Greta Garbo und Salka Viertel* (Berlin: Auflage, 2011), and Salka's papers, in the German National Literary Archive in Marbach, Germany (DLAM).

19. Viertel, *Kindness of Strangers*, 141–143.

20. Betsy Blair, *The Memory of All That: Love and Politics in New York, Hollywood, and Paris* (New York: Alfred A. Knopf, 2003), 138.

21. Michael Schnayerson, *Irwin Shaw* (New York: Putnam, 1989), 152. Marlene Dietrich also came to Salka's salon; they had been together in Max Reinhardt's acting company in Berlin. The rumors of Garbo's affair with Dietrich in Berlin are inaccurate. Moreover, it was Salka, not Garbo, who knew Dietrich in Berlin.

22. George Schlee, in Benchley, "This Is Garbo."

23. Fred Zinnemann, *An Autobiography* (New York: Bloomsbury, 1992), 24.

24. Nottelmann, *Ich liebe dich*, 64.

25. Jack Larson, interview with the author, January 23, 2014.

26. For Mercedes de Acosta, I have especially relied on Robert A. Schanke, *"That Furious Lesbian": The Story of Mercedes de Acosta* (Edwardsville: Southern Illinois University Press, 2003). I have also used Patricia White, "Black and White: Mercedes de Acosta's Glorious Enthusiasms," in *Reclaiming the Archive: Feminism and Film History*, ed. Vicki Callahan (Detroit, MI: Wayne State University Press, 2010), 231–257; Mercedes's autobiography, *Here Lies the Heart*; and the drafts of the autobiography in the Rosenbach Museum.

27. While reading through *Vogue* magazine, I came across a photo of Mercedes as a debutante in the January 1914 issue.

28. Basil Rathbone, *In and Out of Character* (Garden City, NY: Doubleday, 1962), 143.

29. Beaton, Diary, February 3, 1930, Beaton-Cam.

30. Gavin Lambert, *Nazimova: A Biography* (New York: Alfred A. Knopf, 1997), 179.

31. Elisabeth Bergner, *Unordentliche Erinnerungen* (Berlin: 1987), 173.

32. Salka Viertel to Berthold Viertel, September 18 and 19, 1931, DLAM.

33. If you look closely, the hump is apparent in many Garbo films. Garbo eventually practiced the Butler method of exercises to straighten it.

34. James H. Jones, *Alfred C. Kinsey: A Public Private Life* (New York: W. W. Norton, 1997); Alfred C. Kinsey, *Sexual Behavior in the Human Male* (Philadelphia: W. B. Saunders, 1948); Kinsey, *Sexual Behavior in the Human Female* (Philadelphia: W. B. Saunders, 1953).

35. Broman, *Conversations with Garbo*, 162.

36. Gilbert's failure in his first sound film has occasioned a debate over its causes; I follow the anti-Mayer position taken by Leatrice Joy, Gilbert's daughter, in *Dark Star*. According to Fleming, *Fixers*, 82, MGM employees used Mayer's treatment of Gilbert as a cautionary tale against crossing Mayer; Irene Mayer remembered her father throwing a newspaper with an article detailing Gilbert's problems on the dining room table and saying with glee that the announcement should finish Gilbert in films. On the other hand, authors sympathetic to Mayer claim that he wouldn't have attacked Gilbert because Gilbert had the support of the New York office.

37. Fred Niblo, "Crashing the Sound Barrier," *Screenplay*, March 1929.

38. De Acosta, *Here Lies the Heart*, 138; Garbo, "My Life as an Artist," 43; Broman, *Garbo on Garbo*, 121; Raymond Durgnat and John Kobal, *Greta Garbo* (New York: Dutton, 1967), 80.

39. For Marx on Garbo, see Daum, *Walking with Garbo*, 149; Clarence Brown, "An Intimate Look at Garbo," in Haining, *Legend of Garbo*, 173.

40. Carr, *Four Fabulous Faces*, 121; Jacques Feyder and Françoise Rosay, *Le Cinema, Notes* (Vésenaz-près-Genève, Switzerland: Editions Pierre Cailler, 1946), 53–55; David Lewis, *The Creative Producer* (Landham, MD: Scarecrow Press, 1993), 93.

41. Basil Rathbone, "A Journey with Karenin," *Film Weekly*, September 1936, in Haining, *Legend of Garbo*, 224.

42. Alexander Walker, *Stardom: The Hollywood Phenomenon* (New York: Stein and Day, 1970), 142.

43. Foster Hirsch, *Acting Hollywood Style* (New York: Harry N. Abrams, 1991), 169–172.

44. Durgnat and Kobal, *Greta Garbo*, 80.

45. Parker Tyler, "The Garbo Image," in Conway, McGregor, and Ricci, *Films of Greta Garbo*, 12; Walker, *Stardom*, 144.

46. Maurice Rapf to E. J. Fleming, in Fleming, *Fixers*, 105. Rapf was the son of Harry Rapf, a close associate to L. B. Mayer.

## Chapter 8  Understanding Adrian

1. On illustrators in general, see Susan Doyle, Jaleen Grove, and Whitney Sherman, eds., *History of Illustration* (New York: Bloomsbury, Fairchild, 2019), and Susan E. Meyer, *America's Great Illustrators* (New York: Galahad / Harry N. Abrams, 1978). On the "pretty girl" artists, see Caroline Kirsch, *The Girl on the Magazine Cover* (Chapel Hill: University of North Carolina Press, 2001), 137–146, and Norman Rockwell, *My Adventures as an Illustrator* (New York: Harry N. Abrams, 1988), 10, 175.

2. Mimi Miley, *Howard Chandler Christy: Artist / Illustrator of Style* (Allentown, PA: Allentown Art Museum, 1977), n.p.

3. Brian Gallagher, *Anything Goes: The Jazz Age Adventures of Neysa McMein and Her Extravagant Circle of Friends* (New York: Times Books, 1987), 90.

4. Kirsch, *Girl on the Magazine Cover*, 121–122; Shelley Armitage, *John Held, Jr.: Illustrator of the Jazz Age* (Syracuse, NY: Syracuse University Press, 1989). On the flapper, I have relied on Linda Simon, *Lost Girls: The Invention of the Flapper* (London: Reaktion, 2017), and "Exit the Flapper," *New York Times*, January 25, 1922.

5. Mears, "Arc of Modernity," 62.

6. Patricia A. Cunningham, *Reforming Women's Fashions, 1850–1920* (Kent State, OH: Kent State University Press, 2003).

7. Mark Knowles, *The Wicked Waltz and Other Scandalous Dances: Outrage at Couple Dancing in the 19th and Early 20th Centuries* (Jefferson, NC: MacFarland, 2009).

8. Fletcher, "Why Is Garbo Love's Stepchild?"

9. De Acosta, *Here Lies the Heart*, 128; Michael Arlen, *The Green Hat* (New York: George H. Doran, 1924), 12.

10. Louella O. Parsons, "What's Happened to Greta?," *Los Angeles Examiner*, August 18, 1929.

11. *New York World* of January 5, 1913, cited in Banner, *American Beauty*, 239. See, for example, "New Flapper Modes for Spring," *Harper's Bazaar*, April 1917, 4–5; "Smart Flapper Models for the In-Between Years," 1922, in *Everyday Fashions of the Twenties: Pictured in Sears and Other Catalogs*, ed. Stella Blum (New York: Dover, 1981), 92. Blum includes photos of the flapper rainboots.

12. Katie Sutton, *The Masculine Woman in Weimar Germany* (New York: Berghahn Books, 2011), 1–50.

13. Joshua Zeitz, *Flapper: A Madcap Story of Sex, Style, Celebrity, and the Women Who Made Modern America* (New York: Crown, 2006), 93.

14. Poiret cited in William Wiser, *The Crazy Years: Paris in the Twenties* (New York: Atheneum, 1983), 75. See also Cecil Beaton, *The Face of the World: An International Scrapbook of People and Places* (London: Weidenfeld and Nicholson,

1957), 167; Aldous Huxley, "Beauty in 1920," in *On the Margin: Notes and Essays by Aldous Huxley* (London: Chatto & Windus, 1923), 116; and Joseph Howard, "She's Not the Type," *Screenland*, December 1929.

15. "Nita Naldi," *New York Herald Tribune*, July 39, 1922, Nita Naldi file, BRTC; Anne Rittenhouse, *The Well-Dressed Woman* (New York: Harper and Bros., 1924), 104–105.

16. On corsetry, see Jill Fields, *An Intimate Affair: Women, Lingerie, and Sexuality* (Berkeley: University of California Press, 2007).

17. Mary Lynn Stewart, *Dressing Modern Frenchwomen: Marketing Haute Couture, 1919–1930* (Baltimore: Johns Hopkins University Press, 2008), 4–7; Billie Melman, *Women and the Popular Imagination in the 1920s: Flappers and Nymphs* (New York: St. Martin's, 1988).

18. "Hail, the Flapper!," *Picture-Play*, March 1924; Bruce Blower, *Becoming American in Paris: Transatlantic Politics and Culture between the Two World Wars* (New York: Oxford University Press, 2011), 135.

19. Colleen Moore, *Silent Star: Colleen Moore Talks about Her Hollywood* (Garden City, NY: Doubleday, 1986), 135.

20. Margaret Reid, "Has the Flapper Changed?," *Motion Picture*, July 1927; Grace Margaret Morton, *Art of Costume and Personal Appearance* (New York: J. Wiley & Sons, 1943), 233.

21. Georgina Howell, *In Vogue: Sixty Years of International Celebrities and Fashion from British Vogue* (New York: Schocken, 1976), 1–45; Mildred Adams, "Now We Say Farewell to the Flapper," *New York Times*, January 20, 1929; Diana de Marly, *The History of Haute Couture* (New York: Holmes and Meier, 1980).

22. "Paris Yields to None in the Fashion World," *New York Times*, December 2, 1928; Larry Engelmann, *The Goddess and the American Girl: The Story of Suzanne Lenglen and Helen Wills* (New York: Oxford University Press, 1988). On Patou, see Meredith Etherington-Smith, *Patou* (New York: St. Martin's, 1983).

23. Virginia Nicholson, *Among the Bohemians: Experiments in Living, 1900–1939* (New York: William Morrow, 2002).

24. Nicholson, 159; Valerie Steele, *Paris Fashions: A Cultural History* (New York: Bloomsbury, 2017), 232.

25. Susan A. Glenn, *Female Spectacle: The Theatrical Roots of Modern Feminism* (Cambridge, MA: Harvard University Press, 2000), 189. See also Linda Mizejewski, *Ziegfeld Girl: Image and Icon in Culture and Cinema* (Durham, NC: Duke University Press, 1999).

26. Andrea Stuart, *Showgirls* (London: Jonathan Cape, 1996); Derek and Julia Parker, *The Natural History of the Chorus Girl* (Indianapolis, IN: Bobbs-Merrill, 1975).

27. Florenz Ziegfeld, "Picking Out Pretty Girls for the Stage," *American Magazine*, December 1914.

28. John Emile Hirsch, "Glorifying the American Showgirl: A History of Revue Costume in the United States from 1866 to the Present" (PhD diss., New York University, 1988). The *New York World* quote from 1905 is contained in the Ned Wayburn Scrapbooks, BRTC (Billy Rose Theater Collection).

29. Marjorie Rosen, *Popcorn Venus* (New York: Avon, 1974), 96–97. Frequent movie magazine articles discuss the success of Broadway chorus girls in Hollywood films, especially those from the Ziegfeld Follies. See, for example, Paul Yawitz, "Girls from the Follies Who've Made Good on the Screen," *Motion Picture*, February 1932.

30. Mary Astor, *A Life on Film* (New York: Delacorte, 1971), 11–13; Kobal, *People Will Talk*.

31. Adela Rogers St. Johns, "New American Beauty," *Photoplay*, June 1922. See also Harriet Underhill, "The Movies Give the World a Boyish Form," *Motion Picture Classic*, November 1925, and Walker, *Stardom*, 59–81. On Griffith, I have used Richard Schickel, *D. W. Griffith: An American Life* (New York: Proscenium / Limelight, 1996), 33, 57, 129–134; and Bessie Love, *From Hollywood with Love* (London: Elm Tree, 1977). Love was a member of Griffith's company.

32. Addison, *Hollywood and the Rise of Physical Culture*. On the many Hollywood male producers and directors who were small, see Day, *This Was Hollywood*, 19–26. Michael Selsmann, an executive assistant to Marcus Leow in New York in the 1940s and to Darryl Zanuck at Twentieth Century-Fox in the 1950s, told me in an interview that many of these men suffered from a "Napoleonic complex," which made them assume an aggressive male persona to make up for their lack of height. Michael Selsmann, interview with the author, November 13, 2009, Lois Banner Collection on Marilyn Monroe, AMPAAS.

33. Sydney Valentine, "The Heights of Fame," *Screenland*, February 1931.

34. Lady Duff-Gordon (Lucile), *Discretions and Indiscretions* (New York: Frederick A. Stokes, 1932), 77–91; Randy Ryan Bigham, *Lucile: Her Life by Design* (San Francisco: MacEvie, 2012), 325–339.

35. Duff-Gordon, *Discretions and Indiscretions*, 77–91.

36. Lewis, *It Was Fun While It Lasted*, 20.

37. Edmonde Charles-Roux, *Chanel: Her Life, Her World, and the Woman behind the Legend She Herself Created*, trans. Nancy Amphoux (New York: Alfred A. Knopf, 1975), 194–198.

38. Caroline Evans, *The Mechanical Smile: Modernism and the First Fashion Shows in France and America, 1900–1929* (New Haven, CT: Yale University Press, 2013), 212; Robert Forrest Wilson, *Paris on Parade* (Indianapolis, IN: Bobbs-Merrill, 1925), 46.

39. Howard Gutner, *MGM Style: Cedric Gibbons and the Art of the Golden Age of Hollywood* (Guilford, CT: Lyons, 2019), 238.

40. Frank Scarlett and Marjorie Townley, *Arts Decoratifs 1925: A Personal Recollection of the Paris Exhibition* (New York: St. Partin's, 1975), 58–59; Diana Villiers, *Boston Globe*, October 11, 1925; Janet Mable, "Beautiful, but Dummies," *Christian Science Monitor*, November 27, 1935; Carolyn Hall, *The Twenties in Vogue* (New York: Harmony, 1983), 92; Suzanne Lussier, *Art Deco Fashion* (New York: Bulfinch, 2003), 90.

41. Tyler, The Garbo Image," 16.

42. *Harper's Bazaar*, April 1926; "Letter from Edna Woolman Chase, in Paris," *Vogue*, April 15, 1925.

43. Christina Cogdell, *Eugenic Design: Streamlining America in the 1930s* (Philadelphia: University of Pennsylvania Press, 2010); Marie Pochna, *Dior* (New York: Assouline, 2004), 54–60; Adrienne Berney, "Streamlining Breasts: The Evolution of Form and Disguise of Function in 1930s Ideals," *Journal of Design History* 14 (2001): 127–144.

44. Madge Garland, *The Indecisive Decade; The World of Fashion and Entertainment in the Thirties* (London: Macdonald, 1968), 69; *Vogue*, October 15, 1931; Margaret Reid, "Ladies, Be Yourselves!," *Los Angeles Times*, April 26, 1931; Ruth Tildsley, "Curves! Hollywood Wants Them—and So Will You!," *Motion Picture*, July 1933.

45. Adams, "Now We Say Farewell to the Flapper"; Mildred Adams, "Now the Siren Eclipses the Flapper," *New York Times*, July 2, 1929.

46. Marion, *Off with Their Heads*, 74; Christian Esquevin, *Adrian: Silver Screen to Custom Label* (New York: Monacelli, 2008), 22; Katherine Albert, "Hollywood Leads Paris in Fashion," *Photoplay*, November 1929; Eliot Keene, "Willowy Women," *Silver Screen*, November 1931.

47. James Laver, "The Nana Ideal," *London Vogue*, April 18, 1934.

48. On Adrian, I have used Stanley, *Adrian*; Esquevin, *Adrian*; Gutner, *Gowns by Adrian*; and the many articles in the Adrian Collection at AMPAAS.

49. Robert Riley, "Adrian," in Sarah Tomerlin Lee, *American Fashion* (New York: Quadrangle, 1974), 43; Diana Souhami, *Greta and Cecil* (London: Phoenix, 1994), 14.

50. Valentine, "Miracles of Makeup"; "Glamour by Adrian," from Robert Riley, *American Fashion*, clipping, Adrian Collection, AMPAAS.

51. Mayne Ober Peak, "Study the Stars and Dress Your Line," *Ladies' Home Journal*, June 1932, 8.

52. Esquevin, *Adrian*, 13.

53. Margaret J. Bailey, *Those Glorious Glamour Years* (Secaucus, NJ: Citadel, 1982), 171.

54. Helen Louise Walker, unsourced and undated clipping, Adrian Collection, AMPAAS.

55. Stanley, *Adrian*, 112; mss. interview with Adrian, Greta Garbo file, Hedda Hopper Papers, AMPAAS.

56. Adrian, *Hollywood Citizen News*, May 7, 1932, in Hamann, *Greta Garbo in the '30s*.

57. Gutner, *Gowns by Adrian*, 77–78, in *New York Evening World*, July 24, 1930.

58. Reid, "Ladies, Be Yourselves."

59. Stefania Ricci, *Greta Garbo: The Mystery of Style* (Florence: Museo Salvatore Ferragamo, 2010).

60. Elsie Qui, "Blame Hollywood for This," *Picture Play*, May 1930.

61. Sarah B. Marchetti and Emily Thomsen Angstman, "The Trend for Mannish Suits in the 1930s," *Dress: The Journal of the Costume Society of America* 29, no. 2 (2013).

## Chapter 9    The Pre-Code Era

1. On Hollywood censorship and the pre-Code era, see Elena Nicolaou, "Ladies First: The Hays Code Made Hollywood Hell on Earth for Women," Refinery 29, December 6, 2019, https://www.refinery29.com/en-us/women-pre-code-hollywood-movies-before-hays; Mark A. Vieira, *Forbidden Hollywood: When Sex Ruled the Movies* (New York: Hachette, Rising Press, 2019); Thomas Doherty, *Pre-Code Hollywood: Sex, Immorality, and Insurrection in American Cinema: 1930–1934* (New York: Columbia University Press, 1999); Gaylin Studlar, "Marlene Dietrich and the Erotics of Code-Bound Hollywood" in *Dietrich Icon*, ed. Gerd Gemünden and Mary R. Desjardins (Durham, NC: Duke University Press, 2007), 225; and Gregory D. Black, *Hollywood Censored: Morality, Codes, Catholics, and the Movies* (New York: Cambridge University Press, 1994).

2. Ruth Biery, "Garbo's Jinx on Her Leading Men," *Photoplay*, September 1932.

3. Daum, *Walking with Garbo*, 71–72.

4. Brown, "Intimate Look at Garbo," 167.

5. On Jean Harlow, see David Stenn, *Bombshell: The Life and Times of Jean Harlow* (New York: Doubleday, 1993); on Joan Crawford, see Crawford, *Portrait of Joan*; Bob Thomas, *Joan Crawford, A Biography* (New York: Simon and Schuster, 1978); and Annette Tapert, "Joan Crawford," in *The Power of Glamour* (New York: Crown, 1998), 11–67.

6. On Norma Shearer, see Lawrence J. Quirk, *Norma: The Story of Norma Shearer* (New York: St. Martin's, 1988); Tapert, "Norma Shearer," in *Power of Glamour*, 68–91.

7. Mark Vieira, *Hollywood Dreams Made Real: Irving Thalberg and the Rise of MGM* (New York: Harry N. Abrams, 2008), 139.

8. Delight Evans, "The Divorcee," *Screenland*, July 1930.

9. Grant Jackson, "Will Foreign Actors Force Down American Salaries?," *Motion Picture*, May 1933.

10. Palmborg, *Private Life*, 139–140.

11. Viertel, *Kindness of Strangers*, 174.

12. Ruth Biery and Eleanor Parker, "Garbo Has Changed," *Silver Screen*, September 1933.

13. Andrea Weiss, "A Queer Feeling When I Look at You: Hollywood Stars and Lesbian Spectatorship in the 1930s," in *Stardom: Industry of Desire*, ed. Christine Gledhill (1991; New York: Routledge, 2003), 283–300.

14. See, for example, Manners, "Even Hollywood Heroes"; de Acosta, *Here Lies the Heart*, 314.

15. De Acosta, *Here Lies the Heart*, 231–233.

16. Swenson, *Greta Garbo*, 258–259.

17. Marx, *Gaudy Spree*, 58; "The Final Fling," *Silver Screen*, September 1932.

18. Beaton, *Wandering Years*, 258–260.

19. Vickers, *Loving Garbo*, 68.

20. Peter Joel, "Garbo's Vacation Romance," *Screen Play*, November 1982, describes the brief relationship between Garbo and Cummings. Patricia Billingsley, who is preparing a manuscript on the relationship between Cummings and the Spanish playwright Frederico García Lorca, kindly provided me with relevant pages from Cummings's diary as well as reports on his interactions with Garbo that he wrote for a local Vermont newspaper.

21. Garbo, "Hollywood Will See Me No More!," October 1932, reprinted in Haining, *Legend of Garbo*, 181–187.

22. Beaton, *Memoirs of the '40s*, 251.

23. Riva, *Marlene Dietrich*, 155–156.

24. Riva, 168.

## Chapter 10    Breaking Free

1. Fred Niblo, "Masculinity Menaces Movie Maidens," *Hollywood*, July 15, 1928.

2. Mordaunt Hall, "Hollywood Hermit," *New York Times*, March 24, 1929. See also Ruth Biery, "Greta Goes Home," clipping, unsourced, GFS; Edwin Schallert, "Are the Movies Scorning Love?," *Picture Play*, December 1928.

3. Tony Howard, *Women as Hamlet: Performance and Interpretation in Theatre, Film, and Literature* (Cambridge: Cambridge University Press, 2007).

4. Gottfried Reinhardt, *The Genius: A Memoir of Max Reinhart* (New York: Alfred A. Knopf, 1997), 301.

5. Laura Horak, *Girls Will Be Boys: Cross-dressed Women, Lesbians, and American Cinema, 1908–1934* (New Brunswick, NJ: Rutgers University Press, 2016).

6. Madeleine Mahlon, "On with the Pants," *Photoplay*, July 1926.

7. Daniel Hurewitz, "Banned on Broadway but Coming to a Theater Near You: *The Captive* and Rethinking the Breadth of American Anti-lesbian Hostility in the

1920s and 30s," *Journal of Lesbian Studies* 17 (January 14, 2013), 44–55. Ruth Benedict and Margaret Mead, who were close friends and sexual partners, were thrilled by *The Captive*. They liked it because it portrayed the lesbian lover of the married woman as powerful and worthy of the married woman's love. Benedict eventually chose lesbianism as her identity; Mead remained bisexual, even after she married the anthropologist Gregory Bateson. See Banner, *Intertwined Lives*, passim.

8. Paris, *Garbo*, 265.

9. Sarah Waters, "A Girton Girl on the Throne: Queen Christina and Versions of Lesbianism, 1906–1933," *Feminist Review* 46 (Spring 1994).

10. See, for example, Andrea Weiss, *Paris Was a Woman: Portraits from the Left Bank* (San Francisco: HarperSanFrancisco, 1995), 111.

11. Mercedes de Acosta, drafts of autobiography, first mss. unpublished, 29–30, Mercedes de Acosta Papers, Rosen.

12. David Shipman, *Movie Talk* (New York: St. Martin's, 1989), 58; Riva, *Marlene Dietrich*, 165.

13. Garbo to Mimi, 1930, Garbo Forever; Hugo Vickers, *Cecil Beaton: A Biography* (Boston: Little, Brown, 1985), 326.

14. Sam Green, interview with Karen Swenson, February 9, 1981, Swenson Collection, UNCW.

15. Beaton, Diary, October 1947–1948, Beaton-Cam.

16. Gore Vidal to Boze Hadleigh, in Hadleigh *Hollywood's Lesbians: From Garbo to Foster* (Riverdale, NY: Riverdale Books, 2016), 200.

17. George Cukor to Cecil Beaton, quoted by Vickers, *Loving Garbo*, 68, undated, Beaton-Cam.

18. Sam Green, interview with Swenson, February 9, 1993, Swenson Collection, UNCW.

19. Jennifer Terry, *An American Obsession: Science, Medicine, and Homosexuality in Modern Society* (Berkeley: University of California Press, 1999).

20. William J. Mann, *Kate: The Woman Who Was Hepburn* (New York: Henry Holt, 2006), 38, 165.

21. Mann, *Wisecracker*, 224–228.

22. On the making of *Queen Christina*, I have used Betsy Erkkila, "Sailing beyond the Frame," *Critical Inquiry* 11, no. 4 (June 1985), 595–615; Waters, "Girton Girl on the Throne"; Jane Gaines, "The Queen Christina Tie-Ups: Convergence of Show Window and Screen," *Quarterly Review of Film & Video* 11, no. 1 (1989): 35–60; and Marcia Land and Amy Villarjo, *Queen Christina* (London: British Film Institute, 1995).

23. Biery and Parker, "Garbo Has Changed"; "Greta Garbo—Her Life Story," official MGM Garbo biography, 1933, Garbo file, AMPAAS.

24. On Christina's life, I have relied on Veronica Buckley, *Christina, Queen of Sweden: The Restless Life of a European Eccentric* (New York: HarperCollins, 2004.)

25. Laurence Olivier, "The Queen I Could Not Conquer," in Haining, *Legend of Garbo*, 191.

26. Ruth Rankin, "Reunion in the Palace," *Photoplay*, November 1933.

27. Larry Reid, "Be Sure to See *Queen Christina!*," *Movie Classic*, June 1934.

28. On Mamoulian, see Mark Spiegel, *Reinventing Reality: The Art and Life of Rouben Mamoulian* (Metuchen, NJ: Scarecrow, 1993).

29. Beaton, *Memoirs of the 40's*, 272.

30. Ida Zeitland, "Garbo vs. Sten: The Battle Is On," *Screenland*, June 1934.

## Chapter 11   Denouement

1. Laver, "Nana Ideal"; Mary Alcorn, "Must Sylvia Go Highbrow?," *Picture Play*, May 1933; James Laver, *Taste and Fashion* (London: Harrap, 1932), 136.

2. "Then Came Garbo," *Vanity Fair*, November 1932; Bainbridge, *Garbo*, 9. The photos also appeared in Henry Jeanson, "Gretagarbisme," *Paris Vogue*, January 1933.

3. Howard Greer, *Designing Male* (New York: Putnam, 1951), 267. Greer was an American dress designer from the 1920s to the 1950s.

4. Blum, *Everyday Fashions of the Twenties*, 86.

5. Swenson, *Greta Garbo*, 351.

6. Ruth Biery, "The New Shady Dames of the Screen," *Photoplay*, August 1932; Qui, "Blame Hollywood for This"; Adele Whitely Fletcher, "Smooth Ladies," *Photoplay*, November 1930.

7. "Notes for a TV Production on Greta Garbo," S. N. Behrman Papers, New York Public Library.

8. Gretchen Colnik, "Why Women Look Up to Garbo," *Movie Classic*, May 1934; Ruth Rankin, They're All Queening It," *Photoplay*, December 1933. See also St. Johns, "Great Garbo."

9. Arlene Hodgkins, "Garbo's Gamble," *Photoplay*, July 1933. On Billy, see Wilhelm Sörenson, "The Day That Garbo Dreaded," *Sunday Express*, June 5, 1955, reprinted in Haining, *Legend of Garbo*, 144.

10. Sydney Guilaroff, *Crowning Glory: Reflections of Hollywood's Favorite Confidante* (Santa Monica: General Publishing Group, 1996).

11. Riva, *Marlene Dietrich*, 255.

12. Mary Anita Loos, interview with Karen Swenson, March 1, 1995.

13. Garbo's letters to Hörke Wachtmeister can be found in Broman, *Conversations with Garbo*, 123–139, 152–201.

14. Broman, *Garbo on Garbo*, 119.

15. Mary Cass Canfield, "Letter to Garbo," *Theatre Arts Monthly*, December 1937.

16. Gutner, *Gowns by Adrian*, 96.

17. Thomas Doherty, *Hollywood's Censor: Joseph I. Breen and the Production Code Administration* (New York: Columbia University Press, 2007); Lea Jacobs, *The Wages of Sin: Censorship and the Fallen Woman Film, 1928–1942* (Berkeley: University of California Press, 1995); Black, *Hollywood Censored*; Matthew Bernstein, *Walter Wanger: Hollywood Independent* (Berkeley: University of California Press, 1994).

18. Vieira, *Greta Garbo*, 197.

19. Viertel, *Kindness of Strangers*, 197; Broman, *Conversations with Garbo*, 152.

20. Scott O'Brien, *George Brent: Ireland's Gift to Hollywood and Its Leading Ladies* (Port Jervis, NY: Bear Mountain, 2014).

21. Souhami, *Greta and Cecil*, 134.

22. Jay Brian Chapman, "Is Mae West Garbo's Greatest Rival?," *Motion Picture*, July 1933.

23. See Maria DiBattista, *Fast-Talking Dames* (New Haven: Yale University Press, 2001).

24. Rudy Behlmer, ed., *Memo from David O. Selznick* (New York: Modern Library, 2000), 75–76.

25. Viertel, *Kindness of Strangers*, 21.

26. Nottelmann, *Ich liebe dich*.

27. De Acosta, *Here Lies the Heart*, 258.

28. Alastair Cooke, *Garbo and the Night Watchman: A Selection Made in 1937 from the Writings of British and American Film Critics* (New York: McGraw-Hill, 1971), 121–123.

29. Emmanuel Levy, *George Cukor, Master of Elegance: Hollywood's Legendary Director and His Stars* (New York: Morrow, 1994).

30. George Cukor to Hugh Walpole, December 25, 1934, January 22, 1935, George Cukor Papers, AMPAAS. On Cukor, see McGilligan, *George Cukor*.

31. On Don Herold, see Zierold, *Garbo*, 16.

32. Vickers, *Loving Garbo*, 62.

33. Erkkila, "Sailing beyond the Frame."

34. Hettie Grimstead, "At Home with Garbo," *Screenland*, April 1939.

35. Abram Chasen, *Leopold Stokowski: A Profile* (London: Robert Hale, 1979), 165.

36. Reinhardt, *Genius*, 303.

37. Niven, *Bring on the Empty Horses*, 173–174.

38. Broman, *Garbo on Garbo*, 171.

39. Garson Kanin, *Hollywood* (New York: Bantam, 1976), 105.

## Chapter 12  Success and Failure

1. Malcolm, "Garbo You've Never Heard About."

2. Nils Asther in Benchley, "This is Garbo."

3. Vickers, *Loving Garbo*, 74.

4. Louella Parsons column, March 11, 1939, quoted by Daum, *Walking with Garbo*, 156.

5. Broman, *Garbo on Garbo*, 172–178; Rilla Page Palmborg, "Garbo Finds Herself," *Photoplay*, March 1942.

6. There is no biography of Hauser. Relevant information can be found in the Garbo biographies and in Nancy Cooke de Herrera, *Beyond Gurus: A Woman of Many Worlds* (Nevada City, CA: Blue Dolphin, 1993).

7. Castelbajac, *Face of the Century*, 64.

8. Broman, *Walking with Garbo*, 157.

9. Herrera, *Beyond Gurus*, 411; Richard Schickel, *Matinee Idylls: Reflections on the Movies* (Chicago: Ivan R. Dee, 1999), 59.

10. Jessica Dragonette, *Faith Is a Song: The Odyssey of an American Artist* (New York: McKay, 1951), 252–253.

11. See "Reality and Myth: A Symposium on Axel Wenner-Gren," Wenner-Gren Center, Stockholm, May 30–31, 2012.

12. Julie Gilbert, *Opposite Attraction: The Lives of Erich Maria Remarque and Paulette Goddard* (Garden City, NY: Doubleday, 1978); Anita Loos, *Cast of Thousands* (New York: Grosset & Dunlop, 1977), 179.

13. Gilbert, *Opposite Attraction*, 241.

14. Interview with George Cukor, in Boze Hadleigh, *Conversations with My Elders* (New York: St. Martin's Press, 1996), 136.

15. *Time*, December 22, 1941; Melvyn Douglas, in *Photoplay*, August 1976, reprinted in Haining, *Legend of Garbo*, 35.

16. Vieira, *Greta Garbo*, 268.

17. Guilaroff, *Crowning Glory*, 132.

18. Laurence Leamer, *As Time Goes By: The Life of Ingrid Bergman* (New York: Harper and Row, 1986), 459–464.

19. Vieira, *Greta Garbo*, 268.

20. On Valentina Sanina and George Schlee, see Kennedy Fraser, *Ornament and Silence: Essays on Women's Lives* (New York: Alfred A. Knopf, 1996); and Kohle Yohannan, *Valentina: American Couture and the Cult of Celebrity* (New York: Rizzoli, 2009), 174ff.

21. Vickers, *Loving Garbo*, 81.

22. Vickers, *Cecil Beaton*, 313.

23. Walker, *Garbo*, 173.

24. Jhan Robbins, *This Week*, October 4, 1959.

25. Niven, *Bring on the Empty Horses*, 156.

26. Jean Howard, interview with Karen Swenson, November 10, 1992, Swenson Collection, UNCW.

27. Clifton Webb, *Sitting Pretty: The Life and Times of Clifton Webb* (Jackson: University Press of Mississippi, 2011), 158–164.

28. Daum, *Walking with Garbo*, 174; Higham, *Merchant of Dreams*, 328. Higham contended that he interviewed William Stephenson, but I cannot find that interview. Higham has been accused of fabricating sources and events. A summary of the allegations is contained in the Wikipedia entry on Charles Higham. With regard to Garbo and spying in World War II, Garbo denied that she did so, but her denial may have stemmed from her fear of having her participation discussed in public. The major Allied spy during World War II, Juan Pojal Garcia, was given the code name Garbo.

29. Daum, *Walking with Garbo*, 172–175. On Garbo's request to see the Danish ambassador, see Sam Behrman interviews, Viera files.

30. Rosalind Schaeffer, "Is Garbo a Nazi?," unsourced clipping, undated, Greta Garbo file, AMPAAS.

31. David King Dunaway, *Huxley in Hollywood* (New York: Doubleday, 1989); Loos, *Cast of Thousands*, 286.

32. Eric Drimmer, "I Was Garbo's Psychologist," in Broman, *Garbo on Garbo*, 172–179.

33. Loos, *Cast of Thousands* (New York: Grossett & Dunlap, 1977), 286.

34. Kathleen O'Steen, "Commitment: A Brief Affair: Greta Garbo and Gilbert Roland," *Los Angeles Times*, November 1991.

## Chapter 13   New York

1. Laila Nylund, interview with Karen Swenson, March 2, 1995, Swenson Collection, UNCW.

2. Swenson, *Greta Garbo*, 451.

3. Beaton, *Memoirs of the '40s*, 243.

4. Christopher Isherwood, *Diaries*, vol. 1, *1939–1960* (New York: HarperCollins, 2000), 67.

5. Gore Vidal, interview with Dick Cavett, PBS, 1991, https://www.youtube.com /watch?v=zgSQaTqSZ2o.

6. Vieira files.

7. Ronald Hayman, *John Gielgud* (New York: Random House, 1971), 156.

8. Joshua Logan, *My Up and Down, In and Out Life* (New York: Delacorte, 1976), 131; Niven, *Bring on the Empty Horses*, 184–187.

9. Dragonette, *Faith Is a Song*, 254.

10. Sam Green, interview with Karen Swenson, February 9, 1993, Swenson Collection, UNCW.

11. Faderman, *Odd Girls and Twilight Lovers*, 71–72.

12. Bainbridge, *Garbo*, 278.

13. Fred Kaplan, *Gore Vidal: A Biography* (New York: Doubleday, 1999).

14. Betty Spiegel, interview with Karen Swenson, June 2, 1993, Swenson Collection, UNCW.

15. Broman and Sands, *Divine Garbo*, 231.

16. George Bernard Shaw to Gabriel Pascal, September 1, 1938, and Shaw to Marjorie Deans, March 2, 1940, in Shaw, *Collected Letters* (New York Viking, 1985), 4:508, 566.

17. Beaton, *Memoir of the 40's*, 283.

18. Tennessee Williams, *Memoirs* (Garden City, NY: Doubleday, 1975), 138–139; Williams, *Letters to Donald Windham, 1940–1965* (Verona, PA: Verona, 1976), 201.

19. Zierold, *Garbo*, 94.

20. Viertel, *Kindness of Strangers*, 300.

21. McGilligan, *George Cukor*, 182.

22. Gilbert, *Opposite Attraction*, 113.

23. Barbara Barondess MacLean, interview with Barry Paris, January 29, 1991, in Paris, *Garbo*.

24. Anne Mochon, *Alexej Jawlensky: From Appearance to Essence* (Long Beach, CA: Long Beach Museum of Art, 1990).

25. Gray Horan, "Greta Garbo," in Architectural Digest, *Hollywood at Home* (New York: Harry A. Abrams, 2005), 50–57.

26. Beaton, *Memoirs of the 40's*, 271.

27. Jean Howard, interview with Karen Swenson, November 10, 1992, Swenson Collection, UNCW.

28. Jan Rehan, "The Secret Life of Greta Garbo," *This Week*, October 4, 1959.

29. George Schlee to Sam Behrman, June 3, 1955, S. N. Behrman Papers, NYPL.

30. Salka Viertel, Diary, October 6, 1960 (DLAM).

31. Lilli Palmer, *Change Lobsters, and Dance: An Autobiography* (New York: Macmillan, 1975), https://archive.org/details/changelobstersdaoopalm.

32. Vickers, *Loving Garbo*, 270–274; Nottelmann, *Ich liebe dich*, 240.

33. Niall Ferguson, *The House of Rothschild: Money's Prophets, 1798–1848* (New York: Penguin Random House, 1999); Ferguson, *The House of Rothschild: The World's Bankers, 1849–1998* (New York: Penguin Random House, 2000).

34. Herrera, *Beyond Gurus*, 422.

35. Gaylord Hauser quoted in Nancy Cooke de Herrera, *All You Need Is Love: An Eyewitness Account of When Spirituality Spread from East to West* (New York: Open Road Media, 2016), https://www.google.com/books/edition/All_You_Need_Is_Love/LaHMDAAAQBAJ?hl=en&gbpv=0.

36. "Greta Garbo's Great Nephew, Derek Reisfield," *Swedish Press*, December 31, 2005.

37. Viertel, *Kindness of Strangers*, 34.

## Chapter 14   Summing Up

1. Broman, *Conservations with Garbo*, 120, 157; Svetlana Alliluyeva, *Twenty Letters to a Friend* (New York: Harper Collins, 1967); Rosemary Sullivan, *Stalin's Daughter: The Extraordinary and Tumultuous Life of Svetlana Alliluyeva* (London: HarperCollins, 2016).

2. Lewis, *Creative Producer*, 107.

3. Ingmar Bergman, *The Magic Lantern*, trans. Joan Tate (New York: Viking Penguin, 1988), 250.

4. I have derived the term "tragi-sexual goddesses" from Peter Bradshaw, "Why Are the Great Director's [Ingar Bergman's] Women All Tragi-Sexual Goddesses?," *The Guardian*, February 4, 2018.

5. In my discussions of drinking habits in New York in the 1970s and 1980s, I draw on my own experience as a Rutgers professor married to a Princeton professor during those years, with many friends who lived in New York.

6. George Cukor to Cecil Beaton, April 15, 1963, quoted by Vickers, *Loving Garbo*, 68. See Chapter 10 for further discussion.

7. I have derived descriptions of Klosters and Davos from Peter Viertel, *Dangerous Friends: At Large with Houston and Hemingway in the Fifties* (New York: Doubleday, 1992), passim; Nicole Nottelmann's descriptions in *Ich liebe dich*, based on Salka's journals and letters in DLAM; and numerous travel guidebooks to Switzerland.

8. Quoted by Paris, *Garbo*, 454.

9. Viertel, *Dangerous Friends*, 123.

10. Gore Vidal, *Palimpsest: A Memoir* (New York: Vintage, 2021), 299.

11. Salka Viertel's diary for the Klosters years is contained in DLAM.

12. Quoted in Paris, *Garbo*, 508.

13. Throughout this section on religion, as elsewhere in this book, I have used my own experience of religion, from having been raised in the Missouri Synod Lutheran Church, to writing a dissertation on Christianity, to experimenting with feminist spirituality, Hinduism, Buddhism, Islam, and the Episcopal Church in later life. See, in particular, Lois W. Banner, *Finding Fran: History and Memory in the Lives of Two Women* (New York: Columbia University Press, 1998).

14. Broman, *Garbo on Garbo*, 162.

15. Paris, *Garbo*.

16. Daum, *Walking with Garbo*, 175.

17. Dragonette, *Faith Is a Song*, passim.

18. Both Swenson and Paris interviewed Nicholas Turner. Turner's most interesting remarks on Garbo's "conversion" to Catholicism are in Paris, *Garbo*, 534–535.

19. Daniel D. Noonan, *The Passion of Fulton J. Sheen* (New York: Dodd, Mead, 1972).

20. Garbo to Salka Viertel, undated, circa early 1960s. Quoted by Paris, *Garbo*, 534.

21. Paris, *Garbo*, 534.

22. Nicholas Turner interview, Swenson Collection, UNCW.

23. My description of Woodland Cemetery and Garbo's grave is based primarily on my own reaction to them. I visited the cemetery in 2017.

# INDEX

Page numbers in *italics* represent photos.

in, 178, 187–188, 193, *198*, 207–215, 212,
279; Garbo's costumes, 174, 201, 207,
212, 213–214; Garbo's efforts to revive
Gilbert's career, 191; Garbo's health
issues during filming, 218, 220, 232;
Garbo's research on, 195, 207, 209; Gilbert
cast in, 210–211, 212, 213; happy ending,
150, 211–212; incorrectly considered as
failure, 263, 265, 280; peak of Garbo's
career, 5–6, 219, 232; produced by Garbo,
193; produced by Wanger, 206; screenplay by Salka Viertel, 141, 184, 194, 206,
207, 209–212; writers on, 109
Queen of Sheba, 22
Qui, Elsie, 174

Racine, Jean, 65
Rainier (prince), 272
Rank, J. Arthur, 264
Rankin, Ruth, 219
Rapf, Harry, 323n46
Rapf, Maurice, 323n46
Rathbone, Basil, 152, 228
Reid, Larry, 211
Reid, Margaret, 174
Reinhardt, Gottfried, 139, 145, 200, 234,
245, 246
Reinhardt, Max, 69, 88, 139, 200, 322n22
Reisch, Walter, 265
Reisfield, Gray (niece), 11, 267, 283, 290, 295
Reisfield, Scott (great nephew), 54
Remarque, Erich Maria, 244–245, 251, 266
*Remember the City* (Fogelström), 42
Renoir, Pierre-Auguste, 267
Rhodes, Cecil, 275
Ricci, Stephania, 174
Ring, Ragnar, 61
Riva, Maria, 120
"roaring twenties," 88
Rockwell, Norman, 158
Rodin, Auguste, 143
Rogers, James, 98
Rogers, Will, 188

Roland, Gilbert, 204, 255–256
*Romance* (film): costumes, 183; Garbo as
courtesan, 178, 180, 182–183, 185; Garbo's
efforts to help Gordon, 191, 283; Garbo's
"glamour," 184; Garbo's hat, 173, 174;
Garbo's introduction to Salka Viertel,
150; Garbo's masculine side, 175; Mayer's
typecasting of Garbo, 154, 179; Oscar
nomination, 282
*Romance* (play; Sheldon), 182
*Room of One's Own, A* (Woolf), 203
Rooney, Mickey, 225
Roosevelt, Franklin, 225
Rosay, Françoise, 135, 151–152
Rossetti, Dante Gabriel, 23, 215
Rothschild, Cécile de, 2, 239, 260, 263, 272,
274, 285, 288–291
Rothschild family, 2
Rouault, Georges, 267
Royal Order of the North Star, First
Class, 283
Rubens, Alma, 100
Rubenstein, Arthur, 139
*Runnin' Wild*, 159
Russell, Bertrand, 255

*Saga of Gösta Berling, The* (film): audition,
50, 78; finding antique furniture for, 266;
Garbo as star in, 1, 55, 73, 74, 75, 138;
Garbo's weight, 83; Mayer's viewing of,
86; showing in America, 93, 99; Stiller
assigned to direct, 79–80; treatment of
Garbo, 83, 101; stamp honoring Garbo,
183; success of, 85; use of makeup, 27
*Saga of Gösta Berling, The* (novel; Lagerlöf),
49, 54, 75
Salome, 22
Salvation Army, 53, 54
same-sex love, 47, 71, 308n25
Sand, George, 201–202, 264, 265
*Sapho*, 185
Sapphic circle, 144, 147, 164–165, 254. *See
also* lesbians

Thalberg, Irving (cont.)
Viertel with best writers, 141; Stiller's
request to direct *Love*, 124; treatment of
Garbo, 121, 150, 179; typecasting
Garbo as vamp / siren, 101–102, 182;
understanding Garbo's audience, 186;
on von Stroheim, 191
theater productions as art, 2–3
*Theatre Arts Magazine*, 221
Theatre Intima, 81, 195
Theosophy, 254
"third sex," 55
*Thomas Graal's Best Film*, 76
*Thomas Graal's First Child*, 76
*Thus Spoke Zarathustra* (Nietzsche), 186
Tiller troupes, 165
*Time* (magazine), 17, 246
Todd, Mike, 283
Toklas, Alice B., 200
Tolstoy, Leo, 228
Tone, Franchot, 180
*Torrent, The*: Garbo as soft woman, 191;
Garbo as vamp, 4, 78, 100–102, *104*,
182, 316n27; Garbo's diva personality,
106–107; hair style, 27; happy ending,
150; identified with Black entertainer,
22; "Latin lover" movie, 102; Mayer
and Thalberg's decision not to have
Stiller direct, 101; premier of, 109;
Stiller's treatment of Garbo, 83,
101, 152
Tracy, Spencer, 205
transvestitism, 88
*Trilby* (George du Maurier), 82
Turner, Lana, 247
Turner, Nicholas, 51, 116–117, 243–244,
260–261, 275–277, 286, 295
Turner, Nikki, 293–294
*Two-Faced Woman*, 120, 150–151, 173, 204,
245–247, 256, 263, 294
Tyler, Parker, 153, 169
"typing girls," 133
*Tyrannical Fiancée, The*, 81

UFA. *See* Universum Film AG
UNESCO World Heritage site, 296
United Artists, 18
Universal Studios, 108
Universum Film AG (UFA), 68, 89
Uppsala University, 40
U.S. Supreme Court, 177

Valentino, Rudolph, 101, 112, 179
"vamp" girl type, 158, 163
vamp movies, 4, 78
*Vampyren*, 78
Vanderbilt, Gloria, 235
*Vanity Fair* (magazine), 10, 15, 28, 34, 97,
133, 217
*Variety* (magazine), 115, 146
Vassiliev, Alexandre, 21
Venice Film Festival, 230
Venus (Roman goddess), 19
Venus de Milo, 7, 19, *20*
Vickers, Hugo, 240
Victoria (queen), 275
*Victor / Victoria*, 5
Vidal, Gore, 204, 259, 288
Vidor, King, 112, 117
Viera, Mark, 119, 248, 319n26
Viertel, Berthold, 138, 139, 140, 145,
226–227
Viertel, Christine, 277, 287
Viertel, Christopher, 138
Viertel, David, 138
Viertel, Peter, 138, 285, 286–289
Viertel, Salka: on *Anna Karenina*, 226–227,
230; autobiography, 287; Beaton on
Garbo's overbearingness, 274; cast in
*Anna Christie*, 140, 185, 227; death, 290;
described, 138–139; description of Berlin,
88; dislike of de Acosta, 147, 226; dislike
of George Schlee, 250–251, 271; face-lift,
282; friendship with Larson, 318n6;
Garbo followed by Parsons to—'s home,
136; on Garbo not resuming career,
265–266; on Garbo as "personality"

# ABOUT THE AUTHOR

LOIS W. BANNER is a founder of the field of women's history and co-founder of the Berkshire Conference of Women Historians. She was the first woman president of the American Studies Association, and in 2005 she won the ASA's Bode-Pearson Prize for outstanding contributions to American studies. She is the author of twelve books, including *American Beauty* and *Marilyn: The Passion and the Paradox*. Banner is a professor emerita of history and gender studies at the University of Southern California.